FOR THE LOVE OF BRASS

*To Martin
Happy Reading
Gary Wines*

Many thanks to Mr. Andrew Catford
for all his help in making this
book possible.

FOR THE LOVE OF BRASS

Gary London

BROWN DOG BOOKS

First published 2018

Copyright © Gary London 2018

The right of Gary London to be identified as the author of this work has been asserted in accordance with the Copyright, Designs & Patents Act 1988.

All rights reserved. No part of this book may be reproduced, stored in a retrieval system, or transmitted in any form or by any means, electronic, electrostatic, magnetic tape, mechanical, photocopying, recording or otherwise, without the written permission of the copyright holder.

Published under licence by Brown Dog Books and
The Self-Publishing Partnership, 7 Green Park Station, Bath BA1 1JB

www.selfpublishingpartnership.co.uk

ISBN printed book: 978-1-78545-259-8
ISBN e-book: 978-1-78545-260-4

Cover design by Gary London
Internal design by Andrew Easton

Printed and bound in the UK

CONTENTS

Chapter One	The Feeling	7
Chapter Two	Poor Relations	27
Chapter Three	Elaine	36
Chapter Four	Dad's Funeral	50
Chapter Five	The Art Gallery	58
Chapter Six	Practical Justice	71
Chapter Seven	Practical Shotgun	92
Chapter Eight	The Rottie	109
Chapter Nine	Brief Encounter	132
Chapter Ten	What Could Possibly Go Wrong?	138
Chapter Eleven	The New Parlour	230
Chapter Twelve	Anal Specialist	297
Chapter Thirteen	Lettsbe Avenue	314
Chapter Fourteen	Jimmy the Dog	368
Chapter Fifteen	Ryan Gets a Piercing	395
Chapter Sixteen	Unwanted Visitor	435
Chapter Seventeen	Spilling the Beans	446

CHAPTER ONE
THE FEELING

Driving along the A3 from London, heading towards Tolworth in Surrey. It was 9.30 in the morning and a lovely sunny day in early March 1993, and I had this strange, compelling feeling: the urge to keep on driving, past the Tolworth junction and keep going, and never return home. Just leave everything behind and keep going. No thought to where I would end up.

I pondered on this for a while as I drove and said to myself, "Yes! That's what I'll do." The thought put a smile on my face and lifted my heart.

Then reality hit home. How the fuck can you just run off? How much money do I have? What clothes do I have? How much petrol do I have in the tank? These things all went through my mind in a flash.

Okay. Let's take stock. If you're going to do this, what exactly do you have that's of any use? I'd about 40 quid in my pocket, credit cards, about £20-worth of fuel. No change of clothes. I did, however, have the survival kit I always carried in the van, along with a shotgun and some ammo, which I'd got on board for a job I was going to do later that day. A quick stock-check confirmed that I didn't have much on board but "Going" still seemed a good idea.

"Hold on, hold on," I told myself. "You may have been in the Special Forces and well trained but you're not a super-trooper. You don't even have a belt kit with you, let alone your Bergan, and this is not an operational mission. You're going to bloody work. How long do you think you will last with what you have on board?"

All these bizarre thoughts came to a close and there was the slip road for the Tolworth roundabout. I took it, telling myself, no matter how you feel now, just go to work and if you've got to think about this sudden adventure, do it another time and when you're better prepared.

I took the third road off at the roundabout, which would take me through the Broadway and on to Surbiton, to where my job was: the restoration of a very large detached Victorian house. I had four of my men there, two plasterers, a labourer and a carpenter. There was a lot of work of all types to do on the house. The lads were working on the bay window where the roof had failed and water had found its way in. This had damaged the bay ceiling, along with the lovely cornice-work to the inside.

The client, his wife, their baby and a nanny were living in the house, moving from room to room as we were doing the work. One of the corners of the main roof, which we still had to replace, had part of the soffit board missing under the guttering. This provided a nice place for pigeons to live, which was why the ammo and shotgun were in my van. The idea was that I'd shoot the pigeons, go up on a ladder to clear out the nesting materials and cover the hole up with a piece of ply to stop any more birds taking up residence in the roof.

From time to time during the day I found myself thinking about this morning's sudden urge. To drive off into the sunset, as it were, and never return home. Wow! Where did that come from and more importantly, Why?

Home for me was a lovely mock-Tudor semi-detached house with six bedrooms and a double garage with an electric door that operated from a button in the car. The car was a signal-red Mercedes saloon. I lived here with my wife Sharon and my two sons, Michael and Lee. Life was good. We had everything we needed. You see, I ran a successful building

FOR THE LOVE OF BRASS

firm, which I'd set up after leaving the Regiment, the idea being that, with my own business, I could earn more to afford a better place to live and a better standard of living for the family. I had men working for me, and company vans and a truck to look after.

At one time I had 16 men working. One of them was Ron. He was the foreman: a foreman bricklayer, a blinding bricklayer and an excellent all-rounder. Having him on board meant I could go and price jobs, meet clients, arrange and source materials. Also, deal with banking and any office work that needed doing. When I wasn't busy with those tasks, I'd be on site helping out and on the tools myself. There was always lots to do. Then, for me of an evening, I'd get home, get cleaned up, have dinner, then get into the office for paperwork. There was always pricing and estimates to do. Once I'd drawn up draft estimates and invoices, Sharon would type them up ready to go out in the post the next day. It was a full on life. I was able to take some weekends off to get out with the boys fishing or out in the country in the summer. Or of course we'd go shooting. I'd always take my boys with me as much as possible: handguns at the pistol club, shotguns out in the sticks, hunting. Camping out in the woods, sometimes all weekend. I'd teach my boys how to hunt and how to prepare game, a skill they still have to this day.

When we bought the house, which was on the border of Sutton and Morden in Surrey (closer to Morden in fact), it had only three bedrooms. It was in a bad state of repair, so much so that in the flank wall there was a crack that ran from the damp course up to the side flank window and on up to the roof plate. It was interesting because when we viewed the house you could stand in front of the crack and put your hand side-on into it. It was just over an inch wide. You could look through and see the orange wallpaper and orange gloss woodwork – highly fashionable in the 1960s.

What had made the house desirable to me was that it had a block of land next to it with an old garage. I could foresee a large double extension on this land. It also had a long garden, some 120 feet, backing onto Morden Way Park. So, with some money and a lot of hard work, I could really do something with this house.

We'd bought the house from a man known as "Slippery Mick" and his wife, Jackie. I'd wanted to move to Morden Way but the houses always sold very quickly, so it was hard to get a look in. Sally, one of the mums from the school, lived in the road, so we asked her to keep an ear open for any news, should one come up for sale. Well, it hadn't taken too long before Sally knocked on our door and said her neighbour was about to put her house on the market. This would be an ideal opportunity to go and have a look.

"Thanks Sally. I'll go straight away."

I turned up at the door to be met by Mick and Jackie who invited me in. The house was in a state but I walked through the kitchen and on into the garden. I particularly wanted to see the garden. I knew this house had a lot of land. It was at this stage they informed me they'd sold most of the garden to a builder for development, seeing as how the land backed onto another road behind their house.

"Okay," I informed them. "It's not really what I'm looking for now. I think I'll give it a miss. Thanks anyway," I said.

As I was leaving Mick piped up again. "We own another house up the road by the park entrance. Would you like to see that place?"

"Yes, I would, please." So off we went. We walked up the road to see the house where Jackie's mother lived. Mick went on to tell me they were selling both houses and moving away to Gloucester.

I looked at the house from the outside. I didn't go in at that point

FOR THE LOVE OF BRASS

because the old lady had dogs and didn't look after them very well. Peering over the side gate I could see lots of dog shit on the path between the house and the garage and on into the back garden. Mick opened the front door calling out to the old lady that it was just him and somebody to look at the house. To my surprise the house smelt of dog shit as well. There was the odd turd here and there on the carpet. I quickly said I'd seen enough for now but I'd like to make an appointment to come back with my wife, so she could have a look. I thought it might give them a chance to clean up a bit.

Sharon came with me the second time after making an appointment but the dog shit was still there along with the smell. Despite a few things that needed doing, like replace the roof and fix the crack in the flank wall, replace the rotten windows, build a new double extension, re-plaster, rewire, re-plumb, sort out the completely overgrown garden and, of course, deal with the dog shit, we agreed a price, £63,000, with Mick and Jackie. We shook hands and bought the house.

"You'll find this interesting," says Sally the next time we met at the school. "You've just bought a house off of one of the robbers from the great train robbery."

"No way, really?" I said.

"Yeah. That's why he's called Slippery Mick." He'd had a part in laundering the money. Old Slippery stayed out of the hands of the Old Bill for quite a while but got nicked eventually and did his stretch inside.

The house sale was put in the hands of the solicitors. Everything went well and time passed. Eventually, the day came when we'd move. It was on a Friday. The solicitors would exchange contacts at one o'clock. The money would change hands. Deal done. We could collect the keys from Slippery and start moving in.

Our previous house had sold to the first couple who'd looked at it. They happened to be a young Japanese couple.

We told them, "If it helps you guys out, you can start moving your stuff in before one o'clock. Maybe from nine thirty to ten." They said that they didn't have much furniture but the offer was welcome and they'd see us on Friday.

At 9.45 the landline phone rings. I answer.

"Hello," says the solicitor. "I'm sorry to tell you the situation with your vendor has changed. Your vendor is saying the price of the house has gone up from £63,000 to £65,000. The extra £2,000 will have to be paid or the sale won't take place."

"Oh for fuck's sake!" I said. "What about the contract?"

"I know, I know," said the solicitor. "There's nothing we can do at this stage. Are you telling me to accept the new price? And if so, do we carry on with the deal?"

"Yes, I guess so. Carry on with things. I'll have a chat with my wife. If things change I'll get back to you before 1300 but carry on for now."

"Sharon!" I called. "That Bastard Mick has put the price of the house up 2,000 quid."

Sharon wasn't impressed. "What do we do?"

Well, we discussed it and decided, fuck it. We took everything into account and would go for it. I still felt it was a good deal. Even with the dog shit. I'd accepted the new price but I wasn't happy. So I thought I'd go around to Mick's to moan about the two grand and see if I could get it back to the original price and while there, arrange to get early access to the front room so I could start moving in.

We'd hired a Transit box van for the move and figured it would take three trips to complete. So an early access to start unloading would be

FOR THE LOVE OF BRASS

very useful. Our Transit was nearly full. We didn't have far to go. Maybe 500yds and we'd be unloading. By this time it was about 10.30. I thought I'd walk around to Slippery's. As I came out of my house, the Japanese couple pulled up in their car.

I greeted them and said, "When is your removal van going to arrive?"

"We don't have one," said Mr Miyagi. "All our possessions are in the car."

"Really? What about your bed?" I said, thinking they must have a bed!

"No," said Mr Miyagi. "We're Japanese. We sleep on the floor. On bedrolls."

"Bloody hell," I said. "It's a good job we're leaving the carpets and curtains. Anyway, no probs. You can put any of your stuff in the front room. We made space for you."

I called them Mr & Mrs Miyagi after the trainer fellow in Karate kid. Also because I couldn't pronounce their surname.

"My mother-in-law's inside. She'll make you a cup of tea if you like."

My mother-in-law, Brenda, was helping on the day. She was keeping an eye on the kids along with Sharon, doing bits and pieces and making the tea. They did like a cup of tea and a fag. Mind you, so did my father-in-law. His name was Harry but everybody called him "H". He was working with me and helping out, loading the van.

Well, what to say about H. What a character he was: a real man's man and a real male chauvinist pig. Let me put it this way, and this is putting it mildly, if there was an awards list once a year for the most chauvinistic male in England, he'd be on the list for a gold medal and very likely win one. He could also be very violent and didn't mind having a fight with almost anyone. I think he was also the original Mr Road-rage. He could go off his nut at a moment's notice. Unfortunately, he mainly vented his anger and jealous rages in the direction of his wife, Brenda.

"Okay," I shouted to Sharon. "I'm on my way to see Slippery."

"Do your best to get that two grand back," She said.

"Oh, I will. Don't worry about that," I shouted from the front garden.

I walked the 500yds to my new house, which was actually built in the mid 1930s. It had a load of inherent problems, along with its own custom dog-shit alley but that didn't matter, it was my new house. Or at least it would be in two to three hours' time.

As I approached I could see there were no curtains at any of the windows. There was a Luton Transit van parked on the front drive. One of the garage doors was open all the way back and the Transit van had been reversed right up tight against it.

I walked up the path to the front door and knocked on it.

"What do you want?" Slippery said from behind the door.

"I've come to have a chat with you, Mick, about this extra two grand you put on the price. That's not what we agreed. Or what we shook hands on," I said.

"Well, I've had a call from my brief. He said you've agreed the new price of 65, so that's it. There's nothing to discuss."

"Whoa, whoa, Mick. I think it's taking the piss what you've done."

"Well, I don't give a fuck about what you think. That's the way it is now. So FUCK OFF," he shouted.

"Look Mick, there's no need to be like that. Just open the door so we can have a chat."

"NO! FUCK OFF!" he shouted again.

"Look, Mick, I'd like access to, say, the front room so I can start moving my stuff in. It'll make my life easier if I can get a load in; then I can go back and be getting on loading the van again for the next load. You know how it works."

FOR THE LOVE OF BRASS

"I've already told you," he said. "Now FUCK OFF. You ain't getting any access early or otherwise. You can have the keys once my brief has called me and said the transaction is complete. Then you can have access, alright?"

Well, I thought to myself. Any pleasantries I might have shared with my new friend Slippery seem to have gone right out of the window. I walked back to the old house, feeling somewhat deflated. All I'd achieved was to feel pissed off about my visit to the new house.

As I walked up my path, H came out through the front door with a box in his arms heading for the van.

He said, "Alright, the van's full now. Are we okay to go round there and start unloading?"

"No, we're not," I said.

"What's that mean? What did he say?" asked H.

I went on to tell him the story as he loaded the last box into the van. In particular the bit about the keys.

"Oh, really?" said H. "Well, how about we go round and drag him out into the front garden and punch the shit out of him? He'll let us go in then."

"No, we can't do that. It'll only make matters worse," I said, "but thank you for your kind offer to help out the situation."

We both smiled. What else could we do?

I went into the house and told the girls the story. While doing so, I looked into the front room and, over to one side there were three boxes, two suitcases and two bedrolls.

"Is that it?" I said to Brenda. "Mr and Mrs Miyagi have moved in?"

"Yes," she said, laughing as she said it. "They've gone off to do some shopping; they will be back a bit later."

"Well," I said, "it seems there's no rush now. It seems there's not much we can do," I said, while putting the kettle on.

"Nope," Sharon said. "Let's have a fag and a cup of tea."

We scratched around, all of us, smoked cigarettes and drank tea sitting on the front-room floor because the furniture was in the van under everything else.

One o'clock came and I called my solicitor.

"Hello, Mr Copley. How are we doing? Have we exchanged contacts?"

"Yes, we have. The two thousand pounds draft from the bank came through to us okay and contracts have been exchanged."

"Thank you very much," I said, "'bye for now. Okay," I said to everyone. "The deal's done. We can carry on moving. We've a new home to go to. Alright then, H, let's drive round there, get the keys and start moving in."

We jumped in the van and off we went the 500yds to the new house. We pulled up at the front on the road. Nothing had changed and their van was still in the same position on the drive as it had been when I saw it earlier.

H said, looking at the house, "Has the old girl gone?"

"Yes," I said. "She moved out a few days ago." She was already at the new place in Gloucester. "I'll go get the keys and ask Slippery to move his van so we can get on the drive."

I approached the front door and pressed the doorbell. Slippery answered from behind the door again.

"Yes," he said. "What do you want now?"

"Well, Mick," I said, "The contracts have been exchanged. I now own the house and I want you to give me the keys so I can start moving in."

"Well, my solicitor hasn't called me," said Mick, "so it's not confirmed. You can't have the keys until he calls me and says it's okay to hand them over."

FOR THE LOVE OF BRASS

"Mick," I said, "stop fucking about and hand over the keys."

"No," he said. "Not till it's confirmed."

"Well, fucking ring him up and check!" I shouted at the door, now with my patience in short supply and my temper starting to build.

"Okay," he says. "Give me fifteen minutes or so and I'll check."

I went back to the van. H said, "What's his fucking problem? I heard what he said from here. He needs a slap."

"Yes, he does," I said. "Fuck it. Looks like we have to wait."

This went on for a further three times with Mick telling us the same story and us waiting.

H said, "When he does let us in, I'm going to break his fucking nose. Just you wait and see." And all this time waiting we could hear Mick and Jackie loading their van.

It was now 2.30 and Sharon had walked round, wondering what was going on and wanting to know why we'd not been back for the second load. We updated her as to what was going on, after which she went back home to her mother and boys to wait it out there, and no doubt they were having tea and smoking, sitting on the front-room floor, while we were sitting in the van getting more and more wound up. The idea of giving Mick a good kicking seemed an excellent idea now. The loading of Mick's van went quiet and we heard the sound of the roller shutter come down at the back of the van.

Suddenly, the front door I'd been talking to for the last two hours or so opened and out came Mr and Mrs Slippery, shutting the front door of my new house behind them. They both got into their van as H and I got out of ours and walked over to them. They locked the doors on their van. Mrs Slippery beckoned me over to her side of the van, holding up the keys for me to see. She wound down her window an inch or so. Dangled the keys out of the gap in the window for me to take and said good riddance to you and the fucking house. With that she wound the window up and Mick drove off the drive and away up the road.

As their van drove off, I could see the front of the garage, where one of the doors had been closed and the other was still wide open. I walked up to the door that was open. Holding the keys, which it seemed I'd fought so hard for in my hand, I looked into the garage and my heart sank. I couldn't believe what I was looking at.

The garage was a real mess. Covering most of the floor was earth from plant pots. There were two or three smashed terracotta pots but mainly earth in the shape of flowerpots where whatever had been growing in them was just dumped out onto the garage floor. Judging by the amount of earth there was, I'd say they must have emptied two hundred pots in there, while, I guess, loading the pots in the back of their van. Along with the earth, they'd also left us an old wooden and metal frame of a bed, with a lovely big wooden headboard and a number of cardboard boxes, loads of newspapers, some lino, a couple of old, metal-frame chairs, an assortment of empty food tins, mostly dog food, and yes, you guessed it, a number of dried-up packages left by the dogs after they'd eaten the contents of the tins.

It was at this stage I realised I should have released H onto them much earlier on in the day. I walked through the rubbish to the side door of the garage and looked across the alley to the back kitchen door, which had a couple of steps up to gain access to the kitchen. The alley was six feet wide. It was almost completely covered in those packages but these ones weren't dry. It was that bad, you wouldn't have got across the alley without treading on one of these landmines, and the smell… Wow!

It was at this point that I decided, Nope, let's go round to the front door and let ourselves in.

H had reversed our van onto the drive while I was enjoying myself inspecting the garage.

"How is it in there?" H asked.

"Well, it lets in water," I said, "over in the back corner, because it's all damp. The Electrics are hanging down from the joists. They look very unsafe and the rest of it… well, you don't want to know."

"Well, we can sort that another time," H said.

"Right then, open up, let's start to unload the van. The time's getting on. I could do with a fag and a cup of tea."

As H opened the back of the van, I opened the front door and stepped in. The hallway was no surprise. I just felt as if I'd been transported back to 1967.

The stairs ran up on the left-hand side. The first door on my right was the front room, the second door was the back room or dining room and the door straight ahead was the kitchen. All the doors were slightly ajar. I opened the front room door and stepped in. The intention was just to check it was clear so we could start unloading our van into the room. All that was in there was the oldish but clean carpet, no bad smells. Brilliant, I thought, in at last. I gave H the thumbs up through the bay window and he smiled. I think he was happy to know his cup of tea and a fag was closer now. I turned to walk out of the room but as I passed through the doorway I noticed on my left, at shoulder height, three wires sticking out of the wall where the light switch should be. I looked again and did a double take. I looked up at the ceiling to where the ceiling rose should have been. Not there. Just three wires hanging down. The wires had been separated from each other, which told me they were probably live. I looked around the room at low level. No power points, just the wires sticking out of the walls where the power-point faces should be.

The power point faces had been a nice brass type when I viewed the house; now they were gone.

"Oh for fuck's sake!" I shouted to H. "You won't believe what the Slippery bastard's done."

H shouted back with an enquiring "What?"

"He's taken all the power points and even the fucking ceiling rose and lamp holder. Just left the wires sticking out of the walls."

"Are they live?" H shouted.

"Yes. I think so," I said. "We'll have to be careful putting stuff in here. Don't touch the wires or we'll get a packet. I'll have to get Tito over to make this all safe." Tito was a Spanish electrician I'd got working for me.

H shouted from the back of the van, "You'd better check the other rooms to see what else he's done."

"Good thinking," I said.

I opened the door to the dining room, walked in and looked up. No ceiling rose. Looked at the light switch, not there. Looked around the skirting line, no sockets, just the wires hanging out where they should have been. I looked out through the French doors into the garden and froze. This, I thought, was Slippery's Pièce de résistance. His Crème de la crème. My mouth dropped open.

I shouted to H. "You've got to come in here and see what's happened. You really won't believe this one."

H jumped down from the back of the van and came through the house and into the dining room. He walked in and stopped, looking out through the French doors and was silent for a moment. He turned to look at me with a surprised look on his face but said nothing. He looked back into the garden and just said "FUCK ME! He's taken the patio."

FOR THE LOVE OF BRASS

We looked at each other and burst out laughing. What else could you do?

The patio had consisted of crazy paving laid on soft sand, with a little retaining wall along the front. Because the patio was about a foot higher than the garden level, it had two steps down onto the lawn. Mick had lifted every piece of paving with a pickaxe and taken it with him, just leaving the sand and the broken pointing all over where the patio should have been. They'd also dug up some shrubs and a couple of small trees for re-homing in Gloucester.

It was at this point I decided I really should check upstairs. I shot out into the hallway and quickly went up the stairs. I checked the toilet first, all okay. Then the bathroom: seems fine, I said to myself. Then I checked the three bedrooms; again, all was fine, except for what it had now become normal to see – the bare wires sticking out of the places where electrical fittings should be.

Last of all, the box room, which had not been decorated since the house was built. It still had original lino on the floor but interestingly enough, Slippery, in his haste to escape to Gloucester, had left behind three gifts for me on the floor, one of which was an 18-inch First World War bayonet, still in its scabbard and in remarkably good condition for its age. The other two were dried-up dog turds sitting in the corner! I still have the bayonet to this day.

By the end of the day we were in at long last. Tito came round with a box of plug faces, switches and ceiling roses and made the electrics safe. Brenda and H had the kids for the night over at their place, which meant Sharon and I could go out for a well-deserved meal and a few drinks. The following morning, Brenda and H returned with the boys and we spent the Saturday sorting things out as you have to do when you move into a new place. The boys thought it was just one big adventure sharing a new bedroom together.

On Sunday morning we woke to a surprising sight from the main drain in the alley next to the house. It had lifted up because of a blockage. The sewerage was all down the side of the house. It had run into the garage and covered the floor. It was also finding its way under the garage door and out onto the drive, and of course it had found its way into the back garden, onto the lawn.

"Never mind," I said to Sharon. "At least we've a nice high patio to stand on while the effluence flows past." What else could you do but laugh?

With no plumber on the firm, I called Dyno-Rod. They were very good and came out quickly to sort our problem, which they did very successfully. They said the verdict was that items of clothing had been put down the drain, blocking the main drain that ran out to the street. I spent the Monday in Wellington boots with a hose-pipe in one hand and a stiff broom in the other. No wonder they say moving is one of the most stressful things you can do. We had one hell of a long weekend.

I guess it shows the level of commitment we had with the new house. The intention was to turn it into our palace and over time we did. We soon got the main house liveable and cleared the garden to find the remains of a very overgrown shed with its roof collapsed in. This was way beyond any repair, so I demolished what was left of it and found a bonus. Once it was cleared it revealed a sturdy concrete base some 19ft long by 9ft wide. The base was a raft footing which meant I could build walls straight onto it, which of course I did, finished with joists and ply roof with three layers of felt all hot-bonded. New fascia boards and guttering put it in the dry, then a nice picture window to overlook the garden.

FOR THE LOVE OF BRASS

Pebbledash finish to the outside and a new frame and door with a sturdy lock for security, what more could a man ask for? Power! I'd install that properly at a later date. For now, if power was needed, long extension leads would suffice.

All this work was being completed on the shed because I'd need somewhere to store tools and materials while we demolished the existing garage to make a clear building site for the commencement of the new extension. All the while, drawings were being prepared by my architect, to be submitted to the council for building regulations and planning approval. Over time all this took place and construction commenced.

I allowed a three-month period for me and my men to work on the extension, after which we'd have to go back to the other paying jobs. From then on my job would be finished on weekends, or if any of my men had spare time with their work, they could come over and work on my site to help bring it to completion. By the time the house was finished it had cost another £50,000, which was a fair amount of money in the mid 1980s. We even built a lovely new patio, larger and grander than the one that had originally been there. One that Mr and Mrs Slippery would have been proud of.

The years were slipping by and the boys were growing fast. Michael had started senior school but Lee still attended junior school. The building trade was going very well for me. I was earning good money from it all, so much so, we could have a couple of holidays a year and plenty of weekends away. I felt very content with everything that was going on in my life, except I'd started to notice more and more gradually the holidays were just me, Michael and Lee, going over to Spain, until in the end Sharon didn't come with us at all. She'd go on holiday with her friends. Sharon didn't attend our weekends away either, although by now our weekends consisted of camping out in the woods. Fishing and shooting would generally be the order of the day. We could always shoot and prepare our food, in fact it was a pleasure to teach the boys how to do this stuff, bush craft that is. They always enjoyed our time away together, whereas this was never Sharon's cup of tea. We did try to get her involved but I'm afraid that was never going to happen. When we came home with game, we'd prepare it in the kitchen. I'd turn the preparation into a biology lesson for the boys to keep it interesting. Sharon would never get involved, cook or eat any of our meats we came home with, which was a shame. We always had a good selection of game in the freezer: rabbits, pheasants, pigeon, duck and even hares. On occasion, we'd add in partridge and woodcock. I'd always be the chef for these dishes.

"Cheers, Ray," I shouted as I jumped into my van and started the engine. Ray was the owner of the builder's merchants where I bought most of my building materials. I pulled out of the yard and turned right onto Grand Drive, heading for Raynes Park. Once I'd got to the Raynes Park lights, I'd turn left onto the A3, heading for Tolworth and the Tolworth roundabout.

I'd loaded up at Ray's with plasterboard, plaster and timber for the lads at the Surbiton job. By the time I get there it'll be tea time, I was thinking to myself. The traffic was light. Probably because it was 9.25 and the DJ on the radio had just said he'd a news update he was going to give us in five minutes' time. More bad news, I thought with a negative attitude as I drove over the flyover at Shannon's corner. I'd intended to spend the day working with the lads at the job, dealing with roof repairs to one of the large bay windows where all the timber-work had to be replaced. Water had been slowly leaking in for many years. The joists that held the roof up were rotten, as were the wall plates they sat on. The previous owner of the property had dealt with problems like this by moving any furniture away from the area and just put plastic sheets down to catch any drips that found their way in through the ceiling. Not an ideal method but a cheap one, at least in the short term.

I felt aware of one of those sudden adventures coming on, as I'd experienced yesterday. Here we go, I said to myself. That feeling again, off into the sunset. I half smiled to myself but in truth it wasn't funny because the feeling was so strong, and they were the same thoughts I'd had before. I kept thinking, what a good idea, just keep going, just keep going. I went through the same questions and answers as I had before with the same outcome. Do this another time, I said to myself. I'm going to the job and that's it. I came off the A3 at the Tolworth junction as I'd done before and carried on to the site.

The day went well at work, no problems. The next morning, after joining the A3, I experienced the same thing again, keep going, keep going. Seemed such a good idea. This went on for over two weeks. It got worse because towards the third week I found myself making excuses not to go straight home. Any excuse would do and I'd go anywhere. Pop into friends' houses. Go fishing, or just go walking in the countryside or Morden Park. Anything but go home. It all seemed such a waste of time. I felt I needed to get to the bottom of this. I approached Sharon with the way I was feeling. I told her we needed to sit and talk about what was happening and how I felt. I also wanted to know how she felt about things and about us as a couple.

We did this. We arranged a night where we'd sit down with no TV on after dinner and the boys had gone to bed so we could have a talk. Our first talk must have lasted three hours. It covered a lot of things. It didn't make me feel any better. All it did, it seemed, was maybe make things worse between me and Sharon. I found myself telling her how I was unhappy with my lot in life, which just seemed to piss her off. Anyway, we agreed to have another chat the following week and I'd come home on time and stop disappearing. This I did but the feelings were still there, stronger than ever, not to come home!

I should talk to someone else. Maybe Sharon's too close to the situation, I thought. Maybe I'm too close to the situation. But who? Who should I talk to? Who could I talk to? I'd no idea which direction to go in! All I knew was that something was terribly wrong and that I didn't feel comfortable with the place I was in.

Well, I did come home after work as I should or as I'd agreed with Sharon. Spend time with the family. Have dinner. Get cleaned up. Sometimes a quick bath or if there wasn't too much to do in the office I'd lie in the Jacuzzi for a while. Then, when it was bedtime for the boys, I'd take them up to bed but, instead of going back downstairs to sit and watch TV with Sharon, I found myself going into the office, looking for something to do. I'd stay there finding something to do until it was time for me to retire for the night.

This situation had been going on for some time now. I'd had a few more chats with Sharon but this had achieved nothing. I just felt more fed up and Sharon was annoyed that I kept wanting these chats. So we were getting nowhere. Except drifting further and further apart. I felt after some time I was wasting my time trying to find a resolution to the problem.

CHAPTER TWO
POOR RELATIONS

While sitting in the office one night, I'd finished any paperwork I had to do. I'd made any necessary phone calls to staff and clients; I'd always make sure I finished my phone calls by 10 o'clock. People are not too keen on calls after ten at night. I found this out on the odd occasion where I'd be abused for ringing late. This particular evening it was 9.30. I sat looking around. I looked at the in-tray. EMPTY. I looked at the phone. No one to talk to. Looked at the year planner, which was pinned out on a large pin board I'd made. This was fixed to the wall in front of me. I could look at it and at a moment's notice know what was going on for the whole year. It was full of work. Enough to keep me, Ron the foreman and all my men busy. What more could I want?

I started to think… As far as business was concerned I'd achieved every target I'd set myself over the last few years. I'd finished all the works on the house; the house had come a long way from the Mr & Mrs Slippery days. I had the car of my dreams, my lovely signal-red Mercedes. I had my two lovely boys, who I loved so much. As a family we had so much, I thought to myself. In fact we had everything, and everything going for us. It was all going in the right direction except, of course, for my relationship with Sharon.

It was at this time I asked myself the question: WAS I HAPPY?

Well, I said. Are you? Yes, of course I am. I thought, don't bullshit yourself. It's me you're talking too. Be realistic. Be honest with yourself.

Tell the truth. How do you feel? Are you happy?

The truth was harder to accept than I had realised. Much harder to accept. The answer was, of course, NO! I think for me it was so difficult to accept the answer of No because to me it spelled failure. It spelled an end to everything I'd worked for. It spelled an end to my life as I knew it. An end to my relationship with Sharon. It was a feeling of being very low. Terribly low. A feeling that made me feel as though my heart was sinking. But what could I do other than face the truth? Maybe, just maybe, if I talked to someone, maybe this situation could be reversed but who? Who can I talk to?

Giving me the answer. WOW! what a thing. I'd no idea how a little word like No would affect my life in such a dramatic and serious way.

I'd still come home from work and do the usual things, ending up with me in the office. Sitting there and wondering, what if this... what if that! Work was still going well. The job at Surbiton was coming to a close after 14 weeks and some £30,000. Other jobs I had running were a total refurb of a cottage house in Wallington and an extension in Beddington Road, Croydon. There were smaller jobs always coming in, jobs that could be from one or two days to a number of days. All this kept all the men busy and, of course, I had Ron the foreman looking after things as well, which meant I could have some freedom to do the other things that needed doing.

One day, sitting in the office, I had this thought, to contact the Relate service. I wondered if they could help me but really I had no idea. I just thought I needed a counsellor of some sort. So I got their number and proceeded to call them for the information on how it works. The lady informed me I should make an appointment for an assessment, which would maybe last 30 minutes. If they decided to help me, I'd then make an appointment to come back once a week for one hour at a time. I'd be assigned a counsellor and I'd see that counsellor for up to 12 weeks.

Okay, I thought, but I don't know if I'll get a counsellor. I don't even know if they will help. Or even if I'd come to the right place but I thought, I need to make a start. I asked for the phone number of their Purley branch. I didn't want to go to the Sutton branch in case I saw somebody that I knew. The reason for that being that I didn't want any people I knew to know of my failure in my relationship or indeed my life. I was that concerned about the situation. I called the Purley branch. It rang and rang; nobody answered but the answerphone did say their opening times. As I was in a rush to find out if I'd qualify for a counsellor or not, I thought I'd drive over there to meet someone and make the appointment. Also it would give me the opportunity to find out exactly where the place was located, also check out the parking situation, so as I would not be late for the first appointment.

The first thing I did the following day on leaving my house was to drive to Purley. I'd decided not to tell Sharon just yet about my intention with the Relate people. I found the address I'd written down on a piece of paper. It was easy enough to find and, as luck would have it, there was a car park next door. I wandered in and spoke to the receptionist, telling her I'd like an appointment for my assessment meeting. She went on to tell me that there had been a cancellation for a 10 o'clock appointment and if I wanted to, I could wait the 15 minutes or so and have an assessment today. Yes, I said. I'd love to. That would be great. I took a seat in their waiting room, picked up a magazine and put it on my lap ready to read. I looked up at the white ceiling which had a beautiful plaster ceiling rose in its centre. It also had a lovely detailed cornice running around the ceiling line, setting off the ten foot high ceiling very nicely. A nice wide pine door brought you into the room. It reminded me a lot of the Surbiton job that had the same type of rooms on the ground floor as the Relate building. The Relate building would in its time have been a very large Victorian family house, sitting in its own grounds.

While sitting there admiring the room's large bay window and the lovely original cast iron fire place, the time passed quickly. Before I knew it, a grey-haired lady, looking very smart, appeared in the doorway.

"Good morning, sir," she said in a very posh accent. "I understand you would like an assessment."

"Yes," I said."

"Follow me," she replied.

I followed her along the corridor into another nice big room. I thought at this stage because of her age she'd be a very experienced counsellor. She seemed to be around 70 years old, which, I thought, can only be a good thing. We both sat down.

She said, "My name's Diana. It's very nice to meet you, Gary," reading my name from a sheet of paper she had on the desk. "Okay, dear," she said, "you start talking. Tell me what brings you here."

"Oh, okay," I said. "I thought you were going to ask me questions. I don't know if I've come to the right place but I feel I need to talk with someone."

"Okay," said Diana. "You carry on."

I went on to explain how I felt, driving to work and wanting to keep driving and not return. Also the feeling of not wanting to go home and not wanting to be around my wife or to spend time in my house. That I was feeling down almost all the time but felt less like it when I stayed out all day into the evening. It seemed I just didn't want to go home. I talked to Diana for about 25 minutes, only stopping to breathe. WOW, I thought to myself. Where's all this information coming from? I must have had more to say than I realised.

After 25 minutes, Diana said, "Okay, your assessment is over for now. We'll book you in to see a counsellor next week."

"Oh, okay," I said. "I've come to the right place, then."

"Oh, yes," she said. "Most definitely. You'll benefit from seeing a counsellor. You've come to the right place. Come with me."

We walked back along the corridor to reception.

"Diana," I said. "Are you not going to be my counsellor?"

"No," she said. "Another lady will guide you. I have someone in mind. We'll just check when she's available."

"Guide me!" I thought. "I wonder what that means!"

"Hello, Jan. We'd like to book an appointment for Gary here," Diana said, while pointing at me. "When is Elaine next available?"

"Hello Gary," said Jan. "What times are you available next week? Can you come along during working hours?"

"Yes," I said, "no problem at all. Sometime in the morning would suit me."

"Elaine is available," Jan said to Diana. "So, Gary, is ten o'clock okay for you?"

"That's fine with me. Yes."

"Okay, then, Wednesday at ten o'clock, Gary. You'll be seeing Elaine; she's a very experienced counsellor. You'll enjoy working with her."

"Is that it, ladies?" I said.

Jan said, "Just before you go, Gary, can you fill in a form please? It's nothing much. Just your details. Home address, phone number and so on. It'll only take a couple of minutes. It's for our records, you understand."

"Yes, sure," I said.

FOR THE LOVE OF BRASS

Diana said, "Thank you very much. Bye for now," and walked off down the corridor.

As Diana walked away, I said to her from behind, "Thank you for your time, Diana." She just lifted her arm and gave a little wave without turning around. She had this air of confidence about her, as though she had done all this a thousand times before. I finished filling in the form and handed it back to Jan.

"Thank you very much," Jan said. "I'll see you next week."

"Thank you," I said to Jan. "Yes. See you next week."

I walked out through the grand entrance, down the five stone steps, turned left and into the car park next door. I opened my car door. Sat inside. For a while I sat there without driving off. Just looking at the dashboard, thinking. I've done this. I've found somebody to talk to! People who had worked at this most of their lives. I felt assured I'd get somewhere now. Which I think is a good feeling, I said to myself. I still felt a little bit sad because the thing I'd done by coming here and arranging a meeting was that I'd accepted that there was a big problem in my life but, looking at the whole thing positively, I'd get help. The situation would get sorted out and YES, I told myself, that can only be a good thing.

I drove round to the jobs I had on the go, making sure everyone was happy and had what they needed. Then, at around 4.30 I decided to go home. As I was driving, I thought, hopefully I can have one of my meetings with Sharon tonight. They became known as my meetings because Sharon thought they were a waste of time and didn't achieve anything. So my meetings could now only take place when it suited Sharon. Which basically meant, if certain TV programmes were on, no meeting. I'd have to wait for another evening and if East Enders was on there was no chance whatsoever of a meeting. The meetings by this time were becoming less and less frequent. So if we had a meeting tonight, I thought, at least I'd something to tell her. I'd no idea how well today's proceedings would be received. Maybe very well or maybe NOT!

So, turning into Romany Gardens and approaching the house, I pressed the garage door control button when I was maybe 100yds away, knowing the door would be up by the time I got there. Or at least almost up. Either way I could drive straight in. Once the car had come to a stop I could press the door clicker, as we called it. While I was getting out of the car the garage door would be on its way down. We had a door from the garage into the utility room. From there a door into the kitchen. As I came in through the kitchen door, Sharon was at the sink preparing the evening meal. We greeted each other with the minimum of words as was usual now.

I walked through to the front room where the boys were and greeted them. Then back to the kitchen to put the kettle and make a cup of tea.

As I switched the kettle on, I said, "You want a cuppa Shal'?" (Shal was just short for Sharon. most people called Sharon Shal. The other name of Shaz had not caught on yet or it had not been invented.)

"Yes, please," she said.

"How long will dinner be?" I asked.

"Oh, about thirty minutes."

"Okay, that's good. That'll give me time to get cleaned up." Not that I was that dirty, after all I had the car with me all day.

I made the tea. While standing there drinking it, I said to Sharon, "Can we have a chat tonight when the boys have gone to bed?"

"Not another chat!" She said.

We had got to the point in our marriage where we didn't talk to each other much. Just what had to be said or about the kids, or if there was any paperwork to be done. That really was about it.

"Okay," she said, "once the boys have gone to bed."

I got cleaned up. We had dinner. It came to Lee's bedtime and I took him up after he'd said goodnight to his mother and cleaned his teeth. Michael went to bed a bit later, being that bit older. Once the boys were down, we made a brew and sat down in the front room.

"We gonna go through the same shit?" Sharon said. "And you telling me about how unhappy you are? Cos I don't really want to hear it all."

"Yes, I know," I said. "You've told me this before, so I'll get to the point. I went and had a meeting, or more to the point, an assessment at a Relate office today."

"Oh yeah," Sharon said, "and so you've gone to Relate."

"Yeah."

"What, the marriage guidance people?"

"Yes," I said. "You think our marriage is that bad we, or you, need guidance?"

"Yes," I said. "We're not happy with each other are we? There has to be more than this to life."

"I'm alright. It's you, you miserable bastard."

"Yes, well, who or whatever it is, it needs sorting."

"Well, don't expect me to go," Sharon said with a hostile tone. "Don't even fucking ask, because I won't go! Okay?"

"Okay," I said. "Well…" I went on to tell Sharon what had happened at the assessment and what the outcome was.

"So, next Wednesday," Sharon said, "and then what?"

"I don't know. We'll find out. It can't get any worse, can it? We hardly talk. We don't go out together. We don't have sex. It's not a very happy life! It's not a happy relationship. We only have one life. So this needs

FOR THE LOVE OF BRASS

sorting."

The days passed. I took the boys fishing the following Saturday over in an area called Newdigate in the Dorking area of Surrey, a place we often went to. The fishing was always good. Sometimes we went to the area just to walk in the countryside with the dogs. There was always an abundance of wildlife to see: an excellent place for teaching my sons natural history. We had two lovely little whippets, litter sisters: one brindle, who we called Jade, the other a blue dog called Asher after her colouring which was an ash blue. When I say little, most people thought they were Italian greyhounds. That gives an idea of their size.

On the Sunday, I went out with the boys and the dogs, over to Morden Park. Most of the time when we went out I'd have four boys and two dogs. The reason for the four boys was that there is a four-year gap between my sons' ages. Michael liked to bring a friend that was his age and Lee also wanted to bring a friend that was his age. So to be fair, they'd each bring a friend, hence four boys.

Monday and Tuesday passed with just the usual things going on work-wise. The same thing at home: me spending most of the evening in the office, so as not to spend time with Sharon.

Wednesday morning came. Sharon did the school run then came home with the car. I didn't have to worry about any of my building jobs. Ron the foreman was in charge. I wouldn't be off the radar for too long anyway. I found myself looking forward to the meeting with Elaine because I figured this would be the start of a happier me. Also I wanted to know the cause of my unhappiness so as, to my way of thinking, I wouldn't go to the unhappy place ever again. Anyway, the time had come for me to leave.

CHAPTER THREE
ELAINE

I drove over to Purley and pulled up in the car park next to the Relate house. Great, I thought, plenty of parking places. I walked up the front steps, opened the large Victorian door and stepped inside. I walked up to Jan who was sitting at reception, sipping on her cup of coffee.

"Good morning," I said. "My name's Gary. I have an appointment with Elaine at ten o'clock."

"Good morning," said Jan. "Take a seat in the waiting room. I'll inform her you're here."

"Okay, thank you." I walked into the waiting room. The door was wide open, the room empty. Hmmm, I thought to myself, no other customers. I was five minutes early. Maybe the other customers were with their counsellors, or maybe this big house was empty, just me, Jan and Elaine. The house seemed silent for some reason. Then I heard footsteps coming downstairs and along the corridor.

Elaine appeared through the doorway and introduced herself, then said, "Follow me, please, Gary".

Elaine was a tall woman, I guessed about 6ft tall, very smart and well spoken. I followed her upstairs. We went into a room at the front of the house, not a large room but about 10ft square. Elaine sat herself down behind a desk, while at the same time saying to me, "Please take a seat."

She faced the window, which meant my seat faced the wall behind her. I noticed there were two boxes of tissues in the room, one box on her desk, also a box on the small coffee-type table next to my seat. Other than that, really not much in the room at all. The tissues made me think this must be a sad place to be.

I'd no idea of how this was going to go, never having had a counsellor to talk with before. Elaine had some notes in front of her, which had been taken by Diana from my previous assessment. Elaine studied these for a few moments. I'd not noticed Diana taking any notes. I was far too busy talking and letting it all out.

Elaine looked up from her notes. "Okay, Gary. I'd like you to tell me what life was like for you as a child. Are you happy to talk about that time in your life?"

"Er, yeah, I think so. Is this how we start?" I said.

"Yes, it's a good starting point."

"Okay. I, I, er, I'm sorry, don't know where to start." My mind was blank, which made me think this is a bit strange. I couldn't stop talking last time. It was like the gate had been opened and everything was escaping. At this moment in time, I couldn't even find the fence let along open the gate. "Elaine," I said. "Can you give me some direction?"

"Okay," Elaine said. "Were you a happy child? Was it a joyous time?"

"Yes. It was, actually. I can say I'd a great upbringing and, yes, I think a very happy time. Everything was such a great adventure."

"That's good," Elaine said. "Happy memories with your parents?"

"Yes. There was only one bit which was very bad for me, well, for the family as well."

"Really. What was that?"

"My father died when I was thirteen."

"That was bad!"

"A very bad and very sad situation. Things in my life changed then."

"Going back prior to losing you father, are there any other bad memories?"

"No, I don't think so. None I can recall anyway."

"Siblings?" Elaine asked.

"Yes, I have one brother and one sister."

"Did you all get along as children?"

"Yes," I said.

We went on with chitchat, nothing too heavy. The questions went back to the time of my father's death.

"So, things changed after losing your father. How?" Elaine enquired.

"Well, I'm not sure where to start. I guess there's a list," I said.

"Okay," Elaine said. "Can we go through the list?"

"Yes. I found myself getting into trouble at school. Not doing as I was told. At home, not doing as my mother asked. I lost all interest in school. I went each day but wasn't enjoying it. I found I was getting into fights at school and in the street. I'd come home with cuts and bruises, with my clothes torn, which my mother wasn't happy about. She said she couldn't afford new school uniforms all the time, she'd have to repair my clothes but I didn't care. I guess I figured no one could hurt me, compared to the pain of my father being taken away from me. It wasn't long before the police would be around to my house, wanting to talk with me and my mother."

I suddenly thought, WOW! The gates have opened. All my thoughts were escaping. I seemed to go on talking for about 20 minutes.

"The police," Elaine said. "Why did the police come round?"

"I'd run away from home for a couple of days. My mother had reported me as missing, so the police came to talk to me and my mother. The police told me off and said not to do it again but it made no difference because in a few days I'd run off again. For three days this time, and of course the police were looking for me again. More trouble when I returned but I didn't care. No one was going to tell me anything, let alone what to do."

"Ran away," Elaine said. "You ran away. Just as you feel you should do while driving to work?"

"Yes, but I can't run away now."

"You can't?" Elaine said. "Why?"

"I can't. I want to but I can't. I have a wife. A home. My sons. My dogs. I have a family," I explained.

Elaine said. "Okay, Gary, our time is up for this week."

"This week," I said. "That went quick. I thought we might have been a lot further along the track than we are." All we talked about was years ago and not the problem at hand, I said to myself. Then I came out with it.

"Elaine," I said, "instead of once a week," if I came, say, three times a week, we could clear this up much faster. Three times faster."

Elaine smiled and said, "It doesn't work like that. It'll be once a week. Then the time in between can be used to ponder and think about things. We'll fix you over time. Time is the key."

"Fix me?" I said. "Can you see that I need fixing?"

"Oh yes, and we'll fix you but it'll take time."

"Okay," I said. "So same time next week?"

"Yes," Elaine said. "I'll see you then."

"Okay. Thanks very much. See you then."

I left the office, went down the stairs and along the corridor to reception, where Jan was still sitting at her desk, looking as though she was guarding the building.

"Hi Jan," I said. "Looks like we're done for this week. See you next Wednesday."

"Yes," Said Jan. "Wednesday at ten o'clock."

"Okay, bye."

I went through the doorway and down the stairs. I turned left into the car park, pulling the keys from my pocket as I approached the car, unlocked the car and sat inside. I just sat in the car looking forward out of the window, wondering where these counsellor meetings would go or how they'd go. I'd started to think about things already.

I would drive home now, to work in the office and, of course, talk to Sharon a bit later on. As I drove, I wondered why we go back so far in time and it seems we start from there! And the interesting thing is the fact that I'm broken but she knows how to fix me. Ha-Ha-Ha. I laughed to myself. Broken, well, well! I'll be fixed. That's even better; at least I'm not going mad or losing the plot. It's a horrible place to be when you're so unhappy. It's like carrying a great weight around with you and what makes it worse is it holds you back and stops you from doing things.

My house was now in sight. As I pulled in to my garage, I thought, there's plenty of time before Lee has to be picked up from school. So maybe Sharon would like an update while we're on our own. I went in through the doors into the kitchen. No one at home.

"Sharon," I called up the stairs! No answer. Okay, on my own as usual, I thought, but then smiled. The critical piece of information I had today: I'd be fixed. I started to feel better already. Maybe this is how it works. I felt it really was worth the trip to Purley. Anyway, later on came. We had dinner as a family. I told Sharon I'd like to chat later when we're on our own.

"Okay, okay, later," she said.

Of course, while this was all going on we were drifting further and further apart. Our friends and family and everyone else thought we were the perfect couple, the best of friends. I suppose that was the image we gave for other people's benefit. Sharon was never the type of person to talk with people or friends about any problems we might have. I don't think she did, anyway. I don't know if she spoke to her friends about her problems. I did ask once. The answer was a frown, followed by "it's none of their business, is it?"

We sat in the front room with a cup of tea, each with a fag and an ashtray in our hand. "Okay, I'll tell you what happened today."

"Do we have to do this now? I'm not really interested," Sharon said.

"Oh, okay. No we don't have to but I think it's important we sort this out, whatever it takes. You know how I feel about this; we've spoken of it often enough."

"Yeah, well, same old shit," she said.

While trying to explain, I found myself getting annoyed and frustrated. I thought, this will only end badly or worse, in a row. My patience had run to its limits so I decided to keep it short. When I had finished talking. Sharon just said "so what was the point of all that? Sounds like a waste of time! Are you going again?"

"Yes," I said, "next Wednesday."

Our conversation was over by the time we'd finished our cigarettes and tea. Maybe ten minutes max had passed. I found myself walking into the kitchen, putting my teacup in the sink and heading upstairs to the office to find something to do. All I could do was wonder how all this would turn out. If Elaine could fix me maybe, just maybe she could fix my marriage. I was sure that was something I would never be able to do alone. I suppose it takes two people to sort out a two-people problem. I felt I had an uphill struggle, just me and the big weight.

Life carried on. Work. Home. Sleep. Time in the office. Shooting at

Bisley on Sunday. I went to work. Sharon went to work. Work. Home. Sleep… work. Home. Sleep.

Sharon worked for a large building company called Gleeson's, doing computer work in the accounts department. It was a full-time job she'd taken on after staying at home for some years bringing up the boys, although Lee was attending junior school.

We had friends who lived opposite the school gate. Julie was a housewife, so therefore at home when school turned out. When she picked her son up she'd also pick up Lee. Lee stayed at Julie's, in her care, until Sharon finished work. She'd then pick Lee up from Julie's house and bring him home. Michael came home from his school around 4.45. Most of the time, if I wasn't working late, I'd be at home between 4.00 and 4.30 to carry on with work in the office. That is, when I did come home and wasn't going through my spell of disappearing after work.

The following week came. Great, I thought, off to Relate. I couldn't wait to see what this visit would bring. Sharon had taken the car, so I'd be driving over there in my trusty builder's van. I arrived in Purley via the Purley Way from Croydon, pulled into the car park and got out of the van with a spring in my step. Up the front steps of the big house, in through the large front door.

"Morning Jan," I said as soon as I saw her.

Jan looked up. "Good morning, Gary. You can go straight up. Elaine is waiting for you. She went up to her room only moments ago."

"Thank you," I replied and went on my way thinking to myself, that's good. I'm a little early. Ha, more time to talk. I smiled to myself. Before I knew it I was in front of the door. Knock, knock.

"Come in," Elaine answered. I opened the door.

"Good morning," I said with a happy tone.

FOR THE LOVE OF BRASS

"Good morning to you, Gary. You seem particularly happy."

"Yes, I think I am. It's the thought of sorting it out. I've not been my happy self for a long time."

"Have you not? How long have you felt like this?"

"Oh," I said. "Six months. Maybe a year. Probably a year if I'm truthful."

"Take a seat, Gary. Would you like a coffee or a tea before we start?"

"Yes, please, a coffee will make a change," I said. "Two sugars and white, please."

"Okay," Elaine said. "I'll be back in a moment." With that she left the room.

I sat in my chair, looking around the room. Hmmm, I thought, nothing has changed. The tissue boxes were still in the same place, with the piece of tissue sticking out of the top of the box, just waiting to be pulled and used. They looked the same as before. Maybe the tissues don't get used much. Maybe this is not a sad place after all.

Elaine returned with two cups of coffee and gave one to me. I put it on the small table next to where I was sitting.

"Thank you," I said.

"You're welcome." Elaine sat down with her coffee and looked at the notes in front of her. While she did this, I was drawn to the tissue boxes again. Yes, I thought. Maybe not a sad place. Maybe people are so happy when they've sorted out their lot in life, they cry with laughter and happiness. I hope that's the case. I guessed I'd find out. The other thing I wondered was why this big house was always quiet. I didn't hear any other voices.

With that, Elaine put her head up, looked at me and said, "Okay, Gary, how was school for you before you lost your father? Which type of classes did you enjoy?"

"Enjoy?" I said. "I don't think I enjoyed any of it. I went because it was expected."

We went on to talk about different things from that time. Just everyday things. I thought, Elaine must have a reason to go through this. Elaine would only ask the odd question, then leave it me to do the talking. I didn't seem to have any problem with the talking side of things. We talked about this and we talked about that. I did ask: the things we talk about seem to be just trivia to me.

"Yes," said Elaine, "they are, but it's all your life story. We need this information to access the out-workings of what is going on now." We continued along the same vein of conversion. Elaine then asked, "How did your father's passing affected the rest of your family?"

"Well," I said, "my brother and sister were very young, I think, to understand exactly what was going on. My mother, she took the whole thing extremely badly. She collapsed and was confined to bed. Two of her sisters came to stay. They helped out with things like making sure us kids got to school, had our meals, shopping and so on."

"Okay, that's it for now Gary. Our time is up. We'll continue with this next time I see you."

"Alright," I said. "How are we doing, Elaine?"

"Very well," Elaine said. "Keep in mind what we've been talking about. We'll start with that next week. Okay?"

"Okay," I said. "Thank you very much. Have a good week. See you next time."

"Next Wednesday at ten!"

"What can I do with the coffee cup?" I said.

"Oh, just leave it there; I'll deal with it."

"Thanks again. See you," I said. I left the room and went down the stairs. "Bye, Jan," I said as I passed her.

She just nodded. She was talking to someone on the phone. Still quite an old house, I thought as I left and went down the steps, round to the car park and my van.

I travelled home stopping in to look at a couple of jobs on my way. I soon arrived home. Things to do in the office, I thought. Especially as I'd just looked at two jobs. I'll sit in there and price them. This was one of the things I did enjoy doing – costings, or pricing and estimating, which is pretty much all the same thing – the reason being, get it right and you'll make money. Get it wrong and it'll cost you money. So there was every incentive to get it right. Sometimes it was like gambling. If I wasn't sure on something I'd guess and put a price against the item anyway, then hope it didn't cost money. For the most part it worked out very well, plus there was always a way of pinching a few bob back if it did go a bit wonky. So a costing was exactly that. I'd have an A4 pad. Write on it. Down one side, a list of materials that I reckoned was needed for the job. Then I'd make a column to the right hand side of the page. In this column the prices would be entered. Under the material list on the same side of the page I'd enter the labour that would be needed to complete the job. This would consist of how many men for how many days. If it was a small job, for example, it might be one man for, say, two days. Then that cost would be entered. There were a few other factors that came into play when doing a costing; these would be whether the access to the job was good or not; maybe you couldn't park at the job or there was a cost to do so, or it was difficult to get access to the rear garden. Plant was another factor. You might need scaffolding or skips in and out of the job. How much rubbish would we have to take away? Deliveries, and so on. You would have to think of any cost that might be incurred and, of course, enter these costs in the cost column. Once you had your materials and labour down in their column, you would then enter the profit figure, which, on a small job, meant pretty much whatever you felt you could get away with below the word Profit. I'd always enter F&F and would also have a price against that. The F&F cost was very important. If people saw it on a costing sheet they would have no idea what it meant. I knew and that was all that mattered. F&F stood for Fuck Factor. You know, when you get one of those moments at work, you look at something, slap the palm of your hand on your forehead and say OH FUCK, I didn't allow for that. Well, that's a fuck factor. Really it's a contingency figure but it's an easier way of writing it on the costing. So when your costing is done, you now have all the information you need to type up the estimate, along with the job specification on your headed letter paper. This is the estimate the client will receive.

A pricing is exactly that. Sometimes a breakdown price is requested to accompany the estimate. I finished the costings for the two small jobs I'd looked at early in the day, then thought I'd take the dogs over to the park. Walking the dogs had become a good thing for me. It gave me freedom away from the office and Sharon. I could walk and think about things while out. Maybe there was a happy solution for me after all.

As I left with the whippets, heading for the park entrance next to my house, I thought about the time my son Lee came into my office. It was a Saturday morning and I was in the middle of preparing a costing for a job.

"Dad," said Lee. "Can we go in the garden and do some archery?"

We had a couple of bales of straw in the garden, which we'd put on top of each other, then fixed a homemade paper or cupboard target to the bails. That was the target set up. The bales would stop the arrows and once set up, archery could commence. Seeing as how it was a sunny mid-morning, I thought this was a good idea. We could have some fun and I could teach Lee to be a better shot.

"That sounds a good idea, Lee," I said. "I'm just in the middle of doing a costing for a job. As soon as this is done we can go out."

"How long will it take, Dad?"

"I should have it done in about twenty to thirty minutes," I said.

"Okay, well, maybe if I help?" said Lee. "We can get it done faster. Then we can start shooting." Lee stood next to me as I was seated. He leaned forward, eager to help, looked at the paper in front and said, "What's a costing?"

"Well, Lee…" I went on to explain how a costing was put together and how we'd come to the end figure, a cost for the job (now, bear in mind, Lee was nine years old).

"So what's that 'F&F' mean Dad, and why is that number against it?"

"Well, Lee," I said. "The 'F&F' is a contingency figure." (Not wanting to explain its true meaning.) "That means it's a figure or an allowed amount in case we find something we didn't price for in the costing. It's like a type of insurance."

"Oh. Okay, Dad," said Lee. "So what if it's not needed on the job?"

"Well, we get to keep it as part of the profit."

"Yes," said Lee, "but the profit is in that column! You get to keep it anyway?"

"Yes," I said.

"Okay," said Lee. He looked at me. I could see the cogs working in his head. "Dad, I want you to write at the bottom of the first column. Lee's 'F&F' and opposite in the numbers column write ten pounds."

"Yes, okay," I said, while grinning. I proceeded to write in the columns: Lee's F&F, then the £10 opposite. I looked up at Lee. He'd the biggest smile on his face.

He then said, "Can I have the ten pounds now, Dad?"

I laughed. "No, you can't have it yet."

"Why not?" Lee said, "It's in the costing."

We were both laughing. "We haven't got the job yet," I said.

"Oh," said Lee. "When will we get the job?"

"Hold on," I said. "What if the extra ten pounds makes the job too expensive and we lose the job? We don't get any money at all. Then what?" I said with a straight face.

"Hmmm," Lee said. His face was straight as well. He stopped to think for a moment. I could see the cogs turning again. Then a big grin came on his face. "It'll be okay, Dad. We'll get the job." Then we both laughed. "So when will we get the job, Dad?"

"I'll ring the client this afternoon if he's in. Failing that I'll talk to him on Monday. Okay?"

"Yes, okay. Then can I have the ten pounds?"

"No," I said. "Because once we get the job, we have to do the job. Then when the job is complete, then I get paid. Then you'll get your ten pounds."

"Okay, Dad. Let me know as soon as we get the job," Lee laughed. "I can't wait to get my F&F. Come on Dad. Let's go and shoot some arrows."

Sharon came in through the garage into the kitchen with Lee. I'd returned home a bit early with the dogs. I was standing by the kitchen sink preparing food for the dogs.

"Hello," she said. "Is Michael in from school?"

"Yes," I said. "He's in the dining room doing his homework."

"Hello, Lee. Did you have fun at school?"

"Yes, Dad!"

FOR THE LOVE OF BRASS

"That's good. What's for tea, Sharon?"

"I'll sort that out once you've finished feeding the dogs. I'm not sure yet. I'll check in the freezer. Oh, by the way, did you go to see your lady today?"

"Yes, I did," I said. "I'll tell you how it went later, if you like."

"No, not really. I'm not that interested. There's stuff on TV I want to look at," said Sharon. "I don't suppose you're much further down the track, talking with her."

"No, not really," I said, sensing it might not go too well if I tried to push the subject of letting Sharon know how it went.

The situation at home carried on as usual. Spending less and less time with Sharon. We were growing ever further apart. I spent more time in the office. Except for a Friday evening when I'd go to the gun club early on in the evening. Then, when we finished shooting, I and some other club members would go to the Yew Tree pub on Reigate Hill for one or two beers and a meal. Weekends were spent doing my own thing with the boys. We'd go fishing or shooting. Running the dogs. By now, whatever we did it didn't include Sharon. She did her own thing.

CHAPTER FOUR
DAD'S FUNERAL

Drifting into the following week, Wednesday soon arrived. Relate day. By now I looked forward very much to seeing Elaine. The reason, I think, was that I'd pinned my hopes and future happiness on these meetings. I believed I was doing the right thing. I also believed that, once I'd gone through this period in my life, things would get better in my relationship with Sharon. It would sort itself out. I'd be happy again.

Off to Purley I went. I arrived at the car park next to the Relate building, jumped out of my van full of enthusiasm for my meeting, locked the van, turned and headed out of the car park entrance. I turned right and right again up the front steps, through the large door, which was closed to but not locked, and stepped inside, pushing the door closed behind me. Jan was sitting at reception as usual.

"Morning, Jan. We have to stop meeting like this," I said with a smile.

Jan looked up from paperwork she was doing at her desk and smiled back. "Hello, Gary. You know where to go by now. You can go up. Elaine is up there."

"Thanks a lot," I said and, before I knew it, I was knocking on the door as I pushed it open at the same time. "Morning Elaine," I said.

"Good morning," she replied. "Take a seat."

As I took a seat, she said, "Same as last week, tea or coffee?"

"Oh, tea please," I said. "Sugar and milk?" said Elaine.

"Yes, please, two sugars."

FOR THE LOVE OF BRASS

Elaine left the room and I looked around. Everything looked the same, the same as before. The boxes of tissues were even in the same places. I couldn't help but wonder, had there been happy people in here during the week? Had there been sad people during the week? There were no clues. Or had there been no people at all? Had Elaine only come in once a week, just to see me? While I was doing all this wondering, Elaine returned with the drinks. She handed me my tea, which I put on the table next to me. She sat down in her chair.

"Thank you for the tea," I said.

"You're welcome," she said. "Okay, you know what I'm going to say?"

"Yes," I said. "Where we left off last week."

"That's right," said Elaine.

"Well, you asked me if I had any favourite lessons at school, to which I answered, not really. That's not strictly true. I was thinking about the answer I gave you. I did have favourite lessons. Woodwork, metalwork and art. Those lessons I did like doing because I felt as though I had achieved something. Maths, English, RE, PE, I couldn't get into at all."

"That's good," Elaine said. "So you've been thinking about our conversations and meetings here."

"Oh yes, most definitely," I said, "although what we talk about now, I can't really relate to my current situation. But I want to be fixed. I want to get back to my old self and be happy with my lot in life. You said, Elaine, 'you'll be fixed'. That's exactly what I want to hear," I said.

Elaine then asked, "How did you feel when you lost your mother?"

"Lost my mother?" I said. "I didn't lose my mother."

"Yes, you did," said Elaine. "Effectively, when you lost your father you lost your mother because she wasn't there for you or you brother or your sister. She was confined to bed. So, effectively, she wasn't there, so who did you talk to?"

"Well, no one. There was no one to talk to."

"How did you feel about that?" Elaine replied.

"I kept it inside, I guess. Who could I talk to? Thinking about it now, there was no one to talk to. Was I supposed to talk to someone?" I asked.

"Yes, of course you were," said Elaine. "The situation was massive, huge, a life-changing time for all of the family," she added.

"No, I'm afraid not. We never ever spoke about the loss of my father between ourselves as a family or with each other. Funnily enough, not even to this day. It's never mentioned. I suppose that's how bad it affected us all."

"Okay," said Elaine. "How long was your mother gone for?"

"What … wiped out you mean? Unable to do anything?" I said. "Oh, I can't recall the time period. All I can remember is the day of the funeral. And I don't remember much about that. I can remember standing at the foot of the grave, looking down the hole at the brass plate with my father's name on, which was screwed to the coffin lid. Then looking around at the people and family members who were there. Most of the faces I was familiar with. The women all seemed to be crying, the men trying to console them with very straight, sombre faces. My mother stood at the head of the grave. She was inconsolable. One of her brothers was on one side of her, holding her arm. One of my father's brothers was on the other side of her, holding her other arm. The priest stood next to them, saying some words which, to my mind seemed to make matters worse. The words he spoke seemed to upset everybody more and more. I have absolutely no idea what he was saying. To me he was just making a noise. It was, for me, surreal. I didn't talk or say a word to anyone. People spoke to me but I didn't answer. I felt as though I had a protective invisible shield or wall around me. It was as though I was an outsider looking in, watching this service take place. Looking back I remember I didn't cry. I just watched everybody else crying. It was as though I was completely detached from the situation.

The next thing I remember while looking around, the people started to move. They seemed to come towards me on my right-hand side. As they passed behind me, they'd pick up a handful or a small amount of earth that was piled up next to the grave, then throw it into the grave as they passed me. I remember the noise the earth made as it bounced on the wooden coffin lid. I thought, why? Why are they doing this? Then a man's voice said, Gary, you can throw some dirt into the grave if you like. This I did. I picked up a handful and threw it in. The noise that handful made seemed to be the loudest as it hit the coffin lid. I felt a hand on my shoulder, which steered me to my left. I was then escorted away from the grave. There was, of course, a church service beforehand at the cemetery. I don't recall any of that service at all. Nor do I recall travelling to or from the cemetery. I know my brother and sister didn't attend the funeral. It was deemed they were too young. That's all I can remember.

The following day, we were back at home in Bermondsey. My two aunts were there. My mother was in bed. The doctor had been to visit her. She was kept sedated. How long this went on for I have no idea. It seemed to me to go on for weeks." Elaine listened to me talking without any input; she just sat listening. I suddenly realised why the tissues were there. I'd one in my hand, wiping the tears that had run down my face from my chin, while telling Elaine the story of my father's funeral. I looked down to put the tissues on the table next to me to discover there were a further two tissues already there. It was then that I thought, this place is a sad place after all but, trying to keep things positive, I said to myself, I look forward to the happy day here, when I'm fixed; when everything will be rosy once again.

"So, Gary," Elaine said. "You said before, you were not happy for maybe a year. Have you thought about how long has it been since you felt things were not right in your marriage?"

"Yes," I said. "I was thinking about that a couple of days ago. I thought it was a year ago but on refection, it was more like a year and a half. For the sake of an accurate answer, I'll pick a point in time and say March 1991… So yes, a little over a year."

"Okay," Elaine said. "Did you not think at some point then that you might do something about the unhappy situation?"

"Well, yes and no," I said. "Really, I should have done something. Even if it was, just bring it up and talk with Sharon but the thing to keep in mind, looking back, is that Sharon's not a talk-to person. Well, not about this subject. She'd go straight on the defensive and become aggressive, turn it around, and then it would be me who had it all wrong. She'd say things are okay, so don't think about it too much. Just get on with it. So for the most part I thought she might be right. I thought things might change as time went on and indeed they might get better. While this was going on I did from time to time think that Sharon wasn't happy in herself or with me. Or with our family life."

"Okay," Elaine said. "We'll stop it here for this week but there's something I want to ask."

"Okay," I said. "Fire away."

"When you get home after our meetings do you talk to Sharon about what has been said or how things may be going?"

"Yes…" I hesitated. "Well… I try to, but last week she showed very little interest, so it didn't get discussed at all, and after that and it wasn't mentioned all week."

"There's something I want you to do."

"Yes… "

"From now on, don't tell Sharon anything about what we talk about here. Can you do that?"

"Yes, I can," I said, "but if she asks?"

"Just say you've been advised by your counsellor not to discuss what is said."

"Okay, yes I can do that," I said.

Elaine went on to say that she did not think Sharon would ask. She felt Sharon would rather let sleeping dogs lie; she's seeing this as a threat to her own world.

Before I knew it, the following Wednesday had arrived. I was sitting in my chair looking around at Elaine's office. The boxes of tissues were still in the same places. Elaine entered the room with a cup of tea for me and coffee for herself. She sat down behind her desk.

"Okay, Gary," said Elaine. "How are things this week?"

"Yeah, all good, thank you. Work's fine. I've been busy with two new jobs starting. My boys are fine. It's all good, except for an argument with Sharon last Friday."

"An argument?" said Elaine.

"Yes."

"Can you, or do you feel comfortable talking about it?"

"Yes, that's fine," I said. "I'd got ready to go to the gun club, having had dinner, when Sharon said, 'I'm going out tonight. You're having the kids.' 'That's a bit sudden isn't it?' I said. 'No, not really. You go out every Friday. Well, it's my turn this week. I'm going out with my mates.' 'You could have given me some notice,' I said. You see Elaine, I run one of the ranges at the club. If I have notice, I can arrange for someone else to run the range so nobody gets let down. So, as it is, I said to Sharon, 'This makes me look bad.' Anyway, one thing led to another and an argument took place which included shouting and swearing and all in earshot of the kids, which I know isn't good, Elaine, but that's what happened. Sharon came in pissed as a pudding later that night, around three in the morning. She stayed in bed most of the day on Saturday, which didn't worry me. I did my thing with the boys. We amused ourselves all weekend. We went off with the dogs on Saturday, and then out fishing Sunday, so we were okay. Didn't see much of Sharon, which suited me fine! The rift's getting wider between us. That's how it is. I hate the arguing in front of the kids, the shouting and swearing but I find I'm doing it anyway from time to time. I really need to get this situation fixed," I said to Elaine.

"Well," Elaine said. "I can't fix the situation but I'm sure I can fix you."

"That's good to know," I said. "Anyway, other than that, everything's fine."

"Has Sharon asked about our meeting over the last week?" said Elaine.

"No, she hasn't," I replied.

"You mentioned once that Sharon would do paperwork in the office. Does she still do that for you?"

"Yes, she does," I said.

"Has Sharon helped you in other ways?"

"What do you mean?" I asked. "Well, within the business," said Elaine.

"No, she doesn't. I do all that side of things. All the business side, that is. Sharon never really helped with business. Mind you, she never stopped me but she just never supported me either, in any of the business decisions. I did ask why that was the case and I remember she answered, 'You run it all very well. You're making the money. It's all working out. So there's no need for me to help.' 'Yes, I know,' I said, 'but it would be nice to get support from your wife.' But I'm afraid that was never there. Not with anything I did."

"That's sad," Elaine said. "When two people are in a partnership, they should always support each other in everything they do. Together or otherwise."

On refection, I know exactly why I married Sharon. I married Sharon because I was madly in love with her. I thought in my own way, that was enough or all that was needed for a relationship. Love would concur all but it seemed at this stage of my marriage that nothing was being concurred. And the love, well, if there was any left now it was also slipping fairly fast into the abyss. Still, I was of the opinion that maybe our situation could be turned around. After all we had two lovely boys and at this stage a beautiful house, which we had worked so hard on. I felt I'd achieved a lot. I felt we had all achieved a lot. I didn't want to let all this go. So I thought this was all well worth fighting for.

CHAPTER FIVE
THE ART GALLERY

Before I knew it, another week had passed. It was appointment time at Relate again with Elaine. The time was passing very quickly for me, as it often does when you're anxious to achieve something important in life. I only wished it could be fixed in half the time. It couldn't be, I know, I'd been told. So just get on with it, I told myself. We'll get there. The past week had been a mixture of emotions. Ups and downs. My boys had had to listen to more arguments between me and their mother while they were in bed. I hated putting my sons through this shit. An argument could start up over virtually nothing and in a short time become all-consuming and loud.

I started to have nights sleeping on the settee or in the spare room because I didn't want to sleep with Sharon. I had evenings where I didn't even want to look at her, let alone talk to her. Our home life seemed to be getting worse by the week. The Relate weekly meetings were not catching up with it in as much as making it better. Maybe what I was expecting was a miracle or something but I certainly expected something. The weekends consisted of me and the boys doing something… something that we wanted to do, something that was fun and educational. Even if we just took the dogs over to Morden Park there was always wildlife there to seek out. And of course there were the outings to the countryside with the four boys in the van.

The chalk hills was a place we went to regularly. It's an area between

FOR THE LOVE OF BRASS

Betchworth and Box Hill; a lovely part of the North Downs, looking out over Betchworth, Brockham and on to Leigh and Newdigate. So that part of the Downs was a wonderful place to explore. Even in the winter, when the snow had settled, we spent time there. I'd teach the boys how to track animals, which was very easy, as everything left tracks. It was a good visual for tracking. The boys could see just how much wildlife actually lived there. Then, once the snow had gone, we'd know the animals were still there. You just had to look a lot harder for the signs. We'd climb sometimes as well. We had a particularly steep chalk hill we would climb. It was always crumbly, so difficult to achieve. All four boys would do very well and keep trying (even after losing their footing and sliding back down a number of times); they'd all keep going until they reached the top.

"Yes, that's a small fly swimming in my tea," I said to Elaine as I was about to take a sip.

"Can you catch it with the spoon?" Elaine asked.

"Yes, I'm sure I can." After doing so, the spoon and fly were put in the saucer. I was then happy to take a sip.

As I did, Elaine said, "So how was your last week at home?"

I went on to explain about the arguments and that I didn't like doing it in front of, or in earshot of, the boys. I told her about the weekend and that we hadn't seen much of Sharon.

"Either we were out or she was. So I see that as a bonus, because we can't argue."

"That's a good point," said Elaine. "So, Gary, do you always have the boys on weekends?"

"Oh no, Sharon takes them to her mother and father's house some Sundays. They'll go there for dinner and to spend the day. Sharon always visits her parents every Sunday. It's just that some Sundays she'll take the boys. On those Sundays I'll be over on the Bisley ranges, shooting. Either that or I'll be field shooting."

"Okay," Elaine said. "Is it a peaceful place for Sharon and the boys when they go to her parents?"

"Yes, I think so," I said. "They enjoy themselves."

"And do you go over to their house much?"

"Yes. I normally always get invited; well, I don't have to be invited, I can just go. Brenda was always very good. Even if she knew I was going shooting she'd say, 'Come over for your dinner when you get back. It'll be waiting for you in the microwave.' That was exactly what I did. Brenda's roast Sunday dinners were second to none."

"Okay," Elaine said. "Can I ask you about Sharon's upbringing? Did she have a normal family life?"

"Err… no, not really… Well, she did for the most part, except for the trouble between her parents."

"Trouble," said Elaine. "Can you tell me about that time in Sharon's life?"

"It's not really a time. It's a thing that started when she was a little kid and carried on while Sharon was growing up."

"And when did it end?" Elaine asked.

"End," I said. "It never ended. It still goes on to this day. The thing is, Elaine, Harry, or H as we call him, can be a very nice fellow, a sort of do-anything-for-you type of man but, and this is a big but, he is, or can be, very violent. He's extremely chauvinistic. He calls it old school but really he's just a male chauvinist. He has these jealous, violent, uncontrollable rages, which can last for days, and it's all directed in Brenda's direction. He can make her life an absolute misery and of course it's just as bad for anyone who's around him while this shit is going on. As adults now, we just keep out of his way until the rage has passed; however, it does leave Brenda in the middle of it all. Sharon was also in the middle of it all up till the age of eight. It was at this time that her sister was born, not that that made the situation any better. I don't think it made it any worse. How could it get any worse? It just carried on through Sharon's and her sister's upbringing. So really, when you think about it, all three women spent their life in fear of her father. I think that must have been a terrible way to live. What do you think, Elaine?" I said, but continued without waiting for Elaine to answer. Elaine wasn't saying anything once this subject came up. She was just listening while I was talking through it. "So I suppose that would make anyone want to leave home as soon as possible." I just carried on talking.

"Harry had beaten Brenda so many times over the years. And some of those times, the beatings were so severe he'd put her in hospital. The police in those days just called it domestic violence and wouldn't get involved. When the neighbours called the police, as they often did, a police car would turn up. A cop would come and knock on the doors. Harry would answer. The cop would say, 'There have been some complaints about noise. Can you keep the noise down? If we have to come back, we could arrest you for a breach of the peace.' The fact that somebody was beating the crap out of his wife was a domestic situation and nothing to do with the police. Not like nowadays. That situation has certainty changed, but not then. It's just how it was."

It seemed once I got on this subject there was no stopping me. It was just all coming out. Of course a lot of the stories I knew had happened before my time in the family but nonetheless I still had plenty of stories of how H would behave and it wasn't just the domestic violence. While driving, he'd get a dose of road rage, and that's putting it mildly.

"I've seen him on many occasions stop a car by pulling in front of it, then jumping out of his own car, pulling the other car's driver's door open, pulling the driver out of their car by whichever part of their person he could grab hold of, then proceeding to give them anything from a few punches to the head to a bloody good kicking. It's just how it was and it didn't stop there. He'd fought with every member of his family at some point or other.

"One incident I remember. He'd arrived up at his sister's house in Sutton, where he was going to park his caravan at the end of her garden. This had all been agreed earlier in the day by telephone but on arrival there was a discussion between him and his sister, which turned very quickly into an argument. The noise of shouting and swearing was heard inside by Harry's nephew, Robert. Robert decided to come out into the garden to see what all the fuss was about, only to see his uncle Harry give his mother a smack in the face. Robert intervened to protect his mother, only to receive a smack to his own face.

"Now, Robert was young and maybe only eighteen years old but he was a big bloke and quite tough. He decided he very likely wouldn't win in a fight with his uncle using just his fists, so he promptly armed himself with a garden spade that happened to be nearby. He told his mother to go inside, which she did, then Robert set about his uncle with the spade, bashing him with it many times. Luckily there were no blows to Harry's head but that didn't stop Robert from trying to strike Harry, with Harry keeping his arms up to defend himself from the onslaught. Most of the blows hit Harry's forearms although he'd also taken blows to his sides and his legs. In no time at all he couldn't fight back, he just had to get in his car, lucky to still be alive. He drove off with his caravan still attached. Needless to say, that ended Harry's relationship with that side of the family." I seem to have a lot to say on this subject, I thought to myself. "Elaine," I said. "Is this becoming boring to you? Shall I carry on?"

"Yes, if you're happy to do so," she said. "The thing is," I said, "when I think about this over the years, Harry has upset just about every member of his family, as well as Brenda's family. Some he's fallen out with forgive him after a while, then they'll be back on talking terms, only for it all to go wrong sometime in the future and maybe on a number of occasions. I remember H was having an argument with one of Brenda's sisters. It got very heated with lots of swearing passing from one to the other. Maure, which was the sister's nickname, was winning the argument when her husband, Bri, stepped in to calm the situation down, which he thought would be the right thing to do. Harry told him to fuck off, it was none of his business. Bri still thought it was reasonable to try and calm things down. The next thing he knew he was getting up from the floor holding his face after Harry had punched him. The situation would get right out of hand and they wouldn't talk for six months, then it would all be forgotten. The sisters would talk on the phone, then all four of them would talk, only for it all to kick off again at some point in the future. It's just how it is with him. Brenda had been to various battered wives refuges but Harry would somehow find her and bring her back home.

I don't know how he found her. I thought those organisations were secret and protected by the police but those homes didn't afford Brenda much protection. Of course, Harry would always promise it would never happen again and he was so sorry and, so she'd go back home. Not, I think, that she believed him. I think it was more the case that if she didn't, she definitely believed he'd kill her. I can remember waking up one Saturday morning to repeated knocking on my front door. I got up, put a pair of jeans on, went downstairs and opened the front door to find Brenda standing there with blood running from her nose from a cut above her left eye, which had been bleeding and had now stopped. On top of that she had a cut mouth and red marks, and bruising to her face and arms. She stood there, just wearing jeans, a T-shirt and slippers. There were lots of blood stains on her T-shirt and a number of blood stains on the front of her jeans. 'Gary,' she said, 'you've got to help me. That fucker has beaten me up again.' 'Come in,' I said.

"She stepped in and I closed the front door. She looked as though she'd been in the ring with Henry Cooper for six rounds and lost all six of them. The only thing I could think of is, once H knows she's gone, this is one of the first places he'll look. 'Sharon,' I shouted up the stairs, 'Come down straight away, your mum's here and she's in trouble.' Brenda was shaking with fear. She kept saying to me, 'When he finds out I've gone, he'll go mad and come looking for me… he'll come here.' Sharon had come downstairs at this point. She put her arms around her mother and said, 'Why, Mum, why has he beaten you this time, the bastard? Where's your clothes? Where's your shoes?' Brenda stood there shaking uncontrollably. 'I'll put the kettle on,' I said. 'Got any fags?' Brenda asked Sharon. 'Yes, there you go, Mum. Here's a light.' Both women lit up a cigarette. 'Where are your clothes, Mum?'

"Brenda said, 'He started again this morning. I'd just got up. He had the hump last night so I was on tenterhooks all evening. Then this morning he starts. I'd not even got dressed properly. He starts punching and hitting me all over the place. I locked myself in the bathroom but he just kicked the door in. He then got all my clothes from the wardrobe and put them in the bath. Then he turned the water on and filled the bath up. Any clothes of mine he could find, he threw in the bath. He got a pair of scissors from the kitchen and cut some of them up. He's fucking mental, you know! The next thing I know, I heard the front door slam and he's gone out. I ran into the kitchen and looked out the window. I watched him get into his car and speed off. Once I knew he'd gone, I got out of the flat as fast as possible. I ran down the stairs and out through the back door and made my way here using all the back roads and alleys so he couldn't find me. It took me about thirty minutes to get here I think, so I don't know how much time we have. He's bound to turn up here once he realises I'm not at home.' 'So what we going to do, Mum?' Sharon said. 'Do you have a plan?' 'Well, not really a plan but I think I might be alright if I can get to Paula and Martin's house. I don't think he'll find me there. Gary, can you take me to their house?' she asked. 'Yes, I can,' I said. 'Here you are girls, here's your tea. Finish your fags and while you drink your tea, I'll get ready. We should be able to leave in ten minutes.' Brenda tried to clean herself up a bit while Sharon went upstairs and sorted out a couple of bits of clothing for her to take and put them in a bag. 'Okay, you stay here, Sharon, with the boys,' I said, 'because when Harry turns up here, you'll be in and you can let him in. You've got to act as though everything is normal. You know nothing about what happened here. That means you have to lie to your father's face. Can you do that?' I said. 'Yes,' said Sharon. 'I've had to do it before and I'll do it again.' 'You sure now? Because you know what he's like if he smells a rat. He'll as likely give you a hiding and we can't have that, especially as the kids are here, although it might not come to that,' I said. 'He'll want to know where I am, he'll notice my car's not there. Tell him I've gone to work and you expect me back sometime in the afternoon. Oh, and Sharon, once we leave here, make sure there is no evidence that your mother was ever here. The tissues with blood on in the kitchen, make sure they're gone. Not just put in the bin but gone. Check the tea-cups and the ashtrays. You know what

FOR THE LOVE OF BRASS

I mean. No evidence at all,' I said.

"Brenda and I were ready to leave now. We said our goodbyes to Sharon, and as we left I said to Sharon once again, 'Don't forget, love, no evidence, alright? Be strong. I'll see you later.' Brenda and I got into my car and off we went, with Brenda waving goodbye from the car window. 'You okay Brenda?' 'Yes,' she said. 'Especially now we're away from your house. If he turns up we're already gone.' 'Okay,' I said, 'where are we going?' 'Do you know the Elephant and Castle?' 'Yes, of course I do,' I said. 'Well, head for there.' 'Okay,' I said, 'whereabouts?' 'I don't know,' Brenda said. 'You don't know where Martin and Paula live?' 'Well, yes, I do. I've been there before,' said Brenda. 'I'll recognise it when we get there.' 'Okay,' I said, 'how many times have you been there?' 'Twice,' said Brenda. 'That's all very nice but if you've been there twice, Harry will also know where to go if he comes looking, won't he?' 'No,' said Brenda. 'Because when I came here, I came with my sister Barb and, as you know, Barb's Paula's mum. We came over to visit when they first moved in. Then one other time, soon after, we got a train from Battersea to the Elephant and Castle on the overground, so when we get to the Elephant train station, I'll know where to go from there. You know where the Elephant station is, the overground?' 'Yes,' I said. 'No problem, I'll get you there. If you came over here on your own or just with Barb,' I said, 'where was Harry?' 'He was away working one weekend and he let me come over and stay at my mum's. He dropped me off and said I'd have to stay all weekend and promise not to go out for a drink or out with my family in the evening. Harry said he'd phone my mum's from time to time to make sure I was there. We took the chance he'd not phone while we were out at Paula's.' 'And if he did?' I said. 'If he did call, the story was, I'd gone with Barb into Battersea High Street to get some shopping for mum and to have pie and mash. Seeing as how we didn't have a pie a mash over in Sutton.' 'Bloody hell,' I said. 'Have you always been ruled and told what to do like this?' 'Yes, I'm afraid so. Ever since Sharon was born. It's a nightmare living like this, fucking terrible, but what can I do?'

"We drove up through Tooting, Clapham, Stockwell, Kennington, basically following the Northern Line of the underground to the Elephant and Castle. We approached the Elephant roundabout from Kennington and took the fourth road off the roundabout onto the road that would take you to the Bricklayers Arms roundabout and on to Tower Bridge. Within 30yds of leaving the roundabout we drove under a railway bridge. 'Yes, this is it. I recognise the bridge. The overground station entrance is up there,' Brenda pointed. 'Good,' she said. 'It's just along here in those big flats on the right.' 'Okay,' I said, 'that's good. Any idea how to get in there?' 'Hmmm… Yeah, take the second right into the flats. We'll find it once we're in there.' I took the second right and found a place to park. We got out of the car and Brenda pointed. 'Up there,' she said, 'on the sixth floor.' 'Okay,' I said, 'get your bag out of the car and I'll lock it up. It's a dodgy area around here. Nothing's safe.'

"We walked round to the end of the block and found the entrance where the lifts were. I pressed the button to call the lift. While we stood there I looked around the entrance area at all the graffiti on the concrete walls. Artists' tags all over the place, even on the shiny metal lift doors. We waited a few moments, then the doors opened. The smell of human urine came wafting out. It smelled stale, which seemed to make it worse. The graffiti artists had decorated the inside of the lift to match the entrance area of the building. I had this visual picture in my mind of a hoodie standing in the lift with his dick in his hand, pissing in the corner while spraying his tag on the wall. We pressed the button for the sixth floor and the doors closed behind us. We looked at each other as we travelled up, not saying a word. I think we were just holding our breath until we got there and the doors opened. We stepped out into what now seemed like pure fresh London air, grateful to be out of that lift. The views were nice as we walked along the landing. Brenda was looking for the right door. I could see out over London, the Houses of Parliament, Big Ben's tower and St Paul's Cathedral. 'This is it,' Brenda said. 'This is their front door, four doors along.' Okay, four doors along from the pissy art gallery I thought to myself.

"Brenda pressed the doorbell and we could hear the chimes sounding inside the flat. Martin opened the door. 'Hello mate,' I said. 'Well, you two were the last people I expected to see at the door. Come on in,' Martin shouted out. 'Paula, we have visitors and you'll never guess who it is.' Paula appeared in the hallway as we were stepping in. She took one look at Brenda and knew exactly what had gone on. She gave Brenda a hug. We said hello to each other and were invited into the lounge. 'I'll put the kettle on,' Paula said. We all sat in the lounge while Paula was making the tea. We lit up cigarettes and, before we knew it, the room was full of smoke. Paula came in with the teas and Brenda began explaining the saga that had taken place earlier on in the day. For the most part I just sat there smoking and listening to them all speaking and offering opinions on the situation. After a while it was agreed Brenda would stay there with them; at least for now she'd be safe. 'It's so nice to see you, Brenda,' Paula said. 'I've not seen my mum for a while. She's only been here twice and that was with you. You remember we went shopping in the Elephant Mall. We had fun,' Paula said. 'We were laughing about the phone call that might come from Harry.' 'He never did call you know,' said Brenda. 'Well, he did but I was back at my mum's by then.' The girls laughed. I just made small talk with Martin about work and so on, while the girls did most of the talking. 'Okay,' I said eventually. 'I'll be on my way. I wonder if Harry's turned up at my house yet?' 'Oh yes, he'd have turned up, that's a cert,' Brenda said. I said my goodbyes, thanked Martin and Paula and left.

"As I closed their front door behind me, I admired the view of London once more. It was a lovely, warm, sunny afternoon. As I walked along the landing, I thought of the smelly art gallery, the thought of descending the six floors in that confined space. No, I thought. I'll give that experience a miss for today. I'll take the stairs. I walked past the lift doors to a wooden door the other side of the lift. It had a sign that said 'FIRE ES'; the rest of the sign was missing. I went through the 'FIRE ES' door and started my descent. It wasn't decorated as well as the art gallery and the front entrance but nonetheless some effort had been made. There was just the odd tag here and there to look at on my way down. Surprisingly enough, not too smelly, just a couple of piss puddles to enjoy while descending the stairs. I was soon at the bottom, out through the door, around to my right and along the road to where my car was parked.

"It's a real shame really, I was thinking to myself. This block of flats was only three or four years old, so very modern and, once inside, very nice and spacious. Martin and Paula's flat was very nicely done out. Martin had done all the decorating himself as he also worked in the building trade. I found my car just where I'd left it. Thank God, I thought. In I got, started her up. Turned around and back down the road I'd come in on, to the end. Turned left along the road a few hundred yards. Under the railway bridge, onto the Elephant roundabout, first left and I was heading in the direction of home. As I drove, I couldn't help wondering if Harry had been to my house. If he had, what had been said? Had he interrogated Sharon and if he had, how had she held up? Was he still going to be there when I got back? I was supposed to be at work but I didn't have work clothes on. I'd have to think of a story. More lies and deceit. All this pressure and bullshit that affected all of us, just because Harry couldn't behave himself. He couldn't be reasonable, it wasn't in his nature.

"The journey back took around an hour and twenty minutes. It was Saturday afternoon. And there's always plenty of traffic, I said to myself. I arrived home and parked the car. I couldn't wait to find out what had gone on and to make sure Sharon was okay. Some people had mobile phones at this point but we hadn't. We only had a landline and I didn't want to phone Sharon through all this in case Harry was there. It was always such a mess when all this trouble started. I let myself in. Sharon was sitting in the front room smoking. 'You okay?' I asked as I came in. 'Yes,' said Sharon. 'Where're the boys?' 'Upstairs, they're fine,' she said. 'Was he here?' 'Yes, he turned up about an hour after you left. He was only here thirty or forty minutes, then went. Said he was going looking for her to bring her home. He asked had she been here. I said no. I made sure there was no evidence left lying around and he accepted that. He just said they'd had an argument and that she'd left. He didn't mention that he'd beaten the crap out of her and of course I couldn't ask any questions. I just had to pretend I knew nothing. That man is a bastard, a real bastard,' she said."

CHAPTER SIX
PRACTICAL JUSTICE

I pulled up at the road junction opposite my house and looked left and right, all clear. No cars or kids in the road. I drove across to park outside my house, parked, got out of the car and let myself in. A nice cup of tea, I think, before I go up to the office, I said to myself. While the kettle was boiling, I was thinking a lot about the meeting I'd just had with Elaine this morning.

I wondered if she was getting bored listening to me going on about the same stuff. I wondered how this could be helping me or my situation and, of course, I had lots more to talk to her about.

She'd said, "Remember where we are at the end of the session. We can continue next week."

Tea in hand, I made my way upstairs to the office, sat down at my desk and looked at the year planner on the wall in front on me. I found myself staring at it, thinking, I've plenty of work. There was lots going on but I couldn't concentrate. My thoughts were all over the place. Work, kids, money, house, Relate, Elaine and the future. Round and round it was all going like a merry-go-round. I need to get off, I told myself. Go on then, off you get. I couldn't take that step, I was still on it. I suddenly thought, hold on, you don't have to step off. Stay on it and stop it from going round. Then walk off.

I walked downstairs and took my empty tea-cup into the kitchen and put it on the drainer. I shouted, "Asher, Jade, come on girls; we're going out."

The dogs came running in from the utility room with as much excitement as ever. If they could speak, I'm sure they'd be saying, we love you, we love you. Where are we going? We love you so much. I laughed to myself because, out of the three girls in my life, there were only two who would be thinking that.

"Okay, where are we going to go? If we take the van it's out in the countryside somewhere. If we go on foot, it's off to one of the parks. Where do you want to go, girls?" I said to the dogs. We love you. We love you. We don't care where we go. We love you, was what I sensed from them. "Okay, then, girls, we're going over to the park and we'll go on foot." Yippee! Yippee! We love you. The dogs were jumping up and down with excitement. I put their leads in my pocket. "Come on girls, we're going out the back way."

Off we went, down the garden, over the back chain-link fence and into the field as we'd done many times before. Once all three of us were in the park the two dogs took off like rockets. They'd run in great big circles around the field. You often see the same people in the park walking their dogs. This day I saw two Labradors, one sandy-coloured, the other a black one, with their owners. There was also the lady who lived about twelve doors down from me on the other side of the road, she'd a big old Rottweiler, and the man with his Dalmatian. As my whippets ran in their large circle, these other dogs would try to join in the race. The Rottie had no chance. He'd give up after maybe a couple of hundred yards and the Labs would slow down after a full lap. The dog that did run very well with my dogs was the Dalmatian. Eight to ten laps of the park. It was great to see them go, before they stopped to just walk here and there, sniffing around with each other.

FOR THE LOVE OF BRASS

Once my girls had calmed down, I put their leads on them and we left the park through the far entrance, crossed over London Road and into Morden Park. This park was much bigger than the two fields behind my house. This was always a great place to be when you wanted some time on your own, some thinking time, and of course the dogs loved it. There were always squirrels to chase and other dogs to run with. Walking around Morden Park, thinking of what was going on in my life, trying to make sense of it all, wondering how these sessions would turn out with Elaine. My situation with Sharon felt as though we were getting further and further apart.

I headed home after about three hours, with nothing really resolved except that the merry-go-round hadn't just stopped, it had gone altogether, which was a relief, a great relief. That evening I spent time with the boys and once they were in bed, I sat in my office finding things to do.

The following day I went out to one of the jobs and kept myself busy all day. Back home, same old same old, with the odd argument thrown into the equation. Sharon came in from work on Friday and informed me she was going out for the evening. That's good, I thought to myself. I can sit in the front room and watch TV on my own once the boys are in bed. I'd not sat in my front room for some time now. I might even have a drink. Drinking was something I didn't do much. One or two pints after shooting on a Friday was about it. I never drank indoors. There were drinks in the drinks cupboard but they'd sat there for a long time. My friend Mark came round one evening. We were discussing something in the dining room.

"Do you want a brew, mate?" I said to him. "I'd rather have a beer if you've got one."

"Yes, of course," I said. "I'll get you one." I went to the drinks cupboard and returned with a Foster's in my hand. "Will that do you, mate?"

73

FOR THE LOVE OF BRASS

"Yes," he said, "that's great." We sat down to carry on and he opened his beer took a swig, and said, "Fuck me! Gary, there's something wrong with that."

We checked the sell-by date and it was two years out of date. That gives an idea of how much I'd drink at home. Mark settled for a coffee.

I did dinner for me and the boys. Sharon did her own, then got ready and went out. I spent time with the boys, and once they were in bed I thought I'd have a drink. I looked in the cupboard. The beer, all eight cans, were out of date. I put all of them into a carrier bag and binned the lot. Vodka I did have, two bottles, a bottle of gin and one of Bacardi. These drinks would have been brought back from Spain, duty free, from our holidays there. All I needed now was some orange for the Vodka. I looked in the fridge and found a carton. Vodka and orange, feet up, watching the TV on my own, no Sharon. Brilliant! I thought. Not much on TV to look at. Hmmm, just my luck. Never mind, there was always MTV, so I sat there drinking my V and O, watching the latest videos. Before I knew it, half the bottle had disappeared and the orange carton was empty. It was around twelve o'clock. That's it, I thought, I'm off to bed. I crashed out in the spare room and had a really good sleep, no idea what time Sharon came in. I never heard a thing.

Saturday morning and we were all up and about. We normally went shopping on Saturday. Well, of late it was either me or Sharon that went shopping. We couldn't even seem to be able to do that together. Sharon wanted to go shopping in Sutton with her mate from work; they wanted to look for clothes. That was okay with me, left us boys free, we'd go food shopping in Morden. We always had fun when we went shopping and afterwards we'd go in the Wimpy bar and have something to eat. By 1.30 we were done and on our way home, having had our Wimpy. We

FOR THE LOVE OF BRASS

unloaded the van and put all the shopping away. It was a lovely warm day and the boys wanted to play outside with their friends, which they often did in the alley. The alley, as we called it, was an area next to our house, maybe 40ft wide and about one 130ft long. Big enough area to build a good size house and garden on, the alley ended roughly in line with the end of our garden. Then there were double gates, 6ft high, the same height as the fence each side. The gates and fence were a chain-link type, so you could see through into the park even if the gates were locked. In the summer a park keeper would turn up around 9 o'clock and lock the gates. Once the gates were locked we could still use the park by getting over the fence at the end of our garden. Our fence was only 4ft tall. It was fantastic then because we had the park to ourselves. My garage door was up, the boys would be in and out of the garage playing with their skateboards and push bikes, and playing war with their water pistols. I'd come out every so often to check everything was okay with them all. There could be as many as ten kids playing out there. Sometimes, if I was doing some work in my garden and the kids were playing in the alley, I could hear what was going on and know they were all okay. I could also stand on the two back steps into our utility room. From there I could see over the wall easily, with a view of the whole alley. Sometimes, if I was looking over the wall watching the kids, or just going in and out from the garden, I'd see people I knew entering or leaving the park with their dogs. Often I'd have a chat with them from the back steps. That day, I saw the two men with their Labradors who often met to walk their dogs. They lived in the same road as me. While I was talking with them, the lady with the Rottweiler and her husband came past. I greeted them with a hello as I often did when I saw them. The boys were out all afternoon until tea time, when I called to them to come in. I spoke to them over the back wall.

I said, "Get all your stuff into the garage, boys. All the bikes, skateboards and whatever else you had out, then come in, please." This they did and the garage door was put down and closed.

The boys came in and Michael said to me, "I've got a problem, Dad."

"What's that, Mike?"

"Er ... well we brought our stuff in," Mike hesitated.

"Yeah?" I said.

"And, well," said Mike, "my bike's gone."

The bike was a Lizard mountain type bike, finished in a nice bright green, which made it stand out from other bikes.

"Do you know how it happened?" I asked. "Were there any strangers out there, friends of friends, anyone you can think of who maybe had a go on your bikes?"

Mike was thinking. "No Dad," he said, "no one I can think of. We did play a lot with the skateboards. It must have got taken then. I don't even know when it might have gone. I didn't miss it until we were coming in."

"Okay," I said, "don't worry for now. I'll sort something out." We'd got the bike for Mike the previous Christmas. It had cost £200, so it would pay me to try and get it found and returned, otherwise I'd be looking at shelling out another £200. Mike's mother returned from her shopping expedition. She wasn't impressed with the news about the bike's disappearance. I told her, "Don't worry, I'll sort the situation out." They were the only words that passed between us until the next day.

Next morning, I got up and ready, collected together the kit I'd need for a day's shooting and headed off out. Sharon went over to her parents for the day.

Monday came and Michael came home from school. I called him up

FOR THE LOVE OF BRASS

to the office where I'd been working.

"Mike," I said. "I've been thinking about your missing bike."

"Yes, Dad," he said, "do you think we can get it back?"

"Well," I said, "out of all your friends and boys you know, who is the hardiest and the biggest?" Mike was thinking. "What about that Simmons boy that pops by sometimes?" I said.

"Yeah," said Mike, "there's one even bigger than him. You know him, Dad, he comes round with his brother. Jay's his name. Jay Sarge. You know him. We were friends ages ago when we lived at our last house."

"Yes, I know. Does he go to your senior school now?"

"Yes, he does." Mike said.

"And will you see him tomorrow?"

"Yes, I see him every day. We're mates."

"Good stuff," I said. "When you see him tomorrow, I want you to tell him to come home here with you, after school. Tell him I want to see him and have a chat with him."

"Okay, Dad I'll do that."

The following day I was keeping an eye out from the office window, hoping to see Michael and Jay coming across the park. There they are, I said to myself. Right, I'll go downstairs to the kitchen and put the kettle on and wait for Michael to come in. Michael let himself in and Jay was with him.

"I'm in the kitchen, boys." They entered the kitchen both smiling.

"Hello Mike, Jay. Jay," I said, "thanks for coming over here, there's something I want to talk to you about."

"Oh yeah," said Jay.

"On Sunday," I carried on, "Mike had his bike nicked from the alley here next door." I pointed in the direction of the alley.

Jay's smile dropped. He replied, "I didn't nick the bike."

I smiled and said, "No, no, I know you didn't but here's the thing, Jay," I said. "Somebody did take it. Now this is where you come into it."

"But I don't know who took the bike," Jay said.

"I know that. What I want you to do is to ask around and find out who took it and where it is, then I'd like you to bring it back." As I was telling him this I was reaching in my pocket. "So Jay, when you return it back here, I'll give you twenty pounds." By this time I was holding the £20 note in my hand for him to see. "Now the thing is also, I don't need to know who took it or where it was when you found it. I don't care who took it. I just want it back."

"Okay," Jay said, with great intrigue.

"Now I do realise you may have to twist a few ears, or even bang a few heads but I don't care about that. I just want the bike back."

"Okay," Jay says, "sounds good to me."

"The other thing is, Jay, if you use your loaf, when you find out who took it, you can tell them that they own you twenty pounds for the trouble they caused you in making you go round there and get the bike back for your mate Michael. So they'll pay you the twenty pounds, or you'll be back to see them. And then you won't be so friendly. You know what I mean, Jay?"

Jay smiled again and said, "I know exactly what you mean."

"Great, no questions asked. I just want the bike back and there's twenty pounds waiting here for you. Thank you very much Jay. Hope to see you again soon." We both smiled and Jay went on his way home. I heard Michael relaying the story to his mother a bit later on that evening.

The following day was my big day again, another session with Elaine. I'd no real idea if these sessions were helping me but I did look forward to going, so they must have been achieving something, even if it was only me unloading, getting things off my chest.

"Good morning, Elaine," I said as I took a seat in her office. "I'm a couple of minutes early as I'm sure you realise."

"Yes," she said, "that's okay."

"Do you not see anybody before me in the morning?" I asked.

"No," said Elaine. "You're the first of the day for me. We get busy in the afternoon and more so in the evening."

"Oh, really," I said, "and what time do you finish?"

"Oh," she said. "I finish at four o'clock but the offices are open until nine in the evening. The evening is our busiest time. With people having to work, they tend to come along then."

"Blimey," I said, "there must be a lot of unhappy couples out there."

"Yes, I guess there are. Okay. Can we carry on from where we left off last week?"

"Okay," I said. "I think I was at the point where I'd returned home from the Elephant and Castle having dropped Brenda off."

"Yes, that's right." Elaine replied.

"That evening, Sharon phoned her dad to see if everything was okay with him but really, she wanted an update to see if he'd found her mother or just what was going on. She finished the phone call saying she'd call back tomorrow or, if he'd any news of her mother's whereabouts, could he call her and let her know. She was worried. She had every right to be worried. Sharon had no idea if the next time she saw her mother it would be in the hospital."

"Sunday morning, around eleven o'clock. Sharon calls her mother's house. No answer. Sharon's now getting very worried because she has no idea what is going on with her mum. She's so frightened to phone around the family to try and find out in case her father is there where she calls or her father finds out she's called and got there first, then she'd be in trouble with him. The whole family seemed to run on fear as far as I could see. Once Harry had lost his temper, everyone was on edge for anywhere from two to about four weeks, then it seemed everyone could relax but only until the next explosion, when all the same stress would start all over again. She called a few more times, probably every thirty minutes. By around half two in the afternoon when she called again, her father answered the phone. 'Hello Dad,' she said, 'have you heard anything from Mum?' 'Yes,' H said, 'your mother's here. Do you want to talk to her?' Brenda says, 'Hello Sharon, you alright?' 'Yes, Mum. Don't suppose you can talk, Mum, can you?' 'No,' Brenda said. Sharon could tell her mum had been crying. 'Okay, Mum, as long as you're okay. I'll call you tomorrow when that bastard is at work, okay Mum? Talk to you then.' 'Okay, love,' Brenda said. 'Bye love,' sounding very nervous. Sharon said to me, 'I've spoken to mum, she's at home with him.' 'Oh dear,' I said. 'That running away lark didn't last too long.' 'No,' said Sharon. 'I'll talk with Mum tomorrow and find out what happened.'

"The following day, Sharon told me what had happened. Harry had started off looking for Brenda at our house, then systematically worked his way through the family, going to everyone's house, telling then in no uncertain terms that he wanted her back and if any of them stood in his way, he'd be back and it wouldn't be a social call, so if they knew anything as to where she was, they should tell him now. He'd visited everyone except Martin and Paula. He didn't know where they lived, so while he was in the Battersea area, he went to see Paula's mum. She wasn't very good at keeping secrets, especially from Harry. He was very intimidating when he wanted to be. He got the information he needed, then went to collect his wife and bring her home, which of course he did. Once at Martin and Paula's, he told them to stay out of this, as it was none of their fucking business. He said, 'If she ever turns up here again, you'll phone me straight away and let me know, or I'll come round here and fucking start on you. Do you understand?' With that he man-handled Brenda out of their flat and down to the car. All the way home, Harry was threatening Brenda, telling her how he was going to beat her for running away and involving other people and, of course, making him drive around south London looking for her. He gave her a number of smacks when they returned home, telling her if she ever ran away again, he'd kill her next time. Sharon would have known what took place when Brenda returned home. Sharon had seen it all before. In fact, she'd lived it all before, many, many times."

"So your father-in-law really is not a nice man at all," said Elaine.

"No, he's not. Not when it comes to women or, to be more precise, when it comes to Brenda. He has a saying he'd use when he was telling Brenda to do something. He'd say, 'You Don't Keep a Dog and Bark Yourself.' Well, it's one thing saying things like that in men's company as a joke but he'd say it about Brenda in front of other people. He also said it to her face, except he wasn't joking, he meant it. She'd do the housework every day, and exactly how he said. If she didn't, or didn't do it how he expected it done… well you can guess how it goes. For the most part I stayed out of the family conflicts."

"Did you find that easy to do?" Elaine asked.

"Well, I had my opinions on things but basically, I kept them just between me and Sharon. So yes, I guess so."

"You never had an argument or a fallout with Harry?" said Elaine. "Did you?"

"Yes, I did, but it was much earlier in my relationship with Sharon and more than an argument."

"Okay," Elaine said. "It might help if you talk it through. Are you happy to do that?"

"Yes," I said, thinking to myself, will this help, or is she secretly enjoying these stories? Well, maybe not enjoying these stories, she must have heard a thousand like my ones. I'm sure this is nothing new to her. "Yes," I said. "It was when we lived at our last house. We were married and had been for two years. Sharon was six months pregnant, carrying Michael. She had passed her driving test and her father had always said when she passed her test, he'd buy her a car, which he did. At some point while she was driving the car, the starter motor decided not to work. Sharon's car was parked outside our house and Harry said he'd come over and fix it on Saturday morning for her. I'd been working nights on a job in Morden, so when I got home at about seven-thirty in the morning, I'd go to bed. On this particular Saturday morning I was in bed asleep when I heard some noise downstairs, which woke me up. I knew Harry was over to fix the car, so I thought I'd get up, go down and see what was going on. I could always catch up on some sleep later on in the day before I went back to work that night. I came downstairs and into the kitchen, and noticed there was no one around. I put the kettle on to make tea, wondering where everybody was. I went into the front room and looked out of the front-room window, to see Sharon with her mother and father at the back of the car with the engine cover up (the car was an Hillman Imp which had its engine in the rear). I thought I'd go back into the kitchen and carry on making the tea. I had the four cups on the side waiting for the kettle to boil. Each cup had a tea bag, with two sugars in two cups. The girls didn't take sugar. The kettle boiled and I poured the hot water into the cups, turned and opened the fridge. There was no milk. Back in those days the milkman would deliver the milk to your doorstep. Okay, I thought, no milk in the fridge. There must be some on the doorstep. I'd only had two-and-a-half hours' sleep at this stage so I must have looked a bit tired and a bit not with it. I walked down the hall to the front door, opened it. Ah, good, three pints of milk waiting for me. I bent down picked up the three pints. I looked over to Sharon and the in-laws and said, 'Morning, just making some tea, who would like one?' All three looked round and the two girls said good morning. They both said, yes, they would love a cuppa. 'Okay,' I said, 'it's on its way.' I turned to go back in and Harry shouted, 'Oi! What do you think you're doing, you lazy fucker?' I looked back around. I could see he was serious. I replied, 'I'm making some tea.' Then I went inside pushing the door shut behind me, thinking to myself, oh dear, Harry's got the hump about something. Oh, well, it is not my problem. I'm having some tea.

"I went back into the kitchen and finished making the tea. I could hear raised voices outside the front door and before I knew it the front door opened quickly. Sharon stepped in, then slammed the front door shut. I could tell by her face, Harry had started an argument out there. I looked at her and said, 'What's going on?' Then I smiled and said, 'Was it about the tea?' Sharon didn't think it was amusing. She said, 'It's not funny, he's going mad out there.' I could hear Harry's voice getting louder and louder. Then, all of a sudden, a kick to my front door. BANG. It sounded so loud from inside the hall. Sharon turned. She slid the large bolt over. 'You lazy fucker, get out here,' Harry shouted from outside. This was then followed by another great kick against the door. Then another kick, then another. 'Sharon,' I said, 'you'd better open that front door because he's coming through it. Open the door, let me talk to him.' 'No!' she said, 'you stay in the kitchen. I'll talk to him and calm him down.' I turned to put down the two cups of tea I was holding. Sharon opened the door. Harry stepped up onto the step, then tried to push pass Sharon. Sharon shouted, 'You're not coming in.' Harry had reached over Sharon and pushed the door wide open. She was pushing him back and shouting, 'You're not coming in, Dad. I told you. You're not coming in. You're out of order. You're not coming in.' Harry was shouting, 'Come out here, you fucker. I'll teach you a fucking lesson.' I walked the few steps from the kitchen along the hall to the front door. Harry seriously wanted me for something. So I thought I should confront him to find out what this was all about. I was at the door with Sharon between us on the step and Harry just outside. 'What's all this about, H?' I said. 'You fucking know,' shouted Harry. 'Get out of the way, Sharon,' Harry said, 'let me come in.' 'No Dad, I told you. You ain't coming in. This is my house, now get out,' Sharon said to her dad as he was trying to push pass her. I still had no idea what this was about. Then all of a sudden, and this did surprise me, there was a sound of a whack. Sharon's head spun around to face me as Harry's hand passed her face and carried on down to one side of her. Harry had hit Sharon in the face.

"For a split second I had to absorb what had just taken place and, just as fast, I found myself moving forward to pass through the gap between Sharon and the door frame. As I stepped down off the step, and with all the power I could muster, I threw a clenched fist, which connected with Harry's cheekbone and mouth, knocking him backwards and off balance. He fell on to his ass, then on to his back, and lay on the garden path for a second wondering what had happened. I turned and grabbed Sharon, pushed her in as I went back through the doorway, then slammed the door closed behind me. 'Sharon, get into the kitchen,' I shouted as

FOR THE LOVE OF BRASS

I followed her through the kitchen door. I noticed the teas still on the side. 'That's a shame,' I said to Sharon, 'the teas are getting cold.' I smiled, knowing full well the confrontation with Harry was nowhere near over. BANG. BANG. BANG. The sound of Harry kicking in my front door… my front door was strong but with a seventeen-stone Harry laying into it from the outside, I figured it wouldn't be long before I'd be face to face with Harry again. A split-second decision had to be made. I went towards the door, which shook on its hinges each time it was kicked. In between the kicks I turned the brass knob of the Yale lock, thinking to myself, if Harry wants to dance let's dance, and with that, the door flew open and in came an enraged father-in-law. Now, luckily for me but unluckily for my wall phone, Harry had the biggest haymaker punch. I bent back and to my right and, with Harry being left-handed, his left fist flew past my face with only one or two inches to spare, and kept going on its trajectory and connected with my phone. There was the sound of the phone smashing apart and the bells becoming airborne, along with Harry letting out a scream. I instantly took advantage of a target and delivered another right-hand punch straight over Harry's left arm into his face again. He found his body travelling backwards. He fell onto his back and his head landed on the doormat. This all happened so fast that, before I knew what had happened, the red mist had taken over. The next thing I was aware of, I was sitting on Harry's chest with my left hand on his throat just under his chin, holding his head still, while in my right hand, fully raised up in the air, I was holding a club hammer and was about to bring it down onto Harry's head. On realising what the hell I was about to do – if I hit him with this, the blow will kill him – I threw the hammer off to one side. Harry's expression went from horror to relief. I stood up and said to him, 'That's it. Get out of my house. Never come back, you're not welcome here.'

"While all this was going on, poor Brenda just stood in the front garden watching events unfold. Harry got up, wiping the blood from his face, stepped out into the garden, grabbed Brenda by the arm and said, 'Come on you, we're going.' They left my garden, got in their car and drove off. The reason Harry's face was losing a lot of blood was that, while I was having my red mist moment and sitting on him, I'd punched him a number of times in the face before picking up the club hammer, which I'd left on the floor with a bolster in front of my hallway cupboard, from a job I'd been doing in the front garden the day before.

"I closed the front door, turned and looked at the spot where my wall phone had been. That's a shame, I thought. I really liked my phone. Well, I guess I still could. It's just that it ended up in twenty-three pieces with just bare wires hanging from the frame, which was still attached to the wall. That's all that was left of my phone. I looked at Sharon and said, 'Shall we have that cup of tea? I think we need it,' and 'What was all that about?' Sharon said, 'I have absolutely no idea.' Needless to say, the Imp didn't get fixed."

Elaine was just listening to my stories, not saying anything. She just let me run with it.

"I had nothing to do with Harry for three years after that event. Sharon carried on going to see her parents on Sundays with Michael once he was born. It was just me. I didn't have anything to do with H."

"So what happened after the three years?" asked Elaine. "Did you end up friends?"

"Yes, we did," I said. "I was refitting and redecorating my lounge. It was a Sunday, late in the day. Harry and Brenda had brought Sharon and Michael home. They all came in, except for Harry. Up to this point he wasn't welcome in my house, so he was waiting for Brenda in his car outside. Brenda said, 'Gary, is it okay if Harry comes in? We can all have a cup of tea and put all this behind us.' Brenda had asked this before but I'd always said no. Today, for some reason, I said yes. 'That's okay, Brenda, tell him he can come in.' He came in and said he was very, very sorry for what had taken place. He couldn't apologise enough. From then on we built a relationship. We even worked together sometimes. He'd work for me if he was short of work and sometimes I'd work for him, especially if he'd a job where we'd go away to work. He did partitioning, so I'd help him out. We might go away all week and just come back on weekends. Normally the jobs wouldn't last more than two weeks. He was still a male chauvinist though. He was always giving me tips on how to have affairs with other women and not get caught, not that his advice was of any use because he'd been caught a few times. He just thought he could do that because he was the man of the house, he thought it was his right."

"It would seem obvious to me," said Elaine, "that Sharon and Brenda would have trust issues with Harry and maybe men in general. Do you think Sharon trusted you?"

"Yes, I think so. Although there was a time a while back when she did something I had a real problem getting over. It turned into an argument that would last a couple of weeks. Well, not so much what she did, more like what she said. I'd finished redecorating one of the lounge rooms after many evenings' and a few weekends' work. I was out at work and, while I was out, Sharon was at home doing something in the bathroom and she left the tap running in the sink with the plug in. She wandered out of the bathroom and went downstairs to the kitchen, totally forgetting about the tap running upstairs. It wasn't until she noticed water running down the kitchen wall she realised there was a problem. She ran into the lounge room to check, only to find the water was running through the ceiling and down the newly decorated wall. She ran upstairs to turn the tap off. She spent the rest of the day being extremely worried as to what I'd say or do when I got home. When I did arrive home from work, she seemed very quiet and not very talkative. I wondered what might be wrong. After I had been home for a while, she plucked up the courage to tell me what had happened and pointed at where the water had come through into the kitchen. 'Okay,' I said, and went into the lounge room to have a look at the damage. There was water damage to the ceiling and down one of the walls. I said, 'That's not too bad. We'll let the water dry out, then just repaint the area.' 'Oh, that's good,' she said. I've been really worried all day as to what you would say or do because if my mother had done that, my father would have beaten the shit out of her. 'Oh yeah,' I said, 'so you think I'm like your Dad?' 'Yes,' said Sharon. 'Aren't all you men the same?' That's it, I thought. Now we'll have an argument. I felt so let down by Sharon thinking I was like her father all this time. It really hurt and really pissed me off." Hurt I thought, yes that was it. "The thought that that was how Sharon saw me really hurt. It took me a while to get over her remark. I had to ask her a few times, 'Can you try and see me for me and not like you father?' Eventually for me, those feelings subsided and I got on with things but it was always in the back of my mind."

"How do you think Sharon sees you now?" Elaine asked.

"Well," I said, "we don't talk too much to each other these days but I think she's probably waiting for me to turn into her Dad. Do you know what I mean? She always seems to have her guard up."

Elaine said, "Okay, Gary, this is what I'd like. Can you talk to Sharon and ask her to come here with you next time?"

"No," I said in no uncertain terms.

FOR THE LOVE OF BRASS

"Why not?" Elaine asked.

"It would be a waste of time asking her because she'll refuse to come along here."

Elaine said, "Has Sharon ever said she'd like your relationship to be fixed?"

"She's said she'd prefer if it was better, you know, less arguing and so on, but then she doesn't see a problem. She thinks things aren't too bad. Then there's me feeling like banging my head on the wall. I feel like I'm flogging a dead horse, as they say."

Elaine said, "I think you could talk to her... maybe one of those talks you have of an evening when the children have gone to bed. No arguing, just talking. You could explain to her that you need her input and together you can make things better between you, which can only be good," said Elaine. "You see I can fix you but I can't fix the relationship for you if she doesn't come along."

"Oh, I see your point," I said. "I see where you're coming from. Okay, it makes sense. I'll talk to her and try my best."

That evening the boys were in bed. Sharon was sitting in the lounge watching the TV. I thought this is the time to ask, to see if I could do this. After all it was a Tuesday evening. Sharon wasn't going out anywhere.

I wandered into the lounge, sat down and said to Sharon, "I want to have a little chat with you."

Sharon was sitting on one of the armchairs with her hand under her chin while resting on the arm-rest. As I spoke, her eyes turned to face in my direction and, with an expression on her face that said, get on with it, she said nothing. I explained in a nutshell why it would be a good idea for her to come along and how we could benefit from it. I also included the counsellor's views.

FOR THE LOVE OF BRASS

When I'd finished, Sharon said, "Okay, I'll come with you if you figure it'll help." Wow! I thought to myself as I left the room. I didn't think that would have happened. Not in a million years.

Friday, around five-thirty. I pulled up outside my house in my van, having finished work. The garage door was up. Sharon had come home from work a little early. The red Mercedes was parked inside. Leaning on the back of the car were Michael and Jay, talking to each other. Further into the garage, up against the back wall, I could see a bright green bike. I got out of my van. As I approached the boys, all three of us were smiling. I put my hand in my pocket getting out some money.

"Hello boys," I said. The boys greeted me in return.

Michael said, "Got my bike back, Dad. Jay brought it back."

"Well done, Jay," I said, "Any trouble?"

"No," said Jay. "Not really."

"That's good." I looked at Michael. "Is it all there, Mike? Everything working as it should be? Nothing missing, I mean."

"Yes, Dad," said Michael.

"That's great, Jay," I said. "There's your twenty pounds. Thank you very much for bringing it back."

"You're welcome, Gary," said Jay.

"Did you have to go far to find it?" I asked.

"No," said Jay. "It was in a garage on the other side of the park."

"What, this park here behind my house?" I said.

"Yeah," said Jay, "some boy had it. Kept it in his garage, thinking if no one saw it he'd not get caught."

I laughed and said, "Brilliant Jay, good work and did you make some money on the side?"

"Yes, of course I did. I told him he'd to pay for my time looking and asking around for the bike! I told him it would cost him twenty quid. At first he said no but I told him if he didn't pay it now, I'd take the bike away and come back later."

"What, with the police?" I said.

"No," said Jay, "not with the police." Jay laughed. "I told him I'd beat him up, kick the shit out of him."

"And what did he say to that?" I asked.

Jay said, "'Wait here,' the boy said. He disappeared through the garage, into the kitchen. When he came back he'd fifteen pounds in his hand. He said that was all he had, would that do? So I took the money and the bike, then walked over here to Mike's and that's it. Here we are."

I said thanks very much to Jay.

"That's alright, Gary. Oh, and I forgot to say, I told the boy if he so much as comes over this side of the park or near Michael's house, I'll come over and get him," Jay laughed, "so everything should be okay now."

"Okay, Jay, see you soon. Bye."

I was glad we were all able to sort out the bike thing when we did because this was the last week at school. At the end of this week, school summer holidays began. That was always going to be an adventure. The boys would either go to Julie's or some days I'd take off work and take the boys out somewhere for our own adventure.

CHAPTER SEVEN
PRACTICAL SHOTGUN

Mark came over on Friday evening. We were sorting out some details for Sunday, when we were going shooting. He arrived at my house at around 7.30. I answered the door to him.

"Mark," I said, before we settled in. "Do you fancy a beer while you're here?"

"Yes," he said.

"Okay, mate. Let's walk up to the off licence and get a few drinks. I don't have any here."

"Okay," Mark said. Sharon was getting ready to go out with her friends later.

"Sharon," I shouted. "I'm going up the road to the off licence with Mark. Be back in about 15 minutes."

"Alright," Sharon shouted back down the stairs.

"Alright," I said to Mark, as I closed the front door behind me. "Come on mate, we'll go now. Sharon's got a cab coming for her soon. She's going clubbing later."

"Oh yeah," said Mark. "Where does she go clubbing?"

"I don't know. Croydon, I think. I don't ask."

"You don't ask?" Mark said.

"No, mate. I don't care where she goes just as long as she goes out. Then I'm happy. That's the reason I've not been shooting over at the Reigate club some Fridays. Sharon goes out and I babysit."

FOR THE LOVE OF BRASS

"Sounds like you two are not getting along very well," Mark said.

"No, mate, we're not." I went on to tell Mark the situation between Sharon and me as we walked to the shops. I pushed the door of the off licence open and we went in. "What beers do you want, Mark?"

"Oh, Foster's, please."

"Okay, mate," I said to the shop-keeper, "Six cans of Foster's and a bottle of Vodka, please, mate. Oh, and a pack of golden Virginia and some green papers, please." I paid the shop-keeper and we went on our way.

While walking back, Mark asked who the Vodka was for with an enquiring tone. "Sharon?"

"No, it's for me. I drink that of an evening. I find it chills me out and I sleep better."

"Oh dear," Mark said. "Things really ain't that great at home, are they?"

"No, mate," I said. "Oh, and the beers that I had in the drinks cupboard the last time you came over, I threw the lot away. They were all out of date. Sharon drinks the Bacardi. She'll have a couple while getting ready to go out, so all that's left is the bottle of gin. That'll still be there next Christmas, I reckon."

"So does Sharon go out every Friday now?" asked Mark.

"No. Just some Fridays and most Saturdays," I said. "Which I think is great because I don't want her here. I prefer to be on my own with the boys. I've no idea if we can fix this but I'm giving it a go."

The doorbell rang. It was the cab for Sharon. She was on her way to a friend's house where the girls would meet and have a few drinks, then go clubbing later in the evening. I heard Sharon say goodbye to the boys.

Then, as she passed the dining room, she said, "See you later, don't wait up."

That was the sarcastic bit. I just smiled as I looked at Mark. Mark and I got on organising our shoot for Sunday while having a drink. Mark only had two cans because he was driving. I went on to have half the bottle of Vodka, with orange, of course. I put my sons to bed when it was their time to go. Mark left. I'd be seeing him on Sunday morning. I crashed in the spare room as usual. Sharon would come home pissed as a newt and, as always, I'd not hear a thing. I found as long as I only had half the bottle of Vodka over the whole evening, I'd feel okay the next day.

Saturday morning, I and the boys were up and about by around 9 o'clock.

"Okay, boys," I said. "After breakfast I have a few things to do in the office but I should be done just before lunch, then how about we go to Morden for the shopping and into the Wimpy for a bite to eat, then back and we can do some stuff here. What do you think?"

"Yes, that's great," the boys said. "We'll play outside till we go shopping."

"Okay, that's fine," I said.

I was working in my office but found after an hour and a half I'd finished what I had to do, so I came downstairs and put the kettle on for a cup of tea. While I was waiting for the kettle to boil I was just standing there, looking out of the kitchen window. I thought I'd find myself something to do in the garden. Maybe cut the grass, that always needed doing once a week at this time of year. Yes, I thought, that's it, I'll cut the grass. I should have time to do that before we go shopping.

While I was setting up the extension lead for the grass cutter, I'd lean over the wall every now and then and talk with the boys. By now a few of their mates had turned up and they were all playing with their skateboards. While talking over the wall, one of the men walked by with his Labrador. We greeted each other as he passed through the alley to the park entrance. That's it, I said to myself, lawnmower all set up ready to start

FOR THE LOVE OF BRASS

cutting. There I was, walking up and down the garden, trying to make sure the fresh-cut lines ran parallel with each other, thinking to myself, if I don't have enough time to finish cutting the lawn, I could always finish it after we return from shopping. As luck would have it, it was around 12.30 when I finished. I stood up on the back doorstep to talk to the boys over the wall and said hello to the lady who was taking her Rottweiler into the park for a walk. She looked and nodded in response to me.

"Okay," I said to the boys. "I've finished cutting the lawn. I can tidy up when we get back. We'll go to Morden for the shopping in about ten minutes."

"Yes," they both said.

"Okay, then, bring your stuff in. We'll go in ten."

"Okay, Dad," they answered. I put the lawnmower and lead back in the shed. I could scrape the mower blades clean later and tidy up any clippings left in the garden. I went inside and the phone started to ring. I answered. It was Tony, a friend of mine from the gun club.

"Gary," he said. "I have the machine game I promised you. You know the Pac-man one."

"Okay," I said, "that's great."

"I have it on the truck at the moment, can I deliver it over to you a bit later?"

"Yes, of course," I said. "Can you make it about three o'clock? I have to pop out but will be back by then."

"Okay," said Tony. "I'll see you then." I thought, the boys will love this game.

Tony had his own business renting gaming machines to pubs and clubs. Every so often he'd change the machines and eventually, when the machines had done the rounds, or maybe didn't make much money for him, he'd sell them off. We'd spoken about this at the gun club. I'd shown an interest in one of them to put in my garage for my sons to play on. It was also a good excuse for me to play on it.

We sorted ourselves out, jumped in the van and headed off to Morden, shopping. Having bought the week's supplies, it was into the supermarket car park, unload the trolley into the van and off to the Wimpy for lunch. When we were finished with lunch, it was back to the van and home. We unloaded the van and took all the bags into the kitchen.

"Is that it, Dad?" Michael said. "Can we go out again?"

"Yes, you can. I want you both to stay in the alley, alright lads?"

"Yeah, will do, Dad," they both said.

I'd decided not to tell the boys about the machine coming over. I thought I would save that as a surprise for them. I finished off tidying the garden, cleaned the mower blades, oiled them and put the mower away in the shed, ready for next time it was needed.

Tony pulled up outside in his truck. I went out to meet him.

"Hi Tony," I said. "I just need to move the car over a bit to one side so we can get this in." I wanted to put it on the right-hand side, near the utility room door. There was a double power-point socket nearby, which was very convenient.

Once I'd moved the car over, we unhooked the tailgate of Tony's truck and lifted the machine off between us. We rested it on the road for a couple of moments, then we lifted it and carried it into the garage and positioned it exactly where it would live. It was a heavy machine, the two-player type. You could have a player sit each side of it. It had a thick glass top, which could be used as a table when it wasn't switched on. Tony gave me the keys for it. They also fitted the cash box on the side.

Tony showed me how to use it. You could leave the cash box cover off;

then, when you wanted to play, all you'd to do was to click the button on the inside of the box for as many credits as you wanted. That was it: you could start playing.

I paid Tony the £100 we'd agreed. He had told me, "When you get bored with this one let me know and we can swap it for a different type of game." That was a very good deal, I thought.

I thanked Tony very much and we put the tailgate up on his truck, and he drove off. I walked around into the alley. My sons were playing with their skateboards. They had another three boys out there with them.

I called Michael and Lee over and said to them, "Come in here for a minute; I want to show you something." We walked into the garage and up to the machine. Both boys had the biggest smiles on their faces. I said, "Check this out," as I switched the power on. Their faces were beaming as the table-top lit up and they saw what game it was. It was a mad scramble as to who could play it first. I was laughing to see the excitement going on between them.

"Okay, Okay. There's no rush. It's a two-player game, you can both play." I'd already clicked some credits on the game.

It wasn't long before the skateboards and the friends from the alley were in the garage. They were all playing Pac-man. As a parent, I've always thought it a responsibility and a privilege to be in a position to put a smile on your children's faces, to keep them smiling and as happy as possible all the time. Without blowing my own trumpet too much, I think I did a fairly good job of keeping them smiling and enjoying themselves with interesting things to do.

Up at 7.30 Sunday morning, I was already downstairs, having slept in the spare room. I'd not had a drink the night before. I needed to get up with a very clear head, as I was teaching practical shotgun today over in

Godstone. So there was time for two cups of tea and two rollups, a quick wash and time to load the van with the shotguns and ammunition needed for the day, along with the clay-throwing machine and a good supply of clay pigeons. My friends Mark and Andy would work with me for the day as range officers to ensure everyone who came along would have a good and safe day's shooting. I'd supply all the guns and ammunition. All the shooters had to bring was their lunch and waterproof clothes, just in case it rained. Everything else they needed for the day I'd provide, at a cost of course.

The club had started out as a venue for myself and a few friends to shoot. I rented the land from another fellow that I knew, called Clive. In the past, I'd built a stable block for his horses, with a large tack room at one end. That's how I knew of his farm. Behind the stable block was approximately five acres of woodland on a steady incline uphill, which afforded us excellent backstops for our ranges. We'd made steel falling-plate targets at Mark's garage and that was us sorted. Somewhere to go shooting. We could walk around the farm rough shooting, or set up some metal targets in the woods and do our own practical shotgun shooting. That's a form of shooting where instead of moving targets, the shooter would be moving. The targets would be placed out in the woods at different intervals, say for example, 12 targets would be placed along a path, some to the left and some to the right, at different distances from each other. On his first run, the shooter wouldn't know where the targets were. He'd start at a given point, with his gun ready and a belt of ammunition around his waist. Then he'd have to reload on the move to save time. The shooter would have a person behind him as he went along the path, as a range officer. They'd act as a safety officer and time-keeper, because they'd also carry a stopwatch. The winner would be the shooter who completed the jungle run, as we called it, in the fastest time from start to finish, having engaged all the targets. By engaging the targets I mean each falling metal plate would have to be fired at, hit and knocked over. Targets missed for any reason would incur a penalty time, added to the run time. Over time, doing these jungle runs, they got a bit more interesting. We'd have different paths going off into the woods, some longer than others. We made dozens of metal targets. The standard type was a target 10x10ins, which we called a chest target. Then we had a smaller one, which was 6x6ins, which we called a head-box target. Even though the targets were this size, with the shooter moving they could still be missed when fired at. Sometimes with the adrenalin flowing, a target could be fired at two or three times and still not fall over, so a keen aim and a steady nerve was required to complete the jungle run in a good time.

The guns we used for this type of shooting were 12-bore shotguns, pumps and semi-autos. Each gun would hold eight or more rounds. The Remington auto, with extension magazine tube, could hold 12 rounds. Due to the nature of the jungle run, the shooter would always have to reload and, to save time, you would have to load in between engaging targets while on the move. This all made for a very competitive type of shooting.

The club at Godstone progressed from three or four of us having fun, to a full-blown practical shooting club. After we'd got started, I invited a number of friends who I knew were not shooters and didn't have gun licences, just to see what sort of interest I might get. To my surprise, the first six guys I invited all said yes, they would attend, so we set a date for Sunday of the following weekend. I knew I would have to teach these guys, so I made sure I took enough guns and ammunition for everyone to use. Before the Sunday, I drew up a list of things I'd be running them through: first, a safety talk in the tack room, teaching them the basics of how a gun works, with questions and answers and the 'dos and don'ts' on the range. From there, once everyone was happy, on to the range where one person at a time would shoot, with me as the range officer standing next to them, giving them instruction, while the rest of the class looked on. Two types of shotgun were used: the side-by-side double-barrel shotgun and the pump-action shotgun, both in 12-bore calibre. I would teach them to fire the guns from different positions: standing, kneeling, prone (which is lying on the floor); how to aim, how to load, shooting from the hip, which they all seem to thoroughly enjoy and, of course, how to stand; how to hold the gun correctly to absorb the kick without injury to the shoulder.

We had a fantastic day's shooting. All the fellows were extremely keen. They really enjoyed their new experience. They all said that they couldn't wait to do it again.

I told them, "We can shoot again in two weeks' time."

The shoot day would be always on a Sunday. I could hold 26 shoots on the farm per year, which is one every two weeks, if we wanted to use that many dates. Any more than 26 shoots in one year would mean I'd have to get permission from the local council. Seeing as how we only had eighteen to twenty shoots per year where club members came along, it was all good and the council were happy. Before long, the original six guys had told their friends and families, which was okay with me. As far as I was concerned, the more new people wanting to shoot, the better.

My friends Mark and Andy soon found themselves working as range officers alongside me on shoot days. There was so much interest, we had to set up another three courses, one of which we called the novice training day, one an intermediate shoot day, and then a shoot day for the more experienced shooters, which we called a club shoot day. For members to attend the club shoot day, they had to have completed the novice and intermediate shoots. It was my way of keeping everything nice and safe. The shooters always had a range officer with them, regardless of their experience. We had around 35 members, of which there was a hard core of some 18 to 20 members who would always turn up for a shoot. We even employed a woman called Anna as club secretary, to deal with the shoot dates for the three courses and do all the club's admin.

Monday and Tuesday passed in a flash. Wednesday, Sharon had arranged half a day off work and had taken the boys round to Julie and Nick's house for the day. She figured we'd be back from Relate and our meeting with Elaine, then she could then go in to work for the afternoon. I could also work at the office or out on site, whichever was needed. I drove that morning, as I often did if we were both in the car going somewhere. I drove off from our drive and started the journey to Purley. We spoke to each other on the way over, which made a change. We had not had much to say to each other for what seemed an age. Sharon asked me, why Purley? Was there not a closer Relate you could have gone too? I told her there was one closer but it was in Sutton. I felt that was too close to home. I didn't want to bump into anyone we knew. Sharon thought that was reasonable. She asked if I felt going to Relate was helping me. I told her I thought it was. She also asked for what I thought was an insight into what was going to happen when we got there. I told her I didn't really know because I had only been along on my own. I told Sharon that Elaine would probably ask one or two questions and then let her do the talking.

"It's pretty easy, no stress," I told her. "Just wait and see." I asked Sharon if she would like to sort out our situation and try to make things happier between us. She said, yes, that was what she wanted. "Okay. I'd like the same thing," I told her. "Maybe with both of us going, we can achieve that goal."

I put my indicator on to turn left into the car park next at the Relate building. The car park was empty. I pulled up and we both got out of the car and, as we headed to the front of the building, I turned back towards the car and clicked the central locking button. The car flashed at me. We turned right and right again, up the front steps and through the large front door. We walked up to reception. Jan was sitting there behind her desk as always.

"Good morning," we all greeted each other.

I said to Jan, "Should we wait or shall we go up?"

"You can go on up," Jan said. "You're only a couple of minutes early. I'm sure it will be okay. Elaine is up there already."

"Okay, thank you."

We headed along the hallway and up the stairs. Before we got to the top of the stairs, Elaine appeared.

"Hello, Gary. Hello, Sharon, it's nice to meet you," Elaine said to Sharon. She went on to say, "I'm just making coffee. Shall we have coffee all around?"

"Yes, please," Sharon said.

"Yes, please, if that's okay," I said as we went into the office.

We entered the office and sat down. There were already two chairs in front of Elaine's table.

Sharon said to me, "Elaine seems very nice."

"Yes, she is," I said. It wasn't long before Elaine returned with three full coffee cups, with the sugar and milk to one side, all on a nice big silver tray. We helped ourselves to sugar and milk and sat back in our chairs.

"Well," Elaine said, "it's very nice to meet you, Sharon. I've heard a lot about you."

"About me!" Sharon said. I could hear her tone was a little off. "I thought you only discussed things about Gary with Gary. I didn't know I came into this."

"Oh yes," said Elaine. "I have to discuss both of you, which is why it's so nice you could come along here today. I'm here to help you both."

"Okay," Sharon said, with a very serious face.

Elaine said, "I've discussed a lot of things with Gary, going right back to when he was a child. How things were for him and, of course, the loss of his father and how that may have affected his life from then until now. Now it's time for me to talk with you and for you to have an input."

"Okay," Sharon replied.

"I'd like to ask you about your childhood. Was it a happy time for you?" Elaine said.

"Well, yes, for the most part," Sharon replied.

"And how were things at home before your sister came along? You know, when it was just you and your parents? Can you remember what took place and how you felt?"

"Well, yes," said Sharon. "I think things were okay. I was a reasonably happy child."

I could tell things could get out of hand if Elaine wasn't careful but then Elaine didn't have to be careful, she was trying to get to the cause of things that had happened in Sharon's life. Sharon was answering Elaine but with a stern tone to her voice, along with giving me the occasional dirty look.

Elaine went on, "Looking back, were you happy to be sleeping with your parents? Didn't you think it was a little strange?" Sharon's face was slowing turning from stern to angry. Her arms were folded and she'd gone into a defensive position. Her legs were crossed and the foot that wasn't on the floor was tapping into the air.

Sharon said, "Well, I thought it was normal at the time, because it was all I knew."

"Well, did your mum ask you to sleep in between them for protection, or did you do this instinctively to protect your mother?"

"I DON'T KNOW," said Sharon in a very hostile tone. "I just did. What has this got to do with my marriage, anyway?"

"I'm trying to establish your state of mind at the time and how this may have affected you," Elaine said.

"Yeah well, why don't we go forward about twenty years and start from there?" Sharon said in a very loud voice. Sharon had realised I'd told Elaine everything and now she was extremely angry.

Elaine said, "I'd like you to understand the working of this and how it may have been brought forward into your marriage with Gary."

"Yeah!" said Sharon.

"How did you feel when your mother and father fought during the day? Did you intervene, or did you stay out of the way? And how did it make you feel?"

Sharon replied by sticking her arm out straight with her index finger pointing right at Elaine, saying, "What the fuck is it any business of yours whether I sleep with my parents or not and what are you implying when you say that? Who the fuck do you think you are?"

Sharon slid her chair back a little. It caught against the coffee table and made the coffee spill from our two cups. We hadn't even had time to drink our coffee.

Sharon stood up turned towards me, now pointing her finger at my face.

"And you," she said. "You fucking bastard. Who the fuck gives you the right to do our dirty washing in public? You've been coming over here week after week, talking with her." Now Sharon pointed at Elaine again. "All about our private life. Well, you can both fuck off 'cos I ain't having any fucking part of this, Gary. This is fuck all to do with her. It's none of her business. This is supposed to be between me and you. You don't involve outsiders; it's nothing to do with anybody else. I'm fucking going. I'm not having any more of this shit. You two carry on. I'm waiting in the car. Gary, give me the fucking keys." Sharon turned, opened the office door and, as she went through it, she said, without turning back, "Fuck you two and don't talk about me or my parents. It's no one else's fucking business." With that, the door slammed shut. I looked at Elaine. She looked at me. There was a silence for what seemed a while.

Then I said to Elaine, "That's what happens when we try to talk at home, except it can turn into a full blown row with both of us shouting and getting nowhere. I hate it. I can't keep this going, so the best way I deal with it is to go out, or just not talk to her when I'm at home. I know it is miserable for the kids, it must be. I just don't know what to do about the situation, which I guess is why I'm here."

Elaine said, "Sharon does have some very serious issues. I think it's pretty obvious she will not come back here again, which is such a shame. It all fits together now, Gary. Although Sharon wasn't here long, I was able to assess a lot from her outbursts."

"Really?" I said. "Is that a good thing?"

"Well, yes, it is," Elaine said. "It brings it all into perspective. All the stuff we've discussed. I thought, actually, some of what you'd told me may have been exaggerated but now it is very clear to me it was not."

We went on covering the same old ground and reiterating information we'd thrashed through before. This went on for about 20 minutes and then I said to Elaine, "I think we should call this session to an end, seeing as how Sharon will be waiting in the car, probably smoking one cigarette after the other. She's not happy. She'll either have a go at me all the way home, or she'll say nothing, I'll find out soon enough."

"Okay," Elaine said. "Yes, that's a good idea. Try not to argue if you can help it."

"Well," I said to Elaine, "you always give me something to think about for the week ahead. What will it be this week?"

Elaine looked at me, hesitated for a moment or two, and then replied, "Gary, I don't say this to many people but this is what I think you should think about. Your marriage has nowhere to go!"

"What does that mean?" I said.

"It means just that. Your marriage has nowhere to go. We'll discuss the situation next week. I still want to work with you and get you fixed. There's the children to think about, too."

"What does that mean," I said? "Oh, you mean dealing with this without it affecting them too much?"

"Yes," said Elaine.

"Good," I said. "That's very important to me. I need to learn how to do that. My marriage has nowhere to go. Hmmm. I have to think about that. Thanks very much Elaine. I'll go now. See you next week." We said our goodbyes.

I walked down the front stairs of the Relate building, turned left, then left again and into the car park. By this time there were three other cars parked in there. Sharon sat inside the car on the passenger side with the window down smoking a cigarette and blowing the smoke out of the window. I approached the car with the same thought going through my mind. My marriage has nowhere to go. I hadn't really understood the enormity of that statement. I'd have to think about that. Of course, what it meant was, my marriage to Sharon was over. Kaput. Finished. The end. Whatever you wanted to call it, it was done but this was not quite sinking in just yet. I opened the car door, got inside and started to roll a cigarette.

"You could have given it at least the hour, just to see!"

"Don't you ever ask me to go there again because I fucking won't!" Sharon said. "It's none of her business and you shouldn't be talking with people like that. Our life has fuck all to do with her. Do you understand!"

"Yes," I said, "I'm beginning to." I lit my cigarette, started the car, turned it round and drove out of the car park.

On the drive home we said very little to each other. Just a few sentences like, "Why the fuck did you take me there?" "I thought it would help." That sort of thing. I did however make a statement.

I said, "You do realise we won't be able to fix this on our own? It won't get better. It'll just go round and round, never getting any better. It'll just get worse."

"That's a load of bullshit," Sharon said. "That woman doesn't know fuck all. We can carry on as we are."

"No, we can't," I said. "I, for one, am not happy. I've not been happy for a long time. You know that and if you were truthful with yourself, nor have you."

Not much else was said on the journey back home. When we did arrive back, Sharon went off to work. I went inside the house, made a cup of tea and sat in the garden, drinking and smoking. Sitting there in deep thought. I kept thinking of the words Elaine had said. Your marriage has nowhere to go! Does that mean it'll never get better? It has no chance of getting better? I guess in some ways I could see what she was saying. I did have very little love left for Sharon, that's if there was any love left at all.

FOR THE LOVE OF BRASS

It seemed to be just habit now and not much else. I kept telling myself I needed to do something about my dilemma. I needed to do something for the boys' sake. But what? I decided, as they say, if you're not sure what to do, do nothing. That gives you time to think on it and maybe come up with a solution. I knew I'd be going back to see Elaine next week, so maybe by then I might think of something. I was pretty sure it would be down to me to sort this out. I really didn't think Sharon would even try. She just did not show any interest in trying to save anything we had.

That evening was the same as any other. Sharon picked the boys up after her work. Back home for tea. The boys went to bed at their times. Sharon sat in the front room watching TV. I sat in the office, then the dining room, drinking my vodka and orange, then going to bed half pissed; it seemed to help.

CHAPTER EIGHT
THE ROTTIE

I was up early the following day and off to one of my sites. Sharon had taken the boys round to Julie and Nick's again for the day. That morning she dropped them off there in the car. When her workday was done she was about an hour early, so she went grocery shopping. She drove home with the shopping, took it all inside the house and put it all away. With it being such a nice day, Sharon decided to walk round to Julie's to pick Lee up. She knew Michael was playing football over in the park with Julie's son, Mick. The girls had spoken on the phone earlier in the day so they knew what was going on with the boys. Michael was older, so when he finished playing football he'd make his own way home from the park for his tea. Julie only lived fifteen minutes' walk away, so it was no big deal to walk there and back. Sharon often had a cup of tea and a catch up with Julie anyway while she was there.

On this particular day Sharon had picked Lee up from Julie's and they were walking home. They turned a corner into our road. At about a 150yds there was a sharp bend to the left. Sharon and Lee had just passed the bend and had maybe 80yds to go to our front door. At this time, the lady who owned the Rottweiler came out of the park entrance with her dog on a lead. She was walking towards Sharon and Lee on the same side of the road. As Sharon and the lady passed each other they both said hello. No sooner had they said hello than the dog in an instant, growling as he did it, went for Lee.

FOR THE LOVE OF BRASS

There were a lot of factors that now came into play that day which helped or hindered the situation, depending on how you look at it. The dog's head was nearly the same height as Lee's head, Lee's head being just a little higher. This all happened so fast. As the dog lunged at Lee, the dog's owner pulled back on the lead. The dog had to cross Sharon's path to get to Lee. As this happened, Sharon was holding Lee's hand. She was able to pull Lee back from the dog, putting herself effectively between the dog and Lee as best she could. Nevertheless, the dog had got as far as Lee. With his mouth open and teeth showing, he chomped his jaws shut in Lee's face. The lady pulled the dog back even further.

Sharon was now between the dog and Lee. Both women carried on and passed each other by a few steps. The lady had stopped to check everything was okay, with the dog still pulling on his lead and growling in Lee's direction. Sharon made sure she was between the dog and Lee. When she looked down at Lee's face to find dog's slobber on it, along with a two-inch red welt mark on his cheek, that was it. No more damage to Lee, other than it had frightened the life out of him and Sharon.

Sharon and Lee walked on, with Sharon looking back over her shoulder and shouting to the lady, "You shouldn't walk that dog anywhere near children or in the park if that is what he can do unprovoked." She went on to say to Lee, "Don't worry now, you're safe. I won't ever let that happen again."

She carried on comforting Lee as they walked the last short distance to the house. Once in, she took Lee straight into the kitchen to clean his face up and make sure he'd no more damage from the dog attack. Luckily he had no further damage to his face or anywhere else, so all in all, a very lucky escape.

A short time later, Michael came in from playing football. Soon after, I arrived home from work. I parked my van out on the road. I noticed the garage door was closed and there were no kids around. I opened the front door and stepped in.

Michael shouted, "Alright, Dad?" from the dining room where he was sitting at the table doing some homework.

"Yeah, alright mate," I replied. I walked on through the house to the kitchen. Sharon was already in the kitchen preparing a meal.

"Hello Shal,'" I said. "I'm making a brew. Do you want one?" I glanced out of the kitchen window to see Lee playing in the garden.

"Yes, please," she replied, "I'll have one."

"Okay," I said.

I started to head for the back door to say hello to Lee when Sharon said, "I need to talk with you. I've something to tell you. You know that big Rottie dog that the woman takes for a walk in the park?"

"Yeah," I replied.

"Well, as I was walking back from Julie's today with Lee, we passed her and the dog on the pavement and the dog went for Lee and tried to bite him." As Sharon said it, I turned to look out of the window at Lee. My heart started to race. He looked okay, busy playing, making something. Sharon said, "He's alright but before you go out there to see him, I'll tell you what happened."

"Okay," I replied. Sharon went on to explain. And as she was doing so, Lee saw me through the kitchen window and made his way in. I heard the back door open then close almost immediately. Lee appeared in the doorway to the kitchen with a big smile on his face.

"Hello, Dad."

"Hi Lee, how are you?"

"I'm okay, I was attacked by that big dog down the road."

"Yeah, Mum was just telling me. Have you got any war wounds?"

"No, not really, just a scar on my face."

"Let me have a look," I said. On inspection I could see it wasn't too bad. Just a red mark. Hardly raised at all by now, but nonetheless a mark still there. "Oh yes," I said. "A scar on your cheek. Just like Action Man. He's got a scar on his cheek." We laughed but it wasn't funny really. "I bet it frightened you at the time, didn't it?"

"Yeah, it did a bit," said Lee.

"Okay, I'll have a word with the people who own that dog. They'll have to keep it away from any kids from now on!"

Sharon told me the whole story in detail, including what was said. I told her I'd go down the road later that evening and have a chat. The lady's husband didn't get in from work till later and I wanted to talk to them both together.

"Okay," Sharon said. "Dinner will be ready in about twenty minutes."

Lee went back out into the garden and was playing with our dogs. I carried on and made the tea. As I did so we continued talking about the situation and how it might go when I went to see the dog owners. I could see it was going to be an awkward meeting, seeing as how the dog owners needed to use the park, and to do so they'd have to pass our house and any children playing in the park entrance.

Michael finished his homework in the dining room just in time to clear it away for me to lay the table for dinner. I called Lee in from the garden. He came in with the dogs but left them in the kitchen and went to wash his hands. All four of us sat to have dinner together. The topic of conversation was of course the dog down the road. Although it was a serious subject we tried to find the humour in it, making a jokes at Lee's and the dog's expense. I kept an eye out down the road to see when the

FOR THE LOVE OF BRASS

fellow who owned the dog was home. I knew the type of car he had so all I had to do was to see if that car was at his house and give it maybe an extra half hour, then I figured it would be okay to go and see him.

Eventually, I noticed there was a large silver estate car on his drive. Hmmm, I thought to myself, I'm sure that's his car. I went out to our front garden to confirm. Yes, it was him.

"Okay," I said to Sharon. "He's home. I'll wait a while, then go and see him."

It was starting to get dark outside. I found I was feeling a bit on edge, an awkward situation. There was I, going to say my bit about Lee and the other children at the park entrance but knowing full well that the dog's owners would want to use the park and the park entrance on a daily basis. I ran some ideas by Sharon again as to how best to approach this, being as reasonable and polite as possible, especially seeing as how we live in the same road. Another fag and a cup of tea was had.

"That's it," I said. "Time to go and sort this out."

I came out of my house and set off the short distance - ten or twelve houses down on the other side of the road. It was now dark and the only light was coming from our street lamps, which were only lit using 100-watt light bulbs. Just enough to see by if you were out walking anywhere or attending vehicles in the road. Through the gate and up to the front door of the Rottie's house. Knock, knock on the porch door. I remember it seemed all the lights in the house were on. The main door of the house opened and out came this big, tall, male figure. He stepped into the porch, then opened the porch door.

He looked down at me and said, "What do you want?"

Now to give you an idea of what I was looking at, this fellow was about 6ft 5in or 6ft 6in tall, standing on the porch floor, which was about six inches higher than the path I stood on. So I'm now looking up at a man that seemed to be 7ft tall and with only the light shining out from his hallway behind him. I couldn't see his face very well, just this big dark figure.

"Yes," I said. "My name's Gary. I live up the road by the park entrance. I want to talk to you about…"

"NOW! You wait one minute," he said, raising his voice, interrupting what I was about to say. "I want to know what your child did to my dog as my wife took him for a walk! What he did to frighten my dog so much and make him behave the way he did and make him go on the defensive."

I stood there, looking. My mouth must have dropped open in surprise. I must say, it was at this point that my ideas of being polite and reasonable seemed to be no longer in existence. I had no idea where they were but they'd gone. All I could feel was a severe sense of humour failure. I'd no idea what this man's name was, nor did I care but from this moment on, in my head at least, he and his wife would be known as Mr and Mrs Rottweiler. So I stood there in front of this man while he abused my son, my wife and then me for turning up at his front door.

"I'd come down here to see you with reasonable intentions," I said, "but seeing as how we're not going down the reasonable road…" I now raised my voice.

"Oh yeah, oh yeah," he said. "Are you going to threaten me now?"

"No I'm not," I said, "but I'll make you a promise. You will keep your dog on a lead and keep it under control while you or your wife go in or out of the park. If your dog so much as goes near any one of those kids playing in the park entrance, I'll kill it. You'll not get another warning. I also promise you that when I get home, I'll be calling the police to report this incident. Then one more report like this about your dog to them and they'll have your dog destroyed, and that will be the end of the matter."

I turned to walk away from his porch down his garden path to head home. As I did, he was mumbling something under his breath as he went back in and shut his door. I walked back up the road to my house feeling really quite wound up by the whole event.

I walked in through the front door and said to Sharon, "Do you want a cup of tea?" She appeared from the sitting room, where she'd been watching the TV.

"How did it go?" she asked. I gave her an update as to what was said.

"He's a cheeky bastard," she said.

I was making the tea while telling her the story. We had a cuppa and a fag, then I called the police and reported the incident. At least this would be on record.

The following day I went down the garden to my shed where I had a fairly big Bowie knife. The knife had been in there a while, so I cleaned it and sharpened it, then put it by my back door, just on the inside. I told the boys not to play with it.

"You know why," I said. "It's for that dog. If he causes any trouble, I have to have the knife at hand." The intention was, if I needed to, I could grab the knife, jump over the garden wall into the park entrance and deal with the dog. From now on I'd keep an eye out in the alley when the kids were playing out.

Over the next two weeks there were two occasions when Mr and Mrs Rottweiler came up the road to the park entrance to take their dog for a walk. Each time they did, I'd make sure I was out by the back door of my house, looking over the wall so they'd see me. Mr Rottweiler would look at me and say some smug remark like, 'It's a nice day to take the dog for a walk in the park.' I'd just lean on the wall looking at him but I'd never answer him, just watch as they went into the park, and of course I would be there when they came out, just watching.

Another Wednesday soon came round. I found myself sitting in front of Elaine's desk while she was returning with the coffee. I looked around and noticed there was only one box of tissues on the table next to me, and that looked half empty. There must have been some sad goings-on since I was here last. Still, the prospect of getting fixed was something I was really looking forward to. I hope I won't be disappointed, I thought to myself. I looked at the tissues again and thought of the day I had sat here telling Elaine about my Dad's funeral, using the tissues to wipe the tears from my chin as I spoke. Then I wondered, why do we have the word FUN in the word funeral? I certainly didn't see any fun at my father's funeral or any other funeral, come to think of it. Strange the thoughts you can have while sitting on your own in silence.

"There we are, Gary," Elaine said, as she handed me my cup of coffee.

"Thanks very much," I said, as I placed it on the table next to me.

"Before we carry on, Gary, can we pick up on where we left it last week?"

"Yes," I said. "My marriage has nowhere to go. Hmmm, I've thought about that a lot," I said to Elaine. "I've taken that to mean my situation with Sharon will never get better. It has no chance of surviving and will probably only get worse for all concerned."

"I'm sorry to say so, Gary, but I think that's the case. But we can still get you fixed. You need to understand the out-workings of this situation, so you can deal with it as a much more rounded person."

"That'll help me and my boys."

"Oh yes," said Elaine. "Most definitely."

"That's great."

FOR THE LOVE OF BRASS

We went on to talk about the week's events. I spoke about work and what Sharon had done during the week and of course Mr and Mrs Rottweiler. Elaine wanted to know if the killing of the dog was just a threat. Would I actually go through with it? I explained that I hoped it was just a threat that worked out and nothing had to be done but if it came to it, I liked to think I'd do it without hesitation.

Elaine listened and nodded. "Hmmm," she said. It wasn't mentioned again. She did, however, go on to say, "During our time together, Gary, I have come to understand and learn a lot about your life. Your achievements, in particular, really are quite amazing for a person of your age."

"Do you think so?" I said.

"Well, you have achieved a lot, with having your family young, buying your two houses, building on to both to improve them, spending time in the Army and with the Special Forces, running your own business successfully. When you think of it, most people in their whole life do not achieve a fraction of what you have. This just makes me wonder if you have felt you had to do all this up until this point in your life because you may feel you won't be here after a certain age, just like your father. It's just something for you to think on. When this situation is behind you and you are fixed, I have a feeling you may slow down. You may become a more rounded person, which will be very good for you and your sons."

Before I knew it, the hour was up.

"I want you to think about your future for you and your sons, said Elaine.

"What, you mean me and the boys without Sharon in the equation?" I said.

"Well," said Elaine. "It's about you and the boys now."

"Yes," I said, "and I must remember my marriage has nowhere to go."

Elaine just looked and raised her eyebrows. "See you next week, Gary," she said.

"Thank you. Yes, see you then."

I left the Relate building and drove home, constantly thinking, my marriage has nowhere to go. What a daunting feeling. Everything I'd worked so hard for was finally at an end but it seemed I had to get used to a life without Sharon. It had been pretty much like that anyway for the last year.

I have a six bedroom house, I thought to myself, trying to keep this on a positive note. I'll do up the other bedroom at the front of the house and move into that. I'll have my own space, then; that will keep me and Sharon apart. We can live our own lives then and hopefully that will mean less arguing and less stress for me and a happier life for the boys. Yes, that sounds good. I'll get on with decorating and fitting out that room as soon as possible.

That evening at home, Sharon didn't say a word about my Relate visit. We both just carried on doing our thing and not talking to each other, only having conversations about the boys as and when necessary. It was as if Sharon had been a fly on the wall at the Relate office and she'd heard the conversation between me and Elaine. She knew we had nowhere to go, I'm sure, so she was acting accordingly. Women's intuition! Or was she just mirroring my behaviour? I didn't know. I thought I'd break the ice and say something to her.

"Sharon," I said, "when the boys go down tonight, can we have a chat for ten minutes? There's something I what to tell you."

"Oh yeah," she said, "what's that about then? Your meeting with that Elaine?"

"Well…" I said.

FOR THE LOVE OF BRASS

"I ain't fucking interested. As far as I'm concerned, you two can both fuck off together for all I care."

"That's nice," I said. "Thanks for that but it's nothing to do with my meeting today. It's to do with the front bedroom."

"What about the front bedroom?" she said.

"Well," I said, "seeing as how we're having such a lovely conversation now, I won't save it for tonight. I'll tell you now. I'm fed up sleeping in the spare room or settee most of the time, so I'm going to decorate the front bedroom, do it up a bit and move into it."

"Yeah, are yer? Good," she said and walked off into the sitting room.

Okay, I thought to myself. At least we don't have to talk tonight now.

Friday night came. I came in from work and opened the front door to the sound of Sharon's voice talking to me as she walked up the stairs.

"I'm going out clubbing tonight with the girls. You're having the kids."

"Well, I'm going to the gun club. We've got a match on."

"Tough shit!" was the reply. "My night's all arranged, so that's that. Right!"

She disappeared off to the right at the top of the stairs. Oh well, I thought to myself as I closed the front door, at least she was out. That meant just me and the kids. I was happy with that, and once the kids were in bed, I could put my feet up and have a vodka or two. Sharon had done the kids their tea. I thought I'd go into the kitchen and make myself something to eat. By this time Sharon had stopped cooking me any meals, which was okay with me because I had afforded her the same courtesy.

The boys were in and out while I was cooking. They were in the front room of the house which we called the dining room, drawing pictures. They would pop in and out of the kitchen from time to time, showing me what they'd drawn. One of the times when the kids came in, I said to them, "Your mum is going out tonight so it's just us. We can do some house clearance if you like." They loved playing that.

"Yes, yes, yes!" they both said. "Can we start now?"

"No," I said. "I'll have my tea, get cleaned up, then when your mum goes out we'll start."

"Okay," they both said.

House clearance was a game we boys played. We had a number of different plastic toy firearms. These guns fired soft plastic darts with rubber stickers on the front end, so if any of these darts hit glass or a flat painted surface they'd stick. The guns we preferred to use were toy sawn-off shotguns, the reason being that you had two barrels, so all you had to do was cock the gun, put a dart in each barrel and that's it, you were ready to go and with two shots. The gun had two triggers, so you could fire each barrel individually. Once we were armed and ready to go, we'd pick sides. One of us would go off and hide and the other two would come looking for him. The skill was to find your target and shoot him without getting shot yourself. This was an exercise for a type of shooting we did in the army. It was great fun, except we used real guns and cardboard targets. I'd pass on a lot of skills I'd learned in the army to my sons. They loved it and I loved teaching them.

We nearly always played house clearance when Sharon was out, or we'd play it outside. The reason for this was that, when we lived at our last house, the boys were a lot younger, and on one occasion, when I was playing with Michael (he was about six years old), he went off to hide and I was upstairs counting. When I'd finished counting, I came looking for him, checking the bedrooms. Michael, however, was hiding in the front room behind the settee. Sharon came through from the kitchen into the front room looking for him. She couldn't see him but could hear this

FOR THE LOVE OF BRASS

giggling coming from behind the settee. She walked over, looked over the top of the settee and there was Michael with his gun. He must have seen his mum as a target or mistaken her for me because in an instant he fired both barrels. One of the plastic darts hit Sharon in the eye and she was not amused. I said the wrong thing by saying, 'That was a good shot, Mike,' and laughing, just trying to make light of it. Sharon did not see the funny side of it and as a result, we did our house clearance training when Sharon was out.

I'd finished making myself something to eat and was sitting at the table in the dining room with the boys when all of a sudden there was this almighty crash and thud, followed by a groan, then a silence. Then swearing. Sharon had been coming down the stairs carrying some ironing in her arms, when she slipped and fell from about three steps from the bottom. She'd hit the bottom step slightly sideways, so she'd landed on the side of her thigh which had connected with the edge of the bottom step. One of her elbows had hit the edge of a step about four steps up.

We jumped up to see what had happened. As we entered the hall there was Sharon, lying on her side, half of her on the stairs and half not. Once I had seen she wasn't too badly damaged, I started to laugh (because of my sick sense of humour).

I said to her, "What are you doing lying there?"

"Fuck off," she said, "and help me up. My arm and leg are numb."

I said to the boys, "Look at your mum lying there having a rest with the ironing all over the place."

We all laughed and as we helped her up. Even she had a smile on her face as she limped off into the kitchen to get her clothes ready for when she went out. We boys were still sat in the dining room. Then the doorbell went.

"Sharon," I shouted, "your cab's here."

"Okay," she said. "Tell him I won't be a minute."

"Okay." I looked at the two boys. They looked at me. We all had smiles on our faces.

"Can we, Dad? Can we?" they said.

"Yes. Go up and get your guns and ammo ready. Then when your mum leaves, the firefight can begin." They were both laughing and went upstairs faster than Sharon had come down.

Sharon appeared in the hallway all dressed for the evening. She said bye to the boys and I opened the front door for her.

As she went through it she said to me with a sarcastic tone, "I'll be late home. Don't wait up."

"Don't worry, I won't," I said, as I watched her limp down the path to the cab. As I closed the door, a dart hit me in the back of the head. A second dart flew past my head and stuck to the glass window of the door. I turned and ran up the stairs shouting, "That's it. You two had best take cover. I'm getting my gun and coming after you." They were both laughing as they ran off to different bedrooms to hide and prepare for the firefight that was about to start.

The good thing about Sharon going out was the fact that we couldn't argue. It definitely didn't do us any good and would be the last thing my boys wanted to hear. Nevertheless, it was something we did all the time. The arguing never got us anywhere. It seemed to be an exercise where one of us would try to shout louder than the other, with as much abuse and swearing thrown in as we could muster. Of course, neither of us would be listening to the other. It was all just noise. The only positive I could find in arguing was that we did not talk to each other for some days after or, if we did, it would only be the odd word here and there, which seemed to suit us both. I spent as much time out as I could to do with work and as much time as I could out with my boys on the weekends. Sharon spent her time at work or out with friends as much as possible. In a strange way this way of life became normal, albeit I was very unhappy.

Really, looking back, it was at this stage one of us should have moved out but that was not going to be me. I loved my sons so much. Why should it be me that leaves? So that wasn't going to happen. It wasn't an option.

I still wondered from time to time about things that had been said between me and Elaine. Mainly of course, my relationship had nowhere to go. I could certainly understand that statement now. I guess I could for a long time but I suppose sometimes you need to be told something by an outsider for it to sink in properly. I'd be going to see her next Wednesday. What else could there be to talk about? Nothing really, I thought to myself. Only maybe how to try and make it a bit easier for my boys. I was rather thinking that my sessions with Elaine might well be coming to an end soon. I thought that would have to be on the agenda as well at our next meeting.

Wednesday morning was here. I was sitting in front of Elaine.

"Yes, Elaine, I think you're right," I said. "It must by very miserable for my sons. I do try my best not to argue with Sharon but it still happens. Maybe, just maybe, one of us should leave but Sharon says she won't go and I am not going to leave my sons to be a one-parent family. I came from a one-parent family as you know. Nearly all my friends come from one-parent families. I've seen what it's like over the years and I don't want that for my sons."

Elaine said. "We have mentioned your sons over the weeks of our meetings and how you can improve things for them, so with that in mind, you'll work it out, Gary, but it will take time. You can't sort out all of the goings on in a short time. It will unfold for you. You will know what to do as you get healed. This is a healing process remember. I am helping you to get better."

"And how are we going so far?" I said to Elaine. "Can you see a change in me?"

"Oh, yes," she said. "Most definitely, a big change from when you first came here."

"That's good," I said. "It's nice to know I'm going in the right direction."

We spoke of the last week's events. I told Elaine I was going to do out the other front bedroom for myself.

She suggested that might be a good idea and maybe next week's meeting might be the last. She said, "We'll talk about that next week."

Before I knew it, I was saying goodbye, see you next week, and heading out the door.

At home, Sharon did not mention the meetings. In fact she did not mention anything to do with me or us but at least there were no arguments for the poor neighbours to listen to. God only knows what they must have thought when it kicked off.

Saturday morning. I called to my sons.

"Okay, boys, no school today. What do you want to do?"

Lee said archery in the garden. Michael said take the dogs out to the chalk hills.

"Okay," I said. "And I have to get some shopping in for the week's supplies. Okay, let's work this out and we can do all three things. I think we should go shopping first, get that out the way. Then we can do archery in the garden, have lunch here. Then all jump in the van and go out with the dogs. What do you say?"

"Yeah, yeah. Ha-ha-ha."

FOR THE LOVE OF BRASS

"Okay, get ready quick; we'll go shopping in Morden."

In no time, it seemed, we were back from Morden. I was unloading the shopping from the van while the boys were playing in the alley.

I said to them, "Talk to your mates and see who is coming with us when we take the dogs out."

By this time more of their friends had turned up. They were all having a good time. Even the skateboard ramps were out. That's it, I thought. All the shopping is away. I looked out over the wall into the alley where all the kids were playing.

"Lee," I called out. "What about the archery?"

"Oh yeah, Dad. Can we do that another time? I'm having fun here with my mates."

"Okay, then," I said. "Do you both know who is coming out with us later?"

"Yes, we do," they both said.

"Okay, make sure they've told their mums so they know where they are."

I went in to make a cup of tea. Once that was done, I rolled a cigarette and was back at the back door smoking and drinking my tea, leaning on the wall watching the kids all play. I had not seen Sharon so far this morning. She was still in bed, nursing a hangover I suspect, which was pretty normal after the Friday night out.

Friends of ours, Deb and Steve, who lived down the road on the same side and only a couple of houses up from Mr and Mrs Rottweiler, were walking through the alley coming out of the park.

"Hello Deb, alright Steve?" I said. "How's things?"

"Yeah alright," they said. They stopped and we passed the time of day, having a little catch up as you do. I had not seen them for some weeks.

"It's nice weather for the kids to play out," Steve said.

"Yeah, it is. It's great because there's no traffic to worry about." In conversation I said, "I've been keeping an eye out for that big Rottweiler that lives near you. It had a go at Lee about three weeks ago. I told the couple I would kill it if it came near any of the children that play here in the alley."

"Oh dear," Debbie said. "Have you not heard?"

"No, heard what?" I said.

"That Rottweiler is dead. It died about two weeks ago." Oh. well that's not a bad thing. I thought.

"What did it die of? Do you know?"

"Yes. Somebody poisoned it, put poison in some meat and killed the dog."

"Oh shit," I said. "Is that true?"

"Yeah," said Steve. I'll get the blame for that! I'd wondered why I'd not seen them go in and out of the park.

"Well," I said to them. "It must have had some enemies other than me."

"Oh yeah," said Deb. "It was a nasty thing. There's a lot of people around here that won't miss it, including me."

"Okay, well, nice chatting. Thanks for the news. I have to do some lunch for the boys. We're off out with the dogs soon."

I came back in to sort out lunch. Well, well, I thought to myself. Somebody killed it. I wonder why. Obviously somebody disliked it enough to do something about it but it definitely wasn't me. A small part of me was pleased it was no longer a threat. It meant I did not have to worry any more about the kids in the alley.

Lunch was made. We three had a quick bite, got the dogs and off we went: me, a van, four kids and two dogs. Off exploring the North Downs.

FOR THE LOVE OF BRASS

We'd always have a great time there.

Sunday, Sharon took the boys to her mum and dad's for dinner. I went off to Bisley, shooting.

Monday morning. Sharon at work, kids at school. I checked the work load. All the men were busy. I'd stay at home and start to get my own room ready. This I was really looking forward to. This room at the front of the house to the left-hand side had not been decorated since the 1960s. It had old-fashioned wallpaper, white polystyrene tiles on the ceiling and lilac gloss paint to the woodwork. Would have been very nice in its day. I removed all the old carpet and the original lino, stripped the walls and ceiling.

It was at this point that I looked at the fire breast. There was no fireplace. It had been removed before we moved in. Just a fire breast that was rendered. I had this idea that if I cut a big tall hole in the breast, I could fit in a nice big gun safe. I thought of my friend's mother, Molly. She'd always say, 'Don't spoil the ship for a ha'p'orth of tar, dear.' It was with that thought that the plan for my new bedroom was hatched.

I contacted a company that made and sold gun safes, found the size I wanted and ordered it. It had to come down from Scotland. They assured me I would have it by the end of the week, so I started to cut out the fire breast in preparation. I thought if I could prepare the room and get the gun safe fitted by next week I could have the room finished a week after that.

Work was still good. Ron was looking after things very well. I could afford to dedicate time to finishing the room. My room. My own sanctuary and away from Sharon. Maybe, just maybe, with my own room we could have even less to do with each other. That should mean less arguing, less for the boys to hear, less trouble all round. Well, that was my way of thinking, anyway.

Wednesday morning. I could afford to take some time off from my new project. I wanted to go and see Elaine. I had a good feeling things would start to change for the better, albeit in our own directions but for the better.

Sitting in front of Elaine's desk I said to her, "I've done a lot of thinking this last week and I've a lot to tell you."

"Okay," Elaine said, "you carry on."

I started to talk at almost a hundred miles an hour, knowing I only had an hour to fit in what I wanted to say. I told Elaine about the Rottweiler being dead and my new idea to separate from Sharon and live out of my own room. I also said my marriage has nowhere to go, which I fully understand now and I intend to do something about that. I'll go to a solicitor get the ball rolling and file for divorce. Hopefully we can get that and just work out of the same house because neither of us wants to leave. Also I would like this to be our last meeting, if that was okay with her.

"Well, well," said Elaine. "You really have been thinking about things. You have attended twelve visits with me. I think you've come a long way in that three months."

"I can see an end to the miserable life I have with Sharon," I said, "whereas before I couldn't. I now have a direction. We can live apart but still have our boys with us, which is the most important thing to me."

"Okay," Elaine said, "but I want you to know I'm always here to help you should you feel you need it. Please don't forget that."

We spoke some more until our time was up. I thanked her very much for all her help and, on leaving the room, I noticed the tissue boxes again. As I walked down the hall to leave the building I couldn't help but think, I was not walking out with tissues, crying with happiness, but I was walking

FOR THE LOVE OF BRASS

out a much happier person than the one who went in. All I could think about now was getting home and working on my new room.

I really did feel a lot happier with myself and things now. I just felt as if I was getting somewhere after all this time. It had been nearly two years, all in all, of not being happy, and being happy is the most important thing in life. If you don't have that, you don't have anything.

The gun safe had arrived. I dragged it into the hall, took all the wrapping off and checked that the locks worked. Yep, all good, I thought to myself. This thing was 2ft wide, 5ft tall, 1ft deep and quite heavy. I pulled it upstairs and into the room and stood it on some of its cardboard wrapping against the wall. When I was ready to move it into position, I could slide it across the floorboards to the new opening I'd created.

I got to work right away, trimming the opening, clearing all the brick rubbish away and mixing up some sand and cement so I could brick this bad boy into place. By mid afternoon it was in. I could now carry on with the rest of the preparation, getting things ready. I'd get one of my decorators to come in for a few days and help me finish the room off.

By the end of that week it was decorated. Lovely white ceiling, lined and painted walls. Magnolia emulsion was the colour to finish the walls and, lo and behold, the lilac gloss was gone. All the woodwork and door were finished in a brilliant white and this brought the room out of 1960 and up to date. Lovely jubbly, I thought to myself. This weekend I'll go shopping for carpet, curtains and a lampshade, of course. I already had two wardrobes and some furniture that had come from the last house, which would do me very nicely. After that, all I'd need was a bed. I don't think I was ever so happy and determined to finish a room off. All I could see was my own room, which for me meant independence, a sanctuary and, more importantly, another step away from Sharon.

FOR THE LOVE OF BRASS

Saturday. Out with my boys, food shopping first, then out looking for my room's furnishings, and while we were out, a visit to the Wimpey. By the time we were done, the items for the bedroom were all ordered.

Sunday. As usual, Sharon was out at her mum's with the boys. I was at Bisley on the 600-yard rifle range, shooting in a snipers' competition which, incidentally, I won, having achieved the most head shots over that distance. I came home with the snipers' trophy, which would sit very nicely in my new room. That week the carpet was fitted and I put up the new curtain rails and curtains along with a nice lampshade. I positioned the furniture, leaving a space for a bed. As luck would have it, my cousin called in to see us. I showed her my new room and she said she was moving and I could have the double bed from her spare room. It was brand new and she'd no room for it at her new house. All I had to do was to pop over in the van and pick it up, and this I did the following day. Before I knew it, I was in my new room, which to me seemed like a palace.

Until this stage of my life, I'd always shared a room with Sharon. Well, for around fifteen years, anyway. To have a room of my own and especially as we were getting on so badly, I couldn't wait to be in there. I had a lovely antique bookcase converted to a display case, which came to live in my room. It would house my antique gun collection under lock and key, which would make sure my sons did not use the guns for house clearance. The guns that were in my gun safe in the loft were bought down and placed in the new safe.

I fitted my six handguns to the inside of the gun safe door, having first lined it with plywood. The rest of the space was taken up with rifles and shotguns, of which there were many. At the top of the safe there was a shelf which housed the ammunition and holsters, so when the safe was

FOR THE LOVE OF BRASS

opened fully, I had a display of guns 4ft wide and with my antique guns in the room as well. It was a real man cave. I was really pleased with my efforts and so happy to have my own space.

CHAPTER NINE
BRIEF ENCOUNTER

Working in my office, sorting and booking in jobs, dealing with costings, phone calls and so on, I pondered, Sharon had had no input about me living in my new room. The whole procedure of what I had achieved over the past few weeks just seemed to go over her head. Maybe she was just as happy to have her room to herself. I certainly took that to be the case. I thought, maybe we have two happy people in amongst the total breakdown of our marriage. I also thought about finding a solicitor. I thought that should be done this week.

The following day, I decided I would deal with this, or start to deal with this marriage breakdown from a legal point of view. I called a company of solicitors, Carpenter and Co. They had offices in the High Street in Wallington. I spoke to a receptionist and told her what I thought I was looking for. I gave her my details. After waiting a short while, she came back on the phone and said I could come along tomorrow to see a solicitor at 11 o'clock, if that was okay with me.

"Yes," I said, "that's good."

She said, "The chap you'll be seeing's name's Steve. You can expect to be here for one hour."

"Thank you very much," I said. "I'll see you then at eleven tomorrow." That's good I thought to myself. Something else under way.

The next day I was in the office dealing with my usual business, when an enquiry came in for an Artexing job at Woodside Green, Woodside. I

FOR THE LOVE OF BRASS

told the lady that I could come over that day, have a look and give her a price for what she needed. It was on the way to the solicitors, so I thought after my meeting, I could be with her at around 12.30. She gave me her address and said she'd expect me then. I checked my watch, it was 10.20. Okay, I told myself, I need to be on my way to see Steve.

I left my house and jumped into my van. On the journey over to Wallington I was wondering how all this would go. I wondered this and wondered that. I wondered if I should have brought any papers with me but then, what papers? I really had no idea. The only time I had used solicitors was to buy a house. I was sure this would be different but how? Oh well, I'd find out soon enough. I pulled into the large car park opposite the Magistrates Court, just behind the High Street. Then all I had was a short walk down Shotfield to the solicitors' office to meet my new friend, Steve.

I arrived five minutes early. The receptionist asked me to take a seat and wait, then she'd take me to Steve's office. I sat there wondering what would happen and what might be achieved in this one hour meeting.

Miss Receptionist suddenly stood up. "Okay, Gary, if you can follow me please, I will take you to Steve's office."

Off we went, down the corridor, up two flights of stairs, the second flight turning back on itself and heading towards the front of the building. We entered an office that looked out over the High Street. No Steve.

"Please take a seat. Steve will join you shortly."

I perched on a large brown leather armchair, the type that had wings up by your head, right in front of Steve's large wooden desk. Behind the desk was his chair, made of brown leather too, but of the swivel type. Behind that were two very large sash windows. No double glazing here, I thought to myself. You could hear the rumblings of the outside noise, traffic, people and so on, down in the street below.

I looked around the room. Such a tall ceiling, maybe 10ft high. This building had been built in the early 1900s so you would expect ceilings of that height on the first floor above shops. The area downstairs, where Miss Receptionist worked, would have been a shop in its day. To my right there was a large fire breast with a lovely cast iron fireplace and surround. It looked as if it hadn't been used for years. A long radiator under the windows would have been the reason why. The alcoves each side of the fire breast were full of shelves and they in turn were full of books. To my left there were filing cabinets with shelves above. They also were full of books, all of the legal type as far as I could tell. On top of the filing cabinets there were what I assumed to be case files. They were tied in bunches with string. There were some of these also on his desk. The wall behind my chair was also full of shelves and more books, almost up to the ceiling. This office seemed to me to be exactly what a solicitor's office should look like. Full of books and paperwork, giving the impression it was a very busy place.

The door opened with a quick motion.

"Hello Gary. I'm Steve. So nice to meet you."

I stood up to greet him and we shook hands.

"Sorry for the delay, I was just helping a colleague get something done. Take a seat." I sat on my now warm leather chair. "Okay," he said as he sat down. "What can I help you with?"

"Well," I began. "I seem to be at a point in my marriage where things have gone downhill quite badly. I feel I need to get divorced. I've no idea how any of this works but here I am."

"Okay," Steve said, as though he'd done this all before, which of course he had! "I will take some basic information from you. Then we can talk about the situation and what can be done about it. By the end of our hour we will have a good idea of which direction this will go. The first hour is free of charge. Only once we agree to work on your behalf will there be costs involved, which of course I will explain to you as we go. Is that okay with you?"

"Yes," I said.

"Okay, name and address?" He went on to ask, wife's name, how long had we been married, did we have children, did we own any properties, what did we do for our jobs, and so on, working his way through his mental list. As he was asking me these questions, I couldn't help thinking this man seemed so young. Maybe he was just lucky and had a young face. He only seemed around 30 to me. I hoped that his age wouldn't affect his ability to act for me. I also hoped he would be up for a good legal fight.

I opened up and once all the questions were out the way, I told Steve how I'd already been to Relate and seen a counsellor. How I'd spent three months attending the meetings and in a nutshell my marriage had nowhere to go, hence I was there because I felt I needed to do something about my situation, hoping this would make me a happier person. I told him how our relationship had slowly gone downhill and as a result we were now living separate lives in the same house. How it had gone from Sharon going out on the odd Friday night to Sharon going out every Friday night, coming home pissed as a newt. Sometimes Saturday night as well, and during the week she could disappear for the odd evening, off to see one friend or the other. Either way, I said, it was good when she was out because it meant no arguing and less stress for the family.

"Okay," Steve said. "It does seem a course of action is necessary and should be taken, although I'm not sure that living in the same house is advisable. We can talk about that another time but for now, I think we as a company can take this case on. I will draft a letter to be sent to your wife's solicitors. Can you give me their name?"

"Oh," I said. "She doesn't have a solicitor yet. She doesn't even know I'm here."

Oh, okay. Should I send it to your home address?"

"Yes, that's fine," I said. That'll put the cat amongst the pigeons, I thought. "I don't think she'll be happy when the letter arrives."

"That's okay," said Steve. "It shows we're serious. She will have to go and find a solicitor to defend herself."

"Defend herself," I said.

"Yes," said Steve. "We'll file for divorce. She will have to defend her case. What grounds are we filing under? What grounds are there, Steve?" He read out a list of reasons widely used.

"Hmmm," I thought for a minute. "Yes," I said, "the third one - unreasonable behaviour. That seems to be the least provoking or offensive on the list. She should accept that without too much of a fight… Yes," I said, "number three. Thank you." I really had no idea how Sharon would react to this letter arriving. She might hit the ceiling and go mad, or she might get her box of tissues out and cry with happiness. One thing for sure, we'd find out soon enough. "Okay, then, Steve," I said. "Can I take your phone number and call you here should I have any questions?"

"Yes, certainly, and as I said, this first hour is free. Your bill will start from when we draft the first letter." Steve went on to tell me the running cost of things, like how much a letter would cost, how much phone calls would cost and how much an hour for his time.

"That's all okay with me," I said. It costs what it costs was how I saw it.

Steve then went on to say that most of this case would be covered by legal aid so I didn't have to worry too much. It could all be settled at the end of the day.

"Have you any idea how long all this would take?"

"No idea at all," he said.

"Okay, then, thank you very much," I said. "I'll be in touch, no doubt."

I stepped out of the solicitors' building onto the pavement feeling light on my feet and with a spring in my step. I started to walk up Shotfield towards the car park where my van was waiting. I felt really happy that, out of a sad situation, something positive was being done. It was like a great weight had been lifted from my shoulders. Something was being done, I kept telling myself, something was being done.

CHAPTER TEN
WHAT COULD POSSIBLY GO WRONG?

Oh, wow, I smiled. I had completely forgotten I had a job to go and look at. I'd been so preoccupied. I looked at my watch. It was five past twelve. That's good, I have time. Now I get to look at a job where potentially I could make a few quid. Artex jobs were known to be good moneymakers. It's not everybody that can repair a damaged Artex ceiling but I could, so it was something I charged a lot for. Especially if it was an insurance job; I'd charge twice as much. I had no idea how much today's actions would turn my life upside down, inside out and change my life for ever, in such a dramatic way!

I drove out of the car park on my way to the job. I knew where Woodside Green was. I laughed to myself. Funnily enough it was in Woodside. I smiled, just the other side of Croydon from Wallington. I'd checked the address in the A to Z book earlier in the day before leaving my office. We didn't have Sat Navs in those days. Well, I didn't anyway. I arrived at Woodside Green. Got here quite quick, I thought. The traffic was good with no hold ups. It was a lovely sunny day, the leaves had only just formed on most of the trees and there was a nice bit of warmth in the sun. Okay, parking alongside the Green, no problem.

I jumped out and looked for the number. The house I was looking for was on the left and there were houses all down that side of the Green.

FOR THE LOVE OF BRASS

I found the one I was looking for and banged on the door. A woman answered straight away.

"Hello," she said, "you must be Gary."

"Yes," I said. "Nice to meet you."

"Come in. The damage is in the dining room at the back of the house next to the kitchen. We had a leaking pipe upstairs. It's been fixed now but it has damaged and stained the Artex in that area. Have a look and see what you think. I'll put the kettle on. Is that okay, love?"

"Yeah, fine with me. White with two sugars, please." As I was looking at the ceiling I was talking to the lady at the same time. We could hear each other because the door to the room was open. "Okay," I said, "yes I can fix this for you. It's about a three-foot-square patch that needs doing. I'll prepare the area back to the plaster, then seal it, and the new Artex can go on to match the existing. Is this an insurance job?" I asked her, rubbing my hands together.

"Nah, love," she said. "I did check the policy but it had run out a couple of months ago. "Never mind," she said, "these things happen. I ain't worried anyway," she said in her London accent. "Me old man's paying for it."

"Is he?" I said as I laughed. "What does he do for his living?" I asked.

"He's a copper," she said.

"Oh, blimey. Good job I wasn't trying to arrange an insurance fiddle with you."

"Ha-ha-ha," she laughed. "That wouldn't have been a problem. We all like to save a few bob, don't we? Anyway," she said, "how much is this gonna cost us? More than a few bob, I bet."

"Yes, I'm afraid so. It'll be one hundred and fifty all in."

"Really?" she said. "That's a result. I thought it would be about two

139

and a half."

"Oh," I said, laughing. "You should have told me. I'd have charged a few bob more."

She laughed as she said, "Don't worry, love. I'll give you a few bob for a drink when the jobs done, alright?"

Smiling, I said, "Do you remember years ago when somebody did give you a drink. You'd get half a crown or five bob if you was lucky."

"Yes," she said. "Well, don't you worry, I will give you a bit more than that. When the jobs done you can have ten bob."

"Ha-ha-Ha-ha. Okay, that's a deal," I said. We finished our tea and made an arrangement for me to come along and do the job at the beginning of the next week. I left her house and walked over to my van, opened the door and sat inside. I got my notepad out and made some notes for the following week. How much material I'd need, what tools and dust sheets I'd need, stuff like that. Just so I didn't forget anything. It's nice to be efficient but, more importantly, it saves a lot of messing about on the day if you forget things.

Okay, that's that. All the notes I need for next week. My train of thought went directly back to the meeting with Steve and what we had discussed, or more to the point the things he'd told me. I thought it must be nice to be divorced so you could do the things you want to do, whatever they are, like when you were single.

I was about to start the van when, all of a sudden, there was tapping on my window. I looked to my right to see a woman standing there, beckoning me to open the window. I wound down the window and looked at the woman. She was maybe 65 to 70 and she'd this real lived-in look of a face with round glasses in a brown frame. The glass in the glasses was very thick, which made her eyes look a lot bigger than normal.

FOR THE LOVE OF BRASS

Benny Hill came to mind when he played Ernie the milkman. She must have pinched his glasses, I thought.

"You do plastering, don't you, love?" Before I could answer, she said, "well, it says so on your van."

"Yes. Yes, I do," I said. I was still looking at her glasses. I thought she must have good eyesight to see through them. "Yes, of course I do. What can I do for you?"

"Well," she said, "I live in the flats over there." She pointed across the Green. "The man who lives above me, well, his washing machine's leaked, the bastard thing, and the water came through my ceiling and damaged it. Will you come have a look, darling, see if it can be fixed?"

"Yes, course I can. We'll have a look right now." I wound my window up and got out of the van with my notepad. "What's your name, love?" I said.

"June," she replied.

"Okay. I'm Gary." We made our way across the Green, over the road to one of the blocks of flats that were there. The flats were only three storeys high, with parking at the back.

"I'm in here," she said, "ground floor at the back." We went into the block, then up to her front door. She rattled the keys as she put one of them into the lock. Her eyes can't be that bad, I thought. She found the key and the lock straight away. I smiled to myself. "Alright," said June. "Come in, love. The kitchens in here."

"Oh yeah," I said. "I see what you mean," looking up at the damage. "Yeah," I said. "I can fix that for you."

"Good," said June. "How much and when?"

"Well," I said, "give me a few minutes to work out the materials and labour and I'll give you a price right now."

"That's lovely," she said. "You wanna a brew?"

"Yes, please," I said. "White with two."

"Alright, darling," came the reply. I made my notes, June made the tea. We sat in the lounge. You could walk into the lounge from the kitchen and the lounge also had a door out into the hallway. I could see through into the hallway and into what seemed to be a bedroom and out through the back window into a car park.

We sat down with notes and tea. "Tea okay for you?" asked June.

"Lovely."

"Okay, how much?" said June.

"Well, labour and materials, cleaning and taking the rubbish away, one hundred and fifty quid all in."

"That ain't too bad, and when can you do it?" said June. "Well," I said, "I'm working on a job just across the Green Monday morning, so I can do this for you Monday afternoon if that's okay."

"Yes, that'd be great," said June.

"How do you want to pay? Oh, and is it an insurance job?" not bothering to rub my hands together.

"Nah, no insurance. I'll pay you in Nelsons!"

"Alright, that's fine with me."

One of the things I liked about working in these South London areas was the people's accent and the fact that a lot of them used Cockney rhyming slang. It reminded me of my childhood, being brought up in Bermondsey. I'll explain: Nelsons is short for Nelson Eddie, meaning "ready" and in turn, ready money or cash, so Nelsons was always welcomed by me.

As I was drinking my tea, I heard the front door open, then somebody walking down the hallway. I looked up in the direction of the hallway and a woman walked past, looking in as she went. She said hello.

"Hello," I replied but she'd already passed the doorway. I had only seen her for a split second but with what I had just seen of her, she looked very attractive.

As I finished my tea I looked at June, wondering who this woman was. June said, "Oh, that's my friend, she's popped in to use the toilet."

"Oh, is that right?" I said, not knowing what else to say. "Well, okay," I said, "see you on Monday afternoon then. We'll get this ceiling sorted out for you and all the mess out the way. "Oh," I said, "I noticed out the window there, there's a car park at the back. Can I park in there on Monday?"

"Yes," said June, "just drive between the blocks and turn right. You'll be right behind the flat."

"Okay, that's great." As I was saying this, I heard a door close and the sound of somebody coming down the hallway again.

June's friend appeared in the doorway, except this time she didn't pass. She stopped in the doorway, put one hand up on the door frame and looking in at me she said, "Hello, who are you?"

June replied, "This is Gary. He's going to fix up the kitchen ceiling on Monday."

"Oh, that's great," June's friend replied. "I may see you on Monday then."

"Yes, you might," I replied. The woman turned and carried on her way down the hall. I heard the front door open the close.

"Thanks for the tea," I said. "Can I use your loo before I head off?"

"Course you can, darling," said June.

I left June's flat and made my way back to the van, checking first how to get into the car park, to make sure I knew the access in and out for when I arrived on Monday afternoon. I sat in my van before I drove off, and found myself thinking about June's friend. She was extremely attractive.

She'd looked to be around 30 and had a very pretty face with blonde, wavy hair just down off her shoulders. She wore a blouse with the sleeves turned up a couple of times and a mini skirt and high heels. I guessed her to be maybe 5ft 3in to 5ft 5in tall, with a figure most women would die for. As she was talking to me I was sure I could see the tops of her stockings in my peripheral vision, not wanting to look directly at her legs.

Wow. I thought to myself, what a day. Two jobs, a solicitor and a stunning-looking June's friend to boot. I've had worse days, I thought as I drove off, heading home.

Once home, same old, same old. Prepare my own dinner. Play with the kids for a while before they went to bed, then in my office to catch up on things and off to my own room, hardly saying a word to Sharon all evening.

Friday night came and Sharon went out, then came back pissed as a pudding. Saturday, me and the boys were out to Morden, shopping for the groceries, then into the Wimpy bar for lunch. When we got home we unloaded the van of the week's groceries.

Saturdays were always pretty much the same, week in and week out. We might see Sharon or we might not. She always seemed to be recovering from her night before. Sundays, I'd generally go shooting with the gun club to Bisley, or go hunting, or if the weather was nice I would go fishing. With either of these events my boys would occasionally attend. Sharon would always go and visit her mum for dinner. That was pretty much my life. I remember thinking to myself, I hope the divorce doesn't take too long to get out of the way. I really was that naïve to think it would be over quickly. I also thought that once it was over we'd all be happy and get on with our lives. How wrong I was. I had no idea, not yet anyway, but of course the day would come. Not only the day but the weeks and the months. I was in for more trouble and aggravation then I could ever imagine but for now, I thought everything was just fine.

I looked forward to the week ahead as there was always plenty to do and this week was no exception. This week was to have a good start. I had two jobs to do, for both of which I'd be paid in Nelsons. I might even get a ten bob tip from the policeman's wife and, you never know, I might even be lucky enough to meet June's friend again. I was hoping that would be the case.

I arrived at Woodside Green with all the necessary tools and materials for the day's work. I got on with repairing the ceiling, then applied the Artex. It all went very well and before I knew it I was clearing up, job done.

As I was finishing up, Mrs Policemen came in and said, "Gary, here's that drink I promised you and presented me with a nice cup of tea." We laughed about that but true to her word, when she paid me she gave me an extra £30 for doing such a good job.

I loaded the van with everything from the job I'd just completed, including all the rubbish. Okay, I said to myself, off across the Green to see June.

I drove between two blocks of flats and turned to the right. Sure enough, there was the car park with lots of empty parking places. Must be because most people were out at work, I thought. I parked directly behind June's flat and used the tradesman's entrance to get into the main hall, then rang June's doorbell.

She answered the door with, "Hello Gary, darling. Come in. Can I get you anything?" she said.

"No, no. I'm fine thanks. Well, a cup of tea in a little while would be nice. Can I keep your door on the latch so I can come in and out while I'm setting myself up?"

"Course you can, darling," said June.

I was soon on my stepladder preparing and cutting out the damage to the ceiling, making it ready so I could install some new plasterboard to the timber joists. After a while of working there, June said, "Want your tea now, Gary?"

"Just give me ten minutes, please, then I'll have finished the prep work, then I can have a cuppa. Okay?"

About fifteen minutes later, June said, "Gary, here's your tea. I'll put it in the front room."

"Okay, I'll join you in there." What I was thinking was, the hole in the ceiling was ready for plastering. It would take two coats of plaster to finish the repair. A bonding coat to build it out to the existing levels, then a thin coat of finish plaster to make it nice and smooth. My plan was to have a brew, put the first coat on, then once that had set hard enough I could apply the finish. It would still take about three hours for me to be done, even with mixing the plaster in some dirty water to make it set quicker. "Thanks, June."

I sat in the front room, making sure first that my jeans were not dirty. June asked how long the job might take. I answered her questions while rolling and lighting a cigarette. We talked about the weather, as you do, then I heard the front door open and somebody come in.

"Oh," I said to June. "I left the door on the latch, is that okay?"

"Yes, no problem, Gary love. That'll be my friend coming in."

Your friend, I thought. I hope it's that lovely looking woman who I

FOR THE LOVE OF BRASS

saw the other day and, to my surprise, the same woman passed the door opening, saying hello as she passed.

"Hi," I replied.

I smiled as I looked at June, wondering to myself has June's friend come to use the toilet again and is Ernie the milkman missing his glasses. The second of the two questions I could answer straight away. Ernie wasn't missing his glasses because Ernie was dead. He was hit with a rock cake underneath his heart, that's what killed old Ernie.

The first question, well, it did seem odd that June's friend would come here to use the toilet. Oh well, I thought to myself, maybe she lives upstairs or nearby and she's having her bathroom worked on and her toilet may not be working. Anyway, what did it matter?

I heard a door open and close in June's hallway, then her friend appeared in the doorway again.

"Hi June, hello Gary," she said. "Can I sit in here with you two?"

"Yes, you can," I said, wanting to have a chat with her.

June said, "I'll make a cup of tea for you."

June's friend said, "Be back in a tick." She went down the hallway but was only gone for a minute, then she walked back into the front room having taken her jacket off and returned with a box of cigarettes and a lighter in her hand. She sat down in an armchair opposite my chair and lit a cigarette.

"Can I use your ashtray as well?" she said.

"Yes, of course," I replied.

"Will you finish your job today?"

"Oh yeah, soon be done," I said. "Should finish about five I think."

"Oh, okay."

"What's your name?" I asked.

"Cindy," she replied.

"Nice to meet you, Cindy."

As she said her name she crossed her legs, putting her left leg over her right. Cindy had a very short skirt on before she sat down, so now she crossed her legs I could see all of her left thigh, which went way above her stocking top, exposing her suspenders, which were black to match her stockings and black high-heeled shoes. Oh, holy shit, I thought and felt my eyes looking at her legs. I did not expect that. She was watching me look her up and down and I realised she'd seen me looking at her.

To try and hide my embarrassment I thought I should say something, so I just came out with it and said, "You'll catch your death of cold walking about like that…" I laughed. Oh shit, I thought and cringed. Did I really just say that? I can't believe it. Oh well, too late now, it's done.

"I don't walk around like this in the winter, only in the summer," she said.

"Oh yeah," I said. "I can see why."

June came back into the room with a cup of tea for Cindy and handed it to her.

"Well, okay," I said. "I've had my tea and smoke. Time to get back to work in the kitchen." We were all still talking, even though I'd mixed the plaster and was plastering the patch in the ceiling. Even as we talked I couldn't help thinking about Cindy's legs and how sexy I thought she was. I thought she was stunning. Right, I said to myself. Get this job done and get out of here, because I found I couldn't concentrate on what I was doing.

It wasn't long before June and Cindy were in the kitchen talking with me, asking questions about the plaster. How long it would take to dry so it could be painted, that type of thing. Along with general chitchat, I asked Cindy if she was having her bathroom refurbished at home.

"No," she said.

The first coat of plaster was on and I'd used dirty water so it would set fairly quickly. Now I just had to hang around until I could get the top coat on. We stood in the kitchen talking and smoking some more. Eventually the base coat was set hard enough to put the finish plaster on. I looked at my watch; it was five past four. I told the girls half an hour or so, then a clean-up and I should be done around five.

"Okay," they said. "We'll go for a drink when you're done. There's a pub just down the road. Do you want to come with us?" What a lovely idea, I thought.

"No thanks," I replied. "I'll head off once I'm done but thank you all the same."

I could hear June and Cindy talking in the front room.

"Gary," June called through to me.

"Yes?"

"The ceiling will be dry in a couple of days, won't it?"

"Yes, it will."

"Can you come back and paint it for us and if so how much will it cost?" Before I answered, June said, "We'll pass the cost on the landlord, so if it's not too expensive we'll just go ahead and do it."

"Oh, okay," I said. "I'll work something out for you before I go." The time was now quarter to five. I was clearing up the kitchen. There was no more to be heard from the girls in the front room. Then I heard the front door open, then close.

June came into the kitchen and said, looking up at the ceiling, "That looks great, Gary love. You're nearly done."

"Yes," I replied.

"I'll sort some money out for you. Oh, and how much will the ceiling cost to paint?"

"Oh, I think a hundred and forty pounds," I explained to June. "The new patch will need sealing with a white sealer paint, then the whole ceiling will get two coats of white emulsion. Once that's done you'll never know there was a leak."

"Yeah, that's fine," said June. "We'll go ahead and get that done, please."

"I think it'll be dry by the start of next week, so if that's okay I'll pop over and see you then."

"You might get to see Cindy again if you're lucky," said June. "She seems to like you."

"Oh yeah?" I said. "How do you know that?"

"Well, I can just tell," said June.

"Has Cindy gone?" I asked.

"No" said June. "She's out the back. Her husband has come to pick her up. She will say goodbye before she goes."

"Oh, okay. Husband," I said.

"Yes," said June. "She's married to a big black man." She laughed.

"Is she?" I said. Lucky old black man, I thought to myself. "She is lovely though, isn't she June? I think she's stunning." I felt I could say that without sounding like a threat, especially as her husband was outside with her.

"Here you are love," said June. "Here's your money."

"Thanks very much," I replied as I put the Nelsons in my pocket. "I'll pay you for the painted ceiling when it's done. Is that alright?" said June.

"Yeah, that's fine with me," I said.

"Yes, you're right," she said. "She's a lovely girl."

"Okay, June, I'll load my van up. Back in a minute." I went out the flat's

FOR THE LOVE OF BRASS

front door then out into the car park. My van was parked around to the right and next to it was a Black BMW five serials. Standing at the back of the car was Cindy, talking with a big man. I just smiled at them both as I unlocked my van and put my tools inside. I went back inside the flat to get my buckets and the two rubbish bags full of my plastering rubbish. I was in June's kitchen.

"Cindy was outside talking to a man next to a lovely Black BMW."

"Oh yeah," said June. "That'll be Ryan, her husband."

"Husband," I said. "He's not black. He's big, mind you, but he's white."

"Yes, I know," said June. "I call him the black man cos he's from Africa. He's a Saffer."

"A Saffer?" I said. "What's that?"

"He's from South Africa. They call them Saffers for short."

"Oh, okay," I said. I had not heard that term before.

"Yeah. I call him the black man," said June, "just to wind him up." She laughed. "I like to wind him up, I do it all the time."

I smiled. "Okay, on that note, June, I'm off. Thanks again," I said. "Oh, can I take your phone number? I'll talk to you in a couple of days and we can arrange a day and time for me to come over once the ceiling's dry."

"Yes, certainly, love." June wrote her number on a piece of paper. "There you go love," as I left the flat with my hands full. I put my buckets and rubbish in the van and said good bye to Cindy and her husband. Cindy said bye in return but her husband just looked; there was no replied from him. I drove off out of the car park and headed home.

Once home it was back to the usual life. Not talking to Sharon, and spending time with my sons. It was staying lighter a lot longer now in the evenings, which was great. It meant we could go out to Morden Park with the dogs after we had had our dinner.

FOR THE LOVE OF BRASS

We spent many an hour in the park. Around the edge of the park there's a woodland trail. I'd walk through there with my boys and the dogs and we'd spend time trying to identify as much wildlife as possible, while every time the dogs saw a squirrel on the ground they'd chase it, trying their best to catch one. The squirrels were always too quick and they'd escape into the trees every time, then come down again once we'd passed but it didn't stop the dogs from trying. I always found stuff to teach my sons in that park. From insects to owls and other birds of prey, there was always something to see. You just needed to know where to look.

Mark had called me to find out if I was at home on Friday evening. He said he wanted to call in to see me to discuss the possibility of going shooting on Sunday.

"Yeah, no problem," I said. "I'll be there."

"Will you be on your own?" he said.

"What, do you mean without Sharon here?"

"Yes, without Sharon being there. I don't like to come round when you're both there. There's too much of an atmosphere. It makes me feel awkward."

"You're awkward anyway," I said, "so what are you worried about?" We laughed. I was trying to make light of his remarks, which of course were true. Mark was one of our friends who knew how bad things were between us. Mark's wife also knew how bad it was. She had stopped coming over altogether. In fact, there were only a handful of our friends that did come over now. Most of our friends, or so called friends, gave Sharon and me a very wide berth. I think what really seemed to be the icing on the cake was when friends knew we had separate bedrooms and lived apart in the same house. That was better than a cattle prod. That really kept them away.

FOR THE LOVE OF BRASS

The other thing that stood out to me, when I'd occasionally get home from work early enough to go to the school and collect Lee, was that I found I stood on my own. None of the other parents (albeit mainly women) would ever acknowledge me, let alone stand with me. This wasn't the situation before people knew our marriage was on the rocks. I would just stand on my own, watching them all and wondering to myself how many of these parents have a perfect home life, or perfect relationship for that matter.

Friday night, 7.30 and Sharon had just left in her cab to go God knows where. I didn't ask, she didn't say. There was a knock on the front door. The whippets came rushing into the hall from the kitchen barking as they went. They had both got to the door before me and were still barking as I opened the door.

"Hello Mark," I said.

"Hello mate, how's things?"

"Yeah, all good, Sharon's out," I said. We looked at each other and smiled. The dogs walked back down the hall, excitement over for them, and we followed the dogs into the kitchen. "Do you want a beer, mate?" I asked.

"Yeah, a Foster's please," said Mark.

"Dad," the boys shouted down from upstairs.

"What's up?" I said.

"House clearance," Lee shouted down.

"Not now, boys. Mark's here. We're having a drink." Silence came from upstairs. I gave Mark his beer. I made myself a large vodka and orange. "Come on, we can sit in the dinner room at the table."

We discussed our week's work and so on and before talking about Sunday's activities. We, or I, got onto the subject of this woman called

Cindy that I'd met. I told Mark all about her.

"Sounds nice," he said. "Sounds like you like her."

"Yeah, I do. Really fancied her as soon as I saw her. Been thinking about her all week. She's married to a Saffer, a big bastard at that."

"Oh well," said Mark, "that's that out the window before you start."

"Yeah, it would seem so," I said.

"Well, Sunday, mate, fancy a shoot at Haywards Heath?"

"Yeah, that would be good," I said. "We could even take some fishing kit and have a fish for a few hours if we go early," I said. Mark agreed. "That's what we'll do then. I'm pretty sure Sharon's taking the boys to her mum's on Sunday."

We carried on talking about this and that and of course Cindy's name kept coming up. I told Mark how I was going back there to paint the kitchen. "I may see her again, you never know," I said.

I put my sons to bed when it was their time to go and told them, "I think your mum's out again tomorrow night. We can do some clearance then." They were happy with that.

I showed Mark my new bedroom. I had been in it for a while now. He was most interested in seeing the new built-in gun safe.

He said, "So Sharon's alright with you both living like this?"

"Yeah, as far as I know. She doesn't say much about it."

"So there's no chance of you two ever sorting this out, then?"

"No, no chance at all. Our relationship is finished. All over bar the shouting," I said. Little did I know how true that statement would be. Bar the shouting…

We went back downstairs to the dining room, getting another drink from the kitchen as we went. I told him all about my solicitor's visit as well.

"Well, what did Sharon say when she got the letter?"

FOR THE LOVE OF BRASS

"It's not arrived yet," I said. "Well, I don't think it has. She hasn't said anything and I've not seen anything like that with the post in the mornings."

"How do you think she'll take it?"

"I'm not sure. She knows we're finished, so she might take it very well."

Mark said, "I have a feeling it'll not go down too well. Best keep your gun safe locked, Ha-ha-ha…"

Saturday night came and I and the boys played house clearance and watched a Schwarzenegger film, *Predator*, after which we were trying to work out a way to get the three red dots, so we could shine them on each other when playing clearance.

Sunday was a lovely warm day, a real bit of escapism, I thought. Fishing for half the day, then out came the shotguns for the second half. Whenever I was out shooting or fishing or even just walking in the countryside, I'd always forget all my woes and troubles. I just found it so relaxing.

Monday morning, kids off to school. Sharon off to work. I found myself in the office, trying to concentrate on the week's work ahead but all I could think of was Cindy over at Woodside. Would I see her again? Would she be there at June's flat when I went to paint the ceiling? I couldn't stop thinking about her and those stockings when she sat down. Oh dear, I thought. You need to have a cold shower. I smiled at the thought. Okay, I said to myself. I need to get some materials over to Ron and a couple of the blokes. We had a job running in a town called Ewell, over near Epsom. I'd go there first, do what I had to do, then see how much time I had left, then phone June to arrange the painting job.

I finished running around getting and ordering materials for the job and found myself finished by 2.15. Hmmm, I thought to myself. Bit late now to go to June's. I'll phone her when I get home to see if I can get the job done tomorrow. I arrived home and the dogs were glad to see me as always, which is more than I could say for Sharon, I thought to myself. I smiled, made a cup of tea then moved into the office. Okay, a quick phone call, then I'm early enough to go to the school and pick up Lee, save him waiting for his mum at Julie's till half five.

I dialled June's number and it rang for quite a while. As I was about to hang up, she answered.

"Hello, who's that?" she said.

"Oh, hi June, it's Gary. Just giving you a call about painting the ceiling."

"Oh, hello love," she said. "Look, can't really talk now we've had some aggro here. Can you call me tomorrow? I have to go."

"Yeah, sure," I said, "talk then." I hung up. Hmmm, I wonder what happened there, I thought as I sipped my tea. Oh well, I'll go and get Lee. I'll probably be five or ten minutes early. Still, that's okay, I said to myself. I can stand there like a leper as I usually do and watch all the other parents with their perfect lives wait for their children.

Lee appeared from the school doorway into the playground, a big smile on his face when he saw me waiting. He ran over and we headed out of the school gate. We crossed the road to Julie's house and banged on her door. Julie came out.

"Just to let you know," I said, "I'm home from work early so, as you can see, I've picked Lee up."

"Okay, Gary," she said. "See you tomorrow, Lee." She went back inside and we wandered off down the road and went home.

"Can we take the dogs out for a run when we get home, Dad?"

"Yes, as soon as we get there, we'll take them in the big field behind the house."

FOR THE LOVE OF BRASS

Next day, I waited until ten o'clock, then called June's number. Somebody picked the phone.

"Hello," the voice said.

"June?" I said.

"No, who's that?"

"Is that you, Cindy?"

"Yes, who's this?"

"It's me, Gary. I'm calling about the kitchen ceiling."

There was a silence, then, "Hello, Gary. How are you? Are you coming over to sort June out?" she started to laugh. "June," she shouted, "it's Gary on the phone. He wants to come over and sort you out." Cindy found this hilarious. June came on the phone.

"Don't take any notice of her. She's in one of them messing about moods. Sorry about yesterday. We had a bloke trying to break in through the front door. He had a knife and was threatening us. We called the Old Bill and they turned up and took him away. I pushed him away from the front door and as I did, he cut my hand with his knife. I needed to go to the hospital and get a couple of stitches in the side of my hand."

"Bloody hell!" I said. "You're okay now, yes?"

She said, "Yes. Anyway," she said, "you want to come over and finish the ceiling for me?"

"Yeah, I do. When is it okay for you? I said. "Tomorrow, Wednesday, is that okay?"

"Yes, fine with me."

"I'll be with you about nine thirty. Is that okay?" I said.

"Yes," said June. "See you tomorrow. I'll let you get on with it."

"See you." I hung up the phone. That all sounds a bit dodgy, I thought. Somebody trying to break in with a knife and to do what? Rob them?

157

Kill them? God knows. Cindy seemed to think the whole thing was funny. She must be a bit of a hard nut. It didn't seem to phase her. On my travels today, I thought to myself, I'll pick up the paint for tomorrow and make sure I put the painting tools I need in the van.

I arrived at Woodside Green, turned left in between the flats, then right again. I parked in the same place as I had before, right behind June's flat, went in through the tradesman's entrance and rang the bell.

"Hello, Gary," June said, as she opened the door.

"Hi-ya," I said. "Can I leave the door on the latch?"

"Yeah, no probs. You carry on, love. Do you wanna tea? I've got the kettle on."

"Yes, please," I replied and set about getting my dust sheets in and getting them laid out around the kitchen without interfering with the tea-making process. I'd noticed as I parked there was no black BMW there. In fact there were hardly any cars at all in the car park.

I brought in the rest of the tools and paint needed to do the job. I wonder if Cindy is here. I wonder if she'll pop in with her husband. I wonder if she'll pop in on her own, I hope so. I would like to chat with her some more. I just kept thinking to myself how lovely she was.

June had finished making the tea. "You alright?" she said to me.

"Yes, fine thanks. I'll drink this tea and smoke this fag, then get started," I said.

"Okay," June replied.

"Oh," I said, "is Cindy popping in to see you today? It'd be nice to see her."

"You like her, don't you?" said June.

"Yes, I do," I smiled. "I'll be here most of the day, June. You know, waiting for the paint to dry in between coats."

"Yeah, that's alright Gary. I have some things to sort out so I'll take the phone in the other room and make my calls from there. Help yourself to tea whenever you want."

I applied the first coat of sealer to the bare plaster. June had gone off to another room. She'd shut the hall door, the one that led into the kitchen. I could hear the phone ringing quite a lot. I heard the front door open and close a couple of times. Each time I wondered or hoped it would be Cindy visiting. Lunch time came and I shouted out to June.

"I will pop out to the shops for something to eat."

"Okay," June said. "When you come back, come in the front way. Press the intercom and I'll buzz you in."

"Okay," I said, then went off to the shops, leaving the kitchen window open. There was no rush for me to go back as I was waiting for the paint to dry. The weather was lovely so I sat on the Green for a while, eating my lunch and smoking. When I got back I pressed the intercom button.

"Hello," said June.

"Hi June, it's Gary."

"Okay, love." The lock buzzed and I entered, walking down the hall, through the lounge and into the kitchen. The other kitchen door had sheets on it. I carried on with my painting. I could hear some activity going on from time to time. Soon I'd completed another coat on the ceiling. I was standing at the kitchen sink washing my paint rollers and looking out over the Green.

Suddenly I heard, "Hello Gary, how are you doing?" I turned to see Cindy standing in the kitchen doorway.

"Oh, hi," I said with a big beaming smile on my face. "I'm fine. I'm glad you're here. I've been on my own most of the day so it's nice to have someone to talk to."

"Well," said Cindy. "Can I move these sheets over a bit so I can get to the kettle and I'll make a cup of tea?"

"Yes, you carry on," I said.

"So you're nearly finished?"

"Yes, won't be long now," I said. As Cindy was making the tea, I was moving all the dust sheets out of the way and folding them up ready for the van along with the rest of my stuff.

"Are you in a rush?" Cindy said.

"No, not at all."

"That's good," she said. "Come and sit in the front room. We can have a cigarette."

"Okay. Sounds good to me." I was sipping my tea and rolling a fag while passing the time of day with Cindy. I could hardly take my eyes off her. I heard movement in the hall and looked up, thinking it was June, when a girl walked passed the door wearing only her underwear. She looked into the room as she passed. It was definitely not June. This girl was tall, slim, she'd long black hair half way down her back and was only wearing a black bra, black knickers and heels. She had tanned or olive skin. I guessed her to be about 25. It's surprising, I thought, how much information you can take in from a quick look. Especially when you see what I had just seen go past the doorway.

"There's a half-naked girl just gone past your doorway, Cindy," I said.

"Yes, I know," as she puffed on her cigarette.

I looked at Cindy and smiled. "I like working here. Would you like me to decorate the whole flat? I'll do it cheap." We both laughed.

"How long before you finish?" Cindy said. "We're going for a drink in a while. Would you like to join us?" What a bloody good idea, I thought.

"Yes," I said, "that will be great. I'll clear up the kitchen." Well, I've never worked so quick finishing up in the kitchen and loading the van.

I called out to June. "All finished June. Come and have a look, please. I just want to make sure you're happy before we go."

"Okay, love." June came into the kitchen, looked up and said, "Bloody marvellous, Gary. Wouldn't know there had been any water damage at all. Yep, really nice."

"Good," I said. "I'm glad you're happy." I received my Nelsons. "Okay, I said, let's go to the pub."

"Well, I won't be going," June said. "I'm on antibiotics for my hand, so you and Cindy will have to go on your own."

"Oh, okay. What about the underwear girl, is she coming?" I said.

"Oh, Mandy, she might join you later. She's got something to do." Okay, I thought. I'm not so happy now. Although I wanted to have a drink with Cindy if it's only me and her, what if the Saffer turned up? He might have something to say about the situation. Oh well, I'm going anyway, just have to keep my wits about me.

"Come on," Cindy said, "let's go." She said bye to Mandy and June as we left the flat.

"Where are we going?" I said.

"There's a pub two minutes' walk along the road. We'll go there." Off we went, leaving my van behind June's flat. As we walked, I asked Cindy about the man with the knife.

"Oh," she said. "Just an arsehole who wanted to have a go at Mandy. He figured she owed him something."

"And what happened to him?"

"The police took him away. I don't expect we'll see him again."

I pushed the pub door open and looked around. I'd never been in this pub before. As we approached the bar I said, "What would you like?"

"Oh, just half a lager for me," Cindy said. I ordered that, along with a pint of lager shandy for me, knowing full well I'd have to drive later. We sat down in a quiet corner.

"So, Cindy," I said. "Will your husband have anything to say about us having a drink together?"

"No," she said, "nothing at all." That's handy, I thought, and smiled.

"I've a few things to ask you, if that's okay?"

"Fire away," she said.

"Who's Miss Black Underwear?"

"Oh, she's a friend of mine."

"And what, was she getting ready to go out?"

"No," Cindy laughed. "She was working."

"Working?" I said.

"Yes, the flat is a massage parlour." I looked at her. It seemed to take a few seconds to sink in.

"A massage parlour," I said.

"Yes." It seemed I needed a few more seconds. Then I burst out laughing. "What's funny," said Cindy.

"You're telling me June is on the game."

"No, no," then Cindy started to laugh. "June's the maid."

"Oh, right," I said. "So who else works there?"

"Well, there's Mandy and sometimes another girl and there's me…" there was a short pause, "I run the place." Well, my mouth dropped open. I couldn't believe what I was hearing. "Well, well," I said after that. "I think I need a drink. I had no idea. I just thought you were just friends."

"Well, we are," said Cindy. "We're all friends."

"You've a husband."

"Yes," said Cindy, "I do."

FOR THE LOVE OF BRASS

"Does he know about the parlour?" I stupidly said.

Cindy laughed. "Yes, of course he does."

"And he doesn't mind?" I said.

"No, of course not. I was a working girl when he met me and a working girl when we got married. I prefer to run the business and organise things now. Look after the girls and so on, you know." I scanned around the pub as though I was on bodyguard duties.

A sudden movement, as the pub door opened; in came a woman with long black hair. She looked around as she came in, then walked with a ladylike gait in our direction. This could be Mandy I thought, but I couldn't recognise her with her clothes on.

"Hello," she said as she approached the table. "Hello," Cindy replied. "What do you want to drink?"

"No, no," I said, "let me get this."

"I'll have a brandy and coke, please."

"Okay, I'll sort that out." I returned with the drink. "There we go, Mandy. Bottoms up! So sorry," I said, "excuse the pun." The girls laughed and lit up cigarettes.

"I'll just have one or two with you. I've a job to go to."

"Okay. Cindy was telling me about the parlour."

"Oh yes," she said. "Have you visited many?"

"No," I said as I rolled a cigarette. "Oh well, you should pop in for a lovely massage. I will sort you out with a happy ending. Ha-ha-ha." We laughed. "I'll even give you a discount seeing as how you know Cindy. Ha-ha-ha."

"I might hold you to that one day."

"Good," she said, "pop in next week. You've got June's number. June works with us you know."

"Yes, yes, I know. She's the maid."

"Well, yes," she said, "our receptionist, really."

"Oh well," said Mandy, "what's new?"

We spoke about June's ceiling, how I ended up doing the job, the pub we were in and of course the man who came calling with the knife.

"Yes," said Mandy. "He was looking for me. Good thing I wasn't there. Still, I don't think we'll see him again. Not now the cops have him. Is Ryan coming to pick you up then Cindy?" she asked.

"Yes, he will do. When I phone him and tell him to come and get me, he will."

"That's good," said Mandy.

"Talking of phones," I said, "Cindy, I see you've one of those brick phones."

"Yes," She said.

"Can I have your number so we can keep in touch?"

"Yes, of course you can," and wrote her number on a piece of paper. "I'd have given it to you before we left here anyway. I want you to keep in touch."

We carried on with the chitchat. I had a lot of questions for these girls about their profession but decided it wasn't the time or place to start hitting them with all that stuff. That could wait for another time. I was sure there would always be something to talk about with these girls. I told them I had my own firm and that I was the boss. I always had lots to do.

"Well," Cindy said, "when you're out and about, make time to pop in and see us. We can have a cup of tea and a chat or go out for a drink. All you've to do is phone first."

"Okay, that sounds great. I don't have a mobile and in some respects it suits me because I'd not get any peace with people wanting to contact me all the time. So for now I keep contact with the clients and staff restricted as much as possible to the evenings. Okay, girls, I'll be on my way now. Say bye to June and tell her I hope her hand is better soon."

Cindy said, "You can tell her yourself next week." The girls laughed.

"Okay, okay, point taken. I'll pop in and see you on my travels."

"Good," said Cindy, "and, oh, don't worry about my husband. I'll make sure he's not around when you come over but don't forget, phone first."

I parked the van outside my house. Our Mercedes wasn't in the garage, it was parked on the drive, which was unusual. Sharon normally put the car away in the garage when she arrived home from work. She must be going out again quite soon. I opened my front door and, as I stepped in, I was greeted by Sharon.

"Where you fuck have you been? I've been waiting to go out. You're normally home earlier than this."

"I was busy," I said, "that's just how it is."

"Well, it's not how it is. If you're going to be late home you fucking tell me beforehand. I've people to meet and you've made me late."

"Well, I'm here now so fuck off, stay out and don't come back. Where are the kids and have they eaten?" I said.

"The boys are upstairs and of course they've eaten," Sharon replied.

"Go on then, fuck off. I won't wait up," I said.

"FUCK YOU!" came the reply. Sharon's passing shot as she slammed the front door shut was, "You fucking wait until tomorrow. I'm going to sort this shit out with you."

"Yeah, yeah, yeah," I said. BANG! the door closed. That was a nice welcome, I thought to myself. An argument could kick off in an instant between us. It didn't take much. Lots of swearing and shouting, normally enough for half the street to hear. It was like my road's version of East

FOR THE LOVE OF BRASS

Enders and almost as regular, twice a week. Although there wasn't an omnibus edition on Sunday because we were both out, thank God. The neighbours must have loved Sundays.

"Hello boys, I'm in," I shouted up the stairs but I guess the boys would have known that. "You alright?" I said.

"Yes, Dad, we're playing in Mike's bedroom."

"Okay," I replied. "I'll be in the kitchen doing something to eat."

I walked into the kitchen. At least my dogs were pleased to see me. As I was cooking my meal, I wondered if the letter had turned up from my new friend, Steve. I thought I should go upstairs and check in case the letter was thrown on her bed or on the side up there. Then I thought, Nah, what's the point? I don't really give a shit whether the letter's here or not. Sharon did seem quite angry but then she was quite angry most of the time anyway. I smiled to myself. I'm sure I'll know sooner rather than later if it is here.

I sat with my dinner on a tray balanced on my lap watching the TV. When it was time to put the boys to bed I did, then sat back down in front of the TV with a large vodka and orange. When I say large I mean half a pint. When it was time for me to go to bed, I let the dogs out into the back garden for a couple of minutes while finishing off my second large vodka and orange, then wobbled up to my sanctuary.

The next morning I was up and out early to the builder's merchants for materials for one of the jobs. There was a bonus to going out to work early. It meant I didn't have to see Sharon, especially as I had had a bollocking on the way in. What's new? I thought. I finished my list of things to do today. I had completed them by lunchtime, so home I went. I called the dogs.

"Come on, girls, we're going out to the countryside for a long walk. I feel I need it. I've a lot to think about," I told them.

We walked along a ridge on the North Downs, heading towards Box Hill from Betchworth, where we had parked the van. It was a lovely warm and sunny day and it hadn't rained for some days so the paths we took were dry and not all muddy. The walk gave me time to think. I'd stop every so often where there was a nice view, sit down, roll a ciggy and just take in my surroundings while puffing away. I thought a great deal about yesterday's events over at Woodside. A massage parlour, working girls, the man with the knife, the big Saffer, having a drink in the pub with Cindy and Mandy after work. Bloody hell, I thought to myself, I only went there to fix a ceiling for an old lady.

"Come on girls. Let's start heading back to the van. We have to go home so I can get my bollocking." I laughed as I spoke to the dogs. I think Sharon was right, I thought to myself, we should talk about things, and tonight was as good as any other night. As long as we could do it without arguing, we could give my sons and the neighbours a night off in the process.

"Good night," I said to Michael as I closed his bedroom door. I'd already put Lee to bed earlier on, so hopefully it was adult time for me and Sharon. Adult time without it kicking off.

We went into the lounge, armed only with a cup of tea each and our cigarettes and our own ashtrays, so we didn't have to share.

"Okay," I said. "No arguing. If things get heated one of us walks out the room. Agreed?"

"Yes, agreed," Sharon said.

"This trying to live our own lives in the same house is not working too well," I said.

"Yes, I agree, we need some rules if it's going to work," Sharon said.

"Okay. Rules?" I said. "I thought guidelines. I was thinking rules might be broken too easily, then we're back to arguing and all that shit. What do you think?" I asked.

"Yeah, okay," Sharon replied. She crossed one leg over the other as she sat there, then started to wave her foot in the air. I noticed the waving out of the corner of my eye and thought, oh shit, she's getting agitated already but carry on.

"Right, I'm going to be blunt, at the risk of wearing your tea," I smiled. "This is how I see it. If either of us is wanting to go out and the other one is in, then the one at home is the babysitter for the evening. Now, if one of us has notice that we're going out, then they tell the other one and if it's okay with them, then they babysit. If they can't babysit for whatever reason, then they arrange their own babysitter. How does that sound? I think that keeps it simple."

"Yeah," said Sharon, still waving her foot in the air. "Run that by me again. I want it to be clear."

"Okay," I said and explained it again.

"Yeah, okay," said Sharon. "That seems like it might work."

Well," I said, "it seems to give the answers for both of us without it being just expected of us and we shouldn't argue if we both know the guidelines. We know the answers to what we want before we go ahead and do it."

"Yes, yes," Sharon said. We both lit up a cigarette.

"Wow, that's good," I said. "We got there quick and I'm not wearing any tea. Ha-ha-ha. Also, if you've any questions or want to change something, just ask! We can sort it."

"This letter I got today," said Sharon.

"Oh yeah, from a solicitor in Wallington?" I said.

168

FOR THE LOVE OF BRASS

"Yes, that's the one." I could see her foot waving the air again, only this time faster. She puffed her cigarette then put it out in the ashtray and folded her arms. I thought I could be wearing whatever is left in the teacup quite soon, along with the cup and the ashtray, if I'm not careful.

"Okay," I said, "this is how I see this situation between us. We don't get on at all well, we live separate lives in separate rooms, we can't stand the sight of each other, we don't like each other, so I thought we should do something about it. You know, from a legal point of view it's only a piece of paper that says we're married, there's nothing else. So I think we should get divorced." Sharon's foot stopped waving in the air and she stared at me without blinking for what seemed to be an eternity.

"Right," she said. She stood up with her cigarettes and lighter in one hand, and with the other she pulled the lounge door fully open, walked out into the hallway then went upstairs. I sat there wondering what was going to happen next. I rolled a cigarette and lit it up. The dogs came walking into the room. One sat on the floor next to me, the other hopped up on the settee and sat next to me. There was just silence. I puffed on my cigarette looking at a turned-off TV screen. No reaction, I thought to myself, was worse than a reaction, particularly coming from Sharon. It was a rare occurrence. I suddenly smiled to myself, perhaps the reaction would come during the night while I'm asleep, after all Sharon had grown up with that sort of violence in her household.

An hour passed and Sharon came downstairs from her bedroom and into the kitchen to make a cup of tea. By now I was sitting in the dining room with one of my little vodka and oranges. Sharon walked past the door, tea in hand.

As she passed she said with a dead calm voice, "Under the new guidelines you've set, you're babysitting tomorrow night because I'm

169

fucking off out."

A reaction at last, that's good. I smiled to myself. I should be able to sleep tonight without worrying.

The usual things happened on the weekend. Shopping with the kids, then out with the dogs. I went shooting. Sharon and the kids went to her mum's for the day.

Monday morning, I sat in my office dealing with running the jobs and found myself thinking a lot about Cindy and the characters of Woodside Green. Also about the letter. I'd hoped I would have been able to talk more about the letter with Sharon. Who was I kidding? It's Sharon we're dealing with here. The letter would definitely come up in conversation again.

I made a phone call to Steve over in Wallington, just to put him in the picture. He just said thanks for letting him know and could I let him know when I received a letter from Sharon's solicitors? That would confirm that the ball was rolling.

"Don't forget," Sharon said, as she headed out of the front door. "I'm having a drink with one of the girls after work. I'll be home by about eight o'clock, so you pick the boys up from Julie's and sort their tea out."

"Okay," I said, "that's fine with me." Tuesday nights as well now! I thought to myself. Mind you, every night would suit me.

"See you later, boys," I shouted to them. "I'll pick you up from Julie's."

"See you."

Okay, here I am, in the office again. Don't really want to be here, I thought to myself. I know, I'll sort out what I can today, then go off to see the girls at Woodside. I called June's number.

"Hello," she said.

"Hi June, it's Gary the builder. How's things?"

FOR THE LOVE OF BRASS

"All good," she said.

"I was thinking of popping by tomorrow, will that be okay?"

"Oh," she said. "Phone here tomorrow, or call Cindy tomorrow. You can't come over today," June said.

"Okay, I'll call tomorrow."

"Okay, then. That's fine. Talk to you then. Bye for now." Her voice seemed normal and didn't sound like any trouble. They must be having a day off, all of them. I picked the boys up from Julie's and made the tea for the three of us. We took the dogs for a run over the park and before I knew it Sharon was coming in. She was driving the car so she'd not have had much to drink, if anything.

She said, "Fancy a drink? We can sit and talk some more about things."

"Yeah, that'd be good."

We sat down around 9 o'clock, both armed with a drink, something a bit stronger than tea.

"Okay," Sharon said. "I've taken some advice from a solicitor. They'll be writing to you in due course."

"Okay, that's good," I said.

"So now we sort out any details."

"Okay," I said. "You want to divorce me for unreasonable behaviour."

"Yes, that seems to be the least messy or argumentative out of the reasons the court accept for granting a divorce," I said.

"Yes," said Sharon. "I agree. They also say we have to be separated for two years before the application to the court can take place."

"Yes, I know," I said. "In talking to my brief, I told him we haven't got on for just over two years. We're separated and leading our own lives, just in the same house. So if you're willing to tell a little untruth in your statement about the time factor, we can both start divorce proceedings straight away."

"Okay, is that what you want?" said Sharon.

"Yes, it is," I said.

"Okay, I'll agree to that. There's lots of stuff to sort out," she said.

"Yes, I know, but that will be done as we go and in due course and, of course, when the time is right, or so my brief has informed me anyway. You see," I said, "the thing is Sharon, we're not a married couple in any way shape or form. The only thing that makes us married is that marriage license or piece of paper we have that says so, as far as I'm concerned. So getting divorced is just exchanging one piece of paper for a piece of paper that says we're not married. It should all be quite simple. We can keep this whole thing easy with no complications and a minimum of fuss or arguing. We'll both be happier people and that can only be good for our boys and for us. In amongst all the crap, a great outcome, so what's not to like? We are both in agreement about something. What could possibly go wrong?"

★★★

"Hello June, it's Gary the builder. Is it okay to call in today?"

"Oh, I don't think so, darling," said June. "You best have a chat with Cindy first."

"Okay, what's up?" I said.

"You talk to her love, she'll tell you. Give her a ring on her mobile. See you," said June.

I dialled Cindy's number. "Hello Cindy, how are you?"

"Oh, okay Gary. Where are you?" she said.

"I'm at home at the moment. I will be out and about later. I was going

FOR THE LOVE OF BRASS

to pop in for a brew."

"You can't do that, I'm not there today," Cindy said. "We had a bit of trouble at the flat, so I won't be there today but I can meet you if you like. We can have a beer later. We can meet you at The Joiners, you know, that pub we went to last week."

"Yeah, sounds good to me," I said. "What time?"

"Oh, aim for two o'clock. Is that okay with you?" Cindy said.

"Yeah, that's fine with me. I'll see you there."

"See you."

I hung up the phone. I wonder what has gone on over there, I thought to myself. Oh well, soon find out, I guess.

I parked the van in a side street near The Joiners Arms. I thought I'd not park at the flat. I'd no idea what had gone on, so thought it best to stay away. I locked the van and walked the short distance to the pub. I went in through the front door and looked around. Okay, no Cindy yet, I'll get a drink from the bar.

"Lager shandy, please," I said to the barmaid.

While I was waiting for it to be poured I heard, "Hello Gary," in a friendly, nice way. I turned round and Cindy was standing there with a big smile on her face.

"Hello," I said. "What can I get you to drink?"

"No, that's okay," she said. "I already have one. I'm sitting over there in the alcove next to the fireplace." I looked over. To my surprise there sat the big Saffer with two drinks on the table.

"Oh, okay," I said. "I'll be over in a tick." I paid for my pint then walked over to join them. This is a strange situation, I thought. Oh well, I'm here now, let's see what happens.

I sat down and the Saffer said hello. I greeted him we shook hands.

Cindy looked at him and said, "Okay, you can drink up now. I don't need you here any more, you can go. Me and Gary have some things to talk about."

"Okay." He finished his last drop of beer and stood up. I got up to let him out; I said bye and he walked out. I thought, this is a strange situation.

I said to Cindy, "Are you two really married?"

"Yes," she said.

"And he's happy to leave you in a pub with another fellow?"

"Yes," she said. "He does as he's told." Okay, I thought. "Don't sit there," she said, "come, sit next to me."

"Okay." So I did. "That's better, we can have a chat now." I smiled. I found her so attractive, so lovely looking. Hopefully I would get to know her a lot better. I told her I thought it was strange to have a partner that did as he was told like that and not question anything. It just seemed odd to me but then again, he knew she was a working girl when they got married, or at least that's what she told me. He also knew she ran a massage parlour. The whole thing seemed odd to me. I've just not ever known anyone or a couple in this situation. Maybe this is how it works in the world of a brass.

"So, what happened yesterday at June's?" I said. "There was trouble."

"Oh yeah," said Cindy. "There was trouble alright. That bloke with the knife from last week."

"Yeah?" I said.

"He turned up at June's kitchen window, shouting in. He's after Mandy. He was saying he was going to cut her. Cut her bad when he gets her. Luckily the window was locked, so it only opened a bit, just enough for him to shout through but not enough for him to get in."

"What happened to Mandy? Was she there?" I said.

FOR THE LOVE OF BRASS

"Yes, she was but she got out the back window and hid in the bushes for a bit while he was shouting through at the front. I was in the kitchen with Ryan, trying to distract him while she was hiding. We called the police and they took so long to arrive. When they did the man had gone."

"Did you see the knife?" I said.

"No, he just kept saying he'll cut her when he gets her. She got her stuff and left after the police had gone. They know who he is, of course, so they are keeping an eye out for him," she said.

"So what about Mandy? What's she going to do?" I said.

"Well, she's not coming back to June's to work, which is a shame because the men liked her. She brought in a lot of business. I'll have to find someone to replace her. June's not too happy either, with this bloke running about."

"No, I guess not," I said. We talked about this and that. I told her of my situation at home and how long that had been going on. I didn't have to worry if I got seen out with another woman. I told her about the solicitor's letter and how Sharon was out a lot of the time. Cindy said she went clubbing in Croydon a fair bit.

I said, "That's where Sharon goes as far as I know and laughed. You may already know each other."

Cindy smiled. I was enjoying my time in her company. The pub had started to get busy with more people coming in all the time. I checked the time.

"Do you have to go?" Cindy said.

"Not for a while. As long as I stay on the shandies I'll be okay to drive. I'm quite happy sitting here. It's not much fun at home once my sons go to bed. I sit in the office finding work to do or drinking vodka and orange."

"Really?" Cindy said. "I like vodka and orange. We'll have to go out one night on the piss together and drink vodka and oranges."

"Ha-ha-ha," I laughed, "what a great idea." She must like me, I thought, because before I can ask for another date or to see her again, she gets in first and asks me. "Yeah, that's fine with me, Cindy. I'd love to come out with you again and what about your husband?" I said.

"What about him?" was the reply.

"Well, you sure he's not going to be a problem?" I said.

"No, not at all," she said. "I can do whatever I want and I would like to do that with you. When are you available next?"

"Err, you caught me on the hop with that one."

"Well… if you'd you like to see me again," said Cindy.

"Yes, of course. I could come over and see you next week. During one of the days."

"Yeah, that's fine with me. Can I see you on the weekend?"

"No, not this weekend," I said. "I've a couple of things to do but definitely next week. I'll look forward to it. Can I call to finalise the day and time?"

"Yes," said Cindy. "I'll look forward to it too. Call me whenever you want." She leaned over and gave me a kiss. "I'll call Ryan he can come pick me up."

★★★

I walked into my bedroom with an armful of my clean washing and placed it on the bed. I went back downstairs and returned with the vacuum cleaner and a damp duster. I was tidying up my room. I'd not done it for a while. Sharon did do housework but she had no go areas as far as that was concerned. I was responsible for cleaning my room, my office, the spare room and what we called the boys' bathroom, which was the main bathroom in the house. Sharon had her own bathroom which we boys didn't use.

This arrangement for cleaning duties was a result of one of our many sit-down evening meetings. As a consequence it didn't work out too badly between us, at least it got done.

My bedroom door was half open and there was a tap, tap on it, followed by Sharon saying, "Can I come in?" She walked in before I replied. "I've something I want to talk to you about."

"Okay, where are the boys?" I said.

"Downstairs, watching something on the TV," Sharon replied.

"Can it wait until later, till the boys are in bed?" I said.

"No, I want to discuss it now, it's serious, plus I'm going out later."

"Oh," I said, then just smiled. "Go on then," I said, "but no arguing, okay? I don't want my evening ruined."

"Okay, okay," said Sharon. She sat on the edge of my bed. "Right," she said. "I don't like the fact that you sleep in here."

"Yeah," I laughed… "so?"

"I don't think it looks good, as far as the boys are concerned. Their mum and dad should be sleeping in the same room in the same bed."

"Yeah, really," I said. "Where has that come from?"

"Well, my mum and dad would sometimes sleep in separate rooms and I didn't like it. So I think our sons should see us sleeping together."

"What, even though we don't like each other?" I said. "I don't think that is a good idea because, just saying I agreed to this and the boys see us together, then we have a fall out and I move back in here. How is that going to look? I think it's a bad idea. We should leave things the way they are."

"Well, I think it would help the boys, so I want you to consider it. Will you do that, please?"

"Okay," I said. "I'll think about." Sharon left the room to get ready for her evening out, wherever that was. I did think about it. I thought about it a lot. It didn't make any sense to me. We had no marriage. We had both employed solicitors. We're getting divorced. I don't like her. I don't even like her as a person, so how is it a good idea we share a bed together? I just couldn't see it. I finished tidying and cleaning my room, then the thought crossed my mind, maybe because we'd employed solicitors, Sharon could now see an end to our marriage. Maybe it was her way of trying to find out if the marriage could be saved and she was using the excuse of 'it would help the boys'. I was spending too much time thinking about this. I was more interested in thinking about Cindy. Her blonde hair, her pretty face, her lovely legs, her sexy figure. I can't wait to see her again, I thought. That was better than thinking about sharing my matrimonial bed with Sharon. That situation had definitely passed its sell-by date. That should be the last thing on my mind.

I called Cindy and we arranged to meet on Tuesday evening at the same pub, The Joiners Arms.

"We could sit in that alcove," I said, "you know, between the fireplace and the fish tank."

"Yeah, that will be nice. That will give us some privacy," Cindy said. Not that we needed the fireplace for warmth. It was just somewhere nice. Out of the way.

Sharon wanted a chat again on the Monday evening, once the boys were in bed. We sat in the lounge with our cups of tea, ashtrays and cigarettes, as we'd done many times before. I thought, it's funny how the dogs never come into the room to sit with us when we have a chat. If anything, they walk out when we chat. It's as though they know something could go wrong. That had happened a lot in the past, or maybe we just had sensitive dogs. I laughed to myself.

"Okay," Sharon said.

"I'll start. Have you thought about what I asked, about moving back in with me?"

"Yes," I said. "Quite a lot."

"And?" said Sharon. "Well, I think it's a bad idea. I think we should leave it as it is, the reason being, our boys know the situation now, as it is."

"Yeah," said Sharon. She crossed her legs.

"I think it would be better for us to try and make sure we don't fall out in front of the kids. I don't like them having to go through all that shit with them listening to all the shouting and hollering. It's no good. It's no good for any of us."

"Okay," Sharon said as she lit herself a cigarette. She put the lighter down and her foot started to tap the air. "You've not taken any notice of what I said, have you? I wanted this for the boys."

"I know, I heard you," I said. "I just don't agree with it."

"So you're quite sure you want to go through with this divorce?"

"Yes, and for all the reasons we talked about. You know it's been shit for probably over two years, so yes, I do want it to go ahead. We spend no time together as a family and haven't done for a long time." I thought, and I don't like you. I don't even like you as a person. I don't want you around me. "Yes, of course I want a divorce and so I said, so there we are. I think separate rooms and separate lives is the way to go, without arguing, of course."

"Okay," Sharon said, "is that your last word?"

"Yes," I said. She looked straight at me then put her cigarette out, stood up and walked out of the room.

I switched on the TV and sat there looking for a while. I noticed the dogs had crept in without me noticing them. I had one next to me and one on the floor by my feet.

Sharon spoke to me from the dining room saying, "I'm out this Friday and Saturday nights, so if you want to go out anywhere, you can sort yourself a babysitter."

"Thanks for that," I replied, thinking to myself, I wonder what other punishments I have coming for not thinking in the same direction as her. I'm sure there will be some. I just don't know what yet.

"I'm going to a meeting with my solicitor tomorrow," said Sharon from the other room.

"What time are you going?" thinking she'd go after work.

"I'm going in my lunchtime."

"Oh, okay." That's handy, I thought. I can still escape to see Cindy.

I parked the van in the same side street as I'd done before, then took the short walk round to the pub. I walked up to the bar. As I went, I glanced over to the alcove. There was Cindy talking to somebody on the phone. She looked over, spotted me, then, with a big smile on her face, she waved. I ordered a shandy for me and a bottle of Pils for Cindy. I was sure that was what she'd want to drink, seeing as how there was a bottle already on the table. I walked over to her and as I got there she finished her phone call. I sat down and she leaned over, put her arm around my neck and gave me a kiss.

"How are you, Gary?" She said.

"Very well and all the better for seeing you," I replied.

"That's good."

We sat there talking about this and that for about an hour and a half.

FOR THE LOVE OF BRASS

The time really seemed to go quickly. Then her phone rang. She answered.

"Yes, yes," she said. "Okay. Okay, then. Pop in The Joiners. I'm in here with Gary. Yeah. Yeah, I've some money on me. See you when you get here." Cindy hung up then put her phone back in her bag. That sound's good, I thought. Mandy must be coming in. She was always a sight for sore eyes. Cindy stood up. "Okay, my round. You having the same?"

"Yes, please," I replied. Off to the bar Cindy went. I sat there looking around at all the people. It was busy now. The front door of the pub opened and the movement caught my eye. In came Cindy's husband Ryan. He looked around, saw me and walked straight over and sat down.

"Hello, Gary," he said.

"Hi."

"Where's Cindy?"

"She's up at the bar," I said. "Give her a shout and she can get you a drink."

"Oh no," he replied. "I'm not staying. I'll be off in a minute." Cindy returned with the drinks.

"Mind out, Ryan," she said to him. "Let me sit down."

Ryan moved and they both sat down. Cindy looked in her purse and pulled out some money. Ryan put his hand out. She counted out eight £20 notes.

"There you go. That'll take care of it."

"Okay," said Ryan. "Thanks for that. I'll see you later, Claire. See you, Gary."

"Yeah, see you mate," I said and in a moment he was gone. I sipped my pint. "Claire?" I said.

"Yes," Cindy answered.

"He called you Claire," I said.

"Yes, that's my name. Do you like it?"

I looked at her with raised eyebrows. "Well, yeah. I guess. Why Cindy, though?"

"Oh," said Claire, "that's one of my working names. I've had a few but Cindy I quite like, so I've been using that for a while."

"Well, well," I said, "and your husband just pops in to see you and you're sitting here with me having a drink and he takes no notice, like it's an everyday thing. You're having a drink with another man."

"Yeah, well, it will be."

I looked. "What do you mean it will be?"

"Well," she said. "I told him that I like you and he'll see more of you around and out and about with me and that's how it is." WOW.

"Really?" I said. "And he's okay with that?"

"Yes," said Claire. "Yes, he's okay with that."

"Well, I'll be dammed. I've never heard of anything like that, you know in somebody's marriage I mean, it's alien to me."

"Well," said Claire, "you do want to see more of me, don't you?"

"Oh yes, of course I do," I said.

"Well, that's good, because now we can do just that and you don't have to worry about my husband saying or doing anything about it."

★★★

"Morning, Gary," Steve said as he walked into his office. I was already sitting in the comfortable leather chair in front of his desk. "Don't get up."

"Okay, I won't," I said. We both laughed.

"Okay," he said, "you've some news for me. I also have some for you. Okay, where shall we start?"

"You go first."

"Okay. I've received a letter from your wife's solicitors. In it she does state that you've both lived apart for more than two years, exactly the same time as we'd stated in our statement. Did you discuss this with her?"

"Yes, I did," I said. "She agreed we should say that because it was true. After we'd worked out how unhappy we'd been, it was longer than the stated two years."

"Okay," Steve said. "Well, that's out of the way. We can proceed with submitting divorce documents to the court. We'll get this case registered, which will give us a case number. The ball will then be rolling in that direction. Are you okay with that?" he said.

"Yes, I am. My turn now," I said.

"Yes, please carry on," said Steve.

"Well, as you now know, Sharon has a solicitor. So I want to ask how this works."

"Well," said Steve. "In a nutshell, the two solicitors, in this case I and your wife's solicitor, will write to each other, dealing with the case. We in turn will send copy letters to you and your wife respectively, so you both have a record of what is going on with the case. So, for instance, if and when you need to tell your wife something, you make your request or you tell me. I forward it in a letter to your wife's solicitors; then, if she's something to say or wants to make a request about the divorce case, she in turn will tell her solicitor. They then write to me. I then copy a letter to you. We all know what is going on and how things are proceeding."

"Wow. Really?" I said. "That all seems very long-winded."

"Well, it may do but it's how the system works or indeed the only way it can work." As I looked at Steve, I found my eyes going from right to left as I could see the top of a red double decker bus go past the windows behind him.

"And you charge fifty pounds for each letter you send out?"

"Yes," said Steve.

"I knew I did something wrong when I left school." Fifty pounds is a bloody lot of money for a letter. I should have been a solicitor, I thought to myself. "Still," I said to Steve, "there is a benefit to all this. Judging by all you've said, I need never to talk to my wife again." I smiled.

"That's right," he said.

"So if something gets a bit awkward, or if she want to discuss something that I don't want to discuss, I can just say 'tell your solicitor to write to mine'. That will save putting either of us on the spot and hopefully save any more arguing," I said, as another red bus passed the window.

"That's exactly right," said Steve.

I asked one or two more questions concerning how things might go but Steve just said, "We'll cross those bridges when we come to them. There are, in my experience, so many ways things can go. We'll just deal with situations as they arise. The one thing I can tell you is not to worry. Don't worry about anything. If you've a question about anything at all, just call me. We can discuss it on the phone or you can come in here."

Looking at the year planner that was on the wall in front of my desk at home, I was aware there were spaces in between the jobs that were booked in. The recession had been going for just over a year now. I had been okay when it came to work. The building work that is. I'd seen some of my friends in the same business as myself get into a lot of financial trouble. One or two lost their nice big caravans down on the coast, or their new Jaguar car. One or two even lost their house. They were living beyond their means, so when push came to shove something had to give and their assets had to be sold to pay the debts. This situation had put a lot

FOR THE LOVE OF BRASS

of pressure on the marriages and one or two didn't survive. I, on the other hand, had been okay till now but I had just started to notice a slowdown in business. This meant I needed to keep myself out there, keep finding the work to bring in, after all it wasn't just for me. I'd staff to look after.

A friend of mine, a fellow called Andy, asked me to look at some work that needed doing on his house. He wanted to dry-line his cellar. It could then be turned into two usable rooms he could store stuff in. I had a look and we sorted out what we'd do with the rooms, which was satisfactory to him. I gave him a costing, which was acceptable, so I could start. I decided to do the job myself. There were three or four weeks work there. If I didn't rush, it would take me four weeks and Andy wasn't worried if it took five weeks; that would give him longer to get the money together so he was happy either way. He also lived in Wallington in a large Victorian house about 15 minutes' walk from the solicitors. We agreed I would start the following Monday.

I knew Sharon was out Friday and Saturday. She might not come home all weekend for all I knew, not that I was fussed, I thought. I could find a babysitter, then meet Claire and we could go out. That sounded like a plan to me.

I asked around to see who I could get to babysit. Andy, who I was doing the job for on the Monday had four children. The oldest, Jack, said he'd babysit. He was happy to stay the night which meant I was free all night if I needed to be. Yes! I thought, this sounds like an even better plan. I called Claire and asked if she was up for a night out on Friday night. She said yes and she couldn't wait to see me. That's handy I thought. I couldn't wait to see her either. I found I'd think of her quite a lot throughout the day, which made me realise I was becoming very fond of her. I spoke with her again on Thursday to arrange for the following night. The plan was we'd meet at The Joiners and have a few drinks there, then get a cab into Croydon and go clubbing; well, that's if we made it that far. After all that, we'd get a cab back to her place and I could stay there the night, sleeping on the settee. Claire said she wanted to talk to me on Friday, just to chat, she said, because she missed me each day.

Friday came and I went to the bank, did the banking then back to my office to do the wages for the men. Once that was sorted and before I went off to the sites to pay the men, I called Claire.

No answer, her phone was switched off. I left it an hour and called again. Still off. Another hour, still off. It got to five o'clock and still off. Doesn't look like we're going anywhere. I had a babysitter booked and it would be a shame to waste it, so I called Mark.

"Hi mate, you going to the gun club tonight and having a beer after? YES! Great I'll meet you down there."

It wasn't what I'd planned but I had a good evening out with the lads from the gun club. I couldn't drink but that was okay, at least it got me out. I had not been out on a Friday night for ages. The good thing was Saturday morning when I woke up, no hangover. That's handy, I thought and went into the kitchen to make some tea.

Jack was just about to leave. I thanked him very much for babysitting and he went on his way but I couldn't help wondering what had happened to Claire. I didn't know where she lived, so it wasn't like I could pop round. Hold on, I thought, I have June's number in the van in my diary. I went out and brought the diary in and called June's. No answer. Oh well, not much else I can do other than try again later.

I did the usual things with the boys that day, shopping, Wimpy, back home with the shopping. It was lovely weather so in the afternoon it was out with four boys and the two dogs to the chalk hills to give us all a good run.

FOR THE LOVE OF BRASS

Back in time for tea. I called Claire again, phone still off. Oh well. I had not seen Sharon all day. She'd not come home from yesterday. She'll be around when she's around. That evening, once the boys were in bed, I sat in my lounge with the TV on and one of my little vodka and oranges. I thought, that's a shame it didn't work out with Claire. I really did fancy that girl. I hope I get to see her again. I wonder what they are all up to, having fun somewhere, I guess.

Sunday, I tried calling Claire again several times during the day. Her phone was off all day. Sharon however did turn up mid-morning, got herself sorted out and took off with the boys to her mother's for dinner. I decided I would go shooting so I got one of my shotguns out of the safe, grabbed some ammo and headed off to the countryside.

I tried Claire's phone again Sunday evening, still no answer. I tried again Monday afternoon.

"Hello," said a voice. It was the Saffer. I could tell his accent. "Hello Ryan, its Gary. Is Claire there, please?"

"She's busy at the moment. Can you call back in twenty minutes or so?"

"Yes, okay mate. Is everything okay?" I asked.

"Oh yeah. Call her back then. She'll tell you." And with that he hung up. She'll tell me, I wonder what that means. I was glad she was alright. I wondered about why I thought about her such a lot. Was I getting too attached? Should I allow myself to get too attached? Then I thought, well, each time I spend some time with her, I'm not at home in my miserable environment, so if it makes me feel happy seeing her, then why the hell not? On the other hand, I thought, she is a brass and that could be a recipe for disaster for the old heart strings. Oh well, I said to myself, I seem to be happy to carry on turning the pages of this story and see what comes out in the wash! Even if we just end up as good friends.

I called back and she answered.

"Hello, Gary."

"You okay?" I said to her.

"Yes, I am. We have had some dramas. I'm sorry about letting you down Friday night. I had no choice. You know June's flat?"

"Yes," I said.

"You know the knife man story?"

"Yes."

"Well, the police seem to think the knife man watched and waited for Mandy to leave June's, which was about four o'clock. Then he followed her up the road to the shops. When she finished at the shops she decided to catch a bus home, she only lives in Croydon above a shop. She got off the bus near to her flat, walked up to her front door, put the shopping down and opened the front door with her key. Then, as she bent down to pick the shopping up a hand came around from behind, covered her mouth and she was pushed inside into the hall. Then the man pushed the front door shut behind them. She dropped all her shopping but by then it was too late, he was in. He pulled out the knife and held it against her throat, told her to be quiet or he'd kill her. Then he pushed her upstairs and took her into her front room. He pulled out some cord and tied her hands behind her back, then he tied her feet together. He pulled a handful of tissues from a box on the side, rolled them up, then suddenly..." There was a pause. "Are you there?"

"Yeah, yeah. I'm here, I'm just listening. I don't know what to say, sorry. Carry on," I said.

"Okay, then he rolled them up, stuffed them into her mouth, then put tape over her mouth. She was terrified and there wasn't a thing she could do. Then he cut her clothes off bit by bit, piece by piece, all the while he was telling her she'd led him on for too long and now it was his turn to lead her on. He said he was going to cut pieces off of her real slowly. By this time she'd pissed and shit herself which he didn't like and was complaining about, he didn't like the smell. Once he'd cut most of her clothes off, he stopped what he was doing and sat on her settee, just watching her. Then he said he'd something to do and left, saying he'd be back later to cut pieces off of her. He went downstairs and she said she heard keys rattle, then the door opening and closing and silence, he'd gone. She got herself into the kitchen and up to the knife drawer. From there she was able to cut herself free. She grabbed what clothes she could, not even trying to clean herself up. Then she ran out onto the street shouting and crying until some passers-by stopped and helped her and somebody called the police. They took her off to Mayday hospital where she stayed overnight with a police guard."

"Yeah, bloody hell, then what happened?" I said.

"Once she'd called us, we went to the hospital, then I went shopping and got her some clothes. She left hospital with the police and they took her to a safe house somewhere.

She said she was never coming back. Of course, we told June all about the attack and what had gone on. Now June's said, that's it, no more working girls at her flat, not even me. She also said she won't work for me any more as a maid or anything else. She's so frightened by the whole thing she's finished with it all. None of us are welcome there any more."

"So what happens now there's nowhere to work from?" I said.

"Well, it's a bit of a pain but I'll sort something out," said Claire.

"Oh okay, so you've had a busy few days with one thing and another."

"Oh yes," she said. "I've sorted out a place we can use as a parlour.

It's not far from Woodside actually but I just need to finalise the details. Hopefully it'll be okay. There's a second flat that's ideal as well but we'll see what unfolds over the next week or so."

"That sounds alright, then. Any chance we can meet up for a drink? I'd like to see you," I said.

"That would be nice," Claire said. "Maybe later in the week. I have a lot to do for now."

"Okay, I'll call you in a few days," I said.

"Yeah, that's great. Talk soon, bye for now."

Well, I thought to myself, at least Claire's okay and Mandy, poor girl. It's a shame she's gone. I thought she was okay. Mind you, after what happened to her, that would be enough to frighten the shit out of anybody. I wonder if she'll come back? I wonder, will we see her again? I think these girls could do with minders or bodyguards, I told myself.

My week just carried on as normal, running the building company. Seeing the men, buying materials and getting them delivered to the various sites. My foreman, Ron, really was a godsend. He looked after everything when I wasn't around or was busy with other things. Each day I found myself thinking about Claire a lot in between all the other things to think of. Sharon and I had a good week in as much as we did not talk at all, so therefore we did not argue, which is always nice. Until the Friday night that is.

I'd spoken with Claire on Thursday and we'd arranged to meet up for a drink on Thursday evening at The Joiners Arms. I was quite excited on the journey over to see her. I had not seen her for a week and I was keen to do so. It was 8 o'clock when I walked in through the pub door. I glanced around as I approached the bar. There was Claire sitting in the alcove between the fireplace and the fish tank, chatting to somebody on the phone. I got the drinks and sat down next to her. She hung up from the phone call, leaned over and gave me a big kiss.

"Hello, darling. How are you?" she said.

"Yeah, yeah. Good thanks. Better for seeing you. I missed you," I said.

"I missed you too," she said. "I've only been here a couple of minutes before you walked in. That's why I don't have a drink yet."

"Oh, okay," I said. "Did you drive here?"

"No, no," she said. "Ryan dropped me off."

"Oh, okay. I like your husband! Drops you off so you can come out will me for the evening. Ha-ha." I laughed. "I can't help but think you've a strange set-up, you and your old man."

"Well, yeah, maybe. It's just how it is," Claire said.

"So, how's things? Looking for a new property to work out of?" I said.

"Yeah, good. We have one just around the corner from here. Well, not too far away. It's in Cobden Road, just off of Portland Road. Down the road from here, past June's, carry on along Portland and Cobden is on your left."

"So who will work out of Cobden Road?" I asked. "Will you work out of it, or put someone in there?"

"Well," said Claire, "I've a new girl to work for me there. I interviewed her yesterday. I think she's ideal. The punters will love her. She's tall with long, bright blonde hair. Maybe a bit on the thin side but I think she'll be okay."

"Has she done this work before?" I asked.

"Oh yes," said Claire. "I could not employ them if they'd not. They have to know what's it's all about. I won't mess about trying to teach them, I've got enough to do just looking after them."

"Okay," I said, "so you still need a maid or receptionist, or will you do that?"

"I can do that for now, until I get someone. I have someone in mind. I can see them next week, then all being well they can start and I can look for another place."

"Oh, okay," I said. "Another place?"

"Yes, if I can get another place, then put staff in that, all I have to do is to look after the flats and the staff, then we can have more time together."

"Oh, really?" I said. "More time for us."

"Yes," she replied. "I don't see why not."

"Wow, that would be great. I like that idea. Well, you know I work in the building business, so if any of the flats need a tidy up, let me know and I can help out."

"Okay," said Claire. "I'll remember that."

"So how do you find your staff? Are they girls you already know?"

"Yeah sometimes," Claire explained, "but mainly I put an advert in the paper and the girls apply."

"So you advertise for a maid or a brass, or is it done all in the same advert?" I said.

"No, no," said Claire, "it's all done in the same advert. I just say in the advert, New massage parlour requires maid and girls. Call us on Blah blah blah, then the punters see the advert as well. They also call in to see what services we do."

"That's good," I said. "So you get them both ways."

"Yes, exactly… anyway what did you say? A brass! What's a brass? I've not heard that before."

"Oh a brass is a prostitute or a working girl, as you call them."

"Where did that word come from, brass?"

"Well," I said, "it's Cockney rhyming slang. It's short for brass nail, which means 'tail' and 'tail' is an old London word for a prostitute. Dates back hundreds of years."

"Interesting," Claire said. She went on to explain how the interviews go for the maids and the working girls. She said most of the older maids were working girls in their time. She also said there was no shortage of applicants. Once the advert went out there would be lots of phone calls. Claire also said that the flat would be hers to use from tomorrow. She'd be sorting out whatever needed to be done over the weekend and that the new phone line was being installed on Monday and the adverts would be in next week's local papers.

I enquired about what happened to Mandy and asked if that sort of problem, or something similar, could happen again.

"Yes, it could," said Claire, "but we do our best to stop the situation going that far. Normally it can be dealt with earlier."

"Is that why you have your husband run you around? You know, for security I mean."

"No, not really, although it is handy having him around because he's a big fellow but that's as far as it goes. Ryan doesn't like confrontation at all. In fact he'd shy away from it. The time the girls could do with security is when they go out on jobs but that type of agency is something I will be looking into in the future."

After a great and very informative evening with Claire, we arranged to talk on the phone over the weekend. Also I said I would pop over to see her at the new parlour on Monday or Tuesday next week.

Friday found me unloading timber I had ordered a couple of days ago from a truck.

"Ron," I said, "I'll have a cuppa with you when this is unloaded, then I have to go to the bank. I need to get the money out for the wages." This I did, then I drove home, sat in my office and completed the wages for the men. Then I was off, driving back around the sites paying the men, all the while thinking of Claire and meeting her next week at Cobden Road and what I would do that evening. I had arranged to go to the gun club but, maybe foolishly, had not told Sharon. I thought to myself, Sharon hadn't mentioned she was going out on Friday. Mind you Sharon hadn't mentioned anything. We weren't bothering talking to each other.

I finished my rounds visiting the sites and thought, well, I'm back early. I think I'll let Sharon pick the boys up from Julie's. I'll take the dogs out for a run to Morden Park to see if they can't catch a squirrel.

On my return home, squirrel-less I might add, Sharon had picked the boys up, brought them home and fed them their tea.

"Where you been?" Sharon greeted me with an attitude to her voice as I walked in the kitchen.

"Over the park," I said, "but then you knew that, seeing as how my van is out the front of the house and of course the dogs were missing when you came in. I think even you could work that out."

"FUCK OFF!" came the reply. "Do your own meal."

"Thank you very much," I replied, "and thanks for the nice cup of tea as well," as I put the kettle on.

Oh well, I said to myself. I think I'll have this, get ready, get a gun or two with some ammo from the safe and head off to the gun club. I'll have some fun shooting, then a pint with the lads at the Yew Tree pub. Can't wait, I said to myself. Just get me out of this atmosphere.

Sharon had different ideas of course. She walked into the kitchen as I was lighting a cigarette and informed me she was going out for the night. Her cab was picking her up at seven and I was having the kids.

I just looked at her with no expression on my face. I thought, this is a Hamlet moment. I should be lighting a cigar not a cigarette and,

FOR THE LOVE OF BRASS

while puffing on my Hamlet cigar, let all my cares and worries go right over me, but instead I replied, "Go fuck yourself and while you're at it, pack yourself an overnight bag and don't come home for a week. Good riddance to you!"

That was that. I was having the kids for the night, which was fine, my shooting buddies would have to have a pint without me. Mind you things were not that bad. At least once Sharon went out, the bad atmosphere went with her. It was just me and my boys again.

My boys had heard all this before and with that they both shouted from the front room, "Get your gun, Dad, it's house clearance time. Yippee!"

My chance came for the real shooting when I went out on Sunday to Bisley while Sharon and the boys were over at her mum and dad's for the day, visiting. I would join Sharon over there less and less as we got further and further apart. I just didn't want anything to do with her.

After my site meeting with Ron on Monday morning, I was free to do what I wanted. It was 11.30 and I called Claire to see if she was at Cobden Road.

"Yes, I am," she said. "Why don't you come over? We're a bit busy but you can see where we are."

"Okay," I said. "What's going on?"

"Well, the BT guys are here fitting in the new phone line and I'm interviewing a couple of girls. You could meet them, look them up and down and maybe give your opinion."

"Ha-ha-ha," I laughed. "Okay, I can do that. Where are you in Cobden Road?"

"You know June's? Well, go past the Green, follow the road round into Portland Road and Cobden is on your left. Turn into Cobden and about a hundred yards down there's a junction with Denmark Road.

FOR THE LOVE OF BRASS

We're there. Ryan's BM is right outside. You can't miss it."

"Okay," I said. "I'll be about forty minutes. See you then."

I pulled into Cobden Road and as I did, I noticed there was a pub on the corner to my left. That could be handy, I thought. The pub faced onto Portland Road and also had a side entrance in Cobden Road. It was quite big and looked a typical, nice old London pub. The thought crossed my mind, I wonder how much time we'll spend in there.

I found somewhere to park in Denmark Road, then walked back to the junction. There's the BM, I thought, that must be the place. It looked to be a decent-sized house. I pressed the buzzer. There was a BT man in the hall, who let me in. There were two front doors. I walked through the one that was open and down the corridor, passing a room on my left. There was a large full-size cupboard in front of me and the hall bent around to the right and on into a large kitchen/diner and sitting area. The bathroom was off that. All in all, it was it basically a good-sized, one-bedroom flat, all on the ground floor. As I walked in, I was greeted by Claire who jumped up and gave me a kiss on the cheek.

"Do you want a cup of tea? I'll make you one."

"Thanks very much," I said, and sat down on the big lounge chairs saying hello to everybody there, Ryan and three women, all chatting away with each other.

Claire brought the tea over and gave it to me. She introduced the women, "and Ryan you already know," she said. "Well, the phones are going in. We can soon be up and running. Not bad, ay?" said Claire. With that, the phone guys drank up their tea and said they were finished and would be on their way. They wrote down the new number on a piece of paper and gave it to Claire, saying the phone line's live and working. The bill for the installation and any details would be in the post but for now they were done.

"So what do you think of these lovely ladies then, Gary?" Clare asked.

"You all look very nice," I smiled, the situation putting me slightly on the spot. Ha-ha...

They were all very nice looking and very well presented with lovely figures to match. I wondered where all these lovely women came from to do this job because I really had no idea. Okay, I had not met too many working girls in my time but the ones I had met so far were stunning.

We had a lovely chat about all sorts of things and after about an hour, and three cups of tea later, Ryan stood up.

"Oh well, I have to go now. See you all next time."

He left the flat, leaving me sitting with four gorgeous women. They did most of the talking, mainly about one or two new parlours that Claire wanted to open. Listening to this conversation was a whole new ballgame for me, a real education. Without realising it, I was learning a great deal about how this business worked, from renting the most suitable flat or apartment and its location, to advertising. From ads in shop windows to running the ads in local newspapers. Even how the girls dealt with some strange clients, which was of particular interest and very amusing. Before we knew it, it was 5.30.

Claire said, "There's no point sitting here when we can be in the pub having a drink." We agreed. Claire locked up the flat and we all walked the short distance to the pub. In no time we were all drinking, smoking and having a laugh. The girls were so easy to get on with and all so friendly. I guess their job made them that way, or maybe it was the other way around. You could swear and talk about anything and you didn't have to mind your Ps and Qs. Whatever it was, they were bloody good company. I thought, a few more people like this in my life would make things a lot better.

"I'm going now girls," I said. "It's half seven. I'm going home."

"Okay," they all said. "Nice meeting you, Gary, see you again."

I headed for the door but as I got there, I was grabbed from behind. I turned; it was Claire.

"You didn't give me a kiss goodbye."

"Okay," I smiled.

After I had kissed her goodbye, she said, "If you're around tomorrow, pop in and see me at the flat. I have Chantel coming in to work and I'll be doing the phones. Also you can get to meet her. She's a nice girl."

I smiled again. "Sounds good to me. I'll phone before I drive over, just to let you know I'm on my way."

"Okay, great," she said.

I left the pub to walk back to my car. Having only had shandies in the pub I was good to drive.

I opened my front door and stepped in. Sharon was just going upstairs with some ironing in her arms.

"Where you been?" she muttered.

"What do you care?" I said.

"I don't. I don't give a shit," she replied.

"Thanks for that," I answered. Oh, it's nice to be home, I thought. Still, I can spend some time with my boys before they go off to bed. Then my usual evening. Something to eat, which this evening was a kebab I had picked up on the way home. Office work or sit in the lounge with one of my vodka and oranges. No contest. It was sit with my feet up in the lounge with a V and O. I knew if I was in the lounge first, before Sharon, she would go to another room and sit on her own. Either way, I'd have time for peace and quiet.

The following day I did what I had to do in my office. That was all

FOR THE LOVE OF BRASS

going well and everyone was happy work-wise. I went downstairs and walked into the kitchen. My two dogs were curled up together, lying in their bed.

As I walked past them, I bent down close to them and said, "Come on dogs we're going out for a walk." They both jumped up like rockets, tails wagging and crying with excitement.

Off we went to Morden Park. I liked Morden Park. It was a great place to walk and think. I spent a lot of time over there, thinking and trying to iron out problems, especially after big arguments with Sharon. Today wasn't like that. I had a lot to think about but good thoughts, mainly about Claire and her world. I found her world very exciting. I felt I had embarked on a new adventure but had no idea where or how far it would go. Was it a good thing, was it a bad thing spending time with working girls? I really didn't know. All I could see was it was a great thing for now. I would have to continue my journey for as long as it took to see where I'd end up. I not only wanted to continue my journey but I seemed to be going into it with a full-on enthusiasm. Claire showed a big interest in me, as I did for her. I had not experienced affection like this from a woman for a very long time and I guess it must have shown. I was really quite taken back by it all.

On returning from the park, having done all my thinking, I called Claire to see if they were at the flat, and of course there were. Claire had told me the day before that they'd get there for about 9.30 to be ready for 10.00. I drove over to Cobden Road, buying and eating a sandwich on the way. When I got there, I pressed the bell. Nothing happened for about 20 seconds, then suddenly the door opened half way. This lovely, pretty face with long, blonde hair looked around the door at me, while concealing the rest of her body behind the door.

She said, "Hello, Babe, you must be Dave, yeah?"

"No, no," I said, "I'm Gary."

"Okay, darling," she laughed. "Come in. I was expecting Dave, one of my clients."

I stepped in and shut the door behind me. She walked down the corridor and I followed. All I could see in front of me was this tall girl, about 6ft, with her white high heels, white suspenders and stockings, white underwear and long, blonde hair, moving her bum from side to side as she walked, not that I was taking much notice. I followed her into the back room.

"It's Gary," she said to Claire as she walked into the room.

"Oh good." Claire jumped up and greeted me with a kiss. "This is Gary, the man I was telling you about, Chantel. Gary, this is Chantel."

"Very nice to meet you, Chantel," I said, and smiled while looking at Claire. "I don't have many women like Chantel open the door to me dressed like that."

Chantel laughed. "Well," she said, "You'll have to get used to it."

We all smiled as Claire said, "Cup of tea, everyone? I'll put the kettle on."

"Chantel," I said, "you've customers already?"

"Clients, Gary. Clients we call them."

"Oh, okay," I said.

"Yes. I've clients from other parlours where I've worked in the past. Plus Claire has a list of clients in her phone who call and want to pop in to meet me, seeing as I'm the new girl on the block."

We all sat, the three of us drinking tea and smoking cigarettes.

"So girls, how does this work? The procedure, I mean, when a punter comes in."

FOR THE LOVE OF BRASS

Chantel smiled. "Client, Gary."

"Oh yeah, sorry."

As Claire was making the tea, she explained she'd put some cards in shop windows in the surrounding areas. The two ads in the local papers would be out on Thursday so, from then onwards it would get a lot busier on the phones and hopefully a lot busier for Chantel. Chantel then started to talk.

"How it works," she said. "The clients phone in and make an appointment to come along, so we're expecting them. When the client arrives, I let him in. I take him into the front room, which is the bedroom."

"Yes," I said.

"I ask him which service he'd like. Then I take the money for that service and leave the room, telling him to get himself ready and I'll be back in a couple of minutes. Then I come back in here and finish my fag or tea, or whatever. Then I go back into the room and give him his service," she laughed, "whatever that may be. Then he gets dressed and I see him out. Then I tidy the room and myself and, Bob's your uncle, I'm ready for the next one, hee-hee." She smiled. "It's that simple."

I looked at Claire and said, "You sit here manning the phones, landline and mobiles booking in the clients?"

"Yes," said Claire. "That's exactly right."

"Okay," I said. "So when you talk about another parlour, you'd do the same thing there but with a working girl there and a reception to run and book appointments in."

"Yes, exactly right again," said Claire. "The girl gets half of what she takes in the room. The rest I get for providing the flat and being the maid."

"So another parlour is just a money-making machine," I said.

"Yes. That's right," said Claire. "The overheads are slightly more but yes, that's how it works."

"Wow, sounds good to me and you don't get any trouble," I said.

"No, not too much. You get the odd nut like the Mandy situation but no, generally not too bad at all."

Chantel piped up, "The bastards I don't like are the Old Bill, coming in thinking they can get a freebie."

"Oh really," I said. "Does that happen often?"

"Well, yeah," she said. "That can happen anytime."

"And do you give them a freebie?"

"Well, yes," she said. "You have to, or they can make your life miserable, cause you a lot of shit, and they know that, so we have to give them a freebie from time to time."

"Okay," I said, "and the service you provide, how does the client know what service you provide?"

"Well," said Chantel, "that's easy. I give them the menu. Ha-ha-ha."

I started laughing. "A menu!" I said. "Can I see the menu?"

She smiled. "No you can't, you silly sod."

"Why not?" I said.

"Because it's not written down. I tell them what it is."

Now all three of us are laughing.

Claire said, "You're nosy, ain't you?"

"Well, yeah, I guess. I'm interested in how it works, that's all."

Chantel carried on, "We don't write it down because it could be evidence against us, or say for instance, I have a sore fanny from some position I was doing, I don't put that on the menu. I only put on the menu what I'm prepared to do with that client."

I sat talking with the girls for some time. It seemed every time they'd something to say about their trade, it was an education for me. Claire told me about how they'd get an estate agent on their side by offering sexual favours. How that would work is, Claire and one of her girls would go into an estate agent's office (rather than answer an ad in the newspaper) and pick a male salesman aged between say 25 and 45. They'd sit at his desk with him and ask what flats he might have available in the area they wanted to work in, all the time flirting with him. They'd then ask to view the flat. After all the flirting they'd done, the salesman was only too keen to show the property to the girls as soon as possible. He'd normally take them straight away; if not, an appointment would be made at the earliest opportunity. Once at the property, the girls would check the entrance way to see if it was concealed at all or maybe slightly concealed. This could be achieved with plants, shrubs or hanging baskets and sometimes that mattered to the clients, so that would have to be taken into account. Once inside, they'd walk around viewing all the rooms and discussing with the agent what exactly they had in mind for the apartment and how it could be used. By this time the agent knew exactly who the girls were and what they wanted the flat for, and of course all the time they kept flirting with the man. By this time, he'd be getting very excited at the whole prospect of it all and he'd be only too keen to help out in any way possible. After all this, if they figured yes, the flat would be ideal for their use, one of the girls would stand very close to him making a physical contact with him in a very friendly way, while discussing the details of the terms and so on for the flat. By this time, the salesman's getting very aroused by the whole idea so it would be suggested that the agent might like to talk to the landlord on their behalf to arrange a discount on the rent and any other outgoing there may be. Once that all seemed to be out of the way, one of the girls would say they wanted to check out the garden, or go outside to look at the street and the parking situation. While they were outside, the other girl would perform some sort of sexual act on the salesman and that would pretty much clinch the deal and of course this would mean the agent was in their pocket for the future, so when another flat was needed, they'd contact him and of course he'd go out of his way to find them a suitable place. Chantel went on to explain that the situation had a double ring to it for the girls, because the agent would often become a client and visit the establishment regularly under the pretext he'd be checking the property for the owner.

I asked the girls, did this work every time, are men really that gullible?

"Oh yes," they said. "Very much so. It works every time. In fact, we've not had a situation where it hasn't worked. If the situation is adapted," Chantel said, "you can get anything from a man. Anything at all, whether it be a car or diamonds. Men are very gullible. All us girls have to do is know how to use what we have between our legs. Sex is a currency, and with ever-changing values. It can be worth £20 or it can be worth thousands of pounds. It just depends how you apply it and to whom."

I spent the rest of the afternoon with the girls, drinking tea and smoking cigarettes. In between our conversations there were phone calls coming in, which Claire answered. On a couple of occasions the doorbell would ring. Chantel stood up, took off her little jersey to reveal just her white underwear, then walk of out of the room to open the front door. A couple of minutes would pass and she'd come into our room and put some money on the chair next to Claire, finish her cigarette, if she was smoking, then disappear off into the bedroom for a while. The next thing we'd hear was the front door closing as she showed the client out.

On one occasion, Chantel came into our room, put the money on the chair and said, "This client is quite hot. I'll give him some extras free of change." She laughed as she turned to go back into the bedroom.

FOR THE LOVE OF BRASS

The thing I thought was funny was the fact that, when Chantel went into the room after collecting the money, it didn't seem long before she was saying goodbye to her client and closing the front door.

I found myself saying to her, "He wasn't in there long with you."

"No," she said, "sometimes they're not. Ten minutes max sometimes. I do tell them there can be a half-hour massage and then their treat." She laughed as she was telling this. "But normally," she said, "once they've had their happy ending, they're happy to go. I like to send them off with a smile on their face."

"So you give them half an hour's massage, then the happy ending?"

She smiled. "No, half an hour all in. Some I massage for a while, say fifteen minutes, then make them happy. Then by the time they get dressed again, that's their half an hour up."

"Sometimes," I said, "does a client want to stay longer?"

"Yes," she replied, "sometimes they can have an hour, for which I charge them nearly double. Most of that extra time is spent giving them massage and talking with them. I have one client," Chantel went on to say, "who comes in, sits on the bed for an hour and just talks."

"What, nothing else?" I said.

"Nope, nothing else. Just talks. Doesn't even take his clothes off. He's just lonely, so that's what he does."

"Wow! Really?" I said.

"Yes, you'd be surprised, Gary. That happens quite often. Sometimes people are just lonely and want someone to talk to." She smiled. "Sometimes we're like counsellors. They ask for advice on things in their life. Then we get some who are really quite strange. They ask for odd things. That is what's fun about this game. You never really know who is going to come in and sometimes you've got to try very hard not to laugh

205

at their requests. I'll tell you some of that another time." Chantel jumped up. "Who's for tea?" she said. "I'm putting the kettle on."

"Yes, please," we both said together.

"I'll have this tea with you both, then I'll be heading off home. Oh, and yes, Chantel, I'd definitely be interested to hear some more of your stories."

"We'll go over to the pub after you've gone, Gary. Ryan can come pick us up," said Claire.

"Oh what, from the pub?"

"Yes," said Claire.

"Will he drop you off, Chantel?" I asked.

"Yes," said Claire, "she doesn't live far away, only about two miles or so from here but we'll all have a drink first. You're welcome to join us, Claire said."

"Yes, thanks but I'll go home, I think. I'll have a beer with you next time."

"Oh yeah," said Claire. "When will I see you again, then?"

"Friday," I said. "I'll pop over and see you Friday afternoon."

"Okay, that's good," said Claire. "That's a date."

"Okay, girls. See you both Friday."

"Okay," said Claire. "I'll see you out."

She walked me to the front door and once there she put her arms around my neck and gave me a big kiss. It seemed to last for a long time and when it finished I said (not quite knowing what to say), "Thanks for that," and I smiled. "I am definitely coming see you on Friday now," laughing as I walked out through the gate.

On my drive home, I couldn't help myself thinking of the things we'd talked about that afternoon and the kiss Claire gave me as I left. I thought

FOR THE LOVE OF BRASS

about how she always made the first move to kiss me on seeing me or when I was leaving. Even if her husband was there. As much as I had really enjoyed kissing her in that hallway, I was very unsure of the situation. After all, she was married, not that that seemed to matter to her; anyway, it mattered to me. Or was it really the fact that she was a working girl and maybe, just maybe, I was very unsure about that. Maybe, deep down, I was concerned, if I entered into a relationship with her, would I be able to handle what she did for a living? I shook my head. What are you thinking, for fuck's sake! It was only a kiss in the hallway as you left. What are you thinking? I said to myself again.

I made a conscious effort not to think about that any more. All I did know was being friends with Claire and her people was fun. I liked it. It put a smile on my face when I was with her or them, so why not continue to keep smiling. That's exactly what I am going to keep doing, I thought.

I arrived home, came in through the front and I could hear my sons playing upstairs with the synthesiser I had got them for Christmas last. Sharon passed me as she went from the kitchen to the lounge.

As she passed she said, "There's some dinner in there for you if you want it."

"Okay, thanks," I said. "I'll help myself after I've said hello to the boys."

That evening was the same as any other. Sharon in the lounge watching her soaps, me sitting in the dining room drinking one or two vodkas, smoking and thinking about my new found friends, particularly Claire. After a couple of my large V and O's, I thought I would soak in the Jacuzzi and maybe have a third V and O while I was in there, then retire to my own room for some peace and quiet. This I did and, while lying in bed, I thought about the estate agent scenario and how it worked. Then I wondered about Claire. She touches me a fair bit and she kisses me. Is she working me in some way and, if so, to what end, I wondered. I don't have a flat to give her. I won't be giving her a car or diamonds. In the end I had to tell myself, stop this. Too much thinking all the time. Go to sleep.

Okay, Friday morning, I said to myself. Things to do today. Go to the bank, come back and do the wages for the men. Get them over to Ron so he can pay everyone later. Go over to see Claire. Hmmm. I thought that's all the important things to do, then if I'm lucky and can get my friend's son to babysit for me, I could go to the gun club for a shoot. I was sure Sharon would be going out, as sure as eggs is eggs she will be, so I'm not even going to ask her. I just realised, I have to pay for the babysitter each time. Oh well, it's well worth it and at least Sharon is out. I babysit most of the time anyway, which is good because it means when Sharon's out I'm on my own at home. Just me and the boys, which suits me. I thought to myself, it's a shame Sharon is not out every night. I smiled.

I called Claire to make sure it was still okay to come over. I parked in Cobden Road near the pub, then walked along to the flat and pressed the doorbell. Claire answered.

"Hello Gary," she said as she gave me a big hug and an enthusiastic kiss. "Come in. So nice to see you. I missed you."

"I missed you, too," I said as we went down the hall and into the back room.

"Hello Gary," Chantel said. She was in the same place as when I'd last seen her, wearing exactly the same as last time, except instead of white this outfit that all matched was bright red.

"You look very sexy, I must say," I said to her.

Claire said, "It must be the outfit. Everyone likes it, even Ryan commented on it earlier today when he dropped me off here and the thing is," Claire continued, "the ad's in the paper, came out yesterday. We were fairly busy then but today, being Friday I guess, it's been very busy. We've taken a shit-load of money."

"Really?" I said, feeling that they wanted me to ask how much. "Go on then," I said, "how much?"

"Thirteen hundred today, whereas we only took eight fifty yesterday. Must be because, yes it's Friday and people have money."

"Bloody hell. That's good going," I said. I looked at Chantel and smiled as I said it. "Have you had to change the menu because of any sore bits?"

She burst out laughing, then said, "No. It's all good, thank you." Then we all laughed. Chantel said, "I'll put the kettle on."

She walked up and down in her red outfit and I couldn't help but watch her. I looked at Claire and said, "I think you'll do well with Chantel here."

"Yes," she said, "and we still have a couple of hours to go!"

The plan was that in a couple of hours the girls would be joined by Ryan. They'd all go to the pub for a drink or two before they went home. Of course I was invited but I decided I would go home. Earlier I had been able to get Jack, my babysitter, booked for four hours this evening, so I was going to go to the gun club, then have a beer afterwards with the lads. I really wanted to go for a drink with the girls but I just wasn't sure about the situation. I found myself hanging back when it was going out time with them. I still didn't know why I was doing this exactly. It just seemed to me to be that for way for now. The girls did ask a number of times to get me out but sadly, and it did make me sad, I declined.

I had arranged for myself and the boys to go fishing on Saturday at one of our favourite fishing spots in Newdigate, Surrey. This area is over near Dorking and we always caught good fish there, so all three of us were looking forward to it very much. We were up early and got ourselves ready, then off we went. I would often buy fishing medals from the trophy shop, two to be used on the day. One for the biggest fish and one for the greatest number of fish. Sometimes one of the boys might win both but normally it meant the boys would come home with a medal each, which always put a big smile on their faces when they told their mum who had won what and for what. We always took a camera and plenty of photos, all to be kept for posterity.

Sunday morning, we were all up. I was off to Bisley with my handguns for a shooting competition. Sharon would go out a bit later with the boys to her mum's for the day.

Monday came. I was sitting in my office doing paperwork, costings and so on, when I got a call from Ron.

"Hello, Gary," he said. "You know those deliveries we had booked to come in?"

"Yes," I said.

"Well, the Friday afternoon one didn't turn up, due to them being too busy and couldn't make it, and this morning's one isn't coming in till around lunchtime today."

"Yeah, okay," I said.

"Well, here's the thing. John's phoned in here, says he's sick and has to go to the hospital, so I'm here on my own with all this material coming in and you know what this job is like. Everything has to go down that alley at the side of the house. Can you come over and help me unload and get it around to the back of the house?"

"Yes, yes, of course I can. What's up with John did you say?"

"Oh, he's got to go to the hospital. Says he went with some old bird over the weekend and now his knob's sore. Ha-ha-ha, thinks he's got the pox and it's worrying him. Ha-ha-ha." We were both laughing.

FOR THE LOVE OF BRASS

"Okay, mate. Thanks for letting me know. I'll be over with you as soon as possible. Should be there in half an hour."

"Cheers mate, see you then," Ron said.

On my way over to Ron's site I was thinking about Claire. I was thinking it might be a good idea not to go over there as much, I felt, as I was getting too attached to her and I was not sure how to deal with that. I thought about the situation. Yes, I thought, that's it. What I'll do, if I go at all, is I'll only pop over there once a week for a bit of company and a laugh somewhere a bit different. Yes, that's what I'll do.

I arrived at Ron's; we were both laughing about John's situation. I said, "For a labourer, he's picked the best day to have off with all this material coming."

"Yeah," Ron said. "If it had gone to plan, he could have spent all day bringing the materials around on his own while I did something else."

The first truck turned up with sand, cement and a load of blocks, which all had to be wheelbarrowed to the back of the property, then the timber truck turned up after lunch. We unloaded that truck, walking all the long lengths of timber to the back on our shoulders. Once we'd got that done, we set the site up for work to start the following day, by which time John and his pox should have been sorted out. We expected him to be in to work the next day.

The following morning I woke up and had terrible trouble getting out of bed. I had pulled something in my hip or lower back. It wasn't too bad if I sat still but when I tried to move around it hurt, quite a lot. I'd had this type of injury before. I'd had the same pain in the same spot after plastering a ceiling for somebody. I felt I knew what it was. I also knew I would have to visit the osteopath and have it looked at. The last time I had this type of injury I had pulled my pelvis out of alignment and it had to be set back into place and it was something the osteopath had to do, you couldn't fix it on your own.

I made an appointment to go to see him later that day and this I did. I was right, he massaged the area for some time, also applying heat. He then had to twist my pelvis back so it clicked into position. I had trouble walking into his surgery but walked out a lot better. I still had to be careful but basically I was fixed; it just needed time to heal. Judging by the last time I'd done this, it took about two weeks to be back to normal. Before I knew it, I was back in my office wondering what to do with myself. I know, I thought, I'll call Claire and have a chat with her. This I did and she told me how busy they were there. The phone line was busy with the paper ads working well.

I told her about my back and she said, "Well, if you're doing nothing, come over for a cup of tea and do nothing with me." Although I thought it was a marvellous idea, I said no, I'd just wait at home and rest my back. "Well," she said, "I hope it's better soon and if you can, come over tomorrow and see me. I love spending time with you." I said okay and wait and see what tomorrow brings but as I came off the phone I was thinking no, I won't go over there. I will give it a miss.

I picked the boys up from school that day, seeing as I was around, but couldn't do a great deal else with my back the way it was. It was still very tender and all I could do was to rest.

The following day I was in my office doing what paperwork I could find and thinking about what Claire had said. Sit and do nothing with me, she'd said. That seemed such a good idea. I told myself I would finish up here, call Claire and go over to her place. At least I was guaranteed a laugh and a cuppa.

On arrival at Claire's, I rang the bell and Chantel answered. She was dressed in white again, I couldn't help but notice as I followed her down the hall to the kitchen area. She was a real sight for sore eyes. Claire jumped up and gave me a kiss as soon as I walked in and, while Claire was making the tea, Chantel was asking about my back. I told her what the osteopath had to do to put my pelvis back in line.

She said, "That sounds bloody painful."

"Yeah, it is," I said.

"Never mind," she said with a big smirk on her face, "I'll take you into the room and massage you all better."

"Yes, I bet you would," said Claire as she returned with the teas. "If there's any massaging to be done, I'll do it for him." We all laughed.

"As it happens…" I said, smiling. I drank my tea with a couple of pain killers. The girls were telling me how they'd had a busy morning.

As we all sat there smoking, Claire said, "Well, we don't have any clients booked in for Chantel for a while, so we can use the room. How would you like me to massage your bad back for you, Gary?"

"Hmm, let me think about that," I said and, in a split second I said, "Yes, okay. Sounds good to me but you do have to be careful with me."

"Yeah, yeah," Claire said, "of course I'll be," so off we went into the bedroom.

"Okay," Claire said, "strip off and lie on the bed." I took my shoes off along with my t-shirt and lay down on my front. "Okay," said Claire, "just relax and I'll give you a nice massage. It'll do your back the world of good. I'll be using this baby oil, so you might want to loosen your jeans and pull them down a bit off your bum. Don't want to get oil on your jeans now, do we?" This I did, and lay there fully relaxed while Claire massaged the lower part of my back and hips. She was right, it really did do my back the world of good.

We talked about different things. She told me she lived in Shortlands, Scotts Road in the Bromley area. I told her a bit more about my home life and how I was increasingly unhappy living with my wife. I told her about the room I had set up for myself in my house and the fact that we had very little to do with each other. She said she knew I was unhappy and that things were not going well at home and that was why I spent time coming over to see her. I also told her some things about my business, the different things we built and so on.

I couldn't help noticing one or two songs that were on the radio as this massage was taking place. Kym Sims, 'Too blind to see it' and Rozalla, 'Everybody's free to feel good', I guess because I was too blind to see for quite a long time that I was unhappy at home and the Rozalla song – well, I thought, I should be free to feel good. These songs connected with me, although they'd only come out last year, in 1991. I had heard them before and I liked them but today they seemed to register with me and have more of a significance. There was always a radio playing in the room, as the girls called it, the reason being that the music would drown out sound from the other room and, of course, the other way round. We really had a good catch up and got to know each other a bit better. I was intrigued by Claire. It was as though the situation with her was forbidden and this, in some way, seemed to make me want to get to know her even better and spend more time with her.

Massage completed, it was back into the lounge room for tea and a cigarette.

Chantel said, "Feel better for that, Gary? You should do, you were in there forty minutes."

"Yes, thank you," I said, "a lot better." I didn't think Claire would be able to give a proper massage like that and I was pleasantly surprised.

FOR THE LOVE OF BRASS

With that the phone rang. Claire was talking with another girl who was interested in coming to work for her. She set up a meeting with her on the following day. Claire needed to meet her and give her a type of interview, a sort of meet and greet, if you like.

The new girl was interested in being a receptionist. She'd never worked in a parlour before but was keen to learn. She'd come along in the morning at 11 o'clock.

Claire said, "She sounds as if she could be okay and said she had an open mind about things in life. She'll definitely need that if she comes to work here with us lot." We all laughed.

I decided I'd head home to catch up on anything that needed doing. I picked the kids up from Julie's and as it was such a nice warm day, once home, we got the dogs and went to Morden Park for an hour or so. Sharon had already returned home by the time we got back and was sorting out a meal for the kids. She informed me she'd be away all weekend. She was going on Friday after work and wouldn't be back until Sunday night. That's good, I thought. Peace and quiet. If I could get a sitter I could go out on Friday night for a shoot.

I spoke with Jack, the sitter. He was only too keen to come over as it meant a few extra quid for him. He asked if I minded him bring a friend, and could he stay the night and go on Saturday.

"Yes, that's fine with me," I said.

The following day I called Claire about lunchtime. She'd had her meeting with the new girl and the girl was still there. Her name was Abbie and they were having a laugh and all getting on very well. She asked if I was coming over to see them. I said no, I had too much to do and I would have to spend time in the office. Claire said she wanted to meet up at Abbie's house that evening for a drink and she wanted me to go with her. She said her husband wasn't around so I could meet her at the parlour. We could go to Abbie's in my van.

"Okay," I said, "why the hell not?" I didn't have to worry if I didn't make it home because Jack and his mate were there.

Claire and Chantel had finished with work by about 6.30, then went over to the pub. When I arrived at the parlour at around 7.30, I parked and walked up to the door. There was a note stuck to the door with tape. It just said 'PUB'. I walked over and went in through the side door and looked around. There was a table with Claire, Chantel and two other girls, friends of Chantel's. Bloody hell, I thought to myself, this ain't bad. Four lovely girls to sit with. Chantel's friends weren't working girls but were beautiful looking girls, just like Chantel. They worked in an office over in Croydon somewhere. They'd just met up with her for a drink, then they were going out somewhere else.

Claire said, "We can have one or two here, then head over to see Abbie."

"Sounds good to me," I said. "Do you know where she lives?"

"Yes," she replied, "I've a pretty good idea. We'll be okay."

"Okay, great," I said. Seeing as how it was a Friday night, the pub was fairly busy. All the tables were full and there were lots of people at the bar, a friendly place, and we were chatting to the people around us on their tables and to people at the bar each time one of us went up to get a drink.

After a couple of beers we said our goodbyes to the girls and our new friends sitting around us, then left the girls and went to Abbie's. We found her house without too much trouble. She lived on a main road in a Victorian house.

What a big house it was. A lovely double-fronted place set back off the road with a nice big drive up to it. The house had been split, and Abbie

FOR THE LOVE OF BRASS

lived in one of the ground floor flats. Hers had two bedrooms. There were two flats on each floor and it was three floors high, that's how big the house was. I could imagine it in its day with just one family living in it.

We went up the front steps and pressed the doorbell. Abbie answered the door and welcomed us in. To give an idea of her appearance, she was tall, about 5ft 8in, with long black hair, blue eyes, slightly on the slim side and extremely attractive. Her age was approximately 28 to 30.

We went into her flat and met Lee and Courtney. Lee was Abbie's flatmate and Courtney was Lee's girlfriend. Lee went to the kitchen and came back with a couple of bottles of white wine and opened them. We all sat there with a glass and introduced ourselves, then we were away, talking and chatting.

Now, to say we all got along was an understatement. We were having a good old laugh about all sorts of things. These two girls, Abbie and Courtney, had a fabulously wicked sense of humour. We were laughing from the moment we arrived to the early hours of the morning. We ran out of wine at some point and Lee said there was a shop nearby where we could get some more, so he and I went for a walk and came back with another six bottles. It was agreed that we'd stay the night. Lee and Courtney in their own room, Abbie in hers and Claire and I could make up a bed on the floor or the settee. That was that sorted, so we went on the piss. Of course the subject of what Claire did for a living came up and that Abbie would be working for her on Monday morning as a receptionist over at the Cobden parlour. Both Abbie and Courtney found the whole subject of working girls absolutely hilarious and couldn't wait for any stories Abbie might come home with.

We had a fantastic evening, drinking and smoking, and most of the time with tears rolling down our faces with laughter. Abbie became really drunk and went to crash out on her bed, leaving us with Courtney and Lee. Courtney certainly kept the laughter going on her own and when the time came to make up the beds, Lee dropped a load of bedding and pillows on the settee, then they left us to get on with it, which we did. We made up a double bed as best we could seeing as how we were drunk, using six cushions off of the settee and armchair and when we'd finished, it resembled a bed of sorts. The lights were off and we stripped of to our underwear and climbed into the makeshift bed, giggling and laughing.

Claire said, "How's your back?"

"Funnily enough," I said, "there's no pain. It's okay. Must be all the alcohol we've drunk because it doesn't hurt at all," I said. "Thinking about it, that was silly, I should have said you can rub it!"

"What, your back?" Claire said.

"Yeah, well anything you like."

We giggled like two little kids and well, you guessed it, the kissing started and before you could say Mrs Robinson, whoever the hell she is, we were making love. It was absolutely unbelievable, the most fantastic sex I had ever known. In fact it was so fantastic it happened a further two more times. I wanted to make sure, I guess. Yes, yes, Yes! Was the verdict. Brilliant.

Seeing as how I'm not writing *Fifty Shades of Grey* here, or any other colour for that matter, it'll suffice to say sex with Claire was unbelievable and, come the morning, I may have had a bit of a hangover but I remembered every single thing we'd done. That helped quite a lot with the hangover, believe it or not.

We left Abbie's house, having thanked them very much for an excellent evening.

"We must do that again," they said.

"Yes," I replied, "we definitely must, can't wait," with a big grin on my face.

Claire asked would I take her home.

"Yes, of course," I said. "It'll be nice to see where you live. Maybe I can have a shower there at yours, if that's okay?"

"Yes, of course it is," she said, and so off we went to Shortlands.

Claire lived in a two-bedroom flat she'd rented with Ryan. It was very nice, really quite comfortable. I asked her where he was and she just said he was out, giving no more information than that. I didn't ask again, well, not that day anyway.

"He doesn't mind me hanging around with you?" I asked.

"No," said Claire. "He has no say in it, anyway."

"Okay," I said, "it just seems a bit odd to me that he hasn't a thing to say about it."

"Well," said Claire, "let me explain a bit more about our marriage, that's if you're interested?"

"Yes, by all means, carry on," I said.

"We've been married about three years now. I had been married before, when I was younger. I got married when I was nineteen and had a good job. So did he and we even bought a house. Anyway, to cut a long story short, it didn't work out. He went off with someone else so, by the time I was twenty-six, I was single. We sold the house and I spent time on my own, didn't bother with relationships at all. Then when I was twenty-nine, I got to know Ryan. He was over here on holiday and liked it here. He asked me if I'd marry him so he could stay in the UK, offering me ten thousand pounds if I did. He said it would only be for just over two years, then when he got his passport and could stay, he would leave and do his own thing."

"Yeah, so what happened?" I said.

"Well, it's been three years and he's still with me and to make it worse, he only gave me two grand. The bastard still owes me eight thousand quid. He keeps saying he's saving up and he'll sell his car and pay me but it doesn't happen. The only thing he's good for is he runs me around, does the shopping and looks after our flat."

"Oh, okay. So you're still friends," I said.

"Yeah, sometimes and sometimes we fall out, then we're not."

"Okay," I said, "it's all getting a bit serious. Can I use your shower now, please?"

"Yes, I'll get you a towel and show you how to use it. It sometimes can be a bit funny."

"Okay, great," I said.

As I was finishing my shower, the shower curtain was suddenly pulled back and there stood Claire, naked as the day she was born.

"I need a shower too. Can I jump in there with you? You can wash my back if you like."

"Yeah, sure," I said. "I'll wash anything you like," I laughed. Before you know what, we were at it like rabbits again. Things got so intense, the shower curtain was pulled down and we finished up on the floor.

I had no clean clothes to put on when I'd finished my shower but at least I didn't smell too bad. I could get changed when I got home. On leaving Claire's place, I'd told her I was busy on Sunday with the boys, what with Sharon being away, but I would love to come over and see her next week.

"That's great," she said. "Make it as early in the week as you can, like first thing on Monday."

That made me smile to myself and as I drove home, I realised the thing

FOR THE LOVE OF BRASS

was, I was thinking the exact same thing. I just kept thinking of her all the time and especially what we'd been doing with each other and the thoughts I had of her naked.

Well, what can I say? Let me give you a picture of what Claire looked like. She was about 5ft 4in tall, with slightly wavy, blonde hair just off her shoulders, blue eyes and the figure of an athlete. Everything about her body was perfectly proportioned. She even had a six-pack. She was lightly tanned all over, she had her own sun bed in her flat, one of those top and bottom types, so you only needed twenty minutes on it at a time and you were done all over. She was extremely attractive, very sexy but at the same time she had one of the cheekiest faces I'd ever seen. As you can probably guess, I fancied her like mad. There was an advert on TV at the time where they'd say if you can pinch more than an inch, you should eat this particular type of breakfast cereal. Well, with Claire you couldn't pinch a half of an inch of fat because it wasn't there to pinch. I know, I tried many a time. Everywhere she went I noticed people, both men and women, would look at her and more than once, particularly the men. Most of them couldn't take their eyes off of her.

"So, going back to Ryan," I said.

"Yes," said Claire, raising her eyebrow and smiling. "He won't cause you any trouble seeing me or having me hanging around?"

"No, no, not at all. He's no threat to me or you, don't worry. He's okay with things."

"Really? Okay," I said, "that's good. I'll be off home now so the babysitters can go." Claire gave me a big passionate kiss as I left her flat.

I drove home with my thoughts; it was a lovely warm day. When I got back, I thanked Jack and his mate for staying over and gave Jack his money for a fine job.

FOR THE LOVE OF BRASS

Then I said to the boys, "Who fancy's going swimming?"

"Yes!" they both said.

We sorted out our shorts and towels and off we went to the pool at Cheam. It was nicely heated and didn't get so busy on a Saturday afternoon. Our Saturday evening consisted of a kebab, house clearance for a while, then watching the TV.

Sunday, the weather was just as beautiful, so my boys got a friend each to come with us, which gave me four boys, and off we all went to Box Hill, running the dogs. We were all worn out by the time we got home, so it was another takeaway for us and watch TV for a while. Sharon returned home, came in, said hello to the boys, then disappeared upstairs. The boys said goodnight to her when it was their turn to go to bed and I didn't see her again all evening.

Next morning, Abbie arrived to start her new job at the parlour. The three girls, Claire, Chantel and Abbie, were all sitting in the lounge smoking, drinking tea and having a laugh when I pressed the doorbell. Chantel came to the door dressed in black leather. A leather shirt, little leather top and leather high-heeled boots up to her knees. Oh dear, I have to put up with this each time I come over to see Claire, I thought, as I followed her back along the hall.

"Hello everyone," I said as I walked in. I was greeted by all three girls.

Chantel said, "I'll make the tea. Who wants a cup?"

Lovely idea, we all agreed. There had already been a couple of phone calls but no clients as yet. Claire was teaching Abbie what to say and how to say it when she answered the phone.

Abbie looked at me and said, "Don't you make me laugh when I talk all sexy like, will you?" Then she started to laugh, as did we all.

Claire had written out a script for Abbie to follow with the basic information. These calls would come in on the landline from the ads that were in the paper and also those in the shop windows, which brought in a lot of enquiries. On answering the phone, Abbie would have the information in front of her. She'd say, 'We have Chantel here today.' She would then give them her age, her vital statistics, colour of hair and what she was wearing that day and of course what a good time they could expect if they came along to see her and that she was waiting for them, then book a time, give them the location of the parlour and generally have a little chat with them. All the time she'd be doing this with a sexy voice. No laughing, no giggling, just a sexy voice. Some days Chantel would change her name along with her age to try and make it sound as if there was another girl here. Chantel's age was 22 but you would have thought she was older. She could pass for between 25 and 32. The details could change depending on what the client was looking for. She'd been a working girl for some time and knew exactly what to say. She also had all the answers to deal with whatever came up.

Claire got me to go into the bedroom and call the landline, pretending to be a client, so Abbie could practise her technique on me. You can imagine how funny it all became. I'd throw in the fast balls like has she got big tits, or has she got a big arse. Abbie would try her best to answer truthfully but also it was her job to persuade the client he needed to come along. We called this day Abbie's training day; we couldn't help but have fun and a bloody good laugh. Of course, Abbie's training day would last at least a week.

While all this was going on there were genuine clients calling in and coming to visit Chantel, so we had to have a break from training until the client had gone, then all the fun would start again. Claire had said once Abbie was trained she could look at opening another parlour. She already had girls on her books so it was just down to going to an estate agent and seeing what they could get that was suitable. She said I could go with her if I wanted and if the place was suitable she could send two of the girls round to clinch the deal as it were. I said that was handy, I wasn't too keen on doing that part of the deal myself. Ha-ha-ha.

At the end of the training day someone suggested we went for a drink over to the pub, as we called it, and this we did. I'd started to notice some of the same faces in there each time we went. There was always someone saying hello as you went in or while you were at the bar. I left the girls to it after a couple of pints and headed home so I could have my usual exciting evening with Sharon. Still I did get to see my boys and put them to bed, which was always nice. If I was very lucky Sharon would go out, or at least stay in a room on her own.

The following day I decided to go over to see the girls again. The building work was doing okay with Ron in charge so I was free to go. I arrived at around 10 o'clock and true to form we all sat there drinking tea, smoking and having a bloody good laugh.

It got to around lunchtime and Claire said to me, "How's your back? Is it still playing up?"

I looked at her and said, "Well, yes, it's playing up a bit."

"Come on," she said, "there's no one booked in for an hour. Let me sort your back out for you."

I smiled and said, "Yes, please." Off we went into the room.

"Okay," said Claire, "strip off for me and lie on the bed. I'll make your back feel a lot better."

"Yeah, I bet you can," I said. Claire also stripped off naked and sat across me as she massaged my back. With the thought of her sitting on me naked it really did work wonders because my back felt a hell of a lot better.

FOR THE LOVE OF BRASS

Claire worked on me for about half an hour, then said, "Right that's it. You owe me fifty quid. That's what I'm going to charge you for your massage."

"Oh yeah," I said.

"Yes. You can massage me now." She jumped on the bed quickly as I got up. "Come on," she said, "don't mess around. My turn."

"Okay, okay," I said. I started to massage her, rubbing in the baby oil 'thoroughly' of course. I couldn't believe my luck to be able to do this to her. Her body was absolutely stunning.

Claire then says, "This is called a reverse massage. This is what us girls call it in the trade. We strip off and the client massages us all over. They then pay us fifty quid for the privilege, so you now owe me another fifty pounds and when you're done you have to give me one hundred pounds," laughing as she said it.

I obviously had a surprised look on my face and with a big grin I said, "Look, I know you have a lovely body and I must say I thoroughly enjoyed massaging you and I would do it again at a moment's notice but, and this is a big but, I ain't paying you fifty pounds for a reverse massage. If you want me to massage you it has to be fair's fair. I will charge you fifty pounds to do so."

"Okay," said Claire. She was laughing. One thing led to another and before I knew what, we were making love with a full-on passion and intensity. When we were done, we lay there on our backs sweating and trying to get our breath back. Claire said with a laugh and a cheeky expression on her face, you owe me fifty quid mister."

"No, no, no. I'm not paying for the reverse massage. I told you that." This I said while laughing and sporting an even cheekier grin on my face.

"The wonderful sex!" Claire said.

225

"Yes, I think that was worth one hundred pounds," I said.

She laughed and replied, "I would have charged you one hundred and fifty for that and I'm well worth it," smirking as she spoke.

"Yes, you are," I said. "But I'll tell you what. I think seeing as how we both worked equally as hard at it and we got equally the same amount of pleasure from it, I think there shouldn't be an exchange of money. If we can do that to each other and enjoy it so much, we should do that for each other just because we can and because we like each other. What do you think Claire?" She looked at me somewhat quiet, just pulling her cheek to one side and frowning.

"Okay," she said, "you've a deal. That really was very good sex. Yes, okay, you definitely have a deal." Then laughed, "But you still owe me fifty quid for the reverse massage," smiling as she said it.

"Okay," I said as I got a fifty pound note from my wallet and gave it to her.

"Thank you," she said, then gave it right back to me saying, "that's your fifty pounds for the massage you gave me." I smiled and said thank you very much. Little did we know at this point how many times that same fifty pounds would go back and forth between us.

"Okay," I said, "I could do with a shower."

"Yes," said Claire, "well, go have one then. Put a towel around you if you're shy. Take your clothes and go and have one." This meant I'd have to go through the room the two girls were sitting in.

"Okay, then," I said, "just a towel around me."

"Yeah, go on, the girls have seen it all before anyway, what are you worried about?"

"Okay," I said, so with a big, white bath towel around me I went on my way to the bathroom.

FOR THE LOVE OF BRASS

"Hello girls," I said as I passed them. "Who's putting the kettle on?" laughing as I went. Abbie just sat there with her mouth open, not knowing what to make of it.

Chantel burst out laughing and said, "Looks like you two had a good time in there."

"Yes, we did," I replied as I disappeared into the bathroom shouting back, "but she's going to charge me fifty quid for a reverse."

Chantel laughed even louder, knowing exactly what I was talking about, whereas Abbie at this stage didn't, but it wouldn't take long before she caught on.

As I was in the shower Claire appeared and said, "Move over, make room for a little one."

On finishing our showers and getting dressed we came out into the kitchen area. I put the kettle on for us all to have tea and with that, the doorbell went. Chantel went off to answer it and see her client into the room.

After a moment she came back with the money from her client and said, "Hold my tea for me will you, Gary. I'll be back in a while." She sniggered and said I hope I have as much fun as you and Claire did."

"I hope so too," I said. "So, how's it going, Abbie? You getting to grips with it all?"

"Oh yes," she said, "it's good fun. We've had quite a few calls today. Looks like this afternoon is going to be a busy one."

I popped out around to the baker's in Portland Road and returned with some lunch for us all. I sat there all afternoon, mainly with Claire and Abbie as Chantel was busy with clients all afternoon. Abbie was a happy, friendly girl, always seemed jolly. She was good company. I liked spending time with this bunch of girls. It was definitely different from anything I'd ever known.

Chantel finished with her last client at 7 o'clock. It was suggested we went to the pub for a beer or two before going home. Ryan joined us at the pub for a drink. Claire had called him to come over so he could take the girls home. Chantel had a very good day. She'd taken just over £1,000. She was on one in the pub buying everybody a drink. People then wanted to buy us drinks in return, which was alright for them but I had got to drive home.

Claire said after a couple of drinks, "We've had a great day. The company's good in here and the music banging. Why don't you stay and we can all get on one?"

"That would be good," I said "but…"

"There's no buts about it. Ryan's here; he'll drive. You can come over and stay at mine."

"Are you sure?" I said. "Yes, of course."

"Oh, okay," I said. "let me think about it. My round," I shouted. "What you all having?"

"No it's not," shouted Chantel. "I've had a good day so I'm getting them in. You sit down. I want to celebrate you and Claire. I think you're a lovely couple. Let's get the champagne in and get pissed. Ha-ha-ha." She was laughing at having said this in front of Ryan. He just sat there doing as he was told, drinking his shandies. I couldn't help to think what a strange set-up Claire had with her marriage but, with that, two bottles of champagne turned up on ice and were placed on our table with the appropriate glasses for us to enjoy. I noticed the music playing. Claire was right, the music was good and getting better the more we drank. Before long Abbie was singing 'Too blind to see it' and we were all dancing, including the new friends we had made.

FOR THE LOVE OF BRASS

All except for Ryan. He was just sat there half smiling, watching the proceedings.

2 Unlimited, 'Get ready for this'. Oceanic, 'Insanity'. Rozalla, 'Everybody's free (to feel good)'. Kym Sims 'Too blind to see it'. All great tunes and loads more. We all had one hell of a night and so did everybody else sitting around us. I met lots more people and we all ended up drunk and, as planned, Ryan took us all home. I went back with them and was put in the spare room. I crashed out pretty quick. When I woke up I was cuddled up to Claire. She had got in my bed and slept with me.

It took me a while to wake, seeing as how I had a hangover but having Claire next to me made me feel a lot better. We both got up and had tea and breakfast. I asked where Ryan was. Claire said he'd gone out so we showered together and went back to bed so we could pass the fifty pound note back and forth. We had a great time doing so, then got ready and went over to the parlour to meet the girls.

CHAPTER ELEVEN
THE NEW PARLOUR

The girls were fine: no hangovers between them. They were busy on the phones.

Claire said to me, "If it's okay with you I can take an hour or two off. You can come with me and we can look for another flat to set up as a parlour. That'll be exciting."

"Another parlour. Yeah, sounds good. Yes, I'll come with you," I said. "It'll give me a chance to see first-hand how this part of the business works."

Claire made a couple of phone calls to two agents she already had on her books. The first said he had nothing suitable just now but should have in a week or two. The second said he had got a flat he felt was suitable for Claire's needs. The flat was in the Portland Road heading towards South Norwood Hill. We could walk there in 10 minutes or so. The agent gave us the address and we arranged to meet him there. We had time for a cuppa and a fag before we set off.

The landline phone was ringing continuously with Abbie busy booking in appointments. It seemed to me that Chantel would be busy all day, provided all the bookings turned up. Sometimes, of course, the odd one might not arrive.

Claire and I left the parlour and started our walk to meet the agent. Portland Road is quite a busy road, always lots of traffic and people, all going somewhere. We met the agent at the agreed number. The flat was

FOR THE LOVE OF BRASS

above a shop, of course. The entrance was about 25ft down a side alley, then the door was on the right. We all walked down the alley to the front door. The agent opened it and we went in. Once inside, the stairs went up to our right to a hall and landing, off which were the rooms. There was a lounge at the front of the building and a bedroom in the middle. Towards the back of the flat there was a kitchen and bathroom. The flat was fully furnished.

"What do you think?" I said to Claire.

"Well," she said, "it's not bad. Not bad at all. It's in good condition and we could operate out of here straight away. In some respects its better than Cobden because you don't have to go through the lounge area to go to the bathroom. The clients can come in and out without having to go through the lounge. I like that idea." She turned to the agent and said, "I like the flat but I don't like the entrance."

"What's wrong with the entrance?" I said.

"Well, it's good for the clients, it gives them privacy as they come in, which they'll like, but I don't like it for the girls. It not safe for them when they come in and out. I don't like the long alley."

"Oh, okay," I said, starting to get an idea of what to look for. Trying to keep in mind what the clients might be happy with and also that the girls have to be happy. If they're not or feel unsafe they won't work there.

Claire said to the agent, "Okay, what about the second flat you said you have or might have?"

"Yes," he said. "That's just up the road from here. I have the keys. Would you like to see it?"

"Yes," said Claire. She smiled and said, "Let's go," pinching my bum as she walked behind me on the way out. The agent locked up and off we set to the next flat, which really was only about 300yds away on the other side of the road. We arrived at a large Victorian house some four floors tall, which also had a basement flat. The flat we were going to look at was on the first floor. As you went in the hallway there was a front door to your left, which went into the flat we were going to look at. Next to that front door was a fairly grand staircase going up to the floors and flats above.

The agent got out his keys and opened the front door, saying as we went in that the owner was doing a little bit of decorating so the flat wouldn't be ready for a couple of weeks. As we went in, we both looked around, impressed. The flat was in very good condition and fully furnished. I looked at Claire and she raised her eyebrows. I could tell she liked it. As we walked down the hall, the front room was on our left. A large room, it was as long as the house was wide. Past that was a bedroom, then on to the bathroom which had its own door off of the hallway. Finally, the last room in front of you was quite a big kitchen with a nice view over the garden. It was these two rooms the owner was redecorating, explained the agent. It looked to me not to need redecorating but if that's what he wanted to do, then fair enough, I said.

Claire said, "Yes. I like this place. It's ideal. How much is it?" she asked the agent.

"A monkey a month plus the De." The agent was a Londoner from Kennington, it turned out.

Claire looked at me, smiling, and said, "You understand that slang he's using?"

I said, "The flat is five hundred pounds a month, plus the De which is the deposit."

I looked at the agent and said, "Incidentally, how much is the De?"

"A monkey," he replied, "and that will have to be in cash."

FOR THE LOVE OF BRASS

"Fair enough," said Claire. "We'll take it," she said while smiling at me.

"That's great," said the agent. "Can you pay the De now? You know, so I know you're serious about the place."

"Yes, we can do that," said Claire. "Also, I'd like you to keep an eye out for any other suitable flats. You know the type of thing we're looking for now."

I noticed Claire seemed to be including me in almost everything she did, or was I just imagining it? Either way it felt quite nice. I had not felt that feeling for a good number of years.

The agent piped up, "The De would ordinarily be more expensive than that but I'll make sure the owner knows I've dealt with you before and you're trustworthy and reliable, and he does not have anything to worry about with you taking this place on."

"Yes, yes, that's right," said Claire. "Thank you for all your help. I take it the flat's on a year's contact. Is that right?"

"Oh yes, yes," said the agent.

"That's good," said Claire. "Once I've signed for the year, you must come and visit us at our new parlour. I have a new and lovely girl there. She'll sort out your bonus and commission." Claire laughed and so did the agent.

"Yes, I understand," he said. "That'll be great."

We all three left the property.

The agent said, "Bye for now and hope to see you both soon."

"Okay, thanks again," we said, then went our separate ways.

We started our walk back to Cobden and I said to Claire, "Can we stop on the way back for a coffee so we can have a chat? There's something I want to talk to you about, you know, on our own without the girls being there."

"Yes, of course we can," said Claire. We stopped at a Broomfield's baker's. Although it was a baker's, you could also get something to eat there. Seeing as how it was such a nice day it was an ideal spot. We ordered coffee and sat outside in the sun, chatting and smoking. I just came out and said it.

"I would like to know what you think of me, or more to the point, how much you think of me."

"Well, that's easily answered," said Claire. "I think you're lovely," she said, "and I think a great deal of you! Why? Does it not show?"

"Yes, it shows," I said. "I think so much of you. I really like you."

"Yes, I know," she said with that cheeky grin she has. "I know you do and it's nice. I like it and I really like you."

"Well," I said. "This is where I'm going with this. Chantel, when she was drinking, said, 'Cheers to you and Claire. I think you make a lovely couple.' Also when you talk to people you include me in everything by saying us and we."

"Yes," said Claire.

"Well, I just need to sort out with you what type of relationship are we having, or are we even having one?"

"Well, yes. Of course we're having one but I know you're not sure, or where this might be going because I'm a working girl. Most men can't handle that, or they won't or can't have a relationship with a working girl."

"Yes, that's exactly right," I said. "That is, I guess, what I was trying to say without offending you."

"Well," she said, "that's where we are and to show you I care about you, I won't work any more. I'll just run things and make my money that way. Then I can have a relationship with you, or at least I hope I can. So now it's your turn, Gary. What do you think? Is that okay with you?"

"Er, yes. Wow! Yes, it's very okay with me. I'd love to have a relationship with you. I think you're gorgeous. And you'll stop working for me?"

"Yes, that's right. That's what I said." She laughed as she said this. "So if you don't mind, can we get back? I want to see how much money I made in my new job. Ha-ha-ha. Come on."

"Okay, okay," I said. "Oh, but what about your husband?"

"What about him?" said Claire. "Don't worry about him, he's just there in the background. He'll be happy for us. He knows what I think of you. I've already told him."

"Wow, really?" I said. "Okay, well that's great. You've made me really happy." Claire lent over the table gave me a big kiss and said, "Come on then, let's go."

"Okay," I said.

We left the baker's to start our walk back. Claire called Abbie from her mobile phone to check it was okay to come in, which it was, so in we went.

"You've got to be quiet as we go in. She has a client in there with her."

Once in the lounge we said hello to Abbie and I went to put the kettle on.

"So, have you been busy?" Claire said to Abbie. "That's good, oh and good news, me and Gary have got another flat not far from here. Only a good fifteen-minute walk away up on South Norwood Hill."

"Ah, brilliant," said Abbie.

"And the other thing is, Gary and me had a chat on the way back and we're now officially a couple. We've sorted out what we're doing."

"Oh, that's great news," said Abbie. She jumped up and gave us both a kiss. "I'm really happy for you both."

I said to Abbie, "So you knew what Claire thought about me?"

235

"Yes, of course. We all do. She talks about you all the time, to all of us. She just didn't know how things would go between you."

"Yes," said Claire. "Gary brought the subject up, so I made the most of the situation. I told him I'd stop working and that was that."

Chantel came back into our room after seeing her client out and she joined us for tea and to hear the good news. She was just as happy for us as Abbie was and suggested we should go over to the pub again tonight to celebrate.

"I can't," I said. "I've not been home for two days. I need to go home and catch up on whatever is going on with my business. In fact, I should go now. I'll call you tomorrow, Claire. Talk to you girls later. Bye."

Claire saw me out and gave me a big kiss to be getting on with. As I left she said, "I'm so pleased we sorted that out. I'm a happy woman."

"Okay, Babe, me too, very happy, talk later."

Off I went home. Sharon never once asked where I'd been when she saw me. I just did the normal once I was home. Had some fun with my boys, then after, something to eat. I spent the rest of the evening in my office. I spoke with Ron and a couple of clients. I was calling them clients now, which of course they were. I had things to do the following day and I knew I'd not have time to pop over and see the girls. Anyway, the following day, while out, I called Claire, just for a chat. I told her I couldn't make it over but we arranged to meet over in Croydon on Saturday to go shopping. Not for anything particular but just for the hell of it. Saturday afternoon and early evening was the only time I'd got spare that week as I was going to Bisley on the Sunday, shooting the handguns on the pistol ranges. I had no mobile phone in those days, not many people did. You have to bear in mind it was 1993, so if you needed to call someone you did it on a landline or from a public phone box out in the street.

FOR THE LOVE OF BRASS

I called Claire on Friday, just to sort out where to meet on Saturday. She asked if Abbie could join us as she wanted to get a couple of things. The three of us could go shopping and have a late lunch.

"Great," I said. "That's what we'll do."

I spent Friday evening in, playing with the boys, then sitting on my own having a drink while Sharon was out somewhere. I had a site meeting on Saturday morning, so couldn't go food shopping with the boys but Sharon could and did a little later in the afternoon. After my meeting I went over to Croydon to meet the girls at the Whitgift centre. We met at McDonald's and the girls had only just got there when I arrived, so all three of us went walkabout in the centre as well as along the main high street. We had a good look in the Ann Summers shop.

Abbie wanted to buy some bits but then said, "I don't have a boyfriend so it's a waste of time really."

We were laughing at all sorts of things. We had a great afternoon and Abbie was great company. You couldn't help but like her. After all our nosing around the shops we had a late lunch at an Italian pasta restaurant. By this time, of course, we did have a few bags between us.

I said, "Come on Abbie, I'll drive you home. What do you think, Claire? We can have a cuppa at Abbie's house."

"Great idea," they agreed, so off we went to Abbie's.

Once at Abbie's drinking tea, we had not been there long when Courtney and Lee came in and that was it. Once we all got together, the laughter would never stop. Courtney and Abbie were the funniest girls you could ever want to meet. Out came the wine and the spliff's and that was my cue to go, before I got involved and had too much fun. Ryan would come over and pick up Claire later on, so I left them all to get on with it.

Sunday morning and I was up early to let my dogs out into the garden

237

FOR THE LOVE OF BRASS

while I put get the kettle on. I had tea and breakfast, then opened the gun safe and packed my holdall bag. A Browning high power 9mm, a Smith and Wesson .357 magnum and my Smith and Wesson .38 snub nose pistol. I made sure I also packed the appropriate amount of ammo I would need for the day, along with the necessary holsters, both hip and shoulder type. Then finally, armed with a flask of tea and a couple of sandwiches, I was sorted for the day and off I went to Bisley to meet up with some of the lads I had served with in the Regiment. We met on the close quarter or the CQB Ranges, which in the Army stood for Close Quarter Battle. At Bisley they were known as the gallery pistol ranges. We had two ranges booked. One had two firing points, which were under cover. There were two sturdy firing tables for you to put your kit on, then at the side of each table fixed securely to the floor there was a frame, and fixed within it a large wheel with a handle on it, sticking out one side of it. This had two cables which went down the range to a target frame to which you could attach a target by means of pegs or tape. We used a staple gun, having found that more secure at holding the targets up. In the past, if you used the pegs, one on each corner, your friend on the shooting point next to you might, and often did, fire at your pegs. The bullet on impact with the pegs would smash them to pieces and your target would fall down, to the great amusement of your friend. If you didn't have more pegs to replace them with you were in trouble because you couldn't secure your target to the frame. In the past, when this had happened to me, I would to go and break little branches off nearby trees. I could push them through the paper targets to hold them to the frame. Sometimes that would work and sometimes not that successfully, especially when your friend started shooting at the twigs. So for me, I used a staple gun, the large type. The type that a carpet layer might use to lay underlay. Stapling

FOR THE LOVE OF BRASS

it to the floorboards. I found this worked very well.

The things I particularly liked about this type of range were that you could shoot at your target from anything from 3yds to 15yds, depending on what you wanted to achieve, and you could also put up different targets. You could use bullseye-type targets for more accurate shooting, or you could put up a figure 11 target, which was the military's version of a soldier coming towards you with his rifle across his chest. This was a different type of shooting because the kill area was the centre of the target, the centre being a square, which was a ten score, leading outwards, the squares getting bigger and the score value getting less as they went. Then, of course, you also had what we called the head box, which was basically a six-inch square covering the target's face. If you put a round in that area, that would be known as a head shot, wherever that six-inch box was hit.

The second range we booked was next door to the CQB range. This range had four firing points with four individual study tables. The targets on this range were 15yds out. They didn't move back and forth but they did move from side to side. They'd turn away from you side on and when one moved, they all moved. This worked by means of an electric motor, off to one side of the range. The controls were on one of the tables at the shoot point. You could set the time that the targets would be on show and also set the time the target would turn away from sight, or of course you could have somebody controlling the movement by hand at the controls. The really good thing about this range was that you could shorten the distance you were shooting at by moving forward in a line and engaging the targets as they showed themselves. The targets were figure 11s glued onto quarter-inch plywood, so there were nice and sturdy. The figure 11s were approximately 18ins wide by 4ft tall.

FOR THE LOVE OF BRASS

These ranges were great because the firing points were under cover, so on rainy or sunny days, you could train without getting wet or burnt by the sun. You could start shooting at 9 o'clock in the morning until the siren went off at 1 o'clock, then everybody would stop shooting across all the ranges to have lunch. Then you'd resume shooting after the siren again at 2 o'clock for the afternoon session. We'd spent a lot of time on these ranges. Sometimes I'd book the CQB for a couple of hours and bring my sons down here for a shoot. I enjoyed teaching my sons to shoot and they became very good at it. At other times I would attend Bisley with the gun club. We might shoot on other ranges, sometimes up to 50yd pistol competitions. For anything over that distance we used rifles. The club always had a shoot day once a month with the morning being one type of shooting, then in the afternoon a different type and sometimes on a different range. There were always plenty of members on those days and a good selection of firearms and we'd often use each other's weapons.

When I met up with the Regiment guys, we'd always be honing our skills for bodyguard firearm training, just in case we ever needed them. Other than the fact that it was great fun training together, it was also a social thing. It made sure we all stayed in contact and was a good place to find out what was going on in the world of security and close protection, as that is what most of these guys did for their living.

We really did have a fantastic day's shooting. Once that siren went off, some of the guys went off to find a pub or a clubhouse on the Bisley site, of which there were many. I, on the other hand, would just get out my sandwiches and flake, sit in the sun and enjoy the break, waiting for the siren to sound so the fun could commence again.

All in all, we spent a lot of rounds between us. I fired all the ammunition I'd brought with me for the day, which was over 600 rounds. An excellent day's shooting was had.

Monday morning and Sharon had got the boys ready and took them to school, then went to work herself. I sat in my office catching up with things that needed doing. I had another enquiry that had come in, and a couple of the lads I was shooting with on Sunday had mentioned they did a bit of close protection work through an agency. They said they sometimes needed a hand if I was interested, which of course I was. Always nice to do something a bit different.

I finished in the office and went off to help out on one of the jobs, putting up some guttering and replacing a few tiles on a roof. I spent all day doing this and didn't get home till 6.30.

That evening I called Claire on her mobile. She said they had had a good day at the parlour and she was sitting at home now with her feet up watching something on the TV, just catching up, she said. They had ended up having a big night on Sunday evening. She and Abbie had gone out for a few drinks over to a bar in Croydon. They were tired at work all day, so they'd taken some speed to keep them going. Now it was just time to recover, so she was chilling at home with Ryan. I told her I'd pop in to see her tomorrow. She said that would be great and she looked forward to seeing me.

I arrived at the parlour and Chantel let me in, looking as lovely as ever, all dressed up in yellow today with white stockings. I could understand why the men liked coming to see her. We sat there drinking tea and smoking. Abbie was telling me about the laughs they'd had on Saturday night after I went home. They were all stoned and giggling, she said.

"So," I said, "Abbie, you're into your second week now. Do you still like your new job?"

"I love it," she replied. "It's great."

Then, unexpectedly, Claire said, "The room's not busy. Come on, Gary, you can give me a reverse massage." I smiled and, with a grin, said, "Okay, let's go but I ain't paying you for it." Claire laughed as we walked out of the room.

Once in the bedroom, it was like a whirlwind. We couldn't wait to get each other's clothes off and in no time we were making love and rolling around like two Chinese wrestlers. The excitement and passion was almost overwhelming. Afterwards, as we lay there sideways across the bed, smoking a cigarette, Vanessa Williams played on the radio, 'Save the best till last'. I commented on the song and how nice I thought it was.

Claire said, "You certainly did save the best till last," then laughed. "Come on," she said. "Let's go, get cleaned up and have a shower together."

"Come on, then," I said as we put our towels around us. As we were in the shower, Chantel went in and tidied up the room, she'd a client due any minute. As we emerged, one after the other from the shower, the kettle went on for a cup of tea and we all lit up cigarettes. It just seemed to be what everybody did in those days. Drank tea and smoked cigarettes. Any excuse to put the kettle on and pass the fags around.

With that, the doorbell went and Chantel went off to answer. She saw her client into the room, then came in to us with the payment. She was laughing.

"What's so funny?" said Abbie. "You won't believe it," she said. "He's only a young fellow, maybe seventeen! Look what he wants to pay me with."

"What is it?" I asked, my curiosity showing. "What have you got?"

Chantel handed over a piece of paper to Abbie who looked at it and burst out laughing.

"What is it?" I asked again.

FOR THE LOVE OF BRASS

"It's his fucking dole cheque," was her response. The pair of the girls were laughing, then we all started laughing.

"It's only for fifty quid," said Abbie. "I thought you charged more than that?"

"Well, yes I do, but he's only young so I said he can have a little quickie." We all found this hilarious. "Okay," Chantel said, "I'm going back in there. Wish me luck." We were all giggling and in no time at all we heard Chantel closing the front door. She came in and said, "That's the best fifty quid I've ever earned for thirty seconds' work and, to top it all," Chantel said, "he enjoyed himself so much, he's coming back next week when he gets his next cheque." Now we were all laughing. Better have another cup of tea, someone said.

Abbie had brought in the ingredients to make a Chilli con carne for us all for lunch, and this was well on its way and about ready. The rice went on and in 15 minutes we were all eating lunch, and lovely it was too, with the nice French bread that came from the baker's out on the main road. We sat there eating while the phone calls were still coming in. Chantel was truly up and down like a whore's drawers. While she was in the bedroom with a client, we heard the front door open and close, then the door to the room we were sitting in opened and in came a man with plaster on his clothes. He looked like he'd been plastering.

Claire knew him and said, "Hello, Lee." Abbie and I had no idea who he was. Claire said, "Sit down. I'll make you a cup of tea," which she got up to do.

Lee looked at us and said hello.

"Hello, mate," I said. "Looks like you've been plastering."

"Yes," said Lee. "I'm a plasterer."

"Well, that explains that," said Abbie, as she started laughing.

Claire then introduced us. "Lee, this is Gary and Abbie. This is Lee's flat."

"Oh, okay," I said. "Nice to meet you."

"Yeah, nice to meet you guys too," he said.

"I finished work early today so instead of hanging around, I thought I'd come home."

"Oh, okay," I said, "you live here then."

"Yes," he replied. "Claire only has the flat from nine till about half six or seven."

"Oh, okay," I said. "I didn't realise that. Not that it's any of my business, but okay." Claire came over with his tea and we all sat there smoking and chatting. Lee thought Abbie was the working girl but no, we explained, Chantel was and she was in the other room.

A bit more time passed then Chantel came into our room with her little yellow undies on, passed us and went off to the bathroom. After a couple of minutes she came back out and sat with us. Lee couldn't take his eyes off of her. We all sat around talking and laughing about things. The doorbell went again and Chantel was up and off again into the room.

"That's your bedroom in there, Lee?"

"Yes," he said.

"And you don't mind people using it?"

"No, I just change the sheets each night, that's good enough for me."

"Oh, okay. You been plastering long?" I asked.

"Yeah, quite a while. A few years now." I guessed him to be 24 to 26 years of age. "I lost my driving license and I'm on a ban for a year, so that's a pain in the arse," Lee said.

"I have to get a bus or a train to go to work, then someone to get my tools from one job to another. It really is a pain but I only have about seven months to go." He laughed. "So it's not too bad. It's so hot out there today, when I finished early, I thought I'd come home and get cleaned up. I'm glad I did now," he said as he looked at Chantel. I could see he was really interested in her.

Claire said, "Maybe we should all go for a drink after work. What do you think everyone?" We all said yes, won't that be nice.

Lee looked at Chantel and said, "Are you going?"

"Yes," she said.

"That's a result," said Lee. "I'm going for a shower." He got up grinning from ear to ear.

Once he was in the bathroom, Chantel said, "He's quite nice." We all smiled.

"That just leaves you then, Abbie. We'll have to sort you out a bloke."

Abbie just laughed. "Don't worry about me, I can soon pick one of them up," she said.

"Looks like we're going to the pub then," Claire said.

"What time do you want to go?" I asked.

"Well, we've one more client, then we can go. Should be at about six."

"Lovely jubbly," I said. I thought about Mandy and said to Claire. "Did you hear anything about Mandy or has she been in contact?"

"No," said Claire, "nothing at all. I don't think she will now. I think she's gone."

"Who's Mandy?" asked Abbie.

"Oh," said Claire, "a girl we had working for us." She went on to tell Abbie the story of what had happened.

Chantel's last client had arrived and while she was in the room sorting him out, Lee finished in the shower. He had most of his clothes in the big cupboard in the hallway, so he was soon dressed.

He pulled some beers out of one of the cupboards and said, "Shall we start now?"

"Why not?" Claire said.

I asked Claire, if we're going to get on it tonight can I stay at your place like I did last week? You know, come home with you?"

"Yes, of course you can. I'll phone Ryan to pick us up so we don't even have to worry about a cab. You can sleep in the spare room again and I'll come and snuggle up with you. Ha-ha-ha." Smirking as she laughed.

"Sounds good to me."

It wasn't long before Chantel had finished her work. She disappeared into the bathroom to get ready and once she was done we all went up the road to the pub. They always seemed to have a good attendance. Although it was early in the evening it wasn't so much busy with people coming out for the evening like us but more with people who had popped in for a drink on their way home from work.

By the time it got to 7 or 7.30, the pub was really rocking, the music was good and most people were fairly pissed. It was a lively place and we soon took over a couple of tables. Although there were only five of us, the other seats at the tables were soon taken by other people and it was as though they were part of our group. We were all laughing and chatting with everybody else. Everyone seemed to get along in this pub. It had a great atmosphere. Every so often two or three people from our tables would go outside to smoke a spliff, then come back in with their eyes looking stoned but with a big grin on their face. Claire would always introduce me as her boyfriend when we met people. She even did it in front of Ryan, so it was clear to everyone we were together.

Lee was really enjoying himself. He and Chantel got along really well. You could just tell by looking at the way they behaved with each other. It

FOR THE LOVE OF BRASS

was a great evening. Everywhere you looked people were smiling. From time to time I noticed a man standing at the end of the bar with his back against a wall, so when he leant on the bar with his left arm, it put him naturally facing in our direction but also put him in a good position to be able to scan around the pub at everybody but without looking suspicious. I remember thinking to myself, if I had to plot up in here to be able to watch everything that went on but without standing out, where would I go to do it? I looked all around, taking into account where the entrances and the toilets were and also where the big windows were. Yes, I thought to myself, I would stand exactly where this man stood. I wasn't feeling worried or threatened by him in any way but I was aware he was there and made a mental note of details. Size, shape, clothes and so on. I also remember he wasn't white but not black either. He seemed to be a light brown colour but with white features and dark hair.

Anyway, while I was doing this, I was also chatting quite a lot with Claire. She was always very touchy-feely around me, which I really liked. I took it to mean she really liked me, which I was very happy with because I felt exactly the same about her. I think I was touchy-feely with her too, if you know what I mean.

After another hour or so, we were all getting plenty of drinks in and all quite pissed. I had been drinking pints but couldn't keep up so I'd switched to the vodka and oranges with Claire, only having the odd pint. We were all having a bloody good night. When it was my turn to get some drinks in, I decided to go towards the brown man's end of the bar to get served, just to see if there would be a reaction of any type. As I walked towards him with some glasses in my hands that I was taking back to the bar, somebody had been served who was standing right next to him. They turned and walked away leaving a space I promptly filled. I put the glasses on the bar and waited to be served. I was sure I could feel his eyes burning into the side of my face.

I turned, looked at him and said, "Hello, mate, you alright?"

He looked back and said, "Yeah, alright." That was it.

I got served and, with all my drinks, left the bar and returned to our tables. If nothing else, I knew he was now conscious of me. We had made contact. Before long we were all fairly drunk and even up dancing. The music seemed to be getting better and better as it does when you're pissed. Kym Sims, 'Too blind to see it', 2 unlimited with 'Get ready for this', and when Chesney Hawks came on with 'I am the one and only', the whole pub erupted into song; it was just like being at a big party.

Before we knew it the pub was about to close and we were all filing out onto the pavement all saying goodbye to all our new friends. I found Claire pulling my arm and steering me over to Ryan's car where Abbie was already getting in.

"Where's Chantel and Lee?" I said.

"Don't worry about them, they're okay. They're sorted. Come on, Ryan, let's go," said Claire.

Ryan drove off in the direction of Abbie's house. I remember trying to roll myself a cigarette and talk to Ryan. I was in the front of the car and the girls were in the back, giggling while rolling up a spliff.

"So what do you do during the day, Ry?" I said.

"Oh," he said, "I know a guy who has a prestige car chauffeur service. I do some work with him in this BM of mine."

I laughed and said, "What, like a posh minicab service?" He just looked at me and gave no answer. I was smirking. "Sorry, Ry," I said. "I'm just taking the piss. I've had too much to drink."

"That's okay," he replied.

FOR THE LOVE OF BRASS

We dropped Abbie off and waited till she went up the long path to her front door to make sure she was safe, then turned around and went on our way to Shortlands. I finally finished rolling my cigarette by the time we pulled up outside Claire's flat. I tried to light it as I got out of the car. The next thing I knew, I was sitting in her kitchen drinking a cup of coffee.

"Here we are," said Claire. "Have a puff on that," giving me a new spliff that was already alight.

"Okay, don't mind if I do." After about three puffs I said, "That's it, I have to lie down. My head's spinning."

Next thing I knew, I was waking up in the morning with Claire snuggled up to me. I wandered off into the kitchen to get the tea on and looked out the back. There was no BMW out there. That's handy, I thought to myself, we're on our own. Maybe we could exchange that fifty quid with each other. Claire walked into the kitchen with just her G string on, stretching her arm out and rubbing one of her eyes with the other hand. What a sight for sore eyes she was.

"I'm just making some tea," I said.

"That's good," said Claire, "I'll see you back in the bedroom."

"Oh yeah," I said. I never made a cup of tea so quick. We were soon rolling around together, seeing who could get the best value out of the £50 note.

We soon got cleaned up and had something to eat. Claire called a cab and off we went to the parlour. We got there around 10 o'clock and Chantel was already there on her own. She'd gone back with Lee and stayed the night so she didn't have far to go to get to work that day.

I said smirkingly, "You and Lee get on well, then?"

"Oh yes," she said. "I really like him."

Abbie piped up, "I have a Lee at home who's my flatmate. Now, seeing

249

as he's a little older and a bit taller than Lee who lives here, I think we should call him big Lee, and your plasterer Lee we can call little Lee, you know, so there's no confusion."

"Ha-ha. Okay," Chantel said smiling. With that, the landline phone rang. Claire answered and gave her sales pitch and booked an appointment.

"He'll be here in fifteen minutes," she said to Chantel.

"That's good," she said. "It's always nice to get the first one of the day out of the way. I'll just go get the room ready." She came back into the lounge dressed for work. A little short top and a black leather mini skirt with knee-high boots. Her hair and makeup were already done by the time we had arrived.

The doorbell rang and Chantel went to answer. Two minutes passed and she came back into our room shutting the door behind her. "He's a fucking copper. I thought he might have been when I saw him. He waited until he was in the room then produced his warrant card. Said he could help me but I had to give him a freebie. Then asked who else was here."

When Chantel had finished with the cop she came in and said, "That bastard reckons he can help look after me. He said he'll be calling each week to check on me. Fucking arsehole."

The doorbell rang. It was Abbie, who had been out shopping. "Hello to you all," she said as she came into the lounge. "I've got some nice ham and a French stick we can have for lunch."

We all sat there drinking tea and smoking cigarettes and talking about the police and how some of them like to visit parlours. Of course, Claire and Chantel had seen all this before. I asked if he was in uniform.

"Oh no," Chantel said, "they always come in plain clothes. You don't know if they are CID or what. Well, not unless you read the details on

FOR THE LOVE OF BRASS

their warrant card, which I never do. All I see is the police badge. That's enough for me to know it's freebie time.

When lunchtime came, we had our nice fresh bread and ham, then sat around talking all afternoon, while the phone calls kept coming in and, along with the clients, it was a busy afternoon. We discussed the Chantel and Lee situation, which we all thought was cute. Claire said she'd not mind betting Chantel would move in here with Lee. It will only be a matter of time. It got to around 5.30 and I said I would have to be going home.

While driving back, I wondered on the idea of the policeman coming to call and what he meant by looking after Chantel. I started to wonder, if the police came to the parlour in an official capacity, could I be nicked for anything? Maybe I could, just by being there. This was something I should remember to ask Claire about when I saw her next.

While at home, I asked Sharon if she was going out on Friday. Her reply "Is the Pope a Catholic?" I took that to mean she definitely was, which was fine because now I knew if I wanted to go anywhere, I would just arrange my own sitter. I had things to do in the building business to keep me busy until Friday evening, so I made the arrangement for Jack to come over and babysit for me then and I could go to the gun club for some shooting.

I called Claire. I'd wanted to see her Saturday night but she had arranged to meet up with her sister, who she had not seen for a long time. Ryan was going to take her over to north London somewhere. They could then catch up and have a drink together.

Friday evening and Jack pulled up outside my house as Sharon got in her cab and drove away. That's a fair exchange, I thought. I smiled at Jack as I greeted him. He came in and asked where the boys were and what

251

they were up to. He'd got some sort of new computer game he wanted to show them.

I opened up my gun safe, put on the shoulder holster for my .22 auto and slipped the gun into it under my arm. I picked up a box of 100 rounds and put the silencer in my Jacket pocket, locked up the safe and headed downstairs to said goodbye to the three boys. I jumped in my car and was on my way to the gun club. The good thing about only having one gun on you was you could carry it with you all the time, I did anyway. Even when we went to the pub, as long as it was concealed, no one was any the wiser. This made it secure; no one could steal it from your car if you were wearing it.

I might not have been seeing Claire that weekend but I sure thought of her all the time. I could always call her whenever I liked, she said, but I thought it best to give her space, at least for now. I told myself, I didn't want her to think I was too keen. Ha-ha, who was I kidding? It was far too late for that. I was keen, I was really keen. It seemed to ooze out everywhere, just how interested I was in her. I don't think I realised it at this stage but I was falling head over heels in love with her.

Once back home, I paid Jack for a job well done, then got my favourite little tipple out and poured myself a lovely V and O, put my feet up on the coffee table and watched the TV. Every now and then I would find myself thinking about Claire, wondering what she was up to and looking forward to seeing her again. I thought it was good she'd got her own business. It meant I could see her whenever I liked, well, certainly any weekday, especially during the day and most evenings, and going over to stay at her house, even when her husband was around, well, that was beyond me. How did that work? I have no idea, I told myself again, it just does. Can't say I was going to complain, because I wasn't. I told myself it might be better if she wasn't a prostitute, or hadn't been one, but then again I would never have met her at June's flat. She said she'd given up working for me, so all I could do was take that for what it was. Probably quite a big deal for her in money terms because I had seen the amount of money Chantel could take in a day. The thing I needed to remember was what she was doing for me. Don't think about her past, only think about the now, which seemed to be enough for me. I hoped that would stay the same. Another thing I liked about her was her tremendous passion for life. She just got on and did it. The additional parlours she talked about, she just got on and made it happen. There were people on her books that wanted to work with her, people she had worked with in the past, so it seemed all that was needed was the premises to work from. She had it all mapped out. I found business interesting. I found her business more so. I was keen to learn how it all worked, which I seemed to be doing without even trying very hard. It just seemed to be unfolding in front of me, day by day.

Saturday morning. "What do you fancy doing boys?" I said, while we sat around the table having breakfast. The boys wanted to go out into the countryside. It was a lovely day so why not, I said. "We'll take the dogs and go over to Newidgate brick fields. There were three lakes there I knew really well. We could take the survival tin with the fishing kit in it and I said I would teach them how to fish using only the kit that fitted inside a tobacco tin. We sat on one of the banks of the small lake, catching fish constantly all day, using our homemade fishing rods, and maggots as bait. We were lucky, as we got the maggots from a deer carcass we found nearby.

I stayed at home on the Sunday, doing a few jobs around the house. After going to the supermarket for the week's groceries, I cut the lawn in the afternoon. Sharon had other things to do on Saturday, so she hadn't picked the shopping up while we were out for the day but that was okay. She left it for me to do while she went with my sons to her mum's for the day.

I phoned Claire the next morning. The three girls were at the parlour and of course Claire invited me over. I arrived just before lunch. As I drove into Cobden Road I saw the brown man standing on his own outside the pub. He seemed to be busy looking one way then the other as though he was waiting for someone to turn up. I passed him and parked my van. Chantel answered the door all dressed in black underwear today.

"Hello ladies," I said as I entered the lounge, "what's new?" The girls were talking about what they did over the weekend, which didn't sound too exciting. A bit like my Sunday, I thought. Claire said the estate agent had called and the new flat was ours. All she had to do was to go to his office and sign the paperwork.

"You can come with if you like."

"Yeah, when shall we go?"

"Oh, sit and have a cuppa first, then we'll go sort it out."

I asked Abbie how she felt with being the maid, as they call receptionists in this business.

"Yeah, really good," she said. "I have the hang of it all now. I've all the confidence in the world," smiling as she said it.

"Oh, Claire," I said. "While I think of it, how does the law stand with us all being here?"

"What do you mean?" she said.

"Well, there must be laws on running a brothel," I said.

"Oh yeah, there is," she said. "You can have two girls in the property, one working girl and one maid, that's okay, but if you've more than one working girl, it's classed as running a brothel."

FOR THE LOVE OF BRASS

"And what about having a male here?"

"Well, we'd say you were a client, otherwise you would be arrested and charged for living off immoral earnings."

"But if I'm a client or maybe a friend that's just popped in to visit, that would be okay?" I said.

"Yes," Claire said, but if the police did their homework and had the place under surveillance, they would know you were here a lot and would arrest you anyway, regardless of what you told them." All the girls started to laugh.

"That's it, Gary, you're nicked," Chantel said, smiling as she said it. "Mind you Gary, I have to say, I like it when you're here. I feel secure with you here. I've noticed when we go drinking over to the pub, you get a certain respect from people in there. Maybe it's the way you carry yourself, or the way you talk to people, or both, but you give off this 'don't fuck with me' attitude. You carry that well because you're tall and a fit-looking bloke."

"Oh, okay," I said, "Thanks for that."

Abbie agreed. "That's what's nice about you, Gary."

"Thanks girls," I said. "That's nice to know."

"We talked about this the other day," Claire said. "We feel safe around you. We all feel safe around you."

"Thanks girls, thanks," I said. "Well, okay, I've finished my tea. Shall we go get another flat, Claire?"

"Yes, come on then. Chantel, I'll send the agent down here to see you. Don't take any money from him, just give him a good time. I'll cover it for you."

"Okay," said Chantel, smiling. "I'll sort him out."

We went for a walk along Portland Road, seeing as how the weather wasn't too bad. The sky was a light grey all over but it was quite a warm day. Claire was excited at the thought of getting this particular flat. I must say, I thought it was very nice. At the agent's office, we sat at his desk. He was smiling from ear to ear, probably looking forward to his visit to see one of the girls.

"Okay," he said. "A monkey a month and a monkey up front."

"So that's two monkeys," said Claire, laughing.

"Yes," he said, "I think that makes it a gorilla." We laughed. "The five hundred a month," said the agent. "I was able to negotiate for you, that's all in. You just pay your own service bills and that has to be cash each month. This paperwork I want you to sign is for three months, renewable each quarter and that's it. Once that's done, you can have the keys the place is yours."

"Okay," Claire said, "here's your thousand pounds cash." She pulled the notes from her handbag.

"Don't forget to get your gas and electric on from today," the agent said. "Thank you for that, sign here and here's the keys, the place is yours."

Claire leaned over his desk and said in a quiet voice, "Here's the phone number of the parlour. Just call, book yourself in and the maid will give you the address and any details you need. Thanks once again, and don't forget we would like another flat for our purpose, so call me as soon as you've got one." He was only too happy to oblige. We stood up and left. "Come on," Claire said, "Let's go have another look at the place." So off we went.

Once inside, we checked the kitchen and bathroom. All the decorating had been finished and it really looked very nice.

"Yes, lovely," she said. "I have the two girls in mind that'll run this place. It will make a lot of money for us."

FOR THE LOVE OF BRASS

"Well, for you," I said.

Claire smiled. "No, for us. Let's check out the bedroom."

In we went. It was a lovely big room with a big double bed over by the window. Claire leaned over and pulled the curtains together, then said, "Get your arse on here and let's test this bed."

I laughed and said, "You can massage me."

"No, no, no," said Claire. "I want a reverse one."

After a while we both lay there getting our breath back and lit cigarettes. I was looking at the big ceiling rose and the cornice work around the edge of the ceiling.

I said to Claire, "I love these old buildings, they've so much character."

We just lay there talking about whatever came up. She asked me if I went shooting on Friday night. I told her I had.

"Will you take me with you one day soon? I think I would like that. I'm sure I could shoot the bullseye out."

We laughed as she said this and she went on to ask me about what type of gun I had got. When I told her I had a lot of them, she wanted to know all about them and what they were for and why. This, of course, I was happy to tell her. She seemed to find it all really interesting. She asked why I had military guns and I explained because these types of guns we had used when I was in the army.

"Really?" she said.

"Yes, I was. A while ago."

"What did you do and what regiment were you with? Did you shoot anyone?" I thought it's funny how people always ask that question: did you shoot anyone?

I answered that I was a small-arms specialist, or an Armourer as some people call it; I served with the Special Air Service Regiment.

"Isn't that the SAS?"

"Yes," I said, "and no, I didn't shoot anyone."

"Wow," she said. I could see her brain ticking over.

"Since leaving, have you done any bodyguard work?"

"Yes," I said.

"So you're good with security, that type of thing?"

"Yes," I said. "I know quite a lot about that type of thing."

She'd the biggest smile on her face. "You know what that means?"

"What does it mean?" I said.

"We can work together. I knew it. I knew there was something about you. I knew it. Sort of knew we could work together but I just didn't know why. Ha-ha-ha. That's it." She was excited. "You must be good with those guns of yours. Will you teach me? When can we go? I can't wait."

"Okay, okay. Calm down a bit," laughing as I spoke. "Yes, I'll train you."

"Oh great!" she said, raising her voice. "I can't wait. Turn over," she said. Let me give you a reverse massage.

"Well," I said, "I can't refuse that," as I turned. "You carry on."

"Do you know what?" Claire said. "We are in the oldest professions in the world: prostitution and body-guarding. Did you know that?"

"No," I said. "I'd not heard that before."

"Well, there you go, we can learn stuff off of each other."

By the time we'd finished making love again it was definitely time to head back to the parlour. As we were walking, Claire was telling me about the girls she'd got in mind to work out of this new flat.

Samantha and Justeen, both around 30 years of age, one a redhead and one a brunette, Claire went on to tell me. They were very good at their jobs, they both loved sex, they both loved turning a trick with men, they could wrap a man around their finger in seconds and have him eating out of their hand in no time, but their biggest love in life was each other. You couldn't separate them, they were always together.

I asked, "So how would it work with the two of them there?"

"Well," said Claire, "they are both working girls, one of them will be the maid and the other working. Then they'll change it around to suit themselves. The good thing about them is, they'll do a double turn if a client asks for it, so they can really put on a show, send the men mad. Once they let their clients know where they are, they'll be busy all the time and of course word of mouth will bring even more business in, so it's all good. We'll make thousands of pounds a week out of this parlour," Claire said, smiling. "And the other thing is, they don't mind a bit of S and M, the old Sadomasochism."

"Really?" I said. "Oh yeah, they will have special nights for that, normally on a weekend. We can go if you like!" Claire laughed. "You might like it, you never know." I laughed. "Don't knock it till you have tried it," Claire said.

"I think I might give it a miss, thanks anyway. I don't fancy anyone beating me." Claire was laughing as I spoke. "We'll see," she said, "you could do the beating, or the tickling."

"Tickling?" I said. "Do people pay for that?"

"Yes, of course," she said. "You name it, whatever it might be, and there is someone who will pay for it, big money sometimes."

"And how much would somebody pay to be tickled?"

"Well, I was paid five hundred pounds once to tickle someone for two hours, I thought that was good money, don't you?"

"Yes," I said, "I guess so."

We arrived at the front door of Cobden Road and Claire put the key into the lock and opened the door. As we went in we could see that the room door was closed.

"Chantel must be busy," Claire whispered.

We went through into the lounge and Abbie said hello with her hand over her mouth, she was giggling and trying to mask the sound.

"What's up?" I said to her.

"Chantel's got a man in there, he's naked and she's hitting him with a stick. I can't believe it. I find it so funny."

Claire looked at me and said. "There you go." Then she looked at Abbie and said, "We were just talking about that kind of thing, I was telling Gary. Abbie, put the radio back on quietly."

"I just find it so funny," Abbie said. "If somebody did that to me I'd fucking hit them back, ha-ha-ha. He's paying two hundred pounds for it, he must be mental," laughing as she said it.

Abbie put the kettle on and we all sat there with a brew. Claire was telling Abbie about the new parlour and how well she thought it would work out. Then the door opened to the lounge and in came Chantel. All she had on was her suspenders, stockings and high heels.

"Oh, hi Claire, hi Gary," as though greeting people virtually naked was an everyday occurrence. I smiled at her as I thought, in her case it would be.

"Abbie," she said, "the client wanted to know who was in here, so I told him about you. He asked what you looked like, so I told him. He got all excited and asked if you'd come in and let him look up your skirt while he lay on the bed and I beat him. He said he'd give you twenty pounds, so here I am. Do you want to earn some money?" Abbie looked at Claire, who looked back with approval on her face.

"Okay," Abbie said, "what do I do?"

Claire said, "Take your tights off, so when he looks up he's got something to see. Chantel will tell you where to stand and what to do."

Abbie was laughing as she took her tights and her knickers off. "Come on," she said, as the girls went out through the door. Three minutes passed before Abbie came back into the lounge, laughing just as much as she was when she left. "I can't believe what I just saw." She offered the money to Claire. "No, no," Claire said, "it's yours. You keep it."

"Thanks very much," Abbie said as she tucked the £20 note in her bra. "One of those every day would be handy," she said.

A few more minutes passed and Chantel came back into the lounge, having seeing her client out. Abbie was still sitting there beaming from ear to ear.

Chantel sat down in her underwear and said to Claire "Okay, tell me all about the new place." This Claire did whilst I just sat there watching the three girls chat. I found these situations very amusing. I seemed to have a constant smile on my face when I was around these girls, and there were more to meet.

"Oh, Abbie," I said, "did the estate agent call?"

"Yes, he did. Said he couldn't get here today but would tomorrow. He sounded all excited by the prospect, just talking about it."

Claire made a phone call to Samantha and Justeen, who said they'd call in tomorrow.

Chantel said, "The client I had today, the one with the stick. He asked if we could put a bracket up on the wall. He said he'd like to be hit while standing upright. He suggested he could be tied to it by his hands or wrists, then have a hood on his head and Abbie could come into the room as well and hit him." She smiled as she told us this. "So Gary, you're a builder. Can you fit a metal ring or a bracket of some sort for us to tie him to?"

"Yes," I said, "I should think so. Let's have a look in there to see the best place to put it, Chantel," I said. "Will it be okay with Lee, seeing as how it's his flat?"

"Oh yes," she said, "don't worry about that. He'll be fine with it."

I had a look in the room. The only place suitable for the ring was on the fire breast. I said, "I could fit it above that picture, then all you have to do is take the picture down when you want to tie the fellow up to the ring."

"Great," she said.

"I'll go to B&Q on my travels and find something."

The girls said they'd be going to the pub after work and Ryan and Chantel's Lee would be joining them. I told them I had things to do at home and said my goodbyes. Claire saw me out, giving me the biggest kiss and cuddle as I went.

She said, "Come over tomorrow, I want to see you and I want you to meet Sam and Justeen. You'll get on well with them, we all have the same sense of humour."

"Okay, Claire," I said. "I'll call you first in the morning before I head over."

"Okay, that's great," Claire replied.

Once I was home, I spent time with my boys until they went to bed, then had my usual evening's portion of unhappiness with Sharon, mainly spending our time in the house avoiding each other. We hardly said three words now and that was if we were lucky.

The following morning I spent an hour in the office, did about half an hour exercising with my dumbbells, got the dogs and went for a run over the park. Then I got cleaned up and called Claire. I told her I had a few tools in the van and I would stop at a hardware shop on the way over. I thought to myself I had the time now, so I might as well find and fit the ring for Chantel. On the way over I stopped at a shop in Carshalton, where they have a large range of metal fittings, and I found a ring I thought would be appropriate for tying a person to. I was smiling as I bought it because only I knew what it was going to be used for. The ring was attached to a square metal plate with a hole in each corner for a fixing, so when it had its four fixings in place it wasn't going to go anywhere, the stick man could hang around all he wanted. Once I was there with the girls, I showed them the ring and we laughed about how it might be used. I brought my tools into the room, took down the picture, then installed the ring.

"There we go Chantel, all done." The girls came to have a look.

"That looks just the job," Claire said. "Okay, Gary, take your clothes off and we'll tie you to it so we can test it out."

"Yeah, go on," said the other two.

Laughing, I said, "Thanks for the offer girls but I think I'll give it a miss today. I'm putting on the kettle." We went back through to the lounge and sat around smoking and chatting, waiting for our two visitors to arrive.

The doorbell rang and Chantel jumped up to answer it. We could hear her greeting someone, and Samantha and Justeen came in. We all introduced ourselves and the kettle went on as usual. Sam and Justeen sat down and out came the cigarettes. Everyone was smoking so I had to open an extra window to let fresh air in. As we all sat there talking, the phone rang. It was the estate agent wanting to call round for his bonus.

Claire heard who Abbie was talking to and said, "Tell him to come round as soon as poss. There's some ladies here he can meet." Then she said to Chantel, "Before you take him in, bring him in here to meet us all. When he sees all us girls, he'll think he's spoiled for choice. He'll work even harder to find our next flat and tell all his friends."

"Ha-ha," the girls all laughed.

Within ten minutes he was ringing the bell. He said hello, then disappeared into the room with Chantel. I don't know what she did to him but it didn't take long before she was seeing him out, all within 15 minutes.

She said, "He had a big smile on his face when he left and said he would be back soon."

I think at this point I should describe Samantha and Justeen.

Samantha had lovely, flowing, dark-red hair and an extremely pretty face. She was a very attractive young lady in her early 30s. She dressed sexily but very smartly. She was voluptuous, with the top of her bust on show. I couldn't help but notice on her right leg a tattoo of flowers, twisting and winding their way up her leg from her ankle and disappearing under her skirt.

Justeen was a brunette, her hair four or five inches off her shoulders, again a very attractive woman indeed. Medium build with a big bust, very shapely legs on show from her mini skirt. She also was very smart, looking like she was on her way to a business meeting. I would say they were both about the same height, 5ft 5in to 5ft 6in tall. In a nutshell, a real pair of gems. I could see what was meant by saying they could twist men around their fingers. They also had very sexy voices.

The new girls asked if Abbie was the maid, to which Claire replied, "Yes, and Gary over here is our bodyguard, he looks after our security. He's also my boyfriend."

"Oh, okay," said Justeen. "What happened to Ryan?"

"Oh, he's still around," said Claire, "but we're just friends."

"Oh, okay," said Justeen.

"Well, Gary," Sam said, "Can we call on you for all matters of security?"

"Yes, you can," I said.

Claire said to me, "Shall we take the girls up to the new flat and show them around?"

"Yes, sure," I said. "Why not?"

"That'll be nice," Sam said. "Can we also get a set of keys off of you today, Claire?"

"Yes, of course. We'll get a set cut on our way."

As we walked to the new flat, I mainly walked with Sam; she wanted to talk with me.

She said, "I like the look of you, Gary. You look as though you would be perfect for the job of security and minding. We sometimes go out on jobs, mainly of an evening. Would you be up for driving us and looking after our welfare?"

"Yes, of course," I said.

"We'll look after you financially, you won't have to worry about money, working with us. We'll tell Claire all about what we're doing, so we all know what's going on."

"Yes, sounds good to me." We stopped at a shop and got some keys cut. I asked the girls where they came from because they both had London accents. They came from north London originally but now lived in the Crystal Palace area, so didn't have far to come to work.

We entered the flat and the girls looked around. They loved it.

"It's just perfect," Sam said.

"Do you like it, Justeen?" I asked.

"Yes, I do, very much. Oh, Gary?" said Justeen. "My name's Jessie, I use the Justeen name for work, so you can call me Jess."

"Okay," I said, "nice to meet you, Jess." We both smiled.

FOR THE LOVE OF BRASS

Claire and the two girls talked, Sam and Jess would be in tomorrow and start to set themselves up, working from their new premises. Although the girls had mobile phones, the landline would be connected early the following week. All four of us jumped in a black cab back to Cobden Road. It was a warm day and the girls didn't want to walk.

Once there, they all decided it was a good idea to go over to the pub for a few drinks, as this would give Chantel and Abbie a chance to get to know Sam and Jess.

All four girls went to the pub after locking up. Ryan and Lee would join them a little later so I headed off home, telling them I would have a drink with them all on Friday evening.

While at home, I had some friends call and ask if we could have a practical shotgun shoot at the farm on Sunday, seeing as how we had not had one for a while. I said yes straight away and that I would sort out what was needed: targets, the ammunition, and also arrange with my friends Andy and Mark to be range officers on the day. I said I'd get on the phone and let people know and we could have a shooting competition, and all the shooters were invited.

I spoke with Claire on Friday and arranged to meet the girls that evening. I had already sorted my babysitter the night before; I was making tea in my kitchen when Sharon walked in. I looked at her and thought, yes, the Pope's still a Catholic, no point in asking, so I called Jack.

I saw Sharon off and asked her not to wait up for me; then, as the cab took her away, Jack turned up. I drove over to the pub and parked up the road a bit, near the parlour, then walked back to the side entrance. By this time the five girls were fairly charged. They had been there since about 6 o'clock and it was now around 8 o'clock. I went up to their table, said hello to them all and asked who wanted drinks, then went to the bar. The

FOR THE LOVE OF BRASS

pub was fairly busy and while I was waiting to be served, I looked along the bar; there was the brown man standing in his usual place at the end of the bar. He kept looking over, then looking away; he seemed to be watching the whole pub, scanning everywhere. I started to get served and when I looked back over in his direction he was gone. Off to the toilet, I thought, then a voice to my right side said, "Alright mate, alright Gary?" I turned to see Mr Brown.

"Yes, I am, mate," I said as I paid the barman. "Do I know you?"

"No you don't, but I know you."

"How do you know my name?" I said.

"Your girlfriends told me about you and what you do for them."

"Oh," I said, "let me get these drinks over to the girls and I'll chat in a minute." I placed the drinks on the table and looked around but he was gone, only to reappear back in his corner at the end of the bar. Oh well, I thought, he seems a bit strange but if he wants to talk he'll come over. The girls moved round, making a seat for me between Claire and Chantel. As I sat down, Claire gave me a big hug and a kiss on the cheek.

"It's a wonder you're not all drunk."

"No," said Chantel, "we all had some speed early on and that's kept us going."

"Oh, okay." I could tell all five girls were all getting on very well. Abbie was having a whale of a time. She seemed not to stop laughing.

"Where's Lee and Ryan?" I asked.

Chantel said Lee had gone out with his mates from his work, over in Chelsea somewhere, and Claire said Ryan wouldn't show till much later as he was working.

"Oh, okay," I said.

Chantel then said, "That fucking copper was in again today. Came in this afternoon and said he wanted his freebie. He keeps saying his wants to look after me.

"Well, maybe he's in love with you," I said.

"No, no, it's not that, there's more to him than that. He was in here earlier on."

"Did he see you?" I asked.

"Yes," she said. "I pointed him out to Claire; he saw all of us sitting here together."

"Okay, point him out to me on the quiet if you see him in here again."

"Okay, I will."

It wasn't long before I was as merry as the girls. The music was as good as ever. I kept hearing the tunes I liked: 'Too blind to see it', 'Everybody's Free', 'Insanity', 'Get ready for this'.

"These songs are brilliant," I said to Claire and Chantel. Abbie was up dancing each time she heard 'Everybody's free to feel good'; in fact, it wasn't long before we were all dancing in our own corner of the pub and being joined by people we had got to know on previous nights. We were all having a great time. Ryan turned up at closing time, Sam and Jess had a great evening. They said goodbye and got a cab home. Chantel went back over to Lee's where she was staying the night, while Claire, Abbie and myself got into Ryan's car and, as before, we took Abbie home. As usual, I'd had too much to drink, so went back to Claire's to stay the night. Once there, I was wrecked, so had to go to bed, and I left Claire and Ryan up talking. When I woke, Claire was cuddled up to me, which I thought was nice. I loved it when I woke up with her. I stood in the kitchen looking out of the window over the car park, when I had déjà vu.

Claire walked into the kitchen and said, "Bring the tea and come back to bed."

FOR THE LOVE OF BRASS

After a fantastic session of making love, we got ourselves showered and I jumped in a cab back over to Cobden Road to pick up my van. Then back to my house for a Saturday with the boys, shopping over in Morden, then into the Wimpey for a bite to eat and out in the afternoon with the dogs.

On Sunday Sharon went to her mum's with the boys whilst I went to Godstone for a day of practical shotgun shooting. We had 15 people turn up, so a very busy day for us range officers.

I called Claire on Monday and she told me how all the girls had got together and gone out for a big night out in Croydon, so the Cobden Road parlour wasn't opening too early, if at all.

"Okay," I said, "have fun. I'll call you tomorrow."

Next day, I called Claire on her mobile and she was still at home. She said she would be over to Cobden Road in an hour or two. I expected to be there about 11 o'clock. We spoke about what we had been up to the previous day. I told her I'd been swimming at Morden baths. Claire thought that was a great idea.

"Shall we go swimming today? I'll bring my cossie and we can go to the baths in Beckenham. You'll like it there. It's a lovely old Victorian building."

"Sounds good to me. Yes, I'll bring a towel and my shorts."

I rang the doorbell at Cobden Road and Chantel answered, dressed all in white today. I went into the lounge and sat talking with the girls, drinking tea and smoking. They knew I was coming over as Claire had already called. They were telling me about their Sunday night out in Croydon. They had got on the cocaine and, what with drinking a lot, they said they'd probably overdone it and had too much of both, so they weren't too good that morning. Abbie said she had got home at 4.30am after being dropped off by Ryan and, once there, she had been drinking with big Lee and Courtney. They'd been up all night drinking and having their own little party. I thought to myself, these girls certainly party hard, much harder than I ever did.

Claire arrived with her extra bag of swim things and, after another cup of tea, we left Abbie and Chantel to get on with things while we went to the Beckenham baths. Claire was right, the building was very old. It was the type that had little individual changing booths around the edge of the pool and above the booths, a viewing balcony where you could sit and look down on the swimmers. I guessed this was used when there was a swimming gala on. It had a very high roof, which was mainly glass, which let in loads of natural light. The water was kept lovely and warm. We found a booth that was vacant and both squeezed in together and changed into our swim wear. The door of the booth was only about 4ft tall, starting at about your knees and finishing at about my shoulder level, so I could see over the top. We laughed because Claire couldn't see over the top. Once I was ready, I opened the little door and called "come on, short arse" as I dived in.

We spent about an hour in the pool, swimming and just playing around with each other like two kids. Then it was time to get some lunch, which we did as we went back to the parlour. As we walked, I told Claire how sexy and gorgeous I thought she looked in her swimsuit. Then I went on to tell her I couldn't wait to see her in it again and we must go swimming more often.

"I fancy you like mad," I told her. She really did make me very happy when I was in her company, whatever we did. I guess that explained why I wanted to spend so much time with her.

When we got back, Abbie said, "We've been busy while you were gone, we've had four clients in already and the phone keeps ringing. We've three booked in for this afternoon."

Claire smiled and said, "Well done. Keep it up." They always laughed when there was some sort of sexual innuendo like "keep it up." "Bottoms up." "Keep your head down." or such like, of which there were many.

Chantel came in, sat down and said hello.

"How are you?" I asked.

She laughed and said, "My fanny's a bit sore. Other than that I'm okay." We all laughed.

I found it fascinating to hear these girls talk, so did Abbie, she told me. Neither of us had been around working girls before now, so it was a new experience, a learning curve and we were learning fast.

The following day I stayed at home, working from my office, catching up with stuff. I got a call from Claire saying she had heard from Sam and Jess; they wanted to know if I was available that evening. They wanted me to drive them out to a job.

She gave me their number, saying, "This is Sam's mobile, give her a call." Which I did. Sam explained she had a job to go out on but she did not need to be there until 11 o'clock. She wanted me to mind and drive her, would I do it?

"Yes," I said, "I'd love to."

"Great, don't worry about money, we'll look after you."

"Okay, great," I said. "What time and where shall I meet you?"

"Well," Sam said," meet us at our parlour, South Norwood Hill."

"Okay, what time?"

"We won't leave until ten thirty but you can come over earlier than that. In fact, come about nine if that's okay. "We can have a drink and get to know you a bit better."

"Okay," I said, "that's fine with me."

"Good," she said. "I'll tell you where we're going when you get here. It's not far away."

"Alright Sam, see you then."

Later that evening I told Sharon I was going out to see some people. Now I know the Pope's a Catholic, I told myself, but Sharon wasn't going anywhere that evening, so I told her I that I would be taking the car. I thought my nice Mercedes might be better than the van for the first job with the girls.

I tapped on the small glass window of their front door.

Jess answered. "Hello, love," she said, "come in." I walked through to the kitchen/diner and sat down.

Sam came in. "Hello darling," she said. "What do you want to drink?"

"Oh, just a coffee," I said, "cos of driving, you know."

"Yeah, of course," Sam said. "There's been a change of plan. It's only me and you going, Gary. Jess is staying here. She has a client coming over."

"Over where?" I asked.

Jess said, "Over me, hopefully." We all laughed.

"So you'll be here on your own and working?"

"Yes," Jess replied.

"Well, if you girls want me to mind you, I'm telling you this is not a good idea to be on your own."

"Yes, I know that love," said Jess, "but I know this man, he visits me quite a lot; he's okay, he won't be a problem."

"Okay," I said, "you girls know best. I was just saying."

"Thank you for that but it's just you and me tonight," Sam said.

"Jess," I said, "will I be safe with Sam in the car?" We all laughed.

"Yeah, you should be," she said smiling. "Drink your coffee, Gary. It's only nine o'clock, my client is due at ten."

"Okay."

"We can leave about ten thirty," Sam said. "We're only going to South London."

"Oh, okay Sam. Whereabouts?"

"Deptford," Sam said. "Do you know it?"

"Yeah, I do. I know South London pretty well."

"Oh good," said Sam. "Then on to Catford."

"Yeah, that's good," I said. "I know that as well."

We three sat there talking till Jess said, "Changing the subject, when we were in the pub last, us girls, we talked about you. They told us you were in the SAS and that you're good at body-guarding and very good with guns. Is that right?"

"Well, yes," I said. "Who was saying that?"

"Claire was telling us about you."

"The Special Air Service, she told you?"

"Yes," Jess said, "Told us all. She even told some of the other people in there, after she told them you were our bodyguard. That was why you were with us a lot. At one point a man came over and was trying to chat up Chantel. Chantel told him nicely to leave her alone or she would have to tell our bodyguard and that you would have a word with him."

"Oh dear," I said. "I could do without that. I bet everybody knows now."

"Yes," said Jess. "I expect they do."

"I don't like the look of that man," Sam said. "I think he sells the drugs in there."

"Who are we talking about?" I said.

"He hangs around the end of the bar, looking all suspicious," Sam said.

"Has he got a tanned skin?" I said.

"Yes," said Sam.

"I know who you mean. I thought he was just a bit nutty. Oh dear." Then I laughed, "I wonder if he is the local drug dealer? I should keep an eye on him, then."

There was a knock on the front door and Jess went off to answer it saying, "Bye for now" to us two. We sat there smoking till Sam said with a smile on her face, "Do you fancy me?"

"What?" I said, then started to laugh.

She was still smiling. "It's just that you keep looking at my forty double Ds."

"Do I?" I said. I'd not noticed I did that and I found myself feeling self-conscious.

"I'm just winding you up. I know you think the world of Claire. I can see it."

"Really?" I said, "Does it show?"

"Oh, yeah," said Sam. "It shows alright. We can all see it."

"Thanks for sharing," I said with a smile on my face.

"Come on," Sam said. "We should be going. I like you, Gary, I don't see you as a threat. Most other men are constantly on your case. It's nice I can relax around you."

"Well, thanks for that," I said. "I think that's a compliment."

"Yes, it is." Sam said. "Take it as such." We got to the car. Sam said, "This is nice. Is it yours?"

"Yeah, its mine. My wife uses it a lot of the time, which is why you see me in my van. Next time I drive you anywhere, I might only have the van."

"That's okay," Sam said, smiling. "I'm not a posh bird."

FOR THE LOVE OF BRASS

We arrived at the address in Deptford and I parked across the road from the house to have the front of the house in full view. "Okay," I said. "How do you want to do this?"

Sam said, "I'm going in for one hour, so time me. If I'm not out in one hour, come and knock on the door. I'll tell him I have my minder waiting for me; that way, if he looks out of his window, he'll see you sitting over there, so things will be okay. If I'm out sooner, then that's okay too."

"Okay," I said. "See you in an hour."

Sam went over to the client's house and went in. That was it. All I had to do was wait and watch the front of the house.

After a while I noticed the front door of the house open and out came Sam. The door closed behind her. I checked my watch. Only 40 minutes had passed. She walked over to the car and got in.

"Is everything okay?" I asked.

"Oh yes," she said, "he was just finished a little sooner than he figured. Okay," she said, "we can go to the Catford job. I had best ring the client because we'll be a bit early. I'll just check to see if it's okay." This took a moment and yes, the job was a go, so off we went. Same procedure on arrival.

"See you in an hour," I said.

I sat in the car. It was a quiet road, nothing much happened. I watched a fox travelling from house to house, inspecting the rubbish bins and occasionally finding a tasty morsel to eat. Eventually I checked my watch and the hour was up, the front door opened and out came Sam. She walked over to the car and got in with a smile on her face.

"Everything okay?" I asked.

"Yes, of course," she said. "Home, James."

I smiled and off we went.

It didn't take long to get back to Sam's parlour, seeing as how it was nearly 1 o'clock, and we were back by twenty past.

"Are you girls staying here tonight or do you want a lift home?"

"Oh no," said Sam, "we'll stay here. No point in going home now. Do you want to come in for a drink?"

"No thanks," I said. "I'll head off home."

"Okay," said Sam. "Here's your money," she said, sorting out from her bag. "Here's a oner and a tip. Thanks very much," she said. I looked down. She'd given me one hundred pounds and a ten pound tip.

"Thanks, Sam, thanks a lot." She leaned over and gave me a kiss on the cheek.

"That's okay," she said as she got out, "talk to you soon. We have some more work to do together. Bye."

I drove off, heading to Croydon and home, thinking to myself, when I work on the tools, I earn £10 to £12 an hour. I just did a job where I got paid £50 an hour. Well, I thought, how bad is that? And with hardly any traffic on the road I would be home in 20 minutes.

The following day I called Claire.

"How did it go?" she asked. I told her. "That's good," she said, "we'll have to find you more to do so we can keep you on the firm," laughing as she said it. "What are you doing today? Are you coming over to see me?"

"Well," I said, "I have a bit to do in the office."

"Well," said Claire, "get on and get it done, then pop over here. It's my turn and I want to give you that fifty pounds."

"Oh, really, do I have to? Let me think about it." It took one second. "Oh, okay then. See you this afternoon."

We were all sitting in the parlour that afternoon laughing and joking, drinking tea and smoking. In between Chantel's clients, Claire and I went

FOR THE LOVE OF BRASS

into the room to exchange the £50 note, which by now was just a term we used to get each other into bed. We took it in turns to massage each other before having sex, the original £50 note was long gone and I don't even know who ended up with it.

I went off home that evening to good news. Sharon told me she was out for the evening. Marvellous I thought, a bit of house clearance before the boys go to bed.

Friday night came around. I had arranged to be the range officer at the gun club this night for an in-house shooting competition, so I had Jack babysitting. I can't really call it babysitting anymore, because my boys were quite big. It was more like looking after them, or minding them I guess. We had a great night's shooting, then off to the pub for a couple before going home to pay Jack so he could then go home. I knew that on the Saturday evening Sharon would be home; she had two friends coming over, as they wanted to arrange a holiday abroad for themselves. I thought this was a great idea when she mentioned it. My input was yes, you should go, and go for as long as you like, a month or two would be fine.

I did the shopping with the boys, then went for a run. Sharon took the dogs out walking in the afternoon with my sons and one of her friends went with her. Her friend wanted to talk about the holiday. Her husband told her she couldn't go but she was going anyway, so she was talking with Sharon about how to make it happen. I don't know what made Sharon an expert on the matter but then I didn't care.

I called Claire from a pay phone while I was out shopping. She said she was at the parlour with Chantel for the afternoon, doing Abbie's job as the maid. Chantel had a few clients booked in and they were there making some extra money. Chantel's boyfriend, Lee, was away all weekend, so Chantel was making the most of it.

Claire said, "If you're at a loose end, come on over."

Once Sharon had gone, I jumped in the car and over I went. I sat with Claire talking about whatever, while Chantel was in and out of the room. She saw eight clients that day, which netted her £850, of which half went to Claire. There's me thinking my £50 an hour was good. Mind you I said to myself, I don't have a little honey pot to sell.

I drove home after arranging with the girls I'd be back to have a drink with them in the pub. Well, I say a drink, I was actually coming back over for the night, just as I had done before. Once I was back home, I got ready for my night out. I left the car and returned in my van by 7.30. It was a lovely warm evening, one of those evenings where you could drive with your window down and your arm resting on the door. The girls had got ready for the evening by the time I arrived and we went over to the pub almost straight away. It was fairly busy, what with it being such a nice evening. There were quite a lot of people drinking outside in the back garden as well as out the front. Most of the people were at the bar, so we were able to get our usual table near one of the corners. Chantel wanted to get the drinks in first and wouldn't take no for an answer. We sat at the table and the girls said to keep a few extra chairs near us as Abbie, Sam and Jess were coming to join us. That's good, I thought, another mental night this will be.

We three sat together, enjoying or first drinks.

"You had a good day?" I said to Chantel.

"Yes," she said, "very good. Earned a nice few quid," she said, smiling.

"Oh yeah, Gary, that copper was in again during the week," Chantel said. "He's still saying he wants to look after me. Did I tell you?" she said. "I saw him in here."

"Yes, you did tell me."

FOR THE LOVE OF BRASS

"Oh yeah," she said. "I'll tell you if I see him again."

It wasn't long before Sam, Jess an Abbie came in. The pub was already buzzing. It looked to me as though they'd taken some Charlie, laughing and giggling all three of them.

"Okay, girls, what are we drinking?" I said.

As I went to the bar Jess said, "I'll help you." While we were waiting to get served, she was telling me they'd had a good day, very busy at their parlour with lots of clients. I placed the drink order and looked around the pub while talking with Jess.

'Too Blind to see it' was playing and Abbie was singing along with the song, I could hear her from the bar. We took the drinks back to the table carrying two each, then I came back for the last two. As I picked them I up looked along the bar and there was Mr Brown standing in his usual spot, looking in the direction of the girls. I sat down next to Sam and Claire, which meant I had my back to a wall, giving me all around vision. I could see all of the pub at a glance. I decided to ignore Mr Brown and just get on with having a good time, as we all were, all smiling and laughing.

Sam leaned over and said to me, "Next week, will you take me out again one night? One of those jobs we went on, the client wants to see me again."

"Yes, of course I will."

"Good, I'll talk to you Monday to let you know what's happening."

"Yeah, great," I said.

Chantel was sitting the other side of Claire. She leaned forward and beckoned me with her finger. I leaned in towards her and she said, "That bastard's in here."

"Who?" I said. "The copper?"

"Yes, he just walked by and winked at me as he passed." She indicated he was down at the other end of the bar with a couple of other men.

"Okay," I said, "point him out to me when you see him again."

"Okay," she said, then she looked down suddenly, which made me look up. A tall man with a brown suede jacket passed us. Chantel looked back up and said, "That's him. That's the copper, the one in the brown jacket. Yeah," she said, "he's the one who comes in for his freebies."

Claire joined in the conversation, "Yeah, I know him. He gets around all the parlours. He came in once to me and wanted a freebie. I had to tell him to fuck off and made him leave. I told him if he didn't, I would go to the station and report him."

"Did that work?" I asked.

"No, not really," said Claire. "A couple of days later we were raided for drugs. They came and turned the flat over."

"Oh, he's a serious character then."

"Yes," said Claire, "although after that we never saw him again, till now."

The copper walked to the end of the bar and stopped next to Mr Brown. The pair began to talk, occasionally looking over in our direction. Then it dawned on me, how friendly were these two guys? How much did they know about me? I had a feeling I would be finding out sooner rather than later.

The copper walked back past us, winking at Claire as he went, which annoyed me. Then I thought, if this copper visits parlours for freebies and is friendly with Mr Brown who is very likely a drug dealer, he's obviously on the take and very bent indeed.

Abbie had now got down from standing on her chair singing, and I said to her, "How much is a gram of speed?"

"Why?" she asked. "Do you want some?"

I laughed. "No," I said, "I just what to know how much it costs."

"About a tenner," she said. "I'll have some if you get any."

"Okay," I replied. I said to the other girls "Who wants some whizz?" It was called "Billy Whizz" or just Billy sometimes. All the girls said yes, they'd have a dip. A dip meant that you licked your finger, stuck it in the little bag that the Billy came in, then whipped your finger around your gums. Within ten minutes it would be working. Claire heard all that was going on.

I said to her, "I think it's best if one of the girls goes to see Mr Brown and asks if he'll sell us a gram.

"Yes, ok," she said. "I'll go!"

Claire stood up walked over with a big smile on her face. I saw him look her up and down. She stopped, spoke to him, gave him something from her bag then walked off in the direction of the toilets. On her return she stopped briefly next to him, then carried on over to our table and sat down. Out came the little sealed plastic bag, which she opened, licked her finger and had a dip. The various fingers appeared for their dip and wipe.

Abbie said, "Ain't you having a dip, Gary?"

"No," I said, "I tried that stuff years ago, it made me feel sick."

"Okay. Claire," she said, licking her finger again, "let's have a little dip." Claire opened the bag and Abbie had a dip, then stuck her finger in my pint.

"Oi, Oi!" I said.

"Too late," Abbie said. "You got it, now get on with it," laughing as she said this.

"Oh, well." I carried on drinking but this did prove a point. Mr Brown was the resident drug dealer and friends with the copper.

FOR THE LOVE OF BRASS

We were all merrily drinking away and getting drunk as time went on. The copper did come by once more and have a chat with Mr Brown. Then, while I was at the bar with Chantel, a voice said in my right ear, "I know what you're doing! I know who you are." I turned, it was Mr Brown. He'd get very close when he wanted to talk to me, not that he said much but what he said, it was like he was a French secret agent during the Second World War: 'I'll say this only once.' This amused me.

By the end of the evening we were all standing on the seats singing along with everybody else in the pub. It seemed everyone in there was drunk. Next thing I knew, Ryan had turned up to take us home. On leaving the pub, Abbie, Sam and Jess hailed a black cab in Portland Road. In they jumped, after giving us all a big hug and a kiss goodbye. Those girls all lived in the same direction whereas we were going in the opposite direction. Chantel didn't have far to go. She just wandered along the road to Lee's flat.

Once at Claire's, Ryan went off out again and it was just myself and Claire kissing and cuddling with each other while drinking coffee in her kitchen. The next thing I knew we were naked in the shower trying to sober up a little before climbing into bed for some serious love-making.

The following morning I had a whopping hangover. I said to Claire, "You'll have to go and make the tea."

I couldn't get up for a couple of hours and by the time I did, it was the afternoon. A nice hot, sunny afternoon. Claire and I went out walking into Bromley and got a late lunch, then sat around in the sun in the park until tea time. We spent a lovely day together. I didn't want to go home, not yet at least, so we went for a Chinese meal, then sat in a local pub just drinking shandies and talking about anything. Eventually, it was time for me to go home. I got back at about 12 o'clock to a quiet house, everyone was in bed.

FOR THE LOVE OF BRASS

Monday morning and Ron was taking care of the jobs. I wasn't doing much when it came to the building work. It seemed all I wanted to do was spend as much time as possible with Claire. She was becoming all I could think about every day.

I called her as soon as I could and we arranged to meet a little early at Cobden Road to go swimming again. This we did. We didn't have much to worry about, Abbie and Chantel were fine on their own. We had fun swimming, then went to a café for breakfast. It's funny how you're always hungry when you've been swimming. After breakfast we went to see the girls. We all sat as usual, drinking tea and smoking cigarettes. Sam called Claire to talk with me about the evening job. She told me it was one of the same jobs we did last week, although at this stage there was only the one job. She said if any more came in she'd book them for the Wednesday, if Wednesday night was good for me. She went on to say it would be the same time as the one last week. This was all good for me and I told her to let Claire know if there were any changes.

A little while later Claire's mobile phone rang. It was a woman called Holly. Claire and Holly had a long conversation. Holly had her own house not that far away, where she lived with her boyfriend of some two years. They'd split up now and he'd gone, leaving her on her own with the bills. Before she'd met this guy, she had been a working girl, in fact that was how she'd met him. Once their relationship started, he had asked her to stop working as he didn't like the idea of her brassing and she'd said yes. All was fine until they just split up, so Holly knew Claire from three or more years ago. She was wondering if Claire could help her get back to work and of course Claire would be happy to do so.

She went off and sat for a while in the bathroom for privacy so they could sort out the details of how Claire would help her. It seemed to go very well. Holly wanted to work straight away, so it was just a matter of sending clients there from the adverts. This meant more adverts had to go out but we would deal with that. A meeting was planned for the next day, we'd go to meet Holly at her house, to check just how suitable it was for working from. Claire wanted me with her so I could meet Holly and also see where the house was.

By now there were phone calls coming in constantly from guys who wanted to see Chantel. In between these, Abbie took a call for Claire.

"This is a man for you."

"Who is it?" Claire whispered.

"Wayne."

"Wayne," said Claire. "Who the fuck is Wayne?"

"I don't know," Abbie replied.

"Hello," Claire said, taking the phone from Abbie.

"Hello, Claire," the voice said.

"It's the monkey man, you know, Wayne, the estate agent." Wayne did like his little silly jokes.

"Oh, hi Wayne."

"I've another flat for you. I think it's ideal for your needs."

"Oh, that's great," said Claire. "And it's a monkey?"

"Well, thereabouts," said Wayne.

"Where is it?"

"It's up along Norwood Road."

"Okay," said Claire, "can we see it tomorrow?"

"Yes," he said. "When?"

"Well, we have another property to look at, so we'll call you as soon as we've finished. Shall we meet at your office?"

"Yes, that'll be great. Just give me as much notice as you can, please."

FOR THE LOVE OF BRASS

"Okay," Claire said, "I'll be with Gary. We'll see you tomorrow."

We left Cobden Road and went over to Claire's flat. I didn't fancy going home but then, what was new? We went to an Indian restaurant over in the Bromley area, then back to a local pub where we just sat together, like a couple of lovebirds, drinking shandy, discussing the new properties and the opportunities they'd bring.

I told Claire, "I'll come over early to your flat and pick you up, if that's okay with you. If Ryan's not about we can jump into bed for a while, then eat and go to Holly's afterwards."

That was the deal and that was exactly what we did. Driving along Portland Road, we passed Cobden Road, carried on into South Norwood Hill, then, not far from Sam and Jess's place, we turned right into Holmesdale Road and Holly's house was just a little way down on the left.

"There it is," Claire said. "The white painted one, okay?"

We parked nearby and walked over to the house. The front garden was about 20ft long, there was no cover of any sort. Just a clear walk up to the front door. We rang the doorbell and Holly answered.

"Oh, hello," she said, "come in."

"This is Gary," Claire said. "He's my boyfriend and partner. He looks after the girls, drives them from A to B when needed and generally looks after our security."

Wow, I thought to myself. I've a job title now and a lot of responsibility, it would seem. I smiled as I looked at Holly. God knows what she thought.

I was quite surprised at what I saw. Holly looked so normal, she was medium height, medium build, short dark hair, probably in her 30s. She wasn't ugly but then, nor was she pretty. She was just a very normal looking person, rather plain, I guess. She didn't stand out in any way, well not like the other girls I'd met. Even so, on spending time sitting with her while we drank tea and smoked, she was a very pleasant woman. One you'd never guess was a working girl. She talked about her ex-boyfriend quite a lot. She obviously missed him, although she said she knew he'd never come back, so she wanted to start working again. Claire told her if she needed a driver at any time she could ask or book me. I understood how the business worked and I was trustworthy and I'd look after her.

Claire asked Holly if it was okay for me to have a look around the place, just to check windows and doors locks and fittings, to check how secure the place was. This I did; it all looked fine to me. I asked her if she was going to work from here on her own. She said no, and that she had a friend who would come in and maid for her.

"Okay," I said. I couldn't see I'd be any use now, so I said to Claire I needed some tobacco and that I'd go to the shops to get some.

"Okay," Claire said.

"Holly," I said, "nice to meet you. Hope to see you soon." I left to give the girls a chance to sort out their financial arrangements. I didn't quite know how it would be sorted out but I was sure Claire would fill me in another time. I was gone about 20 minutes, then walked back and sat in the van smoking.

Claire came out of Holly's by the time I had finished my cigarette. She got into my van.

"That's good," she said. "We should be able to make a fair bit of money out of Holly working from home but we need to get her some business to get her started. It's from this point I think we need you on the firm, Gary, full time. Come on, let's go back to Cobden and see the girls. We need more adverts out there. I'll talk with Abbie when we get back." Claire was talking as I drove. "I've got some blank white cards there. I'll get Abbie to make up the ads for the shop windows. She's good at that, she's done them before. I can let her go early one day so she can put them up in shop windows on her way home and in her area."

"How well will they work?" I asked.

"Oh, really well," Claire said, "We'll get calls from the first day we put them in."

"Really?" I said. "Oh yeah, don't forget, it's summer! Men are always hornier when it's hot."

"Yeah, yeah," I said. "I guess they are."

"Men approach their wives more for sex in the summer, or just when the weather's warm, the randy buggers." Claire laughed as she said this. "And of course the wives refuse. Most wives really ain't into sex with their husbands. It's all too boring for them. They'd rather have a glass of white wine with their friends. Ha-ha-ha." Claire laughed but it's true. "So the husbands come to visit us girls. It's great for us, we know how to work them, so we can make a lot of money if we do it right."

"So most of your clients are married?"

"Oh yes," said Claire. "Definitely. Maybe 80 or 90 per cent are married. That's why, if a client likes a girl and she works the situation right, he'll come and see her time and time again and keep spending his money. They sort of look at it as an affair but with no strings. Some men are naughty and might want two or three affairs at once and they can. That's the service we provide."

"You keep saying we and us," I said. I felt a streak of jealousy coming out of me. "I hope you don't mean we and us literally. You know I don't want you working while we're together. I've told you that before."

"Yes, yes, I know that. Don't be silly. I won't work any more. I have you now, I've no need to. This is why we're setting up the parlours, to make money. Which brings me on to the point of you working with me all or most of the time, us I mean, us working together." She was looking at me, smiling as she said this.

"Okay," I said, "sounds good."

As I pulled up outside Cobden Road, Claire leaned over and gave me a kiss. "Come on," she said. "Let's go have a cuppa. We can talk about this more later."

We got out and, as I was locking the van, I said, "Don't forget, we have the monkey man to see."

Claire laughed. "I won't, I'll phone him when we get in."

When we got in we found Chantel had already seen one client and there was a second booked. Abbie was making the tea as we sat down. Chantel was sitting there with hardly any clothes on, just her little, skimpy bra and G-string which didn't leave anything to the imagination. When she leaned forward to flick the ash from her cigarette into the ashtray on the coffee table, I thought about Claire's job offer. I looked at Claire and Chantel and smiled.

I've had worse jobs, I told myself, but I really couldn't remember when. Abbie came over with the tea and placed the mugs on the table. Claire explained what she wanted her to do.

"The blank cards and felt tip pens are over there in that drawer," she said. She went on to say about the layout and colours of the adverts she thought would look best. I thought the cards were just like any other advert in a shop window: if you're selling something, you want people to see your advert straight away. The girls spoke amongst themselves, saying they figured they'd get a response from each card within an hour. I thought, that's a pretty cheap way to get your business in, when it only costs £1 a week per card and each call is potentially worth £100 a job. Ha-ha-ha, I laughed to myself, happy days. It's way better than the building business.

The extra business that came in would be directed to Holly at her address. Abbie would have the extra work to deal with.

Chantel then told me, "The stick man's coming to see me soon. We'll be testing the ring you fitted to the wall." She laughed, we all laughed.

"This is one weird job you girls have."

"Ha-ha, yeah, never a dull moment."

"Abbie," I said, "you might get to let him look up your skirt."

We all laughed at the thought of that, then Abbie said, all seriousness, "I hope so, I could do with the extra twenty quid." The laughing continued.

"Oh, Claire," I said, "Ring the monkey man, he wants as much notice as possible to show us that flat."

"Good thinking," she said. "I'll call him now." She got up, lit a cigarette and walked to the other end of the kitchen for some privacy. She opened a window and was blowing her smoke out of the room. The doorbell rang and Chantel got up to answer it.

I laughed and, looking at Abbie, I said, "This could be your twenty pounds coming in." We both laughed. "Will you do it again if he asks?"

"Yeah, fucking right," Abbie said. "He don't touch me, he just looks. He can look all he wants for twenty pounds a go." She was highly amused by the prospect.

Chantel came in with the money from her client. "Yes, its him," she said, smiling, to Abbie.

Abbie smiled and said, "I'm taking me fucking tights off." We were all laughing now. Chantel went back into the room. She was gone about 15 minutes, then she came back into the lounge.

"Go on Abbie, you're on," I said jokingly.

"Listen," Chantel said, smiling as she spoke, "I have him handcuffed to the ring on the wall with a pillowcase over his head as a hood. I've a piece of rope tied around his head. It's tied in a knot behind him and it holds his mouth open, so he can talk but not very clearly. He wants you to come into the room and hit him with the cane. I've already hit him a few times but he wants you to hit him as well, while I talk dirty to him."

I sat there with my hand over my mouth and couldn't stop laughing.

"Will he pay me?" Abbie said.

"Yes, of course he will, for each whack you give him, but you have to hit him hard, as hard as you can. Do you want to do it?"

Abbie looked at me, laughing.

"Go on girl," I said. "Give it to him," I said, with my hand still over my mouth.

"Yeah, fuck it," said Abbie. "Let's go."

The girls went into the room, Claire came back and sat down, having finished her phone call to the monkey.

"How did that go?" I asked.

"Yeah, all sorted. We can meet him at his office in an hour."

"Oh, okay that sounds good," I said.

"So what's going on?" Claire asked.

"Well, Abbie's gone in to hit the fellow with a cane."

"Oh yeah?" Claire said, then she started to laugh. "I've got to see this, I'm just having a creep in to see how she does."

The door was left ajar. I heard a whack, then another whack, then another, and all the time Chantel talking dirty to him. With his muffled voice he was saying 'Harder, harder,' each time.

With that, Chantel came in to where I was sitting. "Gary," she said, "Come and hit this bloke. He wants a really hard whack."

I laughed and said, "Are you sure?"

FOR THE LOVE OF BRASS

"Yes," she said, "he'll think it's Abbie hitting him. Come on, we can have a laugh." I went into the room and sure enough, there was a man hooded and handcuffed to the metal ring on the wall. He was bollock naked, with big red welt marks to his back, his buttocks and the top of his legs. I'd seen similar scenes to this with resistance to interrogation in the army. I laughed as I had that thought because the army didn't have lovely half-naked girls interrogating you. Chantel was calling him names.

"You dirty fucker. You're just a piece of shit. We're going to beat you to death." He was groaning with pleasure. Chantel took the stick from Abbie and gave it to me, then said, "Go on, Abbie, hit the fucker." She pointed to the top of his legs and I swung the stick and hit him across the top of his legs. It made a loud cracking sound on impact. "Go on Abbie, hit the bastard again!" She pointed at the same spot and the cane connected with his skin again. He slumped down almost on his knees but he couldn't quite reach the floor, so he just hung there by his wrists, the handcuffs digging into him. He was still groaning with pleasure. Chantel looked at me and indicated that was enough and took the stick from me. I left the room, and went and sat down with Abbie and Claire. We were all giggling.

"How could anybody like that?" I said. "He must be fucking mad!"

"No," Claire said "They love it. He would have got his rocks off with that."

"Really?" I said.

"Oh, yeah." Claire lit a cigarette. I kept looking at Abbie, we were both smiling. We couldn't believe what had just happened. Claire said, "Oh, it happens all the time. Well, you both made a good job of that." She laughed as she said, "He'll be back to see you both again, Ha-ha-ha." Abbie and I found the situation very funny and quite surreal.

Chantel came into our room and said, "I've got him down. He had a great time. He loved it but he's bleeding a bit from his welts. I want to take him through to the bathroom and clean him up a bit.

Abbie said, "Is he okay?" sounding all concerned.

"Yeah, yeah. He's fine, just wants cleaning up a bit before we send him on his way."

"Gary," she said, "can you hide somewhere so he doesn't see you when I bring him through?"

"Yes, of course I can."

"Just give me ten or fifteen minutes, then I can send him on his way."

I grabbed my tobacco and went out into the back yard to wait there and have a cigarette. I finished and came back inside. Chantel was still cleaning him up in the bathroom.

Claire said, smiling, "Don't worry, she'll let us know when she brings him through so you can hide again."

The call came from Chantel. "Okay," she said, "we want to come through." I jumped up and instead of heading towards the back yard because they'd be coming from that end of the kitchen, I went out to the hall. The first place I thought I'd go and wait was in the large storage cupboard. I'll just stand in there until they've passed, I thought. I turned the catch on the cupboard door, pulled it open and jumped. I had the fright of my life. I pushed the door shut quick and turned the catch. Where the fuck should I go? I couldn't think clearly. Bedroom, go into the room I told myself. This I did and with the door ajar I heard Chantel and the stick man go past to the front door. She let him out and as she walked back towards me, I opened the door laughing.

"Chantel," I said, "Who the fuck is that in the cupboard?"

"OH SHIT!" She said. "I forgot about him with all the excitement going on."

FOR THE LOVE OF BRASS

We walked back into the lounge. I looked at Claire and said, "Did you know there's a man in the cupboard?"

"Yes, she said." "We weren't going to tell you." All three girls were laughing now.

"He frightened the shit out of me and on top of that, he ain't got any clothes on. He's just standing there with a carrier bag." The girls were really laughing now. "What the fuck is a naked man doing in the cupboard?" I said. They could hardly talk for laughing.

"We thought you might not understand."

"Are you kidding me?" I said. "After the stick man, a man in the cupboard's fuck all!" They were holding their, stomachs with tears rolling down their faces, they were laughing so much. "Come on, tell me now. What's he doing in there?"

When they eventually composed themselves, Chantel said, "It's the man from this morning. He was the first client today. He's not got a carrier bag. Well, yes, he has actually," she said smiling. Abbie was crying while listening to this. "He'll be in there for a couple more hours."

"Why?" I said.

"Well," Chantel said, "the carrier bag is tied to his balls and inside the carrier bag there are tins of baked beans."

"Bollocks!" I said.

"No," said Chantel, "beans!" That was it, now all three girls were crying with laughter.

"Oh, I'm putting the kettle on. I can't get any sense out of you lot while you're all laughing like this."

It turns out the client liked this sort of thing. He got Chantel to tie string around his balls, then she tied that to a carrier bag. Inside the bag were tins of beans, soup and that sort of thing, making the bag heavier, so

293

once he stood up the weight of the bag caused him pain and this he liked. Because it would go on for a long time, they put him in the cupboard and he would just stand quietly in the dark on his own with his pain, that was it. The only changes he would make or could make, would be to add or subtract the various tins depending on the pain level he wanted. For this service, Chantel would be paid £150. Once his time was up, she'd untie the bag and his balls, then he'd then get dressed and leave. He had to come to a place like this because surprisingly enough, his wife didn't understand. Ha-ha-ha, I wonder why?

Chantel said, "Abbie this is for you," and gave her a £50 note. "It's from the stick man. He said when you hit him it really hurt so much but he loved it. He'll be coming back for more."

"There you go," Claire said, "see, they love it."

Abbie looked at me. "Gary," she said.

"No, no, no, you keep it. You earned it." We all smiled, "That's better than a little look up your skirt ain't it?" I said.

"He can come back whenever he likes," said Abbie.

"Well," I said. "We need to go to meet the monkey man."

"Yes, you're right Gary. We should be going."

We jumped in the van and drove the short distance to the estate agent's office. We parked in a side street. On meeting him, he was keen to go in his car, which we did. Monkey Wayne drove us over to Norwood Road then along it towards Brockwell Park. We were in the Herne Hill area and as we got near the park there were some shops on our left. At the junction of Trinity Rise he parked near the shops. He wanted to get himself a drink. He was always drinking Coke or root beer. He'd drink two or three of them each time we were with him. No wonder he was a short, fat fellow. He had the face of a weasel. I smiled to myself as I thought this;

in other words, a proper estate agent.

"Whereabouts is the flat from here then, monkey?"

"Just over the road there." He pointed to the houses opposite. "Give me a minute and I'll be with you," he said in his best London accent.

"Okay, no rush," I said.

Claire turned to me as he went into the shop. "I get the impression you don't like him much." Then she laughed.

"No, I don't really but that doesn't matter; he serves his purpose in life."

"Come on," he said as he came out the shop with a can of root beer in his hand. "It's only over there. We can leave my car here." So over we went.

The houses here were all in a good state of repair. He pointed at the one he was going to show us and we went up a few steps onto the path. The front garden was raised about 3ft, as indeed were all the gardens on this side of the road. There were bushes to one side of the path, which belonged to the house next door. We carried on along the path to a side door which was handy.

"A bit of privacy for the clients," I said to Claire.

"Yeah," she said as we went in. It was a converted house with three floors, so a one-bed flat on each floor. Our one was the ground floor. The monkey man had done us proud, lounge room to the front, bedroom in the middle then out to the kitchen and bathroom, which was a little small. It just had a shower toilet and sink in there but that's all you need. It was nice, very nice and fully furnished.

"Lovely and clean," Claire said. "I like." She looked at him and smiled. "Go on then, how much?"

"A monkey a month." He laughed. "By the way, good news is the deposit is only four hundred. The monkey is all in. Just pay your own bills."

"Yes, okay," Claire said.

"Lovely," he said as he took another swig of his drink. "I knew you'd take it. It's ideal for you."

"Yes, you've done well. Thank you very much. Same as before? Can we pop in your office and tie this up tomorrow morning some time?"

"Yes, of course," he said. "It's a three monthly contact, same as before. Sign for it, pay the month's rent and the four Dep. and you have the keys, it's all yours.

We left, locked the property up and walked on to his car. He drove us back to the office, just exchanging small talk as we went, then brought up the subject of his bonus.

Claire laughed and said, "Yes, you like Chantel, don't you?"

"Oh yes," he said, "she's lovely."

"Okay, make yourself an appointment, then come and see her. She'll make your toes curl up." He laughed, you could see the anticipation on his face, love him.

As we left Monkey, Claire said, "I'll get the money from the bank and we'll see you tomorrow."

"Great," he said. "See you both then."

I nodded at him and as we walked to the van I said to Claire, "He likes a bit of cash. He must have some deal with the property owners where he gets a kickback."

"Oh yeah," Claire said. "I'm sure he does. Come on, let's go back to Cobden. We can have a cuppa. I want to phone a friend of mine, Maria, to see if she is in. If so we can go and see her, she only lives over in Dulwich."

"Okay, then."

CHAPTER TWELVE
ANAL SPECIALIST

"Do you have to go home this evening?" Claire asked.

"No, not really. Why? What you got in mind and let me see what I can sort out, I'll let you know."

She looked at me and said with a sexy smile, "You'll like it."

I smiled and said, "Sounds good."

We walked into the lounge. "Hello, girls," I said. Abbie still had the biggest smile on her face. I looked at her and said, "Has that man come out of the closet yet?"

She laughed. "Yeah, he's gone now."

Chantel said, "We weren't sure how you would take it, so we thought we'd keep it quiet."

"That's okay, just tell me next time. It frightened the shit out of me." We were all smiling.

Claire got on the phone to her friend while we all sat drinking tea and smoking, and talking and laughing about all the things that had taken place that day. Claire told the girls about the new flat over at Brockwell Park and that she'd taken it on. She was just waiting for her friend Maria to call back. With that, her mobile rang.

"Hello, Maria," Claire said. In a few minutes, she'd sorted out the details. "Okay," she said, "we can go now to Dulwich." So off we went.

On the drive over she said, "We'll meet Maria, probably go and have a drink, then later get something to eat and go back and stay at my flat."

"Okay," I said, "but I don't have a change of clothes."

"Don't worry about that. We can buy you some tomorrow."

"Okay," I smiled. "I was going to suggest we went swimming in the morning."

"Yes, that's a good idea," Claire said.

"I don't have anything to swim in."

"Well, that's okay. If we're going shopping for clothes first we'll buy you some trunks. I want to pick them out for you."

"Do you? Why's that?" I said.

"Because I'll pick you a pair of those small Speedos, ha-ha-ha. You can show off your lunch box." We both laughed.

"Well, we'll see about that," I said.

We were going to Maria's address. She lived in Melford Road near the junction with Lordship Lane. Claire said there was a pub nearby we could go to. A nice big old pub called The Grove on a corner.

"I know that pub," I said. "Yes, it's a nice place."

We pulled into Maria's road. Parking wasn't that easy but we eventually found somewhere to park the van. We walked back to the house.

"This is it," Claire said.

"This looks nice," I replied.

It was a London house, one of those ones where you can't see the roof, just a parapet wall along the top of the roof line, with at least three bedrooms. You could tell that just by looking at the layout of the front. Probably built in the late 1900s. It looked very nice and with the area it was in, would have been a very sought-after property. We knocked on the big iron knocker and the door opened.

"Hello, Babe," said Maria, "how are you?" She spoke as though they were long lost sisters. They gave each other a hug. I just stood there, thinking I wish I knew you better, I'd love one of those hugs. Maria was stunning, she looked at me.

Claire said, "This is, Gary, my boyfriend, ain't he lovely?"

Maria said, "Hello, love." Then my wish came true as she leaned over and gave me a big kiss and a hug. I had the biggest smile on my face. Temporarily, I felt a bit weak at the knees but soon got my composure back and carried on.

"Hello, Maria. Yeah, lovely to meet you."

"Come on in," she said.

Let me tell you about Maria's appearance. She'd long black hair with bluey-green eyes, she stood about 5ft 10in tall with her shoes on and had a medium build, with quite large breasts and a sun tan. Her age was approximately 25 and she dressed as though she had a million dollars. On entering her house, the interior confirmed it. She really was a particularly beautiful woman, stunning I'd say. She carried herself beautifully, walking like a model. In fact, to sum her up, she looked like one of those models off of the TV. One who should be advertising the latest perfume from Paris.

We went through to her kitchen.

"Tea or coffee?" she said in her broad Manchester accent.

"You're from Manchester?" I enquired.

"Yes," she said, "I grew up there. I came down to the smoke for work when I was eighteen. Been here eight years now and don't intend going back." I could smell the coffee was already percolating.

"Yes, thanks, coffee will be great," Claire agreed.

We three sat drinking coffee and smoking. The girls were doing most of the talking. Claire was telling Maria how she'd taken on this new flat over by Brockwell Park.

Claire said, "It'll be ideal for you to work from."

I coughed on my coffee a bit and my jaw dropped open as I listened. I couldn't believe what I was hearing. Maria was a working girl. She must earn a fortune, I thought to myself. Well, yeah, as I looked around her house and at her.

I waited for the time to be right, then I then said, "Maria, do you drive?"

"Yes," she said, "I have a Porsche but I don't use it much. I tend to use cabs a lot; it saves me the trouble of trying to park."

"Oh," said Claire, "that brings me to a point. Gary here, as well as being my man, he's also a bodyguard. He looks after me and drives the girls and minds them. So when you need a driver, just talk to me or Gary and he'll be up for it."

WOW, I thought, drive Maria around to jobs. I'd drive her for nothing. No, no, don't be silly, I told myself. Of course I have to be paid. It's business after all and what a business to be in! I knew I'd love this job.

We never did get over to The Grove but I didn't mind. I was happy sitting here listening to these two beauties having their conversation.

We left Maria's about 9.30, then headed over to Claire's area. I was quite happy Maria was on the books. She'd start working out of the Brockwell Park flat at the beginning of next week.

We were both a bit hungry, so we stopped on the way and bought a chicken kebab. As we sat in the van eating, I brought up the subject of our new girl, Maria.

I said, "She must make a lot of money from her work because from her house and car it looks like she's worth a fortune."

"Oh, she is," said Claire. "She's an anal specialist."

"A what?"

FOR THE LOVE OF BRASS

"An anal specialist."

I laughed, "Oh yeah, and what's that, exactly?"

"Well, anything to do with anal sex."

"Wow, really? I would never have expected you to say that. I would never have thought she was on the game, let alone an anal specialist. I've not even heard of one."

Claire went on to say, "There's a lot of money in that side of the business, especially working with the Arabs. She has clients who pay her three to five or even six thousand pounds a night."

"Wow! Holy shit, Batman, I can't believe it."

"Well, it's true," Claire said, "but never mind all that, I have something to say. I know you want to work with me, so what I'm going to ask is this, you earn about five hundred pounds a week from your building business."

"Yes, that's right," I said.

"Now, I know from time to time you have to pop out to the jobs or sometimes have to go and look at jobs and of course on a Friday you do your banking and pay your staff."

"Yes," I said. "Well, if you could spend the rest of your time with me, driving me or popping around to the parlours doing what's needed, or we both go to the parlours or whatever, I'll pay you five hundred pounds a week Monday to Friday. Then evenings and weekends, you'll make more money from driving and minding the girls, or just taking us out as our minder. You'll be on well over a grand a week. How do you feel about that?"

"I feel great about that," I said. "So basically carry on doing what I've been doing so far since knowing you."

"Yes, that's right," said Claire.

"Ha-ha," I laughed. "Yes," I said, "You have a deal."

FOR THE LOVE OF BRASS

Claire was very happy with the prospect of having me on the books, so much so that she then said, "Get in the back and take your jeans off. I want to give you one."

"Oh," I smiled and raised my eyebrows, "what's a man supposed to do!"

After cleaning the steam off the windows, we went on our way, over to Claire's flat. I asked if Maria had a maid. Claire said she always worked with somebody and she'd probably have someone already but if not she'd find her someone. We sat in Claire's kitchen drinking vodka and orange and smoking till it was time for bed. Ryan was nowhere to be seen, which I thought was a good thing. I could always relax and cuddle up with Claire, more so when he wasn't around.

The morning came as did we both. We got ready, Claire sorted her swim bag and off we went to the pool at Beckenham. Before going in we walked along the little high street looking for some clothes. I bought a T-shirt and some underpants and Claire found the little Speedo trunks and bought them for me. I felt a bit silly wearing them because I was used to wearing shorts to swim in but if she liked them, that was enough for me. We spent an hour or so in the baths, joking as we got dressed.

I said, "You haven't got any taller. You still can't see over the door. Come on short arse, let's go."

Off we drove to Cobden Road to see Abbie and Chantel. Claire talked with Sam; of course, I'd be seeing her that night. Sam said there were no more jobs tonight, just that one, which was okay, we were going anyway. She said to tell me around 9 o'clock was okay. We could have a drink, then go; we were only going to Deptford and it wouldn't take long to get there at that time in the evening. Claire went on to tell the girls about Maria and that she was starting next week.

FOR THE LOVE OF BRASS

It was about this time I started to think about my new job offer and working with these women most of the time. The girls were great, I have to say, they were all good-looking and had a pleasant nature. They all seemed to be very nice, friendly people, and they certainly worked hard and put the hours in at what they did. When it was playtime they played pretty hard as well, in fact I thought their whole life was pretty full on.

I also thought a lot about Claire and my relationship with her. I was spending most of my time with her every day. I just loved being with her. Her company made me a very happy man and with being around these other lovely women, I'd have thought almost any man would love my job. I found I quite fancied all the girls I was with each day and really liked them but for me the special one was Claire. I was in love with her totally.

Let me explain how I saw the situation. I have a bank account, an emotional bank account in which I store all my feeling and emotions as far as relationships with women are concerned. There were no deposits in the Sharon account and hadn't been for some time, they'd long since been withdrawn. I found I'd deposited my whole emotional balance into Claire's account. She didn't ask for it, I'd just done it. I didn't even know when it had happened but it had happened. So my account was empty. Spending time working with these lovely, beautiful women was great and I loved all the attention I received when I was out with them, but it didn't matter to me how lovely they were, I only had eyes for Claire and I'd not do anything to compromise that. I was protecting my investment in her and because it was complete and everything was invested; it had to be looked after and managed properly so my account didn't collapse. After all, no one wants to be bankrupt.

Chantel would be kept busy with clients until 7 o'clock; in the meantime we drank tea and smoked. I went out to a Wimpy bar and returned with a bag full of food for the four of us. Once Chantel had seen her last client out, she went into the bathroom to get herself ready and we all went over to the pub. Little Lee was already in there standing at the bar. He'd only drunk half of his pint, so he'd not been there long. We all greeted him and Chantel insisted she got the drinks in. We took up residence at our usual table. I noticed Mr Brown had already taken up his residence at the end of the bar.

"Okay," Abbie said quietly. "Who fancies some whizz? I'll go see our friendly dealer." This she did and £10 lighter, she sat back at the table. The little bag was opened and passed around under the table. There, appropriately licked finger tips were inserted as it went by. I gave it a miss.

"No thanks," I said, not just because I didn't like it but I knew I was going out to work with Sam in a while. I was only drinking shandies as it was. I wasn't having any whizz, even if Abbie tried to put some in my pint. I'd say that, within ten minutes, the four of them had even more to say to each other. The whizz was working.

When it was time for me to leave, Claire kissed me and said, "See you later."

On arriving at Sam's flat, she informed me another job had come in since we spoke last.

"So if you don't mind," she said.

"No, that's fine with me. Where is it?" I asked as I lit up a cigarette to have with the coffee Jess had made us.

"It's in Surrey docks," she said. "Do you know that area?"

I smiled. "Yes, I do," I said, "It's next to Deptford."

"Great," she said. "I have the address written down."

"Yeah, great," I said. "So, what you up to, Jess?" I asked.

"Nothing now," she replied. "I'm going to have a nice bath and relax while you guys are out."

"Oh, okay. How are you finding it here, you know, working from this flat?"

"Yeah, really good. Better than working in the Crystal Palace area."

"That's good," I said.

"We'll probably move in here soon, it's a lovely flat, don't you think?"

"Oh yeah, definitely," I said.

Sam finished getting her visiting bag ready. "Okay," she said, "we can go."

"Okay, see you later, Jess." We left.

While driving over to Deptford, I told Sam about the man in the cupboard.

She thought that story was great, then said, "It's quite common for men to want to do that sort of thing to themselves. We do a fair bit of S and M stuff ourselves. It's surprising some of the things people like and are happy to pay a lot of money for."

I parked the car opposite the address, so I could see the house. I felt I knew it well; after all, I'd been here before.

"Okay," Sam said, "one hour from now."

"Okay," I said and checked my watch. Three minutes to ten. Sam walked over to the house and knocked. I watched her go in. Okay, I said to myself, smoke time. I sat there rolling myself a cigarette, then lit it up and, with the window open, I sat there puffing smoke. I looked around. I wonder if there are any foxes here? I bet there are, I answered myself. It's just a question of whether I see one or not.

The time passed; there wasn't much to look at. I sat there, rolled another cigarette, then puffed that out of the window. It was 10.45 as I checked my watch. That's it, I thought as I sat up from my slouched

305

position. Surrey docks here we come.

Still no Sam. I checked my watch, four minutes to eleven. I waited, still no Sam. I checked again, 11 o'clock, that's it. I got out of the van and walked over, expecting to see Sam open the door at any moment, but that didn't happen. I got to the client's door and knocked on it loudly. I put my ear closer to it. I could hear muffled sounds along with a man's voice. My instinct told me, there is something wrong, so I stepped back, raising my right leg and gave the front door one almighty kick just below where the Yale lock was situated. The wooden frame on the inside split and the door flew open really quick. So quick, it hit the wall inside and tried to bounce back shut. In that split second I saw Sam in the hall, struggling. A man was behind her with his right arm around her neck, holding her from behind, trying to pull her into the first room on the left. She was only 6ft from me. I took the two paces in and with my left hand, pushed her head to one side. Then with my right hand, with all the strength I could gather, I punched him in the face.

My knuckles connected with his jaw and he let go of Sam's neck as he flew backwards and fell over, his head hitting the floor. I pulled Sam towards me and turned. The front door had swung nearly shut. I pulled Sam past me with my right hand and with my left hand I pulled the door back open, then pushed Sam through it. As I did this, I saw what I thought was a gun standing in the corner behind the door. An umbrella had stood there as well but that had fallen onto the floor. I glanced back quickly; the man was trying to get up but was in a dazed condition. Not knowing how long that might last, it flashed through my mind, what if he fires at us when we leave?

I reached down the side of the door and picked up the gun. It was a sawn off shotgun, just the barrels had been cut so it still had its full stock.

FOR THE LOVE OF BRASS

I swung it round, pointing it at the man. I slid the release bar over but the gun didn't open because the barrels were short; it didn't have the weight to open on its own. I held the bar with the thumb of my right hand and hit the barrels down with my left. The gun opened and I could see through both barrels, not loaded. Thank fuck for that, I thought to myself, but now I had his gun I wasn't going to give it to him back. I pulled the barrels up to the closed position, by which time he'd stood up. I held the gun out, pointing it in his direction. My arm was outstretched, with the gun pointing directly towards his face. He made no attempt to move towards me, in fact he moved backwards away from me, putting his hands up to cover his face as though I was going to shoot him. Surely he must know the gun's not loaded, it's his gun.

He backed off anyway, then, with the most serious, aggressive and determined voice I could muster said to him, "If you so much as come near one of my girls again, I'll load this fucking gun and shoot you in the fucking face. Do you understand? I know where you live, I know your phone number and I know who the fuck you are. I've even got your fucking gun. Fuck with any of my girls again and I'll blow your fucking head off, have you got that?"

"Yes, yes, please don't shoot me," he shouted as he backed off down the hallway.

"Fuck you!" I replied.

Time to go, I told myself, and turned and stepped out, trying to pull the door shut behind me.

Sam was over by the van. I held the shotgun down against my leg to try and disguise the fact I was carrying it. It made me walk as though I had a limp. Sam got in and I walked round to my side of the van, looking back towards his house as I went. He didn't come out. I got into the van quick, threw the gun in the back, started the engine and drove off as though nothing had happened.

"You alright, Sam?"

"Yeah, yeah, I think so."

"Are you alright?" I said again. "Did he hurt you in any way?"

"No, No. Just frightened the fuck out of me."

We got about 500yds down the road, I pulled up and jumped out. I opened the back doors and hid the gun under some dust sheets. The last thing I needed was the Old Bill seeing it if for some reason we got a pull.

I got back in and asked again, "You sure you're okay?"

"Yes, yes," she said. "I am."

"Ok, we're safe now we're away from there," I said.

"Yeah, I'm still a bit shaken. Fuck that!" Sam said.

"You're okay, that's the main thing. What happened, what caused that to kick off?" I asked.

"He said I owed him time."

"What does that mean?" I said.

"Well, the last time I went to see him I finished early, or more to the point he did. Then once he was finished, I got ready and left, as you remember."

"Yes, yes," I said. "So as I was leaving this time he said I owed him 20 or 30 minutes and he decided I wasn't going. When I said I was, he grabbed me, walking down the hallway. He grabbed me from behind and said I should stay and play with him some more. Luckily, just as it was about to become serious, you came crashing in and saved me, ha-ha." She laughed as she said this, then leaned over and gave me a big kiss. "Thank you so much, Gary, you rescued me."

"Oh," I said, "Where are we going next?"

FOR THE LOVE OF BRASS

Sam looked at me. "Are you having a laugh? We're going home. I need a drink. I want to tell Jess how you saved me from a nutter, ha-ha-ha."

"So what about your other job?"

"Oh, I'll call him and say I had a problem. He'll be alright, don't worry about that. I'll sort him out next time." Sam lit two cigarettes and gave one to me.

"Thanks," I said.

Sam called Jess and started to tell her the story, making me out to be the big hero. When we arrived back at Sam's place, Sam and Jess greeted each other with big hugs and kisses. Jess started to cry as she heard the story again. Sam asked Jess to make her a very large Vodka. I put the kettle on for a cuppa and, while the kettle was boiling, I went back out to the van and returned with the shotgun, wrapped in a dust sheet.

"I'll need to leave this here for tonight, girls. I'll take it away tomorrow."

Sam said, "That's okay, Gary, stick it in the airing cupboard."

She was telling Jess the story. She said, "The best bit for me was when I was outside looking in through the half open door. I could see Gary standing there pointing a gun at the bloke and threatening to blow his head off if he came near me again. Gary," she said, "I didn't know you carried a gun."

"I don't, I got it from his house. It was in the hallway behind the door. It's mine now and I'm keeping it. I don't think he can report it to the police because the barrels are way too short. He won't have it on a license, so that's it. He's lost it."

Sam and Jess were incredibly grateful that I was there to save her. Sam paid me for my evening's work, then gave me a £50 note on top, as a tip. I asked if I could phone Claire to see where she was.

"Yes, of course," Sam said. I called. They were all still in the pub. They'd been joined by Ryan and little Lee. I arranged to meet Claire at her flat, as Ryan would give lifts to anybody who needed one. Chantel and Lee would go to Lee's place, then Ryan would take Claire home. She said it would probably be an hour before she was back. I told her I'd wait at Sam's for a while then make my way over. I decided not to mention our evening's adventure at this point. I asked the girls if I could wait there for a while, then head over to Claire's. They were pleased to have me there. We talked the event over a number of times, laughing as we did so. Sam said from now on she wanted me as her bodyguard.

I said jokingly as I left, "You can't afford me. Goodnight, girls, see you both tomorrow."

I drove over to Claire's but while I was driving, Sam had called Claire and told her of the night's events. By the time I arrived, Claire knew the whole story and as I walked into the flat, she said, "Come on, we're having a drink to celebrate." She opened a bottle of wine.

"Where's Ryan?" I asked.

"Not here," said Claire. I smiled to myself, that's good, I thought.

"Yes, okay then, let's celebrate."

As we were drinking and smoking we talked and laughed about the evening's events. They'd all had a good evening at the pub. Claire also said that the copper had been in to see Chantel and they'd had a very busy day at work. Mr Brown had supplied them once or twice more with the little plastic bags and all in all they had had a bloody good evening. It was at least 2.30 and I'd had enough wine; it was time for bed. We had a lot of cuddling to do.

In the morning after our normal routine, I headed off home for a couple of hours, saying that as soon as I was done there I'd be back to meet her at Cobden. This agreed, off I went. It was about 11.30 as I came

FOR THE LOVE OF BRASS

back along Portland Road and as I approached the junction with Cobden Road, I saw two men sitting outside our pub on the corner. Is it, is it? I said to myself as I turned into Cobden. It's Mr Brown and the copper who visits, sitting together. I'd seen them talk before in the pub but seeing them today, well, they looked like mates sitting there. There was only one glass on the table, so one of them had not been there long, or was about to go.

I wonder what those two are up to? I thought to myself as I found a parking space and pulled up. I just kept thinking about the odd partnership; maybe Mr Brown was a grass, a police informant maybe, and in return, he was allowed to carry on his trade unhindered. Who knows?

I rang the bell and Chantel answered in her working uniform as usual. This time she was all in pink, not that I noticed. I walked into the lounge and Claire jumped up and gave me a hug and a kiss.

"Hello, everybody," I said.

Abbie had a big smile on her face, even little Lee was there. He'd heard I had a gun and wanted to know if he could see it and play with it. I told him no because I didn't have it with me. They all wanted to talk about what had happened. The story had definitely gone around, no doubt my reputation had preceded me in this case.

I just said, "It was nothing!" just like I did it every day, ha-ha.

We were drinking tea, coffee and smoking. Chantel said, "Gary, that copper was in again yesterday."

"Yeah, I know," I said. "Claire told me."

"He still says he wants to look after me."

Little Lee piped up, "Yeah, the wanker. I think he's after my bird."

Chantel just looked at me as if I could help the situation.

"Does he still want a freebie each time he comes in here?"

"Yes," she said, "he does. I've fucking had enough of him."

"So have I," said Lee.

Chantel continued, "I feel like ringing up the nick and reporting the bastard."

"No, no," I said. "Don't do that, not yet anyway. We'll see what happens when we see him next in the pub. Maybe the opportunity will come up and I'll be able talk to him."

"Okay," she said, then she laughed. "I want you to rescue me like you did Sam." Then we all laughed.

"I'll see what I can do, ha-ha."

Abbie had come to work with the ingredients for a Chilli con carne and she was up at the sink preparing it in between answering the phone calls.

"Okay," said little Lee, "I have to go now. Got to look at a little job over in Clapham, then see a man about a dog," (which basically meant he was going to have a beer with somebody later).

"That's good," shouted Abbie, "'cos there's only enough food for the four of us anyway," laughing as she said it.

"See you later," said Lee, "and if I can, I'd like to see that gun."

"Okay, mate," I said. "I'll keep that in mind. See you later."

The phone rang. "Claire," Abbie said, "it's Sam, for you."

Claire had a conversation for a few minutes. She looked over at me, "Do you want to have a drink tonight? All of us. Sam and Jess want to come over."

"Yes," I said, "that will be good. Oh, can I talk to Sam for a minute?"

"Yes," said Claire and handed me the phone.

I asked Sam if the new toy was okay at her flat for the next few days (meaning the shotgun). "As long as you don't mind? That's great. I'll take it away in a few days."

"Yes, that's fine," Sam said.

Claire had a massive smile on her face and Abbie and Chantel were both up for it. We were going out again. Wow, I thought, these girls certainly know how to party.

CHAPTER THIRTEEN
LETTSBE AVENUE

Chantel saw her last client out, disappeared into the bathroom and, in no time at all, came out looking stunning. We all had a freshen up, then over to the pub we went. As always, Chantel insisted she got the first round in, which she did. I stood with her to help carry the drinks back. The pub was only half full at this stage. Mr Brown was at his normal spot at the end of the bar and each time I looked in his direction he was looking at Abbie and Claire. Waiting to relieve Abbie of another tenner perhaps, which I was sure he would do quite soon.

While standing there with Chantel, I couldn't help noticing all the attention she got from the men in there. Mind you, saying that, it was just the same if I stood there with any one of the girls. I mentioned this to Chantel as we were getting served.

"I notice in here you girls don't get pestered by men."

"No," she said, "that's right. It's nice and we like it. After working all day, it's the last thing we want when we're out! We just want to enjoy ourselves. We put the word around that you were our bodyguard and didn't take any shit, so if one of them men wanted to talk to us, they'd have to ask permission from you first."

"Oh really? I didn't know that. Ha-ha." We laughed. "It looks like my reputation has already preceded me."

"Yes," she said, "of course, and that's what we want. Come on, let's take the drinks over."

FOR THE LOVE OF BRASS

Claire had a call on her mobile and within 20 minutes, in came Sam and Jess, both looking as lovely as ever. They were served straight away and were soon sitting with us. With a few extra chairs we all fitted around the table, our usual table, and with me sitting in a position where I could see everything going on in the pub.

Claire said, "I fancy a change. Abbie, if I give you the money, can you get some Charlie from Mr Brown. My treat, I'll pay."

"Okay," said Abbie. Claire gave her a £20 note and she went over to see Mr. Brown. They had a little chat and Abbie came back with nothing.

"Said he wants thirty pounds for a wrap."

I thought to myself, okay let's see what my rep is like in here. I stood up and beckoned him over, over he came.

"You know who I am?"

"Yes," he said.

"These are my girls to look after, so I'm looking after them. They'll buy a fair bit of gear from you so don't take the piss. How much is a wrap?"

He looked at me and said, after a short hesitation, "Twenty pounds a wrap to your girls."

"Thank you." We shook hands.

With five girls having a dip, it wasn't long before another £20 was invested with Mr. Brown. I had a feeling this night was going to be a wild one. The music was great as always. KWS, 'Please don't go'. The Pasadenas, 'I'm doing fine now'. Felix, 'Don't you want my love. Kym Sims, 'Too blind to see it'. All the great tunes of the day.

By the time the second wrap had seen its last wet finger, three of the girls were up dancing. The pub was busy, everyone was having a good time.

Chantel leaned over and said, "He's here, he's in here again."

"Who, the copper?"

"Yes," she said, "The copper. I've been keeping an eye on him. He's had a chat with Mr Brown a couple of times, then with me. He caught me coming out of the toilets and gave me this." She opened her hand, it was another wrap of Charlie.

"He gave you that?"

"Yes," she said.

"Okay, thanks for telling me."

Then it was my turn to go to the bar and get the drinks. Abbie came with me, singing as we went. I ordered the drinks and as I was getting served, a man squeezed and pushed his way in next to me. I looked to see who it was, the copper.

"Hello, Gary," he said, "let me buy you a drink."

"No thanks," I said, "I'm in a round with my people."

"Your girls, you mean," he said.

"Yes, that's right," I said.

"I'd like to chat with you, somewhere not so noisy. Can we talk outside after you have got the drinks in?"

"Yeah, okay," I said. "I'll give you the nod when I get this order back to the table."

"Okay," he said, "great. I'll wait by the door."

Two trips from the bar later, all the drinks were on the table. Don't know where Abbie had gone but she wasn't at the bar or table. Claire had been watching us at the bar.

"What did he want?" she said.

"He wants to talk to me outside. I'll roll a cigarette to take with me, then go see what he wants."

FOR THE LOVE OF BRASS

I turned towards the door. He was looking over. I nodded, then walked in his direction through the people. Once we were outside we stood where there were no people immediately around us.

"What can I do for you?" I said.

"This is how it is, Gary."

"Whoa, whoa mate, you know my name. Who are you?"

"I'm John."

"Oh yeah?" I said.

"Yes, I am, and I'm the local Old Bill, from this manor."

"Oh yeah," I said again. "Show me your ID."

With that he flipped open his warrant card. I saw the Met Police badge, along with his name, John Letts, Detective Constable.

"Okay, John, what can I do for you?"

"Well, I keep an eye on all the criminal activity in the manor and there ain't much that goes on that I don't know about. This is where you come into it. Now I know you're their bodyguard, minder, security officer (he laughed), or whatever you call yourself, and I know Claire has two parlours."

"Two parlours," I said.

"Yes, this one here," he pointed along the road, "and the one where Sam and Jess work from, South Norwood Hill."

"Oh yeah, and how do you know that? Have you been there as well?"

"No," said John, "but my colleague has, so I know for a fact that they both work. This is what I want from you. If Claire wants to carry on working out of these addresses, I want £200 a week from each parlour, so £400 a week and I want to deal only with you."

"Hold on," I said. "Are you fucking joking, what the fuck are we likely to get in return?"

"What you get is my protection. I'll look after your parlours. For instance, if you were about to get turned over for drugs or any other reasons, I'd make sure you know about it in advance. If not, I can make sure you get a spin for drugs every week and nick you all for running a brothel and, in time, close you down."

"Oh yeah," I said.

"Yeah," said John, "and you know I can do it, so I want you to talk with Claire and get it sorted. Then, from the end of this week I want four hundred quid in Nelsons and four hundred every week from then on. You can carry on trading in peace."

"Okay," I said as I took my last puff of my fag, then flicked the dog-end into the kerb. "I'll pass your message on. Where do I find you?"

"I'm in here a lot. You'll find me in this pub."

We both walked back into the pub. I approached the table with a smile on my face.

Claire said, "Well?"

I sat down next to her and said, "He wants to be on the firm and be our protection from the law."

"I fucking knew it, the cheeky Bastard. How much?"

"Four hundred a week for the two parlours." I smiled. "This could be a big benefit to us. We can talk about it tomorrow. It'll work out alright, don't worry. Fuck it, come on drink up, we're having a good time tonight," I said as I looked up at Abbie standing on her chair, singing and waving her arms in the air.

Sam said, "Come with me, please, to help with the drinks."

"Okay," and off we went to the bar.

As I was waiting, I could see Claire talking with Jess and Chantel. I figured she must be telling them about our new employee. Abbie jumped

FOR THE LOVE OF BRASS

down to go and invest another £20. The girls were all having great fun enjoying getting off their trolleys. I just kept drinking and getting fairly pissed myself. I didn't see Detective Constable John any more that evening.

When it was throwing out time, we were all outside on the pavement, giving each other a goodnight kiss. Sam, Jess an Abbie got in a black cab and we said our drunken goodbyes. Chantel wobbled up the road to Lee's while we waited for Ryan to pull up and take us home. I had the same problem as before, trying to roll a cigarette when you're drunk is quite a difficult thing to do. Claire was sitting back on the back seat, smoking her spliff and smiling all the way home. Ryan could see her in his mirror.

"What are you smiling about?" said Ryan.

"Oh," said Claire. "We have a new employee." Then she laughed.

"I don't get it," Ryan said.

"Don't worry," she said. "I'll tell you tomorrow or another time."

We found ourselves in Claire's kitchen. Claire was making coffee for us.

"Where's Ryan?" I said.

"He's gone out," Claire said.

I smiled and looked at her. "You wait till I get you in bed," I said.

She laughed. "Oh yeah, what you gonna do? Here," she said, "have a puff of this spliff." After three puffs, I don't even remember drinking coffee, let alone going to bed.

The following morning I woke up, looked around and found I was on my own. Just for a moment I had to think where I was. Oh yeah, Claire's place.

I sat up and "Oh dear," I said, as I held my head with my hands. "I seem to be a little hung over." I shuffled through into the kitchen. Claire was there. I just stood there, looking at her.

"Scrambled eggs on toast and some coffee to help us feel better?" she said.

"Yes, please," I said, still looking her up and down. "You really are a sight for sore eyes," I said. Claire was preparing breakfast wearing only furry slippers and a G string. I waited patiently, not minding if breakfast took a while. Unfortunately, it was soon ready. We sat and ate it together, after which we both felt a lot better.

"Okay," Claire said as we finished. "Get in that bedroom and I'll be in to sort you out before we go to work." I shuffled back down the hall to the bedroom quite quickly.

After we'd showered and got ready, we sat drinking more coffee and discussing the new employee. We talked about the advantages and disadvantages of having a detective on the books and, when you consider, we really didn't have any choice. Claire thought we'd make the most of the situation and go ahead with it. That was that.

"Settled," she said. "We have a new employee."

I said that, when I spoke to John, I'd tell him no more freebies, as much as he might like them. That would stop, he'd pay Chantal when he visited.

Claire called Ryan's office and booked him to come and get us, and take us to work. On the way over Claire was telling him about the copper and his involvement with us. As she did so, I started laughing.

"What are you laughing at, Gary?" Claire asked.

"I saw his warrant card with his name on it. Detective Constable John Letts."

"Yeah, well, what's funny about that?" said Ryan.

"When we were kids in London, we had a joke we'd tell. We'd say, Where do policemen live? And the answer was, Lettsbe Avenue. Ha-ha-ha." I found it funny. Ryan just looked. He didn't get it. "We have our

FOR THE LOVE OF BRASS

own Lettsbe on the firm, that's it. From now on I'll call him Lettsbe. Ha-ha-ha."

We arrived at Cobden Road and Ryan went off to his work. We went in to have tea and sit smoking with the girls while talking about DC Letts and how helpful we thought he could be. After a while, I went off to the Wimpy to get something for us all to eat. By this time it was two o'clock in the afternoon. As I came back, I saw Mr Brown sitting outside the pub.

As I walked passed him, I said, "Is John in the pub?"

"No," he said, "but he'll be here in a while."

"Cheers for that." I returned with the food and told Claire what Mr Brown had said.

"Okay," said Claire, "then maybe you could go see him and pay him."

"No," I said. "I think it might be better to pay him over here. I'll see what he says. I'm going in the garden for a smoke," I said while rolling a cigarette. "Come out there with me, Claire, I want to talk with you." We both stood in the garden, another lovely day. I said to Claire, "Can you afford this copper on the books?"

"Yes, of course I can."

"Oh, okay, it's just that you have Abbie, me and now him. I just wanted to make sure things were okay."

"Yes, of course," she said. "Don't worry, the girls bring in a lot on money. You forget," she said, "that I have Ryan to pay for as well."

"Do you?" I said. "Why?"

"Well, he doesn't pay any rent, I cover all that and in return he runs me around wherever I want to go."

"Oh, okay," I said. "I didn't realise that. Fair enough."

"There's another good thing about having a copper on the books. I already supply the girls with most of their gear, so now I can do more of that without worrying about getting nicked."

"Alright," I said. "Well, I'll go over to the pub to see if he is about."

We went back inside and Abbie said, "I was thinking, why don't you and Gary come over to my house tonight? Big Lee and Courtney will be there. We can have a party, just the five of us."

Claire looked at me.

"Yes," I said, "why not? "It'll be fun, I'm sure."

Claire agreed, "Okay, that's what we're doing."

"Great," Abbie said. "I asked Chantel before she went into the room but she said no because her and Lee were spending the evening together, kissing and dribbling over each other no doubt. Ha-ha."

I went for a walk over to the pub. John and Mr Brown were there outside, talking.

"Can I talk to you, John?"

"Yes," he said. Mr Brown walked off and went inside.

"Okay, Claire says she'll play ball with you."

"That's good," he said.

"But there's one condition."

"Oh yeah, what's that?" John asked.

"No more freebies," I said. "That has to stop. If you're on the books then we have to take money not give it away. If you arrange something with Chantel, well that's up to you both but Claire has to have her cut when you visit."

"Okay," John said, "I understand."

"Okay, then, that's good," I said. "I thought it best you pop into the parlour to pick your envelope up, then nobody sees anything, is that okay with you?"

"Yes, it is," John said.

FOR THE LOVE OF BRASS

"Okay, come over in the next 20 minutes and I'll be there; after that I won't. I have to go out for a couple of hours but Claire will be there and you can collect it from her if you prefer."

"No, no, I'll be along shortly." John said. I walked back over to the parlour.

"Okay, Claire," I said, "It's sorted. He'll pop by in a few minutes for his money. Once we've made that payment, that's it, we've got him in our pocket, which can only be a good thing, especially as he wouldn't have gone away anyway. Once he's been in, I'll have to go out for a couple of hours. I need to go to the bank in Portland Road, then get over to Ron's site with the wages. I've left it a bit late today but he'll be pleased to see me." We laughed.

The doorbell rang and Chantel went to answer. I looked down the hall and saw it was John.

"Come in, mate," I said, in a slightly raised voice so he could hear me. "You might as well come in here. You know everyone anyway from the pub."

"Okay," said Lettsbe.

"Do you want a coffee or anything?"

"No thanks," He said.

"Okay, then, are you back over to the pub?"

"Yeah I am, for a while."

"Okay, let me see you out." Claire handed me the envelope. "There we are," I said as he was at the front door.

"Thanks Gary, you've got me on side now. Things'll be good."

"Okay, mate, that's good. See you later." I closed the door.

"That's it, Claire," I said, "we have him now, oh and, Chantel, no more freebies for him either."

"Yeah, thanks for that Gary. Claire told me you'd sorted that, much appreciated," said Chantel.

"Okay, I'm going out for a little while now, be back as soon as I'm done. Oh, Chantel, do you think I could borrow one of Lee's shirts if I need to? I'll try and buy one if I can while I'm out but if not I may need to because I won't be going home until tomorrow."

While I was out walking to the bank, I thought to myself, another night I've not been home but it is Friday and the Pope is a Catholic. Sharon might be expecting me to be there to mind the boys but, oh well, she'll have to arrange her own minder. I'm not going back, so she can get on with it.

I returned to the parlour having done what I set out to do. I'd also picked up a new shirt for the evening. The girls were all about done. Chantel had seen her last client out and Claire had got herself ready, not that she'd had to do much. I thought she was always lovely.

"Chantel, is it okay to shower here?"

"Yes," she said, "you carry on." In 15 minutes I was ready and we said our goodbyes to Chantel. Claire, Abbie and I were off in the van and on our way over to Abbie's place for our party, ha-ha.

When we got there Abbie invited us in. Big Lee was already in the chair smoking a spliff. Courtney was messing about in the kitchen. She came out and welcomed us all with a kiss.

"Sit down," she said. "What do you want to drink, we've got Vodka, Bacardi, Foster's lager, all the mixers, we even have a bottle of lemonade for you, Gary. Abbie told us you like a top on your beer."

"Well, thanks very much," I said, "in that case I'll have a top please," I said smiling. The others all placed their orders and Courtney made the drinks.

FOR THE LOVE OF BRASS

"Oh and also," Courtney said, "because we'll be smoking puff, I've a chocolate gateau, a tin of Roses sweets, Twiglets and peanuts for when you all get the munchies."

"Ha-ha-ha, that's great," I said. Lee sat up and joined in the conversation with us. We had a lot to talk about; a lot had happened this week. Abbie had the radio on Kiss FM, so the music was great. We all got quite pissed and stoned, then there was a knock on the front door. Abbie went to answer. It was the neighbours, a young couple from upstairs. They'd heard the music and thought they'd say hello.

"Come in," Abbie said, "what are you having to drink?" They soon joined us, smoking and drinking, and soon they, too, were getting stoned. We were all sitting there laughing until we cried; when Abbie and Courtney got together there was no stopping them. They were so funny with the things they talked about, they had us all in stitches. By the end of the evening I had stomach pains, where I'd laughed so much. I think we all had. We had a fantastic time.

The young couple from upstairs went back to their place and we set up a bed for me and Claire. Abbie said goodnight, followed by Lee and Courtney, then there was just us two. We were still giggling and laughing as we got into bed. God knows what the time was but who cares, that didn't matter. We cuddled up and crashed.

Saturday morning we were up without a problem. We sorted ourselves out after having breakfast, then said our goodbyes and left, heading out to Claire's flat. We spent a while sitting out in the sun, in the communal garden behind the flats, then I went home. As I arrived at my house, my sons were playing out in the park entrance with their friends, bikes and skateboards lay around the alleyway. I waved and said hello to them as I went in. As I walked into the kitchen, Sharon walked past me; no words were said between us. She walked down the hall, picked up the bag that was behind the door and out she went, pulling the door shut behind her. That's handy, I thought, no arguing today. I like the silent treatment, it suits me down to the ground.

I opened the back door and spoke to the boys over the wall. I asked if they'd been shopping with their mum and how long they'd been playing out. I asked if they wanted to go out into the countryside with the dogs; that was definitely well received. Okay, then, it was bring all their stuff into the garage and we'd go in ten minutes. Of course, in ten minutes time I had four boys waiting by the van, ready to go. I called the dogs through. Once they knew they were going out with us all, there was no stopping their excitement. We piled into the van and off we went, heading to the chalk hills of Betchworth.

We didn't return until around 7.30, grabbing ourselves a kebab as we got near home. I didn't expect to see Sharon again until sometime the following day. I'd mentioned to Claire about going shooting on Sunday, which she was very keen to do. I called Claire to see if she still wanted to go.

"Oh yes," she said, "can't wait."

"Okay," I said. "Leave it to me. I'll sort out something and get back to you."

I needed a minder for the boys in the afternoon so I called Jack and asked if he could come over for the afternoon and early evening if needed. I explained the situation to him, saying he might not be needed if Sharon came back but I'd pay him anyway, whether he was at my house for 30 minutes or until early evening. I guessed he wouldn't be there long but I had to cover myself because I'd be going to Bisley to shoot and two hours would be needed just to get there and back. Anyway, Jack was happy to come over and mind the boys, however long it took.

I called Claire back, telling her I'd pick her up at 12 o'clock tomorrow from her flat.

Sunday morning, Jack arrived at 11 o'clock. I'd already got my shooting bag ready, I'd be taking two guns, my Smith and Wesson 357 magnum and my 9mm Browning Hi-power, along with associated holsters and ammunition. I said goodbye to the three boys and left to collect Claire. I was carrying my bag with me when I went to her door, not wanting to leave the guns in the van. Claire greeted me with a hug and a kiss as always.

"Come in," she said. "We can have a cuppa before we go." While sitting in her kitchen drinking tea and smoking cigarettes she asked, "What's in the bag?" I opened it up and put the two handguns on her dinner table. "Wow," she said, suitably impressed. She called Ryan in from the other room and he also liked what he saw.

The guns were put back into the bag and we finished our smokes and tea, then left. We drove into Bisley camp and I explained to Claire that we'd have to book a range. We did this over at the NRA office, booking onto the gallery pistol range, a 25-metre range. We were lucky enough to have it to ourselves, so we put up two targets and shot to our hearts' content, until we ran out of ammo. I spent the afternoon teaching Claire the safety procedures and, of course, how to use both guns. She really enjoyed this; in fact, we both really enjoyed it. By the time we'd finished for the day, Claire could pick up a gun, load it and fire it off, hitting the target every time, which I thought was great. She really enjoyed herself.

On the way home she asked, "When can we do that again?" I smiled and thought to myself, she's hooked on shooting.

"We can go as soon as you like, as far as I'm concerned," I said. "We could go during the week, the ranges are even quieter then."

"Yes, yes, yes, let's go, let's go."

"Claire," I said, "you're like a big kid."

She laughed. "Yes, I know," she replied.

As we drove off the M25 onto the Croydon Road, Claire's phone rang. It was Abbie and Courtney. They'd been shopping in Whitgift Croydon and wanted to know if Claire was home and could they pop in for coffee.

Claire explained where we were. "Yes," she said, "that's fine. We'll see you at the flat in 30 minutes."

We parked in the car park and made our way up to the flat, me carrying my bag. We weren't there long before the door buzzer went; the girls were downstairs. Claire buzzed them in and the kettle was already going. We four sat in the kitchen smoking and drinking tea and coffee. Claire was telling them what a good day she'd had with me on the ranges.

"Gary," she said, "show Abbie and Courtney the guns."

They were gob-smacked, not having seen guns before, other than on the TV. They were both keen to put the shoulder holsters on and have their pictures taken, gun in hand. They looked like two gangsters' wives. At some point, the coffee and tea was exchanged for Vodka orange and beers. The guns went away back in the bag, the music came on and, before you knew it, we were partying again, just the four of us. Ryan came home and Claire was telling him all about the day's shooting she'd had and what fun it was.

Eventually the girls were ready to go home and Ryan said he'd take them. We said our goodbyes and off the three of them went. Claire and I went to bed. We were having fun seeing who could give the best body-to-body massage again and who owed who the 50 quid, arguing in fun who was going to pay.

FOR THE LOVE OF BRASS

Monday morning and this was becoming a habit. Wake up, make love, drink tea, smoke cigarettes, eat breakfast, get ready, and today we decided we'd go swimming again at the baths in Beckenham before going over to the parlour. We had great fun at the pool, playing around just like you did when we were kids. I just loved having time on our own, just me and her. It made me feel very happy inside. I felt as if it was only me and her together in the world sometimes and this is how we would always be.

Lunchtime at Cobden Road and today Chantel was making the Chilli con carne. I walked around the corner to the baker's for some French sticks. Chantel was doing her best but she kept having to go into the room so Abbie would step in and help from time to time, although she kept an eye on things.

I laughed with Chantel, she was at the cooker mixing in the mushrooms she'd prepared and putting a squirt of tomato puree into the pot.

I said to her, "I hope you have washed your hands thoroughly. We don't want to be tasting baby oil, or anything else for that matter." We all had a laugh at the thought of that. I said out loud, "Chantel, you look a lot more attractive than Ainslie the TV chief. Mind you, I've not seen him in his underwear, suspenders and stockings, so who knows. Ha-ha-ha." That got us all laughing. Abbie nearly wet herself; she must have visualised the scene.

Once the lunch was ready we all sat together and ate, and very nice it was too.

Claire said to me, "When we're done we need to pop out to see Holly and drop some stuff off to her, then over to see Sam and Jess but before that, we'll go to that shop in Portland Road that sells household goods so we can get a box of large paper rolls, the kind that masseuses use on their beds, and a box of baby oil and one of talc, a dozen or so of each, they normally come in boxes of twelve."

We all finished lunch and Abbie said, "You can go, I'll clear up."

"Okay, that's great," said Claire. "Oh and Abbie, can you call Wayne the estate agent and find out when the rents are due? Tell him we want the rents to be paid at the same time, so there's no messing around and they won't be paid late. In fact," Claire said, "tell him to pop in to see Chantel when they are due, she can give him a little blow job or something, that way he'll always collect the rent from us and that will save me having to worry about it, ha-ha." Claire laughed as she said this.

Bloody hell, you girls certainly have things all sorted out, things and services can be paid with sex, what a currency, I thought. And the girls have so much of it. I smiled to myself.

We left and went to the Indian shop Claire knew of. Claire bought what we needed, I loaded it up in the van and off we went to see Holly. Claire called her from outside her house. We couldn't go in just yet as Holly had a client with her, we were told by her maid.

"Who's the maid?" I asked.

"Don't know today," Claire said. "She uses different friends, it just depends which one of them is available at the time." After ten minutes or so we saw a man walk down the garden path then head off towards the high street. "That's it," Claire said. "We can go in now. Would do you mind bringing the paper rolls? They are a little heavy. I'll carry the other two boxes."

"Hello, Holly," Claire said as we went in her house.

"Okay, who's for coffee?" Holly said.

"Yes, please," we all replied.

"Claire, Gary, this is my friend Amy, well, that's her working name anyway." Amy was just another dead normal looking woman, maybe 40 years old. She had four or five clients of her own and the rest of the time she'd work as a maid in one or two different parlours. I was surprised at how normal-looking these women were.

We said our hellos.

"Holly, is there anywhere you would like me to put this box out of the way?"

"Yes, please, can you take upstairs and put it in the front bedroom?"

"Okay." I turned and walked back down the hall and up the stairs, pushed the bedroom door open and stepped in. I walked across the room and placed the box under one of the windows and looked around the room on my way out, thinking this just looked like any other bedroom you might find, not like a brass's parlour at all. I smiled to myself. I didn't really know what I was expecting, maybe that was in the other bedroom, I thought as I went back downstairs. As I walked along the hall back to the kitchen I could see into the room a little as the door was ajar. I could see Claire's legs with her bag on her knees; she was putting a large brown envelope into it. Bloody hell! I thought to myself, there must be a few grand in there. I entered the room.

"Thanks, darling, take a seat; your coffee's there."

"Thanks very much. How about the other boxes?"

"No, no, they're okay where they are. Thanks all the same."

I sat down and rolled myself a cigarette. The three women were chatting away about whatever; I didn't really take much notice of what they were talking about. Amy would answer the odd phone call, giving Holly's details to a male enquirer. I seemed to be too busy watching Claire, just watching her interact with the other two seemed to be keeping me occupied. All of a sudden my name was mentioned.

"Yes, well don't forget, Gary will always come over and take you where you need to go, whether you're working or not."

Holly and Amy looked at me and Holly said, "We've heard some good things about you, Gary. Seems you're fearless."

"Well, I don't know about that. I just do what needs to be done at the time, that's all."

"Well," Holly replied, "you certainly make the girls feel safe."

Claire piped up, "Well, he is a former SAS soldier. He knows exactly what he's doing, so don't forget, if you need security, Gary's the man. Just let me know. On that note, we should be off."

I said goodbye to the girls and they both gave me a kiss as we left. We walked over and got into the van.

"Okay," Claire said, "off to see Sam, but before we go I just want to call her."

I started the van. A few words were exchanged between Claire and Sam, then off we went. We drove out into Portland Road; even though there was some traffic it wouldn't take us long to get there. Ten minutes later and we were looking for somewhere to park. We found a space about 100yds away.

"This'll do us." I parked the van and we walked back to Sam's place.

"Hello, you two," Sam said. "Come in." She walked through to the kitchen. "I'll put the kettle on." We sat at the table.

"No Jess?" I said.

"No, she's gone out to see one of her family. She'll be back sometime tonight. Oh, Gary, are you available tomorrow afternoon? I've a job on for an hour or so and I'd like you with me."

"Yes, that's fine, no problem."

We sat at Sam's table with another drink, tea this time, and yet another brown envelope was handed to Claire, which also went into her bag. I sat there smoking while the girls spoke. Sam had a short skirt on and my eye was drawn to the tattoo that ran down her leg.

"Oh," I said, "while I think of it, can I take the shotgun with me today?"

"Oh yes," Sam said. "Jess isn't keen on it being here, so yes, by all means take it away. I'll get it for you, it's only under the bed." Sam came back into the room looking like Ma Baker with a shotgun under her arm.

"That's great. If you don't mind I'll pop out to the van and get a couple of tools, I want to saw a piece off it."

"Yeah, that's fine with me."

"Okay, girls," I said, "back in a tick." I walked down the road to the van and returned with a wood saw and a sheet of sandpaper. While the girls were drinking their tea and smoking, I put the gun on the draining board and marked where I wanted to cut part of the stock off, which I then set about doing. Once the stock had been cut down, I sanded it down with the sandpaper so there were no rough edges. "That's it, all done."

I now had one mean-looking weapon. The barrels were already short enough. I disassembled the gun into three pieces, the fore-grip, the barrels and the lock-pistol grip.

"Sam," I asked. "Can I help myself to some of your carrier bags?"

"Yes, love, you carry on." I wrapped each piece of the gun in a carrier bag, then all three pieces in another carrier bag. I needed to be able to go out in public without anybody knowing what I was carrying. The remains of the wooden stock I wrapped and threw into Sam's rubbish bin.

On leaving Sam's place, I told her I'd call her tomorrow to confirm the time to pick her up, then we made our way back to Cobden Road, where Chantel let us in. I was carrying my shopping bag and a screwdriver as we entered the kitchen.

"How have you been, girls, nice and busy?"

"Yes," they both said, "very busy."

Within ten minutes the doorbell rang and Chantel went to answer. She came back into the kitchen and gave Abbie some money, then went back into the room with her client.

Abbie asked, "Would you like tea?"

"No, no," I said, "Not at the moment. I need to fit something under the kitchen units." I got out my screwdriver and unscrewed one of the kick plates and slid my carrier bag of shopping under the unit, then set about replacing the kick plate.

I sat down next to Abbie and, as I rolled myself a cigarette I said to Abbie, "Keep this to yourself, don't tell anybody what you just saw."

"Okay, yes, okay," she said. Chantel came back into the room none the wiser as to what had happened and everything was normal.

The following day I had things to do in my office. The phone rang while I was sitting at my desk. It was Sharon calling from her work.

She said, "I've something to tell you. I'm going away next week on holiday. I go for a week from Monday, so you can have the kids."

"Okay," I said. "Where you going, anywhere nice?"

"Yeah, I'm going to Turkey with my friends."

"Okay, how long for?"

"One week, I just told you."

"Well, that's a long way to go for a week, why don't you go for three or four weeks, or do a Shirley Valentine and stay there on the F plan?"

There was silence for a few seconds then she replied, "FUCK OFF!" and the phone went dead. Oh well, I thought, guess I deserve that, and smiled to myself.

Around mid-morning, I remembered I had Sam to take out this

FOR THE LOVE OF BRASS

afternoon. I called her to confirm a time to pick her up. She'd be happy for me to be there for 12.30.

Sam said, "We're not going far." That suits me, I thought, I'll get the details when I get there. I have to say I was smiling to myself still, but intrigued as to why Sharon called to tell me that from her office. Why didn't she tell me face to face? Oh well, I thought, who cares why, the main thing is that she is away for a week and that can only be a good thing as far as I'm concerned because that means no arguing for the boys or myself to listen to.

Eleven fifteen, time to get on my way to pick Sam up. 12.25 and I was knocking on Sam's door. She was ready and we got into the van.

"Where are we off to, then?"

"Rotherhithe, darling. Do you know it?"

"Yes, of course; whereabouts?"

"Lower Road."

I smiled. "Yeah, I know that. Give me some more direction when we're closer." Sam had an address written down on a piece of paper.

We found it easy enough, it was a little London house on the same side as the Police station, about 400yds along, heading towards Deptford. I parked up so I could see the house, as usual.

Sam said, "He's booked me for an hour, so time me one hour from now."

"Okay, you got it. See you then." Sam made her way over to the house and went in. I sat twiddling my thumbs. I rolled a cigarette and sat there blowing smoke out of my window, while listening to the radio. In no time at all, it seemed, Sam came out with two minutes to spare.

"Lovely," I thought. No dramas, things were all okay and we could head back to Portland Road.

"I'm popping in to see Claire," I told Sam, in case she wanted to come with me.

"Yes, okay."

"We can have another catch up and a cup of tea. Ha-ha." She found that funny but Jess wasn't at home, so why not?

I parked in Cobden Road and Chantel opened the door to let us in in her working clothes. Sam looked at her, then at me and smiled as Chantel walked down the hallway.

Sam said, "No wonder you like coming around here," smiling as she said it. We went into the kitchen and Abbie jumped up to put the kettle on. We all sat around talking and smoking, all five of us. After a while, I needed to head off home.

"Sam," I said, "I'll drop you on the way." We all said our goodbyes.

I pulled up near to Sam's flat and she leaned over and put some money in my shirt pocket and said thank you for today. All I could see was that it was £20 notes.

As she got out of the van she said, "It's so nice to see you two are so in love, you and Claire. I can see you love her to pieces." Sam leant over and gave me a kiss. "Thanks, Gary," she said as she got out. "See you soon."

"Yeah, bye." I drove off into the traffic to make my way home. I checked in my pocket when I stopped at traffic lights, there were five £20 notes. It made me wonder what she did in these houses to be able to pay me £100. I also wondered how my evening at home with Sharon would go, maybe arguments, maybe not. I told myself, I won't argue for the sake of the boys, they've heard enough of that shit.

Surprisingly enough the whole evening went past without anything being said. It was just like a normal evening, Sharon not talking to me, which I thought was great, just how I like it. And soon we'd have a week

FOR THE LOVE OF BRASS

on our own.

I found myself in my office at home, catching up on bits and pieces to do with my building firm. This stuff was now really of no interest to me, it just needed doing and as soon as possible as far as I was concerned. What I was interested in was going to see Claire and the girls. When I was away from Claire it gave me a pain in my heart, that seemed to be how much I loved her. When I think about that feeling, it's not a place I wanted to be in but the feelings had taken over; I didn't seem to have a choice. Still, although I felt vulnerable and sometimes anxious with the relationship, it also made me feel very happy when I was with her. I came to the conclusion it was just the price you have to pay when you love someone.

Eventually, that was it, jobs were done and I was on my way back to see Claire. Before I went, I checked in my van that I had a drill and a few tools, then I went down the garden to my shed to look through a bucket of old fittings. I was after two aluminium coat hooks which I'd need when I got to Cobden Road. Once I found them, I locked the shed up and left the house to head over to see the girls. One of the first things I wanted to do when I got there, other than have lunch, was to arrange a day out, just for myself and Claire, out in the countryside, away from everything. A Wednesday bank holiday, I called it. Also I wanted to fit the coat brackets up.

"Hello girls," I greeted them as I came in.

Abbie was up straight away. "Okay, who's for tea?" and of course we said yes.

I had a carrier bag with the tools in, which I placed by the settee. "Have you been busy Chantel?" I asked.

"Yes," she said. "Done four already today."

"Nice one," I replied. "Abbie," I asked, "are there more booked in?"

"Yes," she said. "Chan will be busy all day."

"Okay. Great." I winked at Claire. We sat there drinking tea and smoking cigarettes till the doorbell rang. Chantel got up to answer it and a couple of minutes passed before Chantel came back in with the money and gave it to Abbie. Then she waited a couple of minutes as normal, finished her smoke, then went back into the room.

"Abbie," I said, "how much has he paid?"

Abbie looked and said, "A hundred pounds."

"Okay," I said to the girls, "she'll be at least half an hour."

"What're you up to?" Claire said.

"I want to fit a couple of brackets on the wall in the back of the cupboard."

"What the fuck for?" Abbie said.

"It's where the shotgun will live." The girls just looked at each other a bit bewildered. "I'll explain soon."

I looked inside the cupboard and removed a few things that were on the shelf, then slid out the drawer above. There was a gap of some three inches between the back of the drawer and the wall. I unscrewed the kick plate to the kitchen cupboard and retrieved the carrier bag that was under there, replacing the kick plate as I went.

"Now Abbie, I'm doing this while Chantel is out of the room. I don't want her to know the gun's under here, because she might tell Lee and he'll get it out and play with it, so you have to keep this to yourself."

I took the shotgun parts from the carrier bags. Now Claire was interested. She came over to see exactly what was going on. She had a big smile on her face.

"Can I put it together?"

"Yes," I said. "I'll show you." She soon had it assembled.

FOR THE LOVE OF BRASS

"This is what we're going to do," I told her. I held the shotgun up against the wall where I wanted it to be when it was fitted, then, with a pencil, marked the wall where the underside of the barrels would be. Next I marked under where the pistol grip was, at the point behind the trigger guard. Then I put the shotgun on the bottom shelf and proceeded to offer up the coat hooks, putting the bottom of the hook on each pencil mark, then drilling and screwing each bracket into position.

"Why is one bracket higher than the other?" Claire asked.

"There's about two inches difference in height and the reason for that is that, when the gun sits on it, it'll sit level, which'll keep it up behind the drawer, out of sight. Should anybody open the cupboard door and look in, they won't see it." We placed the gun onto the brackets, then cleaned up the mess from drilling, put the drawer back in and the items back on the shelf. "There you are," I said. "Bob's your uncle."

Claire laughed. "Show me how to get it out quick." I showed her and she loved the idea of having it there.

"Insurance," I said, with a smile. The kettle went on again and out came the cigarettes. I put the tools back in the bag and Chantel came back into our room, sat with her tea and was none the wiser as to what we'd been doing. She didn't even ask what the drilling was about.

We sat and arranged our day out for tomorrow.

"The weather forecast is dry. We'll take a picnic and stay out all day."

"Brilliant," Claire said, "can't wait."

Abbie said, "It's so nice to see you two, how you are. You love each other so much."

"Yes, I'm afraid so," I replied. Claire just smiled. "Oh, I forgot to say Sharon's away all next week, so I'm not sure what times I can do with you all but I'll let you all know as soon as I know. I should be able to get

339

her sister to help out, so hopefully there might not be too much change. Okay, girls," I said. "I'll be off now."

"Why so soon?" Claire said. "Abbie, what booking do you have for Chantel?"

Abbie replied, "Nothing for about forty minutes."

"Gary," Claire said, "come on, let's go in the room and I'll sort you out before you go home."

"Ha-ha," I said, "it'd be rude not to." So, with a big smile on my face, in we went. We had a fantastic time, as we always did when we had sex. It was always such fun. I'm sure the girls must have heard us laughing from their room.

Once we were finished, Claire said, "Can you do me a favour, please, on you way home?"

"Yes, of course."

"Can you pop over to Maria's flat and pick up some money? She'll give it to you in an envelope. Keep hold of it and I'll get it off you tomorrow. Stay with her for a while, have a cuppa and chat with her, you know, make sure she's alright. It won't hurt for you to get to know her a bit better, you know, build up a working relationship with her. I like her and I know she likes us. I want to make sure she's happy."

I pulled up outside Maria's flat and tapped on the front window as I walked up the side of the house to the front door. As I got to the door, it opened.

"Hello, Gary," Maria said, "come in."

"How's things?" I asked.

"Yeah, good thanks. Claire called and told me you were on your way over. I'll put the kettle on." I followed her through to the kitchen.

"Is Lisa here?" I asked. "No she's not. I'm on my own for a couple of days."

"Oh, okay."

"But I do have an envelope for Claire to give to you. She must trust you a great deal; well, all the girls trust you a great deal, so I'm told."

"Yes, I guess that's the case."

"I've heard the stories of you saving Sam from a gunman and down at the pub you're treated with the greatest respect, even when you're not there. They all say you run that pub and also the area."

"Well, I don't know about that, but it's handy in some ways."

I couldn't help myself from looking Maria up and down as she stood there making the tea. What a sight for sore eyes she was. She sat down at the table.

"There's your tea and there's the money for Claire. Stick it in your jacket pocket so it's safe." The envelope felt thick, there must be two or three grand in there, I thought. "We do have fun when we're all together," she said. "Don't you think?"

"Yes, yes we do," I said. "A really good time," I said as I rolled a cigarette.

"And do you like all the girls?"

"Yes," I said, "they're great."

"And which of the girls do you like the best?"

"What other than Claire, you mean?"

"Yes."

"I'd say Abbie. She seems to be the most fun, or the funniest, she should be a comedian."

"Yes, I know what you mean. And what do you think of me?" I looked up from rolling my cigarette and smiled. I didn't answer. "Well," she said, "what do you think?"

"Well," I said, "you're bloody lovely. In fact you're stunning in my eyes. I think you're absolutely fucking gorgeous if you must know but hold on a minute, why are you asking me this?" She smiled, then she stood up and pulled her chair around the corner of the table and put it in front of me.

She sat down on it and said, "Give me your hand," which I did. She said, "Press on here." She put my hand between her breasts and said, "My heart beats quickly sometimes, can you feel it?"

I said, "My fucking heart's beating quick as well now and you're giving me the popcorn, for fuck's sake, you have to stop this."

"No," she replied. "I'm serious. Can you feel it?" I thought, for fuck's sake, I don't know what to say, I'm literally stuck for words. I said the only thing that came to mind.

"How's the anal business? Still going up in the world?" Oh no! I thought, what have I just said? I wished the ground would open and swallow me. I couldn't believe it.

She burst out laughing and said, "Bloody hell, I do make you nervous, don't I?"

"Yes, you do, or at least you have today, behave yourself. What is this, some sort of test I don't know about? Ha-ha-ha, did I pass it? Has Claire asked you to do this to see if I'd stray?"

"No, no, no," she said. "I just wanted you to check my heart rate." She carried on laughing.

"Let me finish my tea, I need to have this fag, for fuck's sake." I finished my tea and had my smoke. Maria sat there with biggest grin on her face. "Okay," I said. "What's this all about?"

"Well, I wanted to know what you thought of me, because I thought if you like me a lot or fancy me, you'll look after me better."

"Oh," I said, "well you can employ me to look after you whenever you want. I'll come out on jobs with you, you know that."

"Yes, yes, I know that but it has to go through Claire."

FOR THE LOVE OF BRASS

"Yes, well, what's wrong with that?"

"I was thinking you could come and look after me all the time."

"I can't do that, I'm in a relationship with Claire."

"Yes, yes I know but I like you and I thought we could have a relationship and you could look after me all the time. I'll pay you £1,500 a week in cash and you get to have a relationship with me. We can have a relationship with each other. I'll keep working, of course, and you can do what you want in between jobs."

"Well, what can I say, thank you very much for the offer but I can't do that. Anyway, when you need me from time to time to come out with you, just book me through Claire. I'll be happy to come out with you and I'll look after you, you know that. Okay, I should go now I think."

"Yes, okay. I think we should keep this to ourselves and stay friends. I don't want any awkward moments when we're out. We'll stay good friends, agreed?"

"Yes, agreed."

"Good." As I was leaving her house she pulled me close and kissed me. She said, "Thank you, you'll see me again soon."

I went weak at the knees when she kissed me but decided to keep that to myself. I drove home and, as you might expect, the journey went really quick. I couldn't help thinking about what had taken place at Maria's flat.

Once home, a usual evening ensued. I spent time with my boys and sat watching TV, just myself and my V and O. I went to bed thinking what a good day I'd have tomorrow.

Wednesday morning, and I drove over to Cobden Road to meet Claire there for 10 o'clock. On arrival, the first thing I did after giving her a kiss and cuddle was to give her the envelope I'd collected from Maria the afternoon before. Then we went round to the shops in Portland Road for supplies. I brought our shopping back and made up our picnic for the day. I put it all in a rucksack, then we were ready to go. We said goodbye to Abbie and Chantel; they were now in charge and left to run things. Of course, Claire had her big brick phone with her just in case she was needed.

I drove us to Betchworth and parked in a little quiet lane that I knew from my poaching days, then off we went on foot. We walked all along the Pilgrim's Way to Box Hill and a little beyond, stopping in some lovely places for a bite to eat and a bite of each other. We had a fantastic day all on our own with no interruptions. We got back to Cobden Road around 7 o'clock. We met with Abbie and Chantel over at the pub and had a quiet evening in there with just two or three drinks. Mr Brown was standing in his usual spot. We said hello to the locals that we knew. At the end of our evening, Claire made the call and Ryan turned up to take us all home. Chantel went to Lee's while we took Abbie home.

When we pulled up in the drive there was a commotion going on. Courtney and big Lee were in the drive by the front steps of the house having an argument.

Courtney stopped slapping Lee and said hello to us, adding, "I don't have time to talk, sorry, but I'm busy beating him." We just said hi, even big Lee said hi. We drove off to the sound of Lee saying "For fuck's sake!" and Courtney saying something about a Chinese meal and slapping Lee again. He was laughing, which seemed to make it worse for him but no doubt he deserved it. Ryan took us back to Claire's flat, then he headed off back to work. We were both pretty worn out, so we went to bed talking about our great day out and laughing about the Courtney and Lee thing.

After a normal morning at Claire's, making love, tea an breakfast, I arrived home. Sharon had already left to take the boys to school and

FOR THE LOVE OF BRASS

herself to work but the dogs were pleased to see me, as always.

"Come on girls, we're going to Morden park for a run." They were both jumping up at me with excitement. The plan was to walk to the park, then go for a run around the perimeter.

In no time at all, I was through the park gate and walking in the wooded section of the park. I had a lot on my mind, firstly about my relationship with Claire, then with Sharon going away. I didn't have any details of Sharon's holiday but then, that really didn't matter. I don't know why that kept coming to mind. I just told myself it's a good thing she's going away at this stage of our marriage, if you could call it a marriage, because we'd become pretty good at disliking each other and not talking much. I'm sure if it wasn't for my sons, I'd have left her years ago. Then I started thinking that she would have probably done the same. I smiled to myself thinking it might have even ended up as a race as to who could get out the door of our house first.

My thoughts soon drifted back to Claire. Something told me there was something wrong with us but I couldn't put my finger on it. I just had this feeling, a type of dread, but I couldn't work out why, I just did. I started turning things over in my mind but there was no answer to be had. Something felt wrong, and that was all I knew.

I realised I was about to put my key into my front door. Wow, I thought, I've walked all the way around the park then home, deep in thought, not having had a run at all. I decided I'd exercise in my bedroom as I sometimes did, well, most days when I was there - sit ups, push ups, dumbbells, that type of thing - then make some business calls and a little paperwork, estimating. I'd have to go to a job and see Ron but first I must call Claire, just because I missed her and wanted to chat. We'd arranged we'd go out Friday night so I'd call Jack my sitter later that evening when he was home. I'd get him over to babysit the boys because I knew Sharon would be going out; there was no point in asking her that question again, what with the Pope and all.

I told Claire I'd be staying at home tonight and slipped into the conversion, "Is everything alright?"

"Yes, fine. Why?"

"It's okay, just thought I'd ask." I told myself I'd ask her again when I saw her next, if we were okay. The thought of doing that seemed to put my mind at rest.

After my site meeting with Ron, I went home and called Jack. He was fine with the Friday job. I told him I'd not be there but Sharon would be and could he be there for 6.45 as Sharon would probably have a cab coming for her at 7.00. I also told Jack I'd leave his money for him in an envelope from the last time he babysat. He was only there for about 45 minutes until Sharon came home that time. He said don't worry about paying him for that time but I felt I should; after all, I wanted to keep him happy. I knew I'd be asking him to come over a lot.

I spent time with my boys, then, after they'd gone to bed, I sat on my own in the lounge watching TV with my V and O, which seemed to have become my best friend. I could sleep better once I'd had one or two. I felt I could talk to it without getting any abuse.

Sharon walked past the lounge door and as she passed I asked her, "Can we talk for a minute?" She stepped into the room.

"What?"

"I just wanted to ask you about your holiday. When did that come about?"

And with that, she turned and walked out saying, "None of your fucking business!"

FOR THE LOVE OF BRASS

I looked at my V and O and smiled to myself. That's that, then; think I'll finish my drink and go to bed.

I called Claire in the morning to tell her I'd a few things to do, then I'd be over to see her. I said I should be there about 1 o'clock. I went to the Midland bank at Rosehill and collected some cash so I could return to the office and deal with the men's wages. This done, I put a few clothes in a bag that I thought I might need for my night out, then headed over to the job in Croydon. I met Ron there and we discussed the details of the extension we were building. Ron was always happy just to get on with the job; as long as he had finance and some staff, he didn't need me for anything. I left the wages with him to pay the men. That's me done, I thought. I'm off to see the girls.

My intention was to spend the afternoon with the girls, so I couldn't wait to get there. As I pulled into Cobden Road I noticed over on my left-hand side, about 50yds from the pub, DC Letts with another man also dressed in a suit. Hmmm, looks like another copper, I thought to myself. Lettsbe had his back to me so he didn't see me pass. I looked at the other fellow. Don't know him, I said to myself, but I had a feeling I'd be getting to know him and probably quite soon.

I parked on the same side as the parlour, about 100yds along from where Lettsbe had been standing. There was a slight bend in the road, so I couldn't see the two men from where I was. I decided I'd roll myself a ciggy and watch in the mirror to see if they came by me in a car, together or not. No sooner had I lit my cigarette than I could see a car coming down the road towards me and as it passed, yes, Lettsbe and his friend were in the car together and Lettsbe's friend was driving. That's it, I thought. Another Old Bill on the scene. I'll have to keep an eye out for him in the future.

I locked the van up and walked back along the road to the parlour, excited to see Claire. Chantel greeted me at the door, dressed in her best working clothes. Black with knee-high black boots, with a little type of black shawl which barely covered her shoulders.

"Hello ladies," I said as I walked into the kitchen. Abbie sprang up to put the kettle on. The girls were all sitting there smoking and discussing our going out tonight. Claire said she'd make some calls in a few minutes and invite the other girls to join us over at the pub. I asked Chantel, "How's business?"

"Very good," she replied. "We've been busy all week."

Abbie sat down with the teas and said, "It's been great all week."

Claire started making the phone calls. "Sam and Jess say they're busy but will join us as soon as they can." She invited Holly and her maid along and asked Maria and Amy but they were busy all night so unfortunately we wouldn't see them.

When Claire finished on the call to Maria she told us she was going to pop out in half an hour to see Maria to pick something up.

"Okay, I'll come with you," I offered.

"No, no, you stay here with the girls. I want to go on my own."

"Oh, that reminds me," I said to Claire, "I want to talk with you on our own. Can we go out the back to talk in private?"

"Yes, of course." We went into the garden and I said to Claire, "I just wanted to ask if we're alright."

"What does that mean? Of course we're alright, where did that come from?"

"I don't know, I just had a feeling things maybe weren't right."

"Don't be silly, course they are." She leant forward and gave me a big kiss.

FOR THE LOVE OF BRASS

That seemed to be enough for me, so, "That's good," I said.

We went back inside and Claire went on to say in front of us all that she was just picking something up from Maria and helping her out with a problem, so she was happy to go on her own. The doorbell rang again and Chantel got up to answer it in her black get up. I could definitely see what the men saw in her and why they kept coming to see her. Mind you, that was the case with all the girls.

Claire left to go and see Maria. Abbie and I sat there laughing and talking about whatever and especially Courtney beating up Lee. Chantel had another four clients to see before she was finished for the day. Abbie went on to tell me that Chantel would earn between £2,000-3,000 a week and that was after she'd paid Claire, whereas she only got £300 a week and of course the odd bit of money for letting somebody look up her skirt. We laughed at the thought of that.

She lifted up her skirt and said, "There you go, Gary, seeing as we're friends you can have a freebie." Then she burst out laughing. She was definitely one funny person to be around. The thing was, I had such a miserable life living with Sharon, coming over here to see Claire and the girls was just so much fun, the complete opposite to what I had or had ever known. I'd not told any of my regular friends about what I was doing; it was a completely and utterly different world, as though I had two lives running parallel to each other. Well, not as though I did, I actually did and this made me very happy. I saw it as a total escape from everything I knew in life and, as far as I was concerned, it could stay that way.

Claire returned after a couple of hours or so and, as I found myself feeling quite hungry, we went out into Portland Road to the Wimpy Bar for a meal, knowing we should have something inside us for the evening's drinking. We returned about 5.30. While we were out I asked Claire if

FOR THE LOVE OF BRASS

Maria was okay. She said she was and that she'd picked up some money and she'd put £400 in a brown envelope to give to to me, so as when we were in the pub I could deal with giving it to Lettsbe.

Claire and I got ourselves ready, then left for the pub over the road, well, our pub as we called it, telling Abbie and Chantel we'd see them over there when they'd finished work. We wandered in and found the pub was half full of people already and rocking. The music was already on and the tunes were good; it sort of made you feel you were going to have a good night. We sat at our usual table with our first drink. I looked around. Mr Brown had appeared in his usual spot at the end of the bar. He nodded to say hello. As we took the first couple of sips of our drinks, Lettsbe walked past the table, looking at us both.

"Gary, Claire," he said as he walked over to where Mr Brown was standing. I got up and made my way to the toilet. I went in and was standing by the urinal when the door opened behind me. I looked round; it was Lettsbe. He went to the sink to wash his hands and I did the same.

"Hello John," I understand it's your birthday, so here's a card for you, giving him the brown envelope.

"Thank you very much," he said as he tucked it inside his jacket pocket. I walked back out and sat down at my table to sip my beer again.

Claire said, "All okay?"

"Yes, darling, all sorted."

In no time it was up to the bar for another one.

Mr Brown came over while I was waiting to be served and said, "Is it safe?"

I thought, for fuck's sake. "Yeah, yeah. It's safe." He nodded, turned and went to stand in his corner again.

It wasn't long before Chantel and Abbie came in. Chantel got a round

FOR THE LOVE OF BRASS

of drinks in as she always did and we all sat at the table.

Chantel said, "Abbie, do me a favour, please. Here's twenty quid, go and give it to Mr Brown, would you?"

"Yeah, sure," Abbie said. She came back with a smile on her face.

"Come on ladies," said Chantel, "let's go and powder our noses," and off the three of them went.

I sat on my own just nodding and saying hello to people as they went by or stood at the bar. The girls came back from powdering their noses full of good cheer, giggling and laughing.

"Sorry, Gary, we thought you wouldn't want any."

"No, no," I said, "I don't."

"That's good," Chantel said, "'cos we done the lot." They all burst out laughing.

"My round," Abbie said. "Let's get some more drinks in." As she was lighting up a cigarette, I noticed Lettsbe at the other end of the bar. He'd look over every now and then to look at Chantel. The drinks were flowing well.

"My turn girls, I'm going up to the bar."

Chantel said, "I'll come with you, Gary."

As we stood at the bar waiting to be served, Lettsbe turned up and stood the other side of Chantel, talking to her. I couldn't hear what was being said but I could have a good guess. He definitely had a soft spot for her. I got drinks in for everybody including Lettsbe and Mr Brown.

It wasn't long before another £20 was invested in Mr Brown's business. Claire's phone rang a couple of times and she answered the calls, then got up.

"I'm just going outside to call Ryan."

Twenty minutes later, Ryan came in and Claire instructed him go and pick up Holly, then pick up Sam and to bring them both here, and off he went. Next little Lee came in and Chantel told him to get the drinks in.

He looked at her, then at me, and said, "She's off of her tits!"

"Yeah, I know. They all are." We were laughing.

"I want some of what she's had," said Lee.

"Well, go and see Mr Brown and give him twenty quid and you too could end up like that," pointing to Chantel and laughing. "Ha-ha-ha-ha."

Sam and Holly came in with big smiles on their faces to see everybody getting off their nut and having fun. They both came over and gave me a kiss.

Sam said, "Are you on it as well, Gary?"

"No," I said, "just the beers."

Then Ryan came over and before he could say anything, Claire said to him, "You're not needed any more. Go back to work. I'll call you later when we need you, okay?" And with that, off he went.

Chesney Hawks, 'I am the one and only' came on. Abbie shouted "Yip-pee!" and jumped on the seat, dancing and singing along with it, as did most people in the pub.

Little Lee leant over and said to me, "That fucking copper's in here. You know, the one I don't like."

"Yeah, I know who you mean, mate. Just have a drink and forget about him, he's nothing to worry about."

"Yeah, you're right. Fuck it, let's get some more drinks in," said Lee.

By this time, we were all on the piss. The pub was full of people and everybody was having a good time. Sam, Holly and Claire were chatting away to each other.

"What's you three talking about?" I shouted across the table.

"You and your guns. I'm telling them about your guns."

"Oh, okay," I said.

'Everybody's free to feel good' came on and now we were all up dancing and singing. More drinks, more visits to Mr Brown and an absolutely brilliant evening was had by all. Before we knew it, Claire was on the phone to Ryan. Then we were all standing outside the pub on the big wide pavement chatting, smoking and waiting to go home.

Little Lee and Chantel said their goodbyes and walked off down the road. It was decided that Sam, Holly and Abbie would get a cab, but they'd take Abbie home first because she was the worse for wear, then get themselves home. They'd jump into a black cab once Ryan had turned up for myself and Claire.

Next morning, oh dear, I thought, as I opened my eyes. A little too much to drink last night. I lay there for a while, gathering my thoughts, reflecting back to last night's events in the pub. The information was slowly being released from my pickled memory bank. I looked to my side to see I was in bed on my own. Claire was already up, having a shower. I got myself up and wandered through to the kitchen to put the kettle on. Claire appeared in the doorway with just a towel wrapped around her middle; what a sight for sore eyes, I thought.

"Good morning, darling." She leant over and gave me a kiss, then turned and skipped down the hall to the bedroom. How could she be so full of beans after her alcohol- and Charlie-fuelled evening? To that question, I didn't have the answer but I did know that after a mug of tea and something to eat I'd feel a lot better.

"Come on," Claire said, "let's go out. It's a nice day. We can go for a walk over on Bromley common."

"Okay, sounds good to me but what about the shopping? You need a few things here."

"Oh, don't worry about that. I'll send Ryan to deal with the shopping.

I got myself into the shower and by the time I came out, Abbie had been on the phone. She was bored, so Claire had invited her for a walk with us. She was on her way over in a cab.

The three of us went for a walk into Bromley. We ended up walking around the shops, then going into the Glades for lunch. After that, more looking around the shops. We never did get to Bromley Common. By now it was late afternoon and we were making our way back to Claire's flat. She called Ryan and told him to meet us there. When he arrived, she gave him a shopping list and sent him food shopping. I needed a lift to get my van from the pub so she asked him to take me over to Cobden Road first, which he did.

"Thanks, mate," I said, as he dropped me in Cobden Road.

I turned the van round and drove to the Portland Road end. As I pulled up at the junction, our pub was on the left-hand side. I looked across the wide pavement at the wooden chairs and tables. Three men were sitting at one of the tables. I recognised all of them, Lettsbe, Mr Brown and the other Old Bill in a suit. The one I'd seen yesterday. Hmm, that's interesting, I thought to myself. I didn't acknowledge them, just drove off, making my way back to Claire's.

We sat at Claire's, the three of us talking and laughing about last night in the pub. I told the girls who I'd seen outside the pub earlier on but they didn't really show any interest. We decided to have a quiet night and go down to the local Indian restaurant for a meal.

"Thank you very much," the waiter said as he finished taking our order, and with that, Claire's phone rang.

"Oh, hi," she said. It was Maria. She said she'd be in the area in about

FOR THE LOVE OF BRASS

15 minutes and wanted to know if Claire was at home. She had something for her. Claire explained where we were and invited Maria to join us.

Fifteen minutes passed and there was a vroom, vroom outside. Maria had pulled up in her Porsche. The door opened and in she came, looking a million dollars, as always. She sat at our table and, after she'd said hello and giving us all a kiss, the waiter came over to take her order. I noticed he hadn't been able to take his eyes off her, ever since she'd walked in.

The girls were all chatting away. I mainly sat there listening and looking at all three of them, thinking how lucky I was to have these lovely looking women in my company. The thought made me smile. Abbie was telling the story of last night, what a great time we'd had and how it was a shame Maria couldn't make it. Then our meals arrived.

While we ate we started talking about what there was to do tomorrow. I suggested we could all go shooting at Bisley. The girls were highly delighted at the prospect and Claire couldn't wait. She started telling Abbie and Maria all about the fun she'd had there shooting with me and how I'd been training her. With this in mind they were all excited and couldn't wait to go.

"Maria, could you pick Abbie up and come over to Claire's for say 10.30 tomorrow morning, then in the meantime I'll go home for the guns and ammunition, drop off my van and come back over in the Mercedes to pick all three of you up and we can go to Bisley together." I smiled.

"Yes, sure I can," said Maria.

Abbie agreed and Claire said, "Excellent, I can't wait. We'll have good fun and Gary is such a good teacher. You'll learn lots."

As we drove through the main gate of Bisley camp, I said to the girls, "We just have to pop into the NRA office and book ourselves a place." This we did, and it wasn't long before we were shooting on the 25yd range. Once I'd gone through the basic safety procedures with them, out came the ammunition and we were soon putting holes in the targets. The girls were screeching auto pistol and my snub nose .38 special. The .38 held six rounds and the .22 had a ten round magazine. I'd also brought along a silencer for it. The girls were having a ball and seemed to take to shooting like ducks to water. Before we knew it, the range hooter went off to indicate all shooting on all the ranges would stop for an hour.

"Lunchtime."

The girls said, "That's a shame, we were just getting started."

"Come on," I told them, "we'll go over to Fulton's gun shop which is the camp gun store and gunsmiths. We can buy more ammunition for the guns as you seem to be going through it like no tomorrow. Big smiles came on their faces.

"Yeah, can't wait."

"While we're away from the range, we can go over to Jenny's burger van for a drink and something to eat."

Maria saw the second magazine in my bag. "Can we use that as well?"

"Yes, of course. With that loaded you'd now have twenty rounds, you just have to reload. I'll teach you how to do that quickly so you can keep on firing." I'd never seen the girls smile as much as they were when they were firing guns. A little later on I taught them how to use the auto with a silencer fitted to it.

Abbie said, "This is like James Bond or, better still, Charlie's fucking Angels."

"Yes, that's us. Charlie's Angels and you're Bosley," they said, looking at me, all laughing as they said it.

Towards the end of our shooting session I started to teach them defensive shooting, just as I'd teach bodyguards.

FOR THE LOVE OF BRASS

The girls told me they'd had a fantastic time and Maria finished off the last six rounds of .38. On the way back home to Claire's flat, it was all they could talk about and the questions kept flowing. Once at Claire's, we all sat around the kitchen table with our tea and cigarettes. The girls were keen on cleaning the guns. I had a tin of gun oil in my bag and I got a kitchen roll from the cupboard. There wasn't much to teach the girls with the revolver, just a general wipe over would do for now but I could show them how to strip down the auto for cleaning. This they found very interesting, I also had them strip the silencer down and clean that. Once this was done the girls just had to have some photos taken with the guns, just like Charlie's Angels, then Maria and Abbie left for home. I also had to head home but not before we found ourselves in bed vigorously trying to earn the £50 from each other.

Monday morning and once again I was driving over to meet Claire at Cobden Road. We were going swimming at Beckenham baths. Sharon dealt with taking the boys to school this morning and saying goodbye to them, then she'd go home to finish her packing, ready for her holiday to Turkey. I didn't know what time she was going but that didn't matter, all that mattered was I'd be picking the boys up from school.

I had a chat with Sharon's sister whose name was also Maria, although no-one called her Maria because when my boys were young they couldn't say Maria, so they called her Mimi and the name had stuck, so Mimi it was. Anyway, Mimi had said if I needed her for anything while Sharon was away, all I had to do was ask, picking up the kids from school, cooking tea or even staying the night and getting the boys off to school in the morning. She'd offered this to help out in case I had to work.

After our swimming session at the baths we went back to Cobden Road. Sam had called and wanted me to go out on a job with her, which

I was happy to do. Claire was going to go over to see Holly with some supplies and we'd meet back at Cobden Road a bit later.

The job I went on with Sam was easy enough. I took her to see a client over in the Dulwich area, waited an hour, which was uneventful, then drove her back. She gave me 50 quid. When I arrived back at Cobden, Claire was already there. She was talking to the girls about Lettsbe; he'd been in to see Holly. He'd gone as a client and of course they recognised each other from the pub. He had sat and had tea with her, then left, not having used her services.

Claire said to me, "Now he knows for sure she's a working girl and associated with us, we might have to pay more protection money."

"Yes, that's true," I said, "but we'll wait to see if he says anything or what unfolds. I have to say my goodbyes now, girls. I've got to go home and pick my boys up from school. Sharon's on holiday now in Turkey somewhere. Peace and quiet," I said and laughed.

Chantel and Abbie both gave me a kiss goodbye, Claire walked me out to my van, then she too gave me a big kiss goodbye but she seemed concerned about Lettsbe. She mentioned him again.

"Don't worry," I said, "we'll see want happens. I have to go now but I'll call you later."

I made it back home just in time to pick the boys up.

"Dad, can we go out with the dogs?"

"Yes, of course we can. We'll go home to get them, then go to Morden Park. Then can we get a kebab and chips for tea."

"Ha-ha, yes we can." We all laughed.

We didn't get back until about 7 o'clock and after a while, it was time to get the boys ready for bed. Once they'd settled down, I poured myself a large V and O. That's it, I thought, I'll call Claire. She was still at Cobden

FOR THE LOVE OF BRASS

Road with the girls and said they were just chilling and talking.

"Oh," said Claire, "Sam has called. She wants to book you for tomorrow afternoon. Is that okay?"

"Yeah, yeah, that's fine. Tell her that's okay. I'll call Mimi and get her to pick the boys up and cover for me till I get back."

"Okay," Claire said. "See you tomorrow."

I sat down in my lounge to watch TV for a while and thought of the girls sitting over there on their own. Then I thought of the shotgun; that's a point, I thought to myself, there's no ammo there. I'll get a couple of shells now so I don't forget and take them with me tomorrow.

After I'd got the boys ready and off to school, I went home to my office for a while and did a few tasks, then left for Cobden Road. I'd arranged for Mimi to collect the boys, give them their tea and wait there till I got home, so I didn't have to worry about time later. For now we were going swimming again. Swimming was great. It gave us time on our own plus we got to play around like a couple of kids together.

Once back at the parlour, Abbie had made tea and we all sat there drinking and smoking. The phone rang and it was the fellow we called "Stickman". He wanted to come around in half an hour so Abbie booked him in. We sat there laughing about what might happen with him next, then he arrived. Chantel took him into the room and when she asked what he wanted today, he said he wanted to look up Abbie's skirt while Chantel was giving him a wank. Then he wanted to be gagged, hooded and handcuffed to the wall and for Abbie to hit him with a stick because she was so good at it. He wanted to give Chantel £200.

"Okay," she said, "you get yourself ready and I'll be back in a minute." She came back into the kitchen with us, laughing as she told us what he wanted. "Here's the two hundred pounds," which she gave to Claire. "He wants the same as before, Abbie you have a job. Put your short skirt on."

"Okay," Abbie said, laughing as she did so.

Chantel then went on to say, "When we call you, Gary, can you come in and hit him like you did before?"

I laughed. "Yes, okay, just come and get me."

We were all giggling and Chantel and Abbie went off into the room to make a start.

I said to Claire, "Where's the stick?"

"I don't know. Have a look in the hallway cupboard."

"Okay, there ain't no fucker in there is there?"

"No," she said. "I don't think so."

I quietly opened the cupboard door, still half expecting to see a naked man in there. Empty, that's good, I thought, and got out the stick. I put it by the bedroom door, then we waited. After a while the kitchen door opened and in came Abbie. She beckoned me to follow her, with one of her fingers on her lips for me to be quiet. I went into the room and both girls had the biggest smiles on their faces. Mr Stickman was standing facing the wall. They'd gagged and hooded him, after they'd sorted him out on the bed of course. He was naked and had his hands up and tied together and over the hook on the wall.

Abbie said to him, "I'm going to give you a little whack with the stick, just make a noise as best you can if you like it, then I'll hit you again." I gave Abbie the stick she lifted it up and swung it down across his back. Crack! it sounded as it hit him. Both girls were laughing out loud now and he groaned.

Chantel said, "He likes it. Hit him again, Abbie." This she did, even harder. He groaned and she hit him again, he groaned some more.

Abbie passed me the stick then gestured with her hand for me to hit

FOR THE LOVE OF BRASS

him. She was smiling, we were all smiling. I lifted the stick as high as I could, then thought to myself, hit him across his arse. If you hit him in the back you could damage his spine or his kidneys. Yes, I told myself, hit the softest part of him. I brought the stick down as hard as I could and with the loudest thwack it struck him right across his buttocks. He let out one big muffled sound then buckled at the knees and went silent, he was just hanging there.

Chantel looked at me and said, "I think you've fucking killed him." I started laughing and had to smother my mouth. I turned to go out the door and saw Claire had been standing in the hall watching the whole thing. We went back into the kitchen, laughing.

I said, "I think I need a ciggy."

Mr Stickman regained consciousness. One of his wounds was bleeding, so the girls untied him, cleaned him up and sent him on his way.

As he left he said, "Thank you very much," and told the girls he couldn't wait to come and see them again.

The four of us were soon sitting there drinking tea and laughing about Mr Stickman when the doorbell rang with another client for Chantel.

Off she went into the room and I said to Claire, "I've bought over a couple of shotgun shells for the sawn off. I'll load them in the gun now Chantel's out of the room. I opened the cupboard door then slid out the drawer. I lifted the sawn-off out of its brackets, broke it open and put two nice red shotgun shells in the breach. I closed the gun, put the safety catch on, then replaced it back on the hooks, putting the drawer back and closing the door.

I looked at Abbie, "Don't forget, say nothing to anyone about this, will you?"

"That's fine," she said. "I won't say a word."

Sam called and asked if I could pick up her and Jess in half an hour. We finished our tea and I said goodbye to the girls, then went on my way over to Sam's flat.

"Sorry," I said to Jess, "you have to sit in the back."

"That's okay, no problem. It's comfy enough in here." I'd put a big old cushion in there for just this type of occasion.

Sam said, "Do you know Scawen Road, over by Deptford Park?"

"No, but I know Deptford park. I'll head in that direction and if you don't mind, can you look it up in the A to Z?"

We found the address no problem and I parked up. The girls went in saying they'd be out in an hour. I waited as usual. Sure enough, after an hour the girls came out and off we went to the next address, Dunton Road off the Old Kent Road.

"Yep, I know that," and off we went. Once there, the building looked like it had been a pub but now it was flats. The girls said they'd be one and a half hours and while they worked, I sat, bored, smoking and listening to the radio. Once they were done it was finished for the evening, so off we went back to their flat to drop them off.

As I left, Jess said, "This is for you, Gary," and gave me £150 pounds, which I thought really wasn't too bad at all for what I'd done. Sam called Claire to tell her we were back safely and I had a quick chat with Claire to tell her I was on my way home and that I'd see her tomorrow. I suggested we could go swimming again and with that all agreed, I made my way home to see Mimi to thank her for helping out.

I turned up at Cobden Road about 10.30 the next day and, guess what, Claire and I went swimming. We were back in time for lunch, then I went over to Sam's to pick up an envelope. As luck would have it, I had my black leather jacket on. The envelope was quite thick, I guessed maybe two grand in it but it fitted nicely into my inside pocket.

I spent a while there, just enough to have a coffee and a smoke with the girls. By this time I was really getting to know the girls quite well. I saw them all as friends and we were like one big family. We always got along so well.

I took the envelope back over to Claire and she said to me, "You have to go early today, don't you?"

"Yes, to pick up my boys from school."

"Okay, can you do me a favour, please, on your way home with whatever time you have, can you pop in to see Maria and spend a little time with her? She's on her own again this week and it'll give her a little company. Just make sure she is alright."

"Yeah, no problem. I'd would love to. She's a good kid and I like her."

"Kid?"

"Well, yeah, I can call her that because she's younger than me. Okay, then, I'll be on my way." Claire gave me a kiss goodbye, as did Chantel and Abbie.

Chantel said to Abbie, "Have you told him yet?"

"Me? Told me what?"

Chantel said, "Don't look in the cupboard on your way out."

Oh, no, I thought to myself. Who the hell's in there? As I walked past the cupboard I put my hand on the handle, hesitated and looked at the girls. They were sniggering. Nope. I thought better of it. I don't what to see inside. I'm sure my life will be okay without whatever image I'm going to put in my head by looking inside the cupboard. I waved and pulled the door closed behind me.

I looked at my watch and figured by the time I got to Maria's, I should be able to spend around an hour with her. This suited me fine. She was great company, plus I really liked her.

I was soon parking my van by the park opposite her place. I tapped on the window as before and walked up to the front door. Maria opened it, then stood right in the way. I couldn't pass her. She put her arms around me and kissed me. I couldn't help myself and kissed her back.

"Okay, okay," I said. "Nice to see you but don't make me all nervous again, please."

She laughed, "Okay, I won't. Claire called and said you were on your way over. I'll put the kettle for tea."

"That's great." I followed her into the kitchen and found myself watching her as she filled the kettle and got the cups ready.

I sat and started to roll a ciggy. "So you enjoyed yourself shooting at Bisley on Sunday?"

"Oh, it was fantastic. Never had such a good time and learned so much. You know a great deal about all that stuff, don't you?"

"Yeah, I guess so. I've done it for a long time. I was interested in guns when I was a kid and I've had the gun licence for a long time now."

"Well, I have to tell you something. When we were firing that Smith and Wesson magnum, I found that really sexy. It makes you feel like you have a lot of power when you're holding a gun in your hand. Then when you were helping me aim the gun and you had your arms around me as we fired it off, it was making me wet."

"Oh, for fuck's sake, where's the tea?" Then I started laughing. "Are you going to embarrass me again?"

She smiled. "No, no. As if I'd do that."

As we sat with our tea, I asked her if she went home much.

"Oh yeah, all the time. Most nights in fact. I just use this place like my office, I live in Dulwich but I never take clients to my house. I don't think that's a safe thing to do. When I've any clients wanting to see me, they come here but most of my jobs are out calls and mostly on the weekends. I've a number of very wealthy clients and I earn a lot of money. I've no man in my life to enjoy it with or any man to look after me, which is why I'd like to team up with you. I'd like the same arrangement you have with Claire.

"I'll look after you, you should know that," I said.

"I can earn six or seven thousand pounds on a weekend, sometimes ten."

"What, ten thousand quid for the weekend?"

"Yes, and it happens quite often. I've had my house now for nearly three years and it's all paid for. My car's paid for too so from now on it's all profit, or of course I could look for another house. With you being a builder, we could cash in together big time. So Gary, what do you say? Don't answer now, just think about it, please."

I could see Maria was being very serious. I thought to myself, what an offer. Any man would be very grateful to have an offer like that and with a woman who was so beautiful. Wow. I didn't know what to think. The only thing I could think of was that I was in love with Claire.

"Okay," I said to Maria. "Well, thank you. That's all I can say at the moment, other than, can you give me your phone number? I keep a book in the van with the girls' numbers in, just in case, you know, I might need to contact any of you."

"Yes, no problem, here we go." Maria wrote her number on a piece of paper and gave it to me.

"I'll have to go soon," I told Maria. "I'm going to collect my boys from school."

"Yes," she said, "your wife's away, is that right?"

"Yes, that's right. She's back next week, so in the meantime I get to have fun with the boys, just the three of us."

"Bye for now," Maria said as she gave me a kiss on the cheek.

I collected the boys from school and out we went with the dogs for an hour or so, then came back home to cook some tea for us all. Later, when the boys were in bed, I called Claire for a chat, plus I was curious to find out who was in the cupboard. It turned out to be true about the man in the cupboard. It was the same fellow who had frightened the life out of me before. He was in there doing the same with the baked bean tins.

Claire also went on to say a young Irish couple had called looking for work in the business. Claire had asked them to come over for a type of interview, which they had. It had given them all a chance to meet each other and chat about how things worked if they worked for Claire. She had told them about me and how I dealt with the security and the minding of the girls. They had all sat for some time drinking tea and smoking, then DC Lettsbe had phoned in and made an appointment to see Chantel. He was quite sweet on her.

"After he'd gone, Chantel asked us not to tell Lee he'd been, so try and remember, keep it to yourself. It'll only serve to piss Lee off." Plus, I thought, she quite likes Lettsbe now, or she seems to anyway. Lettsbe had also left a message with Chantel to tell me that he's aware of Holly and that she works. "He said he'd be expecting a birthday card from her on Friday. Chantel was bemused when she told me. What the fuck does that mean? Is it his birthday?"

"No, no. Just taking the piss, don't worry. Thanks for telling me."

"So what are we going to do?"

"Well, give him another two hundred quid, I guess. What do you think, Claire?"

FOR THE LOVE OF BRASS

"I think he is a fucking cheeky bastard, that's what I think."

"Okay, let's leave that subject for now, we can talk about it some more tomorrow. I'll call you in the morning. Goodnight, Babe."

CHAPTER FOURTEEN
JIMMY THE DOG

I sat in my office ordering materials from a list Ron had given me for the jobs we had running over in Croydon, then I went downstairs to the kitchen and put the kettle on. I stood there smoking, looking out through my kitchen window and thinking about Lettsbe. Nothing we could do about that situation. He'd now be costing £600 a week. My phone rang.

"Hello Gary, it's Abbie. When are you coming over? Is everything okay?"

"Yes, yes, it's all good," I said.

"We have a dog," she said.

"Have you? When did you get that?"

"Today, we got him today. You should come over as soon as possible. He's so funny."

"What type of dog is he?"

"I'm not sure. You'll know. Come and see him."

"Okay, I'll be over in about thirty minutes." With that she hung up and all I could hear was the dialling tone. Okay, I thought, I'll give the tea a miss and no doubt have one over at the parlour.

Chantel opened the door to me with the biggest smile on her face. "Come in, Gary."

I followed her down the hall, watching her bum wiggle from side to side. As I entered the kitchen, I froze. My mouth dropped open and I couldn't believe what I was looking at. The new pet dog was a man.

FOR THE LOVE OF BRASS

Let me explain exactly what I saw. There was a man on his hands and knees. Around his neck was a wide leather collar with pink studs, and attached to that was a lead, which also had pink studs all along its length. The man was naked, except the girls had put one of Chantel's G-strings on him. The front of the G-string seemed to cover his dick but that was it. His bollocks hung out to one side, and on the other end of the lead was Abbie, taking him for a walk around the kitchen. Once I'd composed myself, I looked at Chantel, then at Abbie and just burst out laughing. I thought it was one of the funniest things I'd ever seen. Abbie was almost wetting herself as she walked the dog over to the back door where there were two bowls on the floor, one with water in and one with biscuits in. She told the dog to have a drink and this he did. He bent down and started lapping the water which sort of left his arse sticking up in the air with his bollocks on display, just like a real dog. I didn't know what to say. I was shocked, yet the scene was so funny.

"Does the dog have a name?"

"Yes," she said, "Jimmy."

"Ha-ha-ha, Jimmy the dog."

I'd never seen anything like it in my life. It was so funny.

As I was laughing, I asked, "Is he house trained?"

"Yes, I think so," Abbie replied.

"Is he naughty?"

"No, I don't think so," Chantel piped up and went on to say, "give me a minute." She went off into the room and came back with a riding crop and said, "If he's naughty, smack his arse with that."

I sat down with stomach pains where I was laughing so hard. Abbie walked him back over and sat down. Jimmy rolled over on his back for a tummy tickle and that was it for me. I had to go outside, I couldn't stand it any longer. I kept looking back in through the kitchen window, I couldn't help myself. What a sight, and all the while Jimmy wasn't laughing. He was carrying out his role as a dog very seriously. Luckily, the kitchen-dining room was quite big, so Jimmy had space to exercise. In the excitement of meeting Jimmy the dog, I'd forgotten to ask where Claire was. She was out getting a few bits and also seeing Holly. She'd be back in a while.

"Has Claire met Jimmy yet?" I asked.

"No, he wasn't here when she left."

After a while, Claire came in with a few bits in her bag from the shops for our lunch. As she walked past Jimmy, he stood up on all fours trying to sniff her bag. She patted him on the head saying, "Good boy," as she passed him, then put the shopping on the side. She looked at me with a cheeky grin on her face and said, "So you've met Jimmy, what do you think?"

After Jimmy had been a dog for a couple of hours, for which he paid £150, Chantel took him into the room so he could get dressed like a human again. Then he left the parlour. Every time I looked at Abbie we laughed. This whole world was new to us.

About four o'clock and a couple of clients later, Claire said, "Come on, let's have an early day and go over to the pub for a beer or two."

By 4.30 we were having our first drink. I was on shandies as I was driving. Lettsbe came walking in.

"Oh Gary, just the man I want to see. Come up to the bar; let me get you a drink."

"Hello John," I said and leaned on the bar next to him.

"You got my message then."

"Yes, yes, I did."

"Well, if you have another parlour in my manor you have to pay for it."

FOR THE LOVE OF BRASS

"So it's six hundred pounds each week now."

"Yeah, that's right. Starting from tomorrow," he said with a big grin on his face. I walked back to the table where the girls sat, with the same beer I went up with. I looked at Claire. "Yup, it's gone up a couple as we thought."

The pub was getting busier now, probably nearly half full. We four sat there talking, mainly about Jimmy the dog. Abbie and I still found the thought of it very funny. Claire and Chantel had seen it before, in fact Chantel went on to tell us about a client she had had a while back. He'd call her, for her to visit him. He liked being a baby. She told us she put nappies on him and fed him and he paid her good money for doing that.

"It takes all types, I guess."

"Gary." I looked up, it was Lettsbe. "Can you come outside for a few minutes? I've someone I want you to meet. Oh, and bring your fags." I followed him out though the side door of the pub. "There's a bit of a breeze blowing along the front," he said. "I thought we could stand round here, out of the way." I started to roll a fag and noticed a man in a suit was crossing the road and walking in our direction. I recognised him as the other Old Bill I'd seen.

"Hello, Gary," he said as he put his hand out. We shook hands. "Nice to meet you at last. I've heard a lot about you and all good stuff I must say. I'm Detective Sergeant Peter Carter, I'm John's boss, we're from the same factory in the manor."

"Yeah okay, nice to meet you, too. What can I do for you?"

"Well, we know all about you. We know your military history with the Regiment, we know about your building company, we know all about your gun licences, we even have a list of the guns you own. We know where you live, where your wife works, we even know where your kids go to school."

"Well, that puts me at a disadvantage because I don't know anything about you or what you do."

"Well, you don't need to know anything about us other than we'll look after you and your girls."

"Hold on a minute, I don't have any girls. I just help out my girlfriend, he knows that." I pointed to John.

"Well, for argument sake, we'll call them your girls because that's how it looks to everybody and you've earned the respect of everybody in that pub and the surrounding area. They all think you run this place. Now that suits us because your presence is keeping things in order and we like things to be in order. We don't want loads of shit and paperwork to do, we like things to be tidy and you seem to be doing it for us. Your girls talk about you in such a way, they tell people you have guns and that you carry guns and you have shot people in the past for trivial things. They tell people you're nice to their faces but won't stand any shit and that you're heartless. Your reputation has spread and with your appearance, people believe it. We want to work with you."

"Yeah, and do what?"

"We want to give you protection. We want to make sure you don't get any shit from anyone including the police. We'll be your insiders and if people start to play up, we'll let you know and we'll nick them and keep them out of the way."

"And how much is this going to cost me?"

"Well, we'll start by looking after your parlours, as we already do. We know you have three, so that's six hundred a week. I think you'll find in the long run it'll be well worth it and should you want to engage in any other criminal activities, let us know and we'll eliminate the competition for you, at a price, of course. We could be partners in a sense, then we all get to make money. As for now, your parlours are protected and you won't get any problems from the police. Should you get problems from other sources, let us know and we'll sort it for you. I have to go for now but keep in contact with John here, as I'm sure you will. We'll meet again." I shook his hand and he turned and walked away.

"Come on," Lettsbe said. "Let's go back in and have a drink."

"Well, John, I don't know what to say. I didn't realise quite what the girls were saying. I knew they said a few things but I didn't realise they said so much, or how far it had spread."

John laughed. "You're the Daddy around here and you didn't even know it. Ha-ha-ha. I find that funny. Anyway, anything we can do to help, just let me know."

John moved away as we went back into the bar and I went over to my right where the girls were sitting. Well, that was interesting. Abbie spoke up first.

"Are you in trouble?" and laughed.

"Yes, I am. He'd information that I had his dog called Jimmy." We all laughed. "Tell you about it later, Babe, when we're on our own. No point discussing it here." Claire smiled.

We discussed Friday night. "How about we get in here and have a big bash of a night?" I suggested.

"What a great idea," Claire said. "But not here, we should go anywhere and have a mental one but we'll go somewhere." The girls all agreed we'd go out together.

"Can I use your phone, please?" I asked. "I want to call Jack, my sitter." I walked outside to use the phone as it was a bit noisy in the pub. As I came out the side door there was Lettsbe and Mr Brown. Mr Brown was serving John up a nice little white wrapper, Coke or whizz who knows, I thought. And who cares?

I called Jack and asked if he could be at my house tomorrow at 6.45 and stay the night. I'm sure he was used to this by now. Yes, he could. Marvellous, I told myself. All I have to do is pick the boys up from school, spend some time with them, cook dinner for us all, then go out about 7.00, once Jack has arrived.

"Yes!" I told the girls as I went back into the pub. "All sorted, we're going out."

I told the girls I'd be off home now but I'd see them tomorrow. I had to pick the boys up from Mimi's. She'd picked them up from school and taken them to her house for tea with their cousins. Mimi's mum had also popped in. She wanted to see the grandchildren and she'd brought a few treats for the kids.

When I arrived at Mimi's house, she said, "The kids want to stay the night, if that's okay?"

"Yes, that's fine," I said.

"Okay, bring their change of clothing over in the morning. I'll get them ready and you can take them to school."

"Okay, everybody happy. Good." I went off home, took the dogs out and fed them and myself, then put my feet up and watched the TV with my good old friend, V and O.

When I arrived at Cobden Road next day, Claire, Abbie and, of course, Chantel were already there. Chantel had already seen two clients so she was off to a good start. Claire suggested it would be a good idea for us to pop round to the shop for a couple of things.

As we left the parlour she said, "Let's go into the Wimpy for a coffee. I want to talk to you on our own. What did the Old Bill have to say?"

"Okay, I'll tell you about it once we're in there."

FOR THE LOVE OF BRASS

We took a seat in the corner by the front window so I could see around me and what was going on outside, which seems to have become a habit of mine. I told Claire the whole conversation that had taken place with DS Carter and Lettsbe. She wanted to know all the details, some of which we went over two or three times. She wanted to get her head around it all.

"Basically, these two coppers are so bent they couldn't lay in bed straight and it seems we can do whatever we want as long as they get something out of it. In exchange for that, they'll protect us." Claire was deep in thought and taking this all very seriously. I could see the pound signs ringing up in her eyes. "So what are you thinking?"

"Hmmmm, this could be a big advantage to us. If we work this right we could make a fortune. Let me think about it. Come on, let's go back to the parlour. I've a job for you."

We walked in and Abbie put the kettle on. "In a little while," Claire said, "the Irish couple will be here. I want you to meet them. I told you about them before. They'll be working with us. They double up on jobs like Sam and Jess do, so I want them to meet."

"Double up?" I asked.

"Yes, they work a lot with voyeurs, you know, the people who like to watch the sexual activity going on while they wank or shag their own partner."

"Really?" I looked at Abbie and we started laughing. "Oh," I said, "I've been missing out in life."

"Me too," said Abbie. We smirked and grinned like two naughty kids, then the doorbell rang. Chantel went to answer, as usual, and in came the couple.

"This is Bridie and Patrick."

375

"Hello," they said.

Claire introduced us all and we sat smoking and talking for a while. Then Claire called Sam and in no time I was driving Bridie and Pat to meet Sam and Jess. The kettle went on again as we went into Sam's flat, then Jess came through. We introduced each other, then all sat around the kitchen table. I noticed they didn't talk much about what they did at work but more about Dublin, which was where Bridie and Pat came from. Sam and Jess had been there, so they had stuff in common to talk about. It wasn't long before I was mentioned as the girls' minder. Sam started to tell the story of how I had saved her from a nutcase with my gun, which the Irish couple seemed very impressed with. Pat went on to explain how they didn't need a minder because he did that for Bridie, he'd go on jobs with her and would wait for her or, if he was booked on the job, he'd go in as well.

"So you drive Bridie?"

"No, I don't drive. Neither of us do."

"Oh, okay, how do you get to the jobs then?"

"We use a cab, or maybe now we can use you."

"Oh, okay." I looked at Sam with raised eyebrows, I wasn't really understanding what was going on or what he meant but it didn't matter I told myself, it would all come out in the wash when they started working.

After some time, we went back to Cobden Road. Claire knew I'd be going to pick up my boys soon and asked if I could pop in to see Maria and pick up an envelope. "Oh, and she's at her house in Dulwich, not at the flat."

"Okay." When I got to the area I had to drive up and down looking for somewhere to park. The parking was always shit here. In the end I had to park down the road a couple of hundred yards away and walk back. By

FOR THE LOVE OF BRASS

the time I got to Maria's front door, there was a man with a parcel for her. He'd knocked but got no answer. He asked if I could sign for it, which I did, and started to turn but before he went, he said he'd been to the house before there was never anyone in.

"Do they go away a lot?"

"No," I said, "they don't. You must have been unlucky, anyway I'm moving in the weekend, she's my sister. I work from home so there'll always be someone here. See you next time."

"Okay, thanks," he said and went on his way. I knocked some more and Maria answered and let me in. She saw the parcel.

I said, "Here you go. I signed for it but that man, he asked too many questions." I told her what I'd told him and suggested she didn't have anything else sent there but had it sent to the flat instead. "You just never know, he might have been eyeing the place up, casing it or whatever."

I collected the boys from school and in no time we were out over the park with the dogs. It was getting slightly colder now the summer had passed but it hadn't rained for a couple of days, so there was no mud to worry about. The only ones that might get wet and muddy were the dogs if they got in the stream but they generally tried to avoid the water.

"Dad," they said when we got back, "can we do house clearance while the dinner's on?"

"Yes, okay."

"Great, we'll get the guns." We hunted each other around the house until the food was ready and soon after that, Jack arrived.

My phone rang, it was Claire. She said not to come to the pub but to meet them at the wine bar in Surrey Street.

"You know where the Surrey Street market is in Croydon. We'll start our evening there. Oh, and don't bring the van. We could end up anywhere." She was laughing as she said it. I thought this sounds like we're going to have a good night out.

I called the cab firm at Rosehill and booked a cab for 7.15. I figured it'd take me till 7.00 to get ready, then a little time spent with three boys would be good. I left the house to the sound of laughing and joking while the house clearance was taking place. The cab driver knew the wine bar we were heading to, and as I got out of the cab I paid the driver and told him to keep the change. I had butterflies in my stomach. The anticipation was nearly too much. I was expecting a very good night out with the girls and couldn't wait to get started.

The wine bar was busy, full, even though it was only a quarter to eight. I think some had got in there after work and just not gone home yet because most of them seemed pissed. The music was good and the place was banging. The girls already had a pint of cider waiting on the bar for me. All three of them were dressed up and looking lovely. I kept getting looks from some of the guys in the place, you could tell what they were thinking. How come that fellow has three of the loveliest ladies in the bar with him?

I was soon onto my third pint and half way through that, and needed to go off to the toilet. "Where's the loo in here?" I asked someone.

"Just down the back mate, you can't miss it." On my return the girls had saved my stool and I sat down. We were talking about all sorts of things including the Dublin couple. They were a handsome pair, it had to be said. I was about to pick up the remains of my pint, when I noticed a small white something fizzing in the bottom of the glass.

I picked the glass up to have a better look and said to Abbie "What's that?" All three of them started laughing. "Okay, what's funny, what is it?"

"Don't worry about it." Claire said. "It's only an E."

FOR THE LOVE OF BRASS

"An E!" They all started laughing.

"Yeah, it'll be okay. Just drink it up. We've all had one and we're going clubbing in a while, around the corner to the Blue Orchid. We'll have a great night." I was slightly apprehensive, having never had one before.

"It'll be okay," The girls said. "You'll love it."

"Okay." Fuck it, I thought as I drank the rest of my pint.

"Come on," Chantel said. "One more drink in here, then we'll go clubbing."

"Yippee!" said all three girls.

The idea of the one more drink here was to give the E time to get into the body's system. It would need 30 minutes or so before you'd start to feel the effects of it. Ecstasy was a drug I'd never tried, so this would be new to me. They told me it would give you an overwhelming feeling of great happiness, accompanied by joyful excitement. It's an amphetamine-based drug with euphoric effects, originally produced as an appetite suppressant. Of course, by now it was highly illegal but nevertheless, here we were finishing off our drinks, having all downed an E, then on our way to the night club. The Blue Orchid was only about 15 minutes' walk away.

"Yes," Claire said, "we'll walk and that'll give us a little more time for the E to work."

As we drew closer to the club Abbie asked if it was working yet.

"I don't think so," I replied.

"Well, let me know when it does. I can't feel anything yet either. This is my first time as well." We were both already smiling big time and as we stood at the kiosk waiting to pay for our entrance into the club, I found my foot tapping to the sound of the music coming from inside. Once I'd paid, we walked up to where the doormen were and they opened the doors. As I walked through I was immediately hit by the effect of the Ecstasy. Wow! What a feeling it was.

I turned to the girls with the biggest smile on my face and said, "You'll have to get the drinks in because I'm going dancing." And off I went to join all the others out there on the dance floor. They were probably E-ing as well. I felt absolutely marvellous and they were right, a feeling of euphoria flows right through you. Years later when I watched a film called *Rise of the Foot Soldiers,* there's a scene where Carlton Leach says to his bouncer friend, "Err, I've only gone and had one of those pills." "Oh yeah?" his mate says. "What's it like?" "Shit, I can't feel anything," but he's tapping his feet, really wanting to move. Carlton turns to his mate, leans over, kisses him on the cheek and says, "I fucking love you," then turns and goes out on the dance floor and starts dancing. That part of the film really, really made me laugh. It brought back so many memoires because that's exactly what it's like. I could certainly understand why people liked this drug. In a very short time I was joined by Abbie. Claire and Chantel put the drinks on a nearby table, then they joined us, all of us having the time of our lives.

Once I'd finished that pint of lager that was it, no more lagers for me; it was bottles of water for the rest of the night. The flashing lights and the coloured laser beams all added to the effect. You just feel happy and as though you want to kiss everybody, and at some point this is what I was doing. I kissed the three girls I was with multiple times, along with any other women who happened to dance by. I'd never known an evening like it. We were still dancing as the club closed and we danced out onto the street.

Claire had arranged for Ryan to pick us up. Once in the car, Claire decided to drop me home first. This they did and I was waving goodbye as Ryan's car drove away down the road. I went inside the house; it was

FOR THE LOVE OF BRASS

about four in the morning and, still buzzing, I got myself into bed.

I couldn't go to sleep at all. When I closed my eyes I could still see and hear the club and the music in my head. I found myself tapping my foot against the bottom of the bed. I lay there for quite a while, still enjoying the effects of the Ecstasy, but eventually I fell to sleep.

Saturday morning and Jack was off home. The boys wanted to go swimming, so we headed off to Cheam baths. Once we'd got changed and passed through the shower section and into the main pool area, I realised music was being played, and up to date music at that. The sound of it put a big grin on my face. It made me feel very happy and I can remember thinking this must be the residue of the Ecstasy pill. We all had great fun there, as always, and afterwards we went to the Cheam Wimpy bar for lunch where the boys could have a milkshake and ice cream. I decided we'd have a night at home, not doing much. I ended up calling Claire and arranging a time to pick her up the following day. We'd decided to go to Bisley again, shooting. Some of the members of the gun club would be there as it was one of our monthly meets. We were shooting on a range called the short Siberia. It was 100yds long, so rifles would be the order of the day. Claire hadn't used rifles before, so this was something else I'd be able to teach her.

Once again, we had a great day. Claire met some lovely people, as she put it. She also got to shoot a number of different types of rifle, which she thoroughly enjoyed. Afterwards we went back to her flat and had a lazy evening, doing very little other than having an Indian meal delivered.

Monday morning and the usual things happened: have sex, have tea, have breakfast, get a shower and go to the parlour. We decided to give the swimming a miss today and go straight to see what was going on at Cobden Road. When we got there, Abbie told Claire she'd seen a sun bed

FOR THE LOVE OF BRASS

for sale in an ad in a shop window. It was quite cheap, Abbie thought. We went for a walk along the Portland Road and found the shop with the ad.

Claire said, "That seems a good deal."

It was the full-size type with a lid that also had tubes in it, so you could get brown all over. The thing was £100. Claire got the details from the shopkeeper and called to chat to the woman who owned it. On the strength of that, she bought the bed, called Ryan and told him to get a friend and that he'd be dealing with picking it up and installing into her flat. It would be living in the spare room. There were a couple of driving jobs for me, so I called Mimi and asked if she could pick the boys up from school and stay with them. This she was happy to do, which meant I could stay out until I was done and could get home to let her go.

I picked the Dublin couple up from Croydon and took them to a job over in Crystal Palace. I waited outside the job for two hours, which I have to say I did find boring. Anyway, once they were done I went back over to Cobden to wait for a while, then out again to an early evening appointment for one hour. This time only Bridie was going in, Pat wasn't needed, which was handy because this meant I had company to sit in the van with. We got talking and I couldn't help myself, I had to ask if he was okay with his girlfriend being a working girl. I chose not to use the word brass as I figured he wouldn't know what it was. He explained he really didn't mind her working as it was a means to an end. Oh, okay. I thought.

"And how does it work?" I had to ask.

"Well," he said, "I can live with it because when she goes into a house or a room on her own, I never ask what goes on in there."

"Don't you wonder a little bit?"

"Oh yes, of course I do, but there's no point in asking because it'll only hurt me."

FOR THE LOVE OF BRASS

"You love her then?"

"Oh yes, very much so."

"And she doesn't ask what happens when you go into a room on your own?"

"That's right, she doesn't ask anything, it saves us having these mental pictures in our head. We don't need that, it would only cause a problem for us."

"Oh, okay. What happens when you both go into a room together? I'm sorry to ask this, it's just so I can understand how these things work."

"That's no problem, I don't mind telling you because your girlfriend works as well."

"Well," I said, "she was. I can't deal with her working, so the agreement was she wouldn't work while we were together."

"Oh, okay. I see."

"I don't mind her working in the business and I even work in it with her. I'm fine with that but I couldn't be with her if she worked."

"Okay, I understand that. I'd like that arrangement with Bridie but we can't do that at the moment."

"Oh, why's that?"

"Well, we're saving up to get married." I really didn't know what to say to that one, I thought.

"Saving up to get married?"

"Yes, we are. We're very much in love and want to get married. The plan's to be over here and work, then when we've enough money, we can go back to Ireland and get married." Wow! How about that.

"I couldn't do that, I'm afraid. So, what will happen when you're married back in Ireland?"

"We'll have enough money for a deposit on a house."

"How will you pay the mortgage?"

"Well, we figure we can come back over here and keep working, which is why we're here. We need to get to know as many working girls as possible, so we have contacts for later on."

"Oh, okay. And do you get much call for you to service the ladies?"

"No, not really."

"So what happens when you both go in, if you don't mind me asking?"

"Well, I have sex with Bridie."

"What and they watch?"

"Yes."

"What, just watch?"

"Yes, well they play with themselves while we're shagging. Sometimes they ask if they can have a little go on Bridie."

"And do you say no?"

"Oh yes, we always say no. Not unless they pay a bit more money, then they can." Fuck me! I thought. Unbelievable! "It's that extra money that we're saving up to get married with."

"Oh yeah, so that happens a lot?"

"Oh yes, all the time."

"So how many jobs do you get where both of you are needed?"

"Well, not that many. Maybe just three or four a week."

"Okay, so Bridie is doing all the work mainly?"

"Well, yes, I guess so."

"Wow, how about that. I'm glad you told me all that. I find it fascinating what other people do." I couldn't help but wonder to myself, the odd things people do. For want of a better word, unbelievable! It's a good job they're in love because this might not all work out. I laughed to myself at this sarcastic thought.

FOR THE LOVE OF BRASS

Before we knew it Bridie was on her way out of the house and over to the van. Now I couldn't help but wonder what she'd been doing, let alone what he must be thinking.

Bridie and Pat were finished for the day so I was going to drop them off home, but before I did I had one more task to do and that was pick up another envelope from Maria. When I got there, I explained I couldn't stop as I had Bridie and Pat in the van and was going to drop them off home in Mitcham, then going home myself.

"If you don't have much to do tonight, you can always come over here and keep me company. Oh, and a message from Claire, can you call her later?"

I looked at Maria and smiled. "You're such a naughty girl," I said as I walked off down her path. I thought any man in this world would have been happy to have her on his arm. Oh well, let's get these two home then I can get home myself and let Mimi go.

I called Claire later that night, she said that the Old Bill had been in for their payment. "Miserable bastards. They weren't happy they didn't get it on Friday."

Next morning I got the boys ready and took them to school, then back home, out for a run, then I took the dogs out. I like to exercise as much as I can. I checked the post when I got back from running the dogs and there was a letter from my brief, Steve. He wanted a meeting as soon as possible.

Okay, I thought to myself, I'll try to talk with him later. Sharon would be coming home today, worst luck – oh well, she is the boys' mum – but as I had no idea when, I'd need to be back in time to pick the boys up from school. She might not get back till nighttime. As I drove over to see the girls, I was thinking about Claire. She loved to be naughty, always pushing the boundaries with things, particularly with Ryan. She had him running all over the place for us and the other girls come to think of it. He was the firm's lapdog. I smiled at the thought.

I met Claire at her flat and we went to the Bromley Glades for lunch. Again she told me about the coppers not being happy with the delay in their payment. They'd said not to be late again but if there was a problem, we needed to let them know in advance and that would be okay.

We also talked about the new couple on the firm. She asked me what I thought of them and I told her about the arrangement they had with each other and how much in love they were. Out of the blue, Claire told me she loved me and that I should never have that worry about her working while we were together. Of course, I agreed.

We left the Glades after a lovely lunch and went back to her flat. As always, we ended up in bed together, working on the £50 massage. Later I left the flat and went over to pick the boys up from school. When we got home we started archery practice in the garden. Sharon came home from holiday in the early evening and the boys were very pleased to see her, which was nice for all concerned. After the kids had gone to bed, I was sitting watching the TV with my V and O when Sharon came into the room and started to tell me about her holiday. It sounded as though she had had a good time; she had a lovely tan, the brownest I've ever seen her. She said she was knackered and had spent all her money and wasn't going out again until Saturday night. That's handy, I thought. No need to come home if I don't want to.

Next morning, after my normal run, I went over to the parlour, where I met Claire. We were going over to see Maria and Lisa but before we did, she suggested we pop around to the Wimpy to chat on our own. She wanted to talk about the coppers and in particular the new one, Carter.

FOR THE LOVE OF BRASS

She asked what I thought and whether we could trust them. "Well, they're as bent as anything but putting that to one side, yes, I think we can trust them. They're in it for the money, that's obvious.

"And who's this new bloke?"

"DS Carter. There was a Carter in the TV series *The Sweeney*, do you remember that?"

"Yes, I do. Then maybe we should call him Sweeney or the Sween."

"Yes, that's a good idea. It'll be like a code," Claire laughed. "Well, if you think the Sween is okay, I might sort out some more drugs and see if we can move them."

"Where, in the pub?" I asked. "Well, yeah, but maybe also through those two dodgy coppers Lettsbe and Sweeney." She laughed at the thought of Old Bill selling gear for her. I thought to myself again, you definitely know how to push boundaries when you have the opportunity.

We finished our drinks and headed over to see Maria and Lisa. When we got there, Claire talked about drugs with Lisa. I said I didn't need to know the ins and outs of this stuff and went into the kitchen to make a brew. Maria joined me.

"They can sort it out on their own."

"Yes," I agreed. Maria told me her heart was playing up again and would I like to feel it?

I smiled. "No, it's okay. I'll take your word for it. You like embarrassing me or telling me stuff that you know full well is going to me laugh and will shock me."

"Yes, of course I do. You're a funny guy, Gary, that's why I like you so much. You have a sort of innocence about you and I find that sweet. You don't see it much in people these days." The two girls finished their discussions in the other room and we said our goodbyes. Claire and I drove over to see Abbie and Chantel, and Claire picked up more money.

Abbie said, "Have a cuppa before you go. I've something to tell you, Gary." She laughed.

"Okay, what is it?"

"The man is in the cupboard."

"Yeah," I sniggered.

"He's got eight tins of baked beans tied to his bollocks."

"No, you're kidding?"

"Nope, tied them onto him myself. We used a piece of ribbon, tied it around his sack then tied the carrier bag to that. He stood up and shuffled into the cupboard and we've locked him in there in the fucking dark. He's not coming out for another two hours, shame you weren't here to see it. Ha-ha-Ha-ha. Oh, and Jimmy the dog's booked his slot at the kennels. He's coming round tomorrow, you should pop in and give him a pat. Ha-ha-ha."

After a cuppa we drove over to see Holly. She was okay and Claire picked up more money. Next we went over to see Sam and Jess for another money collection. We spend quite a bit of time there just catching up and chatting about all sorts, as you do. Once we'd seen all the girls, the plan was to go out to dinner, just us two on our own. It's so nice to be on our own, I love spending my time with Claire.

We went to a lovely French restaurant in Bromley where we spent the next two hours having a great time together. We always enjoyed each other's company, particularly when we were on our own. Part of our conversion was about the money that was now coming in. Claire was taking £10,000–£12,000 a week and now with the Old Bill on board, she figured she could take more, and maybe a lot more.

Having stayed the night at Claire's flat, I got up and went to make the tea. Claire informed me that all the making money was making her stressed and she needed a body-to-body massage. I quickly put the teas down, put my cigarette out, picked up a bottle of baby oil and pulled back the covers to reveal her naked body. I squirted her with baby oil and jumped on top, and we rolled around covering ourselves in the oil, making a right old mess with oil everywhere. When we were done, I had to give her the 50 quid. It has to be said, the massage she gave me was better than the one I gave her. We both lay there quite worn out by the whole experience.

We got ready for the day ahead and went over to see the girls at Cobden Road. Chantel was extra-busy today with lots of bookings coming in. The queue for visits to see her was getting longer and longer, till at one stage it had got to nine bookings and it was only 11.30.

Abbie said, "We need to start sending the clients over to Holly," which she did. She explained to the clients about Holly and how sexy she was and how they should go and see her. She said they'd not be disappointed and if they travelled just that little bit further, she would make them feel very special. This worked a treat and Abbie started to book Holly's clients an hour apart. I made the tea and we sat down, listening to what was going on.

Claire spoke with Holly and told her what to expect; then, in between all the calls, Abbie said, "Gary, you should pop in tomorrow. Your mate Jimmy the dog's coming in at one to see us, he's booked a three hour session."

I had a big grin on my face. "And what if you're busy?"

"That's okay, we'll take it in turns to walk him around the flat and feed him." She laughed. "He's bringing his own dog food. Ha-ha-ha. Also, I want to buy him a tail of some sort and pin it onto his G-string." We were all laughing, I find this stuff so funny.

"Oh, don't forget, Abbie, if he's naughty, smack him with that riding crop."

"Oh, don't worry, I fully intend to."

Claire and I left to do our rounds. We started by going over to Maria's flat. Once there, Maria and I went into the kitchen, leaving Claire and Lisa to it in the front room. After a while Claire appeared in the doorway holding up a big brown envelope and smiling.

"Tonight's fun," she said. I took that to mean it was tonight's drugs. I smiled at the thought of that and wondered what was in the bag.

"You've heard we have a dog," I said to Maria.

"Yes," replied Maria laughing.

"Well, he's coming in today to see Abbie and Chantel." I told Maria about when I'd first met him. She was crying with laughter as I gave her the details.

I found it so funny but Maria found it even funnier. "But you look so shocked, Gary."

"Well, yes, I am. It is shocking. I'm not used to seeing things like this, it's just so strange. How can anybody want to be a dog, for Christ's sake?"

"There are stranger things than that going on, I can tell you. I've had men who want to be 'My Little Pony' and dress up as it. You would definitely laugh if you saw that. I've had men who want to be Barbie dolls."

I pulled a face as Maria was telling me this stuff. "Barbie dolls, what do they do?"

"Well, nothing really. They just like you to dress them up and put their makeup on for them."

"Oh no! You've gotta be kidding me?"

FOR THE LOVE OF BRASS

"Nope, not at all. I'll take you to one of these sexual-themed parties one day. You'll see all sorts there. They're normally based around a theme, My Little Pony or some such thing. I can only imagine your face at one of the parties. Your face would be priceless, it would be great."

Claire decided after talking with Lisa for a while that we should all have a party at our pub tonight. She started to make the phone calls, inviting all the girls and their partners. Everybody thought it was a good idea, even Sam and Jess. They had some work booked but said they'd do their best to be there, even if it was a bit late.

Maria offered us lunch, which was gratefully received. We stayed for a while, actually for most of the afternoon. We were deep in conversation, talking about the different things that took place in the trade. It was all very amusing to me and really quite an education. Eventually, seeing as time was getting on, we headed back over to Cobden Road. We arrived there just after 4.30.

Abbie just kept looking at me and laughing. "You've missed him," she said. "The dog has been and gone. Shame you missed it. We pinned a little fluffy tail on him and walked him around. Oh, and the funniest bit was, we fed him his dinner and soon after, the dirty little fucker went and pissed on the corner of the fridge!"

"I hope you told him off."

"Yes, of course. I smacked his arse with that riding crop. Ha-ha-ha. He was whimpering, so we pushed his nose in it and threw him out into the garden and left him out there for half an hour. Fuck knows what the neighbours must have thought! Ha-ha-ha-ha."

Claire sat at the coffee table and opened the bag of drugs. To my surprise there was quite an amount. There were two plastic bags, the type that have a sealable top, they were about three inches square. One had

Cocaine and the other had Amphetamine in. There was a quarter bar of Cannabis Resin and two hundred Ecstasy pills in another plastic bag. Claire made a phone call to Ryan and told him to come over as soon as possible. When he arrived she told him to leave us 50 Es, take the rest away and start to cut the Cocaine. She wanted him to come back with ten wraps of Charlie. The ten wraps and 50 Es would be coming to the pub with us.

She told us, "The Es are only two pounds each, providing I buy five hundred at a time. This little lot cost me three pounds for each pill but this is our little tester. We'll take them to the pub with us and see what we can move." She was smiling as she said it. "Oh, and Ryan, bring back a change of clothes for me and Gary. Gary," she said, "tell him what you want from the flat."

We left the girls to it and went around to the Wimpy for a bite to eat before our big night out. Chantel saw her last client out by 6.30. The girls then had a quick tidy up and started to get themselves ready for the night's entertainment.

"Come on, then, let's get around to Chantel's and start getting ready," Claire said.

"That's fine with me," I replied.

Ryan had come back by now and it was 7.15. A quick wash and change was all I was going to have; I think Claire had the same thing in mind.

"Fuck it," she said. "That'll do. Are we all ready, then? Let's go, but before we do, we should have an E. Ryan you can't have one because you have to pick us all up later. Ha-ha-ha." Ryan was going back to work once he'd finished with us.

I went into to the kitchen and got a sharp knife out. I cut my E in half,

FOR THE LOVE OF BRASS

that was all I was going to have. By my reckoning, half would be sufficient for the evening. I didn't want the effects carrying on into the night again because then you can't sleep.

As I washed my half down with a glass of water, Ryan came past. He saw what I was doing and said, "Can I have that half?"

"Yes," I said, "knock yourself out." He swallowed it as he lit up a cigarette and sniggered.

"Don't tell Claire." I just smiled.

Abbie suddenly let out a great big, "Woot, woot!", laughing as she did it. "Are we all ready? Come on, we're going now."

We wandered into the pub. Chantel was at the bar first. "Right, what's everybody having?"

The barman took the order. His name was Jamie and we'd got to know him by now. The governor of the pub was a big 6ft 4in fellow with ginger hair; we just called him Ginge. He was walking back and forth filling the shelves with bottles of beer. Once we'd all been served, we sat around our usual table.

Within an hour or so the pub was busy. The Es were working and Abbie was up dancing on her chair, which by now seemed normal for her. The music was great; every time Rozalla came on with 'Everybody's Free', it seemed the whole pub joined in; we were all having a great time. Mr Brown appeared and took up his usual position at the end of the bar.

Claire said, "He never looks very happy. Chantel, give him one of these Es." This she did. He came over to say thank you and wanted to know, is it safe?

Claire said to him, "Here's twenty pills, knock them out for a tenner a pop. We're testing them. Let me know what you think."

Lettsbe came by on his way to the toilet and said "Hi" to us all but mainly to Chantel. Claire nudged her and handed her a pill.

Chantel said to him, "Open up," which he did and she dropped it in his mouth. "Swallow that," which he did, washing it down with a mouthful of Chantel's drink. By the time I went up to for drinks, Ginge was dancing up and down behind the bar and Jamie was serving everyone at double quick time.

I told Mr Brown it was safe and he said, "I've sold all the Es and wraps." The whole pub was dancing, rocking and singing. We'd taken up two tables now, there was myself, Claire, Abbie, Chantel, Holly, the Irish couple as we called them, Maria, Lisa, and Sam and Jess turned up by 10.30. Even little Lee came in, dancing off his face on Charlie.

What a night! It was so funny to see Lettsbe dancing all over the place and, at the end of the evening when we were leaving, Mr Brown came over and handed Claire a roll of money, saying that all the gear he had was gone, he'd sold the lot. Claire called Ryan to pick some of us up and the others were outside waiting and dancing on the pavement for cabs to take them home.

CHAPTER FIFTEEN
RYAN GETS A PIERCING

I woke in Claire's bed feeling slightly hungover from all the drinks I had had the night before. I couldn't remember what time we'd got to bed but I did remember we'd had a good night.

"What day is it?" I asked.

"I'm not even sure, oh yeah, it's Friday."

We slowly got ready and headed over to see the girls. There wasn't much going on for me, just one job to go out on with the Irish couple around lunchtime and that seemed to suit me fine. I was happy to take it easy and sit around. I went home at around 4 o'clock in the afternoon, having reminded Claire to pay the Old Bill later. Sharon would be going out, so I could have a quiet night at home with the boys.

Saturday morning, and it was Sharon's turn to be in bed with a hangover but not me, I felt fine today. I went shopping with the boys to Morden, then into the Wimpy bar. Once we got home, Sharon was floating around. I called Claire to see what they were up to and to my surprise Claire was at the parlour with Chantel. She said she was being the maid for a while till Chantel was done. They'd be finished there by about 2 o'clock and could I meet them in Croydon. She said she'd phone Abbie and, if I could pick her up, we could eat and go shopping for the afternoon. I collected Abbie and we all met up at 2.30 at the Arndale centre. We spent time walking around the ladies' shops so Chantel could buy work clothes, then I dropped Abbie and Chantel off home and went back to Claire's. The plan now was that the girls would make their way over once they were ready, then Ryan would drive us into Croydon; we were going to hit the Blue Orchid again. Once we were in Ryan's car and on the way to the club, out came the Ecstasy.

Well, as you can imagine we had another fantastic night, just myself and the three girls. I still kept getting lots of funny looks from the other men in there, I guess they were trying to work out how it was I had three girlfriends. Each time a guy asked one of the girls for a dance, they'd say "No, I'm with him," and point at me.

Ryan picked us up once the club had closed and we were all singing in his cab on the way home to the music from his car radio.

Sunday morning was like any other morning at Claire's: sex, tea and breakfast. We went for a walk on Bromley Common, then spent the rest of the day relaxing before going out for dinner in the evening.

Monday morning, and sometimes we'd shake it up a bit, tea, sex then a cigarette, or maybe cigarette, tea and then sex, but then you spill your tea. Then off we went to the parlour with our swimming stuff. The plan was to go swimming at some point in the day's fun but first thing was to go over and see Sam to pick up more money. We'd pop in to see Holly while we were out to make sure she didn't need anything; Amy was out getting the bits and pieces they might need. Then it was back to Cobden Road for a cup of tea with the girls; then we decided it was time to go swimming.

When we got back we found out a lot had gone on. While we were away Chantel had been very busy. She told me she had a client who wanted knife sex.

"Which is what, exactly?" I had to ask. The client wanted Chantel to hold a knife against his neck while she sat across him and rode him like a cowgirl.

FOR THE LOVE OF BRASS

"Oh, yeah?"

"He wants to do that the next time he comes to see me and I want you to help me out with the knife thing. We'll need to get one ready."

"Okay," I said. "I'll sort out a knife for you; does it have to be big?"

"Oh yes, the bigger the better."

"Okay, I'll sort one out. How about I get you a Bowie knife? I'm guessing you don't want it sharp or too pointy, just in case something goes wrong."

"That'll be great, Gary. You've obviously done this before." She laughed.

We sat around just chatting, there were no client bookings for another two hours.

"Fuck it!" Claire said. "Let's go over to the pub." But with that, her phone rang; an enquiry came in for a couple. "Yes, we can do that, for one hour's time. Yes, no problem." Claire took the booking, then she got on the phone and called the Irish couple; they'd be over in half an hour and meet us at the pub. Once in the pub, I made sure I drank only shandy and a small one at that. Bridie and Pat arrived, and Bridie had a private chat with Claire. She arranged some gear to take with her so she and Pat could get off their nuts later on this evening. I was thinking to myself, with what these two do for a living, they probably need to get off their nuts every now and then to deal with it all.

I opened the back doors of the van and Pat jumped in and sat on the pile of folded dust-sheets. Bridie got in the front with me and off we went to a job over in Tooting Bec.

"There's the house," she said and we pulled into a road off of Tooting Bec Common. It was a nice big wide road which would have been lovely in its day but now all of the five storey houses had been converted to flats. I parked close enough to be able to keep an eye on the place. I could see on the front wall of the house five gas meters, which meant five flats. We knew the number of the house and we had flat C.

Bridie got out of the van and I said to Pat, "I think you'd better go with her. Stay with Bridie while she presses the door button on Flat C and wait with her till the client answers, so that you know for sure it's Flat C she's going into. Once she's in, wedge the main front door open with something; use a newspaper if you have to. There are always newspapers in the front porch of those big houses. Use a paper or something, so if we have to get in there in a hurry we can, alright mate?"

"Fuck me, Gary, you think of everything."

"Well, just listen and learn, Pat, because in the future it might just be you and her. You'll need to know this stuff so you can look after her. Alright, go on, catch her up and make sure to wedge the door." This he did and in two minutes he was back to the van. "Are we okay?" I asked.

"Yes, she went into Flat C."

"That's good, did you wedge the door?"

"Yes, I did. You were right, there were about eight old newspapers in there. I rolled one up and put it in the door."

"Good, well done, mate."

"Gary, I have a question."

"Yeah, fire away."

"What if the client looks out of the window and sees me?"

"Well, that's a good thing. You want him to really, because then he'll know she's got a minder and that should in itself keep her safe. Also, mate, I recommend you carry some sort of weapon, just in case you have to go charging into a place one day." A weapon, I thought, and smiled to myself and charging in. I don't think Pat could charge into Tesco's quickly to buy a sandwich. He didn't seem to have an ounce of aggression in him. Mind you, if it came to saving the love of his life, who knows what he's capable of? You can never tell with people.

We sat in the van talking about this and that. I gave him a few more security tips he might want to keep in mind. He asked what type of weapon I'd recommend he carry.

"Well, you don't want something that looks like a weapon, you don't want to be turning up to a door with an axe, if you get my drift. Just something small and inoffensive, a screwdriver's a good one. The type with a large palm grip's good because you can use it like a push-dagger, or the small electrical type, you know the sort? The one you'd use for testing with or putting on plugs. They're good because they have a chrome clip on the top so you can wear it clipped onto your shirt and nobody takes any notice of that, plus you can wear it all the time, wherever you go."

"Will that do damage, then?" I looked at him.

"Well, if you stick it into someone's face or neck, I can guarantee they'll not be happy, which gives you time to either wound them again, or make your escape from the property."

"Thanks for your help, Gary. Here comes Bridie now. Everything must have been okay."

"Yeah, everything's fine most of the time. It's only now and then something goes wrong. You just have to be prepared for it if it happens."

Pat got out of the front seat to let Bridie get in and let himself in through the back door, then closed it behind him.

"All okay?" I asked Bridie.

"Yes, no problems."

"That's good. Home now, is it?"

"Yes, please, can you drop us off at our place in Mitcham?" Which I did. On the way I asked her if she'd be talking to Claire later.

"Yes, I will be. Oh, and here's thirty pounds for driving us, thank you."

"Would you mind telling her I've gone home? I'll see her tomorrow over at Cobden Road."

Once I had dropped them off in Church Road, I drove through the back streets and made my way into Morden to get myself a kebab. I sat in the van and ate it; I didn't seem to be in any rush to go home. Once I got there, I put the kettle on for a cup of tea and, while waiting for the water to boil, I looked down the garden to the shed. I started to think about the Bowie knife I had in there, the one I had for the Rottie. That wasn't needed now, so that'd be perfect for Chantel, I thought. I stepped into the shed, put my tea on the workbench and reached up to one of the ceiling joists. I brought down the Bowie knife. It had sat resting on that beam for a while and one side of it had some surface rust on it. I put the sharp cutting edge of the blade on the grinding wheel to make the cutting edge blunt which it did very well. Then I ground the point off the end, giving it a rounded finish. All it needed now was a good clean with some wire wool. After about half an hour's cleaning with the wire wool and gun oil, the knife came up like new. I took it back inside to my kitchen and gave it a good wash up in the sink. Once dried off, it looked great. I wondered how it would feel, so I held it up against the side of my neck and, to my surprise, because the cutting edge was now square and not sharp, it felt sharp when I put pressure on it. This'll be perfect for Chantel's purposes. I wrapped it up in newspaper, then put it in the van ready for delivery tomorrow.

★★★

FOR THE LOVE OF BRASS

"Hello."

"Oh, hi," the receptionist said.

"I have a letter from Steve, my solicitor, he wants me to make an appointment to come over and see him."

"One moment, I'll just check his diary. Yes, okay. He has a slot first thing at nine o'clock tomorrow, Wednesday, for one hour. Can you come then?"

"Yes, that's fine."

"Thank you. See you then." I called Claire on her mobile to ask if she wanted to come out into the countryside today. She was very keen, especially as it was such a nice day. I left my office after a further few business calls and, as I arrived at Cobden Road, I passed the parlour. As I did so, the front door was open and Lettsbe was standing there talking with someone but I couldn't see who it was. I parked up 50yds away and saw Lettsbe come out and head off in the direction of the pub. I just smiled, thinking, he's been in for an early shag with Chantel. With that, Ryan pulled up outside the house and Claire got out and walked into the parlour with some urgency. Ryan pulled away and past me as I sat there. My stomach rolled with excitement, knowing we were going out for the day, or at least for a few hours. I locked the van and walked down the road to the parlour. Chantel and Abbie were in the porch of the flat with a bucket of soapy water and cloths, cleaning the front door and letter box.

They said, "Claire's inside, go and see her and cheer her up a bit. She's pissed off."

"Okay." I went straight in she greeted me with a hug and a kiss. She went on to explain somebody had been spreading dog shit on the front door and pushing it through the letter box, so it was on the inside of the door and on the door mat. They'd also cut the landline telephone cable in two places where it came from the pole into the house. She went on to say she knew a telecoms man and she'd already called him to come over and fix the problem. The girls were cleaning up the rest of the mess in the doorway and they needed to get that sorted before they could start work.

"Why was Lettsbe here, what's he got to do with it?" I asked.

"Oh, nothing. He just popped in to see Chantel for a shag but had to go without because of what was going on. So he missed out." Claire laughed.

"Do you have any idea who did this?"

"No, none at all but I'll find out! Come on," Claire said. "Let's go to the shops and get lunch."

"No, no," I said. "I'll treat you when we're out."

"Okay, then, the girls are sorting this, so we can go. Bye girls." They were almost done with their cleaning duties so we left them to get on with it and headed out over to Newdigate near Dorking.

We walked around the village and visited the church. When we were ready for lunch, we drove along Parkgate Road to The Surrey Oaks where we had a lovely lunch. After that we walked around the lakes at the old brick fields, saying that on a nice day we'd come back and go fishing there. While we were out, there were a number of calls to Claire's mobile phone from the girls using the pay phone over at the pub and, of course, another call after the telecoms man had fixed the landline.

Twiddling their thumbs was all the girls could do while they waited for the landline to come back on. When the telecoms man finished it was 2.30, so a fair bit of business had been missed.

Claire and I got back to Cobden Road around 6 o'clock. The girls were telling us what fun we had missed because Jimmy the dog had been in for an hour. He'd booked two hours but the girls kept blaming him for shitting up the front door, so they kept hitting him with the riding crop on his arse. I guess after an hour of that, he'd had enough and went early but they still charged him for the two hours he'd booked. He'd asked for his money for the second hour so they smacked him some more with the crop. They said he'd left with his tail between his legs.

"Chantel," I said as I unwrapped the newspaper, "a present for you. A nice new Bowie knife."

She got all excited. "Let me play, let me play." As she took it from me, "Wow, that's a big one!"

"Yes, the blade's eight inches long."

"Ain't had one that big for a long time." She and Abbie were giggling. "It's great. Just the job. How much do I owe you?"

"No, no. That's alright. It's a present for you from me."

"Thank you very much. It'll go into my sex toy collection." What a strange place to keep your Bowie knife, I thought to myself.

"Come on," said the girls. "Let's go over to the pub. We've had a bit of a funny day to say the least. We need a few drinks." I left them all to go to the pub, I had to go to Mitcham to pick up the Irish couple, then out with them to two jobs. The first was in Croydon; just Bridie was booked for that. The second was in Sutton and they were both booked on that one.

The Croydon job was alright for me. At least I had some company. I couldn't help myself talking about what these two would do in this industry when they got back to Ireland. The second job was at the top of Sutton on a quiet road. As normal, I sat with my radio on, smoking cigarettes. While waiting, I was thinking about the girls in the pub, they'd all be merry by now, by one means or another or probably both. I knew Ryan would pick them up when Claire called and he'd get them all home safely. No need for me to worry.

Bridie and Patrick came back and got into the van.

"Is everything okay?" I asked.

"Yes, yes fine. Bit of a strange one though, that fellow."

"Why was that?"

"Well, he wanted us to fuck each other in his lounge while he stood in the hallway peeping through the door. The door was just open a little."

"And what was he doing in the hall, playing with himself?"

"Yes, I think so, judging by the funny noises he was making. It was almost enough to put you off." I just started laughing; this stuff never ceases to amaze me.

I drove back over to Mitcham and dropped the couple home to their flat in Church Road. That was me finished for the night. I could go home and put my feet up. When I got there I sat for a while with my V and O, wondering what would happen at Steve's tomorrow. What's happening next? Sharon was at home but she was doing her own thing and didn't talk to me, so I decided there was no point in asking her if she knew what the meeting might be about. I was quite sure she would know but no, I told myself, just wait and see, wait till tomorrow.

The next morning I drove over to see Steve at his office in Wallington. I parked the van in the car park at Shotfield, then walked the short distance down to his office. The receptionist led me into the hall and up the stairs. She indicated with her hand which door I should go through.

"Hello, Gary," Steve said as I entered the office. "Please, take a seat. Can I get you a drink?"

"Yes, please, tea would be nice."

"Okay." Steve made a quick call to somebody and placed the tea order for us both.

FOR THE LOVE OF BRASS

"I've had the letter saying you want to see me."

"Yes, that's right. We've had a letter from your wife's solicitors. As you know they've acknowledged the divorce paper we filed with them and have made a few requests of their own."

"Requests or demands?" I piped up. "Because I can't see Sharon requesting anything."

"Well, we're dealing with defendant's solicitors."

"Defendant?"

"Yes, and you're the plaintiff."

"Oh, okay."

"They want to know under what heading or grounds will this divorce take place. You stated that you didn't care, you just wanted a divorce in your statement. They want a heading, or grounds, that's the least damaging to Sharon's character." A lady came into the office with the teas, then left as quick as she came. I put some sugar in my tea and stirred it. "So," said Steve, "this is a list of reasonable causes people use to sue for divorce."

"Can you read them out to me?"

He started to read and I found myself having no interest at all in what he was saying. He then went on to say, "There are other things you need to take into consideration when choosing your reason, blah, blah, blah."

I just wasn't taking it in. I looked around the office thinking to myself, nothing has changed in here since I was here last. He kept talking. I watched the tops of the buses outside go past his window every so often. There seemed to be quite a few on this busy route.

"So which one would you like, or which do you think is the most suitable in this case?"

"Unreasonable behaviour, that sounds the most inoffensive to me. Yes, that's the one we'll use. Steve, file for divorce under that heading or those grounds and if she doesn't like it, we can find one that is offensive. Okay, mate?" I said as another bus went by Steve's head outside the window. I thought, I've come all the way over here for this, he could have asked me this on the phone. I felt very frustrated with my situation. I really thought things would be moving much faster than they are, it's all so slow. I felt very disappointed with the proceedings so far. "Are we done?" I asked.

"Yes, we are, Gary. I'll put this in writing to the defendant's solicitors and, of course, send a copy to you."

"Thank you very much," I said as I walked out of his office. I was in there a total of 20 minutes; what a waste of time, I told myself. I even thought, I don't like that man much.

Little did I know at that point that in time, I'd be spending a great deal of my life in his office, with him giving me a great deal of help and advice on some very serious matters. He really would go on to become my best friend.

I left the office to walk back to my van. As I walked, I told myself, don't worry about that shit, that's what you're paying him for, he can worry about it. I'm off to see the girls and have fun in their company and see Claire, of course; she doesn't disappoint me, I love her to bits.

I drove over to Cobden Road and the three girls were already there when I arrived. Abbie put the kettle on while Chantel came over to give me a big hug.

"Thank you again for my knife, I love it. Can't I pay you for it?"

"No, that's okay. I told you."

"Are you sure? We could go into the room and I'll sort you out?" she said smirking.

"No, no," I said, "it's okay."

"I know, but how about I get a gram of Charlie and you can snort it off my tits?"

FOR THE LOVE OF BRASS

"For fuck's sake, Chan, you're happy with the knife, ain't you?" We all laughed.

Claire said, "I thought your eyes lit up when she said about the Charlie on her tits." All three girls were laughing by now.

"Stop the windups, please, girls. Behave yourselves."

It turns out it was all Claire's idea to have a windup. She said, "I have a job for you, can you go out with Jess?"

"Yes, of course. When?"

"Pick her up in about half an hour, she's going to a job in South Croydon, then she wants to go shopping in the Arndale centre. She wants you with her for an hour or two, is that okay with you?"

"Yeah, sure. I'll finish my tea and have a ciggy with you all, then go and pick her up."

I rang the bell on Jess's door and she came out. "Where're we off to?"

"I've got a job in South Croydon. This one's a bit different. I'm going to an office, so you can't park outside. You'll have to park nearby but it's in a public car park.

"I don't think I like that idea, Jess."

"No, no Gary. It's okay, the client is okay; I've seen him before."

"Well, if you're happy, that's fine with me."

"You can park, I'll show you where, then I'll walk the short distance to his office." As we drove, I asked if the office was a busy one. "Yes," she said, "and he wants to see you there?"

"Yes, well, that's the thrill for him. I'm booked in under another name and going for an interview with him. When I arrive, the receptionist will show me through, then once I'm in his office, he just shuts the office door and sorts me out over his desk."

"Really? What if somebody comes in?"

"Well, that's the chance he takes. It's that that gives him the thrill, it's all part of it for him."

"And you charge him more for that, I hope."

"Oh yes, of course. This little visit will cost him three hundred quid."

"It's a wonder he doesn't ask for an invoice. Ha-ha-ha."

"Well, he did when I first went. I told him no, so now he pays me out of the petty cash." We both smiled. "He wants to claim it on expenses."

After about forty minutes or so, Jess came walking back into the car park.

"Hi Jess, did it all go well?"

"Oh yes, no problems. If you like we can leave the van here and walk to the shopping centre."

"Yep, that's fine with me." I locked the van and we went for a walk. I don't really know why she wanted me with her this day, after all she was only shopping.

"What is it you're going to buy, Jess?"

"Oh, nothing really. Just having a look around. We can go for coffee when we get there."

Jess told me she enjoyed my company, she felt secure when I was around. If there's one thing I'd learned working with the girls, and they all said the same thing, it was that if they have a man around, even if it's their boyfriend, they need to feel secure in his presence, a woman needs to feel safe.

"Here you are, Gary," Jess paid me. She gave me £150 for the three hours I was with her, which I thought was bloody good money.

I took Jess home and drove over to Cobden Road. The three girls there were all in good spirits, as indeed they had been when I'd left them earlier in the day. Wayne, the "monkey man" estate agent, had been in to collect the rent. The girls were laughing at the thought of his visit. Chantel had said she had him stripped naked on the bed and, while she was giving him a blow job, she stuck her finger up his arse.

"He went fucking mad!" We were all laughing as she told us the story, I didn't think to ask if he went mad with pleasure or pain, I just found the whole thing very funny. Lettsbe had also paid Chantel a visit and of course she said don't tell her Lee.

Claire then said, "How about we stop working for the day and all go over to the pub for a drink?"

This we did. Claire asked me if I'd pick Abbie up from her house tomorrow and take her to the hospital.

"Have a chat with her and she'll tell you the details." Abbie told me she wanted me to pick her up and take her to the Mayday hospital in Croydon.

After a couple of beers, I left the girls and headed home. I didn't think they'd be in there long, probably only a couple more, then they'd also be going home.

The following day, I collected Abbie from her place and we went over to the Mayday. I stayed with her to keep her company while she was having different tests done. I asked her what the tests were for but she just said, "Women's problems." That was enough of an answer for me not to ask any more questions.

When we were done we had lunch in the hospital canteen, then made our way back to Cobden Road. Claire had been there, standing in for Abbie and manning the phones.

We arrived at 3 o'clock and Abbie just told the girls everything was alright. No doubt she might talk to the girls if need be when she was alone with them.

"Okay," Claire said. "Come on, Gary. We're going over to see Maria. We have some business to do."

We were about five minutes from Maria's place when Claire got a call from Maria saying she'd been delayed and would be there as soon as possible. She said she'd call as soon as she was home.

"Okay, what shall we do?" I said. "Let's go and find a cafe and sit in there for a while and wait for the phone call."

About 50 minutes passed before Claire's phone rang. It was Maria, she was home.

"Come round," she said, "I'll put the kettle on."

Maria gave me a hug and a kiss on the cheek as we went through the door. We sat down in the kitchen.

"Here we are, Claire, one brown envelope with money and one jiffy bag with goodies." Claire put them both in her bag out of sight.

We finished our tea and cigarettes. We were going back over to the pub, so we invited Maria but she said she was busy working tonight and would see us another time. She winked at me as she said it, which made me smile.

We walked into the pub; Chantel and Abbie were already there having a drink. I got more drinks in and we joined the girls at our table. Claire was on the phone to Ryan's company leaving a message for him to come over to see us as soon as possible.

Within half an hour, Ryan arrived at the pub. Claire gave him the two bags and sent him away saying, you know what to do with them. Ryan left.

"Oh well," I said to the girls, "looks like a big night coming up."

"I fucking hope so," Abbie shouted, laughing as she said it.

Chantel went to the bar for more drinks and I asked Claire, "Can we

FOR THE LOVE OF BRASS

have a talk on our own?"

"Yes, okay. Now?"

"Yes, let's go outside. I don't want anyone hearing."

We went out through the pub's side entrance; there was no one around. I explained to Claire what was on my mind. I told her that I didn't mind picking up money and running around from A to B but not drugs.

"I won't do that. If you need drugs picking up from anywhere, use Ryan or someone else but not me. I'm not going to be a courier, do you understand where I'm coming from?"

"Yes, yes I do. Not a problem, sorry. I'll make sure next time it doesn't involve you. Come on, let's go and have a drink." Just before we went in she pushed me up against the side wall and kissed me. Then she laughed and turned to go back into the pub.

We sat at the table and Claire leaned over and said, "Open your mouth, I have half for you." This I did and I felt the half pill on my tongue. She smiled and said, "Sorry, Babe, this'll make it alright. It won't happen again."

I smiled as I swallowed the pill, then, taking a swig of my beer, I winked at Claire as if to say thanks.

I noticed Chantel and Abbie would occasionally be licking their fingers so there must have been a little bag of something being passed around between them under the table. They just had those big permanent grins on their faces. Within a short while, the Es were working. Mr Brown was at the end of the bar tapping his feet, nineteen to the dozen. I think he and half the people in the pub were E-ing.

We went on to have a fabulous night with lots of good music, lots of singing while standing on the tables and lots of drinking. Little Lee came in and joined us. He went home later with Chantel. Ryan picked us three up at the end of the evening. We took Abbie home, then he took us back to Claire's flat, dropping us off and then disappearing into the night.

The following morning, I woke in Claire's bed. I immediately rolled over onto her and gave her a good morning cuddle; tea and cigarettes were to follow.

We arrived at the Cobden Road parlour around 10.30. Abbie and Chantel were already set for the day. They said little Lee had called and said he didn't fancy working any more today, so he was coming home early. Chantel wasn't comfortable working when Lee was around, she just felt it would be better if he wasn't there. We four sat and laughed about the fun we'd had last night in the pub and the fools we might have made of ourselves singing and dancing along with everyone else.

Claire's phone rang; it was a job for the Irish couple. She took the booking, then called Bridie. When she finished, she turned to me and said, "That's all set. Gary, could you go and pick Bridie up and take her to a job in Tooting Broadway?"

I finished my tea and cigarette, then went over to Mitcham to pick Bridie up. There was no mention of Patrick but that wasn't unusual when the bookings came in, unless he was booked on the job as well. I pulled up outside the flat in Church Road. She came out on her own and got into the van. I already knew where we were going, Claire had written the client's address down on a piece of paper, which I had in the van.

I gave her the piece of paper and an A to Z map book.

"Can you look the address up, please?" Then I noticed she had a tear in her eye. "What's up, where's Patrick today?"

"Oh, he can fuck off as far as I'm concerned. "We've had a falling out."

"Oh, why?"

"That last job we went on, he asked me questions about the client and what I did with him. I didn't want to tell him but he kept on, so I told him and now he is so pissed off, I wish I'd not said anything. We were arguing most of the night, I think we're going to split up."

"Well, I don't know what to say. I realise it must be a difficult situation with you both working in this game. Anyway, with you out for a while, it might make it a bit better." But as I said it I thought to myself, how can that make it better when he knows she's out doing it all again. I'm just glad Claire doesn't work.

We found the address and she had her hour in there, then we drove back to her flat. As we pulled up, Pat came out. I wondered what might happen now.

"Stay in the van," he said, "we have another job for both of us. Claire called me and gave me the details; she said you'd be alright with it."

"Yes, mate, no problem. Where are we off to?"

"Only Sutton." He said as he pulled the back door of the van closed. He handed me a piece of paper with the address on it, Mulgrave Road.

"I know that." And off we went. There wasn't another word spoken between them all the way there, you could have cut the atmosphere with a knife. It was a flat we were going to and seeing as how Pat would be going in with her, I parked in the block's car park. All I had to do was sit and wait the hour, smoking and with the radio as my company while I waited.

Once we were heading out of Sutton, I suggested to them both, "Why don't you come back to Cobden Rad with me and see the girls? A change of scenery might do you good. I think it might be a good idea for you, Pat, to have a little chat with Claire. I think she can help you in these matters of what's pissing you off." He agreed. "I'm just thinking, you two obviously love each other and it's worth trying to sort it out." They both said okay.

FOR THE LOVE OF BRASS

We walked into the kitchen at Cobden Road. Claire and Abbie were sitting there, Chantel was in the room with a client. Little Lee was sitting there too. He didn't seem too happy and I could guess why. Abbie put the kettle on while I briefly told Claire why I'd bought Bridie and Pat back. Claire got her cup of tea and a cigarette then went for a chat with Patrick out in the garden. They were out there for about 30 minutes, by which time Chantel had come back in with us. She was smoking and laughing with Abbie, and Little Lee seemed happier now Chantel wasn't in the room. After the chat with Claire, Bridie and Pat gave each other a kiss and a hug.

Then I said, "Why don't you both go over to the pub and have a drink and a chat with each other and make it up?"

They thought that was a great idea and Claire then said to me, "How about if we all go over in a while and have an early drink with them?"

"Sounds good to me."

"Okay," Claire said, "We'll come over about four o'clock and have a drink with you." Claire made a call. "Ryan, we're going over to the pub early for a drink. Can you come over here with the gear for selling in the pub, you know what I mean? We discussed it yesterday."

It seemed no time at all before Ryan was at the door. Claire put the gear in her handbag and rolled herself a big spliff which she shared with Ryan. I didn't want any of it and the girls, well, they were still working; I didn't think they'd want to get stoned.

"So, Ryan," I said, "why don't you have some time off, especially as you've had a smoke. Come to the pub with us." He looked to Claire for approval.

She smiled, then said, "Yes, why don't you?"

He was all happy, just like a little puppy. I watched and thought, he's

FOR THE LOVE OF BRASS

allowed out with us. It's about time, I grinned to myself. Abbie and Chantel were staying at work for a couple of hours more, they'd join us later.

Little Lee said, "I'll come with you. Have you got an E I can have or buy off you?"

"Yes," said Claire.

"That's good, I think I'll get off my nut." We walked down the road and as we got near the pub's side door a man said, "Hello, Lee."

"Oh, hello, mate. This is my brother," Lee said to us. "His name's John."

"Hello, John. You coming for a beer?" we said.

As we were about to walk into the pub, a white transit pulled up on the main road. It came to a very sudden halt which seemed out of character for traffic normally pulling up to stop there, which made me look in the van's direction.

Picture this scene, it was a nice bright day with people standing around outside the pub, maybe six or seven in three small groups. Between us and the van there were two blokes chatting, side-on to the van, about 12ft from it. The side door of the van slid open quickly and a man with a black ski mask on stepped out, one foot on the pavement and one still in the van. He swung up a sawn-off double-barrel shotgun from his side and levelled it in the direction of the two men standing side-on to him. I instinctively turned my back and in doing so, put myself between Claire and the gunman. As I did this I tucked my head forward and waited for the bang. Ryan, however, had his left hand on the handle of the pub door. He'd turned to his right, no doubt to say something and was oblivious to what was about to happen. The bang came; it seemed exceptionally loud. People screamed and shouted. I waited for the second bang, then I heard the van door slam shut. I turned towards where the gunman had been standing but he was gone and the van was pulling away fast.

Ryan shouted, "I've been shot!"

I pulled Claire close and said, "Are you okay?"

"Yes, yes," she said. I noticed little Lee and his brother were still standing near the kerb about 8ft from us, they were both staring in our direction with a look of shock on their faces, as though for a split second they couldn't figure out what had just happened. I reached for the pub door handle and pulled the door open. I stepped inside, pushing Claire in front of me, and Ryan stepped in behind us.

He shouted again, "I've been fucking shot!"

"Where, where?" I said.

"In the head!" He turned his head to his right; he had some blood coming from his ear. I burst out laughing. "Are you hit anywhere else?"

"No, no," he said, "it ain't fucking funny!"

"Yes, it is."

Lettsbe and Mr Brown appeared. They passed us to look out of the front window. Outside there were two men on the pavement, one sitting up and one lying on his side. They were both shouting with pain.

Lettsbe said, "Let's get the fuck out of here before the Old Bill turn up," which made me laugh even more.

Some of the people from outside started to come in in a hurry. I guess they wanted to take cover from any other projectiles that might be coming their way. Lettsbe and Mr Brown disappeared out through the back door into the pub's garden. They must have climbed over the back fence to lie low until all the fuss was over. We sat at our table, Lee's brother John getting the drinks in. Ryan was whinging a lot about his ear. Claire got some Wet-ones out of her bag and wiped the blood from his ear, so now we could see where he'd been hit. I kept laughing as I looked. He had two pellets in his ear, one on the outer edge about half way up and one just off centre and slightly high of his ear lobe. Claire was trying to get them out but they seemed to be stuck fast.

I said to Claire, "Get your nail file out."

I folded his ear in two where the pellet was situated while Claire put the point of the file behind the pellet and pushed in an outward motion. It popped out, landing on the table.

"There you go, mate, a souvenir for your troubles." We all laughed. Claire then folded his ear lobe in half and squeezed hard and as she did, the other pellet popped out. Now the two tiny wounds really started to bleed. We sent him off to the toilets to clean himself up, then we saw a blue flashing light outside the pub.

Little Lee said, "We saw you stand in the way of the gun to protect Claire."

"Wow," John said, "are you mad or brave?"

An ambulance arrived and took away the two men who had been shot. The police taped off the area to the front of the pub, looking for clues. Then they wanted to interview people about what had happened.

"My advice to you all is to say you saw nothing, you just heard the bang and took cover as best you could. You didn't see the gunman or the van and after the bang you got in here as fast as you could to hide, end of story. We don't want the coppers around."

"What about my ear?" said Ryan.

"Don't report it, you will just become another gun statistic and nothing will get done about it, so why bother with all the statements?"

With that, Bridie and Patrick came walking into the pub.

"Where were you?" I asked.

"We went for something to eat first. Looks like we missed all the commotion."

"I got fucking shot!" Ryan piped up and we all laughed.

"Two pellets in the ear don't count," said Claire.

It wasn't long before the drugs came out under the table and the party started. Claire went over to get the girls and told them what they'd missed. She also told them I was the hero that saved her life and stopped her from getting shot. She told them about Ryan getting shot, which they found really funny. I must admit the situation did make me laugh but in truth I laughed because I was relieved it wasn't worse, well not for us, anyway.

The three girls came back over to the pub and that was when the party started properly. The pub soon got as busy as it would be for a Friday night. I think Claire made a point of telling everybody in the pub I'd saved her from the gunman. I had people coming up, wanting to buy me a drink for my bravery; it seemed to be all that got talked about for the whole evening. We all had another great night and at 12 o'clock we jumped in cabs and headed into Croydon. We went to the Blue Orchid, to E and dance the night away. Then it was cabs again, back to Claire's to continue the party. I think I went to bed around 6.00 in the morning.

Eventually, after leaving Claire's and getting a cab over to pick my van up, I arrived home. It was some time in the afternoon. Sharon had the right hump because I'd not come home Friday night, so she couldn't go out. My punishment for the crime was she wouldn't talk to me, once she'd called me a selfish bastard, of course. Oh well, I thought to myself, at least we won't be arguing. She did inform me, however, that she was going out and that I would be having the kids. I sat and wondered, should I call Jack to see if he would come over? Then I could go out again. In the end I decided it would be a good idea to stay in for the evening and have a night off, regardless of what Claire and the others were doing. I thought after last night I needed it.

FOR THE LOVE OF BRASS

Sharon came home about 4 o'clock in the morning, pissed as a newt, stumbling and falling up the stairs and mumbling something about what a fucking arsehole I was and how she'd had enough of me and wished I was dead, but then again I was half asleep – maybe she was saying how much she loved me, I couldn't really be sure.

I woke up on Sunday feeling pretty good. I called Claire to see if she fancied going shooting over at Bisley. She loved the idea, so I said I'd go and pick her up. When we got there, we linked up with my gun club who were there shooting rifles all day. We started by going into one of the big club houses there and had a lovely sit-down roast dinner, with only a little drink. Then we joined the ranks at the firing point to shoot some targets. When we were finished shooting, it was back over to Claire's area to sit in a nice quiet bar in Bromley, reflecting on the weekend's events and having a sensible little drink. Needless to say, I didn't go home that night.

I woke in Claire's bed to the sound of Ryan laughing. It seemed to be coming from the kitchen and it sounded like there was a bit of a commotion going on out there. I could hear pushing and shoving, then all of a sudden Ryan let out a scream. It sounded like a girl's scream, then he ran into the bathroom and locked himself in. I could hear him cussing and moaning. I got up and walked through to the kitchen, looking to make some tea. Claire was already there making it. She looked up and smiled, then explained what had happened. Ryan had been making the tea and as he finished stirring his tea, he'd put the hot spoon on the back on Claire's hand for a laugh. It had made her jump and burnt her, which she didn't appreciate, so in return she'd put her cigarette out on his arm, which she did find quite amusing.

I got my tea and turned round to go back to the bedroom to make myself a cigarette.

I shouted out, "Good morning, Ryan."

"Nothing good about it. I've had a shit couple of days; I've been shot and burnt. What'll happen next?"

Claire just laughed at him, she was very much like that. The words of the Billy Joel song came to mind, 'she'll carelessly cut you and laugh while you're bleeding but she'll bring out the best and the worst you can be. Blame it all on yourself, 'cos she's always a woman to me.' In a nutshell, that was Claire. Whenever I heard that song it reminded me of her.

It seemed that from about this time onwards, Claire would be supplying Mr Brown with his gear regularly, namely Charlie, Whizz and Ecstasy pills. He did ask me if it was safe for him to deal with Claire. Of course it was safe. The police told us to do it and Lettsbe also told him he was to deal with no one else but us or he'd be shut down, so he was happy with that situation. We, of course, would go clubbing a couple of times a week over to the Blue Orchid and I had four absolutely gorgeous women with me, who all said when they were approached by men for a drink or a dance, "Sorrys I'm with my man," then point to me. The men were totally confused as to what was going on.

Somebody in London started to have sex parties once a month and Claire had an invite to go to one of these events, which she and Chantel attended. Ryan drove them there and bought them back, so they were safe. I asked if I could go but Claire and Chantel said, "It's probably best if you don't, you might not understand why the people are there." They felt it might be too much for me to handle and assured me they were just going to have a look out of interest and meet other people in the trade. When Claire and I were on our own, she'd often talk about all the money that was coming in. She was more than happy with the situation and she wanted to know if I was happy with my money, which of course I was.

FOR THE LOVE OF BRASS

One of the things I was very happy with in our relationship was the fact that we were like two rabbits and couldn't keep our hands off each other, even at Cobden Road parlour when there was a gap in the booking of clients, we'd often go into the room and make the most of the unbooked time, regardless of what time of day it was. In between jobs, we'd always try our best to go swimming, which was a really good way to keep fit but we were so busy, this meant only a couple of times a week in reality. One of the best things we had going for us was having the Old Bill on side. This pretty much meant that we, or Claire, could do whatever we liked, in our area at least, without having to worry about getting nicked. Our cops were a real asset to us, everybody in the pub thought we were all the bee's knees, everybody knew us and, with our little firm, we were like the kings of the manor.

My week consisted mainly of swimming, two mental nights out and a little paperwork at my office, although that was fast becoming less and less and almost a thing of the past. Most of my time was spent with the girls. If we went drinking, I'd generally stay on the shandies because of driving them around, and most of that seemed to be at nighttime.

I don't think a day went past without Ryan having the piss taken out of him by somebody or other about having his ear pierced on the day of the shooting. Even Lettsbe took the piss out of him each time he saw him. He reckoned the pellets were a ricochet off the corner of the pub wall. He was the only person to get hit other than the intended targets, so really, I was no more of a hero than anybody else who was there. People just seemed to take it that way and of course Claire reinforced it for her own ends.

Another handy thing with knowing Lettsbe was that he sometimes gave us a lift if we were going for a drink in Bermondsey or up to the Old

Kent Road. The first time he offered to take us, I told him we were going to the pub called The World Turned Upside Down, everybody just called it The World. It was at one end of the Old Kent Road near the flyover. I think he was happy to take us in a police car although we found it funny. I'm sure he just wanted to know where we were going and what we were up to, I guess in case he was missing out on something. We might have a drink in there but we'd just wait for him to drive off, then go for a short walk around to the Vic in Pages Walk. All the pubs up there had a DJ and good music playing, so a good night was guaranteed wherever we went.

I'd normally arrange to meet my old mate Bob in the pub, I'd known him since we were kids together growing up in Bermondsey. Probably from the age of ten. He'd join us with his mates, Lee, Steve, Paul, Nicky, Dean and Caroline, then we'd all get on it and have a great night. Some nights we'd stay at Bob's flat in Linton Road or sometimes Ryan would come and pick us up and take us home to Claire's.

Claire's passion for life was amazing. She was always upbeat, happy and jolly, and up for anything, really. We always had a good time wherever we went and these were some of the things I loved about her so much. She loved having a sun bed and the idea of having her own was so she could keep her fit little body brown for the winter. It seemed she was always going on it. She'd get naked and lie there for an hour or more, cooking.

One day she said to me, "Come on, get naked and lay on top of me. We can get brown together, all we'd have to do was change sides half way through so we both get brown at the same time." Of course, as you might expect, that didn't work out too well; once I was on top of her I couldn't keep still and kept burning my arse on the tubes above me, so we had to give that up as a bad job.

Some days we'd go out into the Surrey countryside, walking and looking at the wildlife. This was something she'd not done too much of before but had learned to enjoy with me. We'd explore the North Downs and check out Box Hill, sometimes go fishing in the River Mole. Fishing was another thing Claire was keen to learn.

Somewhere in amongst all that was going on in my life, I received another letter from my solicitor, Steve. He'd copied me in on a letter from Sharon's solicitors stating that the defendant was happy to accept that the divorce could go ahead on the grounds of unreasonable behaviour, which I felt was about time.

Tea seemed to be a big part of our life; there was always a kettle on or a cup being made. We had tea while the stick man was being beaten to within an inch of his life next door in the room. Tea while the cupboard man was suffering with his baked bean tins, tea while Chantel was sorting out clients with her new big Bowie knife, and, of course, tea while Jimmy the dog was being smacked with a riding crop for not doing as he was told. It was all very civilised. It was all very English. I remember thinking, I wonder if Cynthia Paine and her parlour had anything on us lot.

Where Abbie lived there was a young couple who lived above her. One night, when Abbie was at home, they came down to visit her for a drink and brought a few beers with them but after the three of them getting on the Charlie, they ran out of beers, so decided to walk down the road to the off licence. On their way back, the fellow, Chris, was messing around and stepped out into the road. He was hit by a car and thrown up into the air, crashing onto the pavement. He died later that night in hospital. Abbie was very shaken by this and had a couple of days off work.

The following evening, Claire and I went over to see her, as had her father. When we arrived, her father told us he'd been there most of the day, keeping her company and giving some sort of comfort. He said she'd taken it quite badly. We all got along very well; he invited us to go over the meet him and Abbie's mum; we could come for tea one day soon. In the meantime Claire handled the phones while Abbie was off.

After a couple of days, we arranged to go and meet Abbie's mum and dad. I remember on the way there, Abbie was sitting in the back of the van. Elton John was on the radio and she was singing along with him, 'Don't let the sun go down on me, but I don't mind if your dad does', and giggling away to herself.

"Oh," said Abbie, "I've not told my mum and dad what we do, so if my Mum asks, which she probably will, what are we going to say?"

"We'll say we're your friends from the pub you use," Claire said. She'd say she worked in a baker's and Gary's a pimp. Ha-ha-ha. The girls were wetting themselves laughing.

The tea was made and we all sat around Mrs Abbie's table. Almost straight away, Abbie's mum said, "What do you do Gary?"

Before I could open my mouth, Claire said, "Well, he's a…"

I interrupted. "Builder, I'm a builder."

The girls smirked. "And what do you do, Claire?"

"I work on a stall selling clothes."

"That sounds good," she said. "As you know, my Abbie works as a secretary in an office answering the phones and she likes her job very much, don't you dear."

"Yes, Mum, I like it very much."

My turn to smirk. "Do you Abbie, is your job that good?"

"Yes, yes," she said smiling back at me. Little did they know that their daughter took her knickers off some days and let men look up her skirt for £20 a pop. The thought of this made me smile.

The Sweeney had done his homework; he saw Maria in her Porsche driving through Dulwich one day and got her registration number. He'd seen her at the pub with us all a couple of times and, let's face it, if you saw Maria once, you wouldn't forget her.

Through that, he found out where she lived and through that, he found out where the work flat was. He made more checks, we think with the landlord, and found Claire had an involvement. They also knew Ryan would turn up sometimes and collect a parcel. They even knew I went there sometimes, so by the time he had all the evidence, he knew the flat was operational and that it was one of Claire's.

That was it, another £200 to find, so now £800, and with the £200 they charged for letting us work with Mr Brown, our police protection was costing £1,000 a week. On the other hand, although it may be expensive, the parlours were safe and we did what we liked. Lettsbe would sometimes ask if the drugs came in to the firm via Maria's place; I think they might have known but weren't sure. I think they wanted to know, not so as to nick anyone but more so they could hit that source with the police tax as well.

Cobden Road parlour was hit again;, we called it the dog-shit hit. As before, somebody had cut the phone cables and spread shit all over and through the front door. This caused the parlour to be out of use for three days, this time costing a lot of money. Claire had a chat with Lettsbe; she wanted him to help find out who did it. He said he'd look into it. When the phone lines were back on and working, Abbie had a call from a person who said the parlour would be shut down and the sooner the better. She told Claire about the call, saying it was a woman's voice, and within a couple of days the same caller phoned in again.

Abbie answered, and she called Claire to listen. Claire recognised the voice; it was her sister. She grabbed the phone and wanted to keep her talking as long as possible to try to get as much information as she could about what was going on. It turned out that one of the clients from Cobden Road had been and visited her sister's parlour and had told her where Claire was. Jill was her sister's name, and she was a brass too, or a working girl, as she liked to be called. She'd worked for many years and, five years ago, she and Claire had had a really big fall out, which came to blows, many blows.

Jill hated Claire with a vengeance so, on finding out where Claire was working from, Jill decided to cause trouble. Well, Claire kept her on the phone for about one and half hours, talking with her and trying to make things better. The longer they spoke, the more information she was getting from her sister. Eventually, she persuaded her sister they could sort this out and that they should meet and at least be friends again. Jill said she would think about it and call back tomorrow. Claire had made notes as they were talking. Jill now had a new husband but we didn't know who he was or what he looked like. She also knew Jill was in London somewhere; she couldn't find out, however, who'd given Jill Claire's address, not that it really mattered. What did matter was finding out where Jill and her new husband lived. If she could find that out, she could then inflict her retribution for these two dog-shit hits and settle old scores from what had happened in the past.

Claire was really anxious, but at the same time confident her sister would call back and agree to a meeting to sort things out. The call came the next day. The two talked some more, then agreed to meet. Claire said they couldn't meet at Cobden Road, because the parlour had people working in it and she lived upstairs with her new husband of only three years who Jill hadn't met. She said he wasn't well and was at home at the moment and that she'd not told him about her sister Jill, let alone the big falling out that taken place. She felt it would be best if they meet at Jill's house. Once this was sorted, the husbands could meet as well and everyone would be happy. After a lengthy chat Jill agreed they could meet at her place. She gave Claire her address and arranged to meet there Friday afternoon. It turned out Jill didn't live far away, just off of Barry Road, a long road that runs between Lordship Lane in Dulwich and The Rye in Peckham.

This gave Claire just two days to sort out what she had in mind. She spoke to me and said she was planning an attack on her sister's house. She told me why and what was going on. She wanted me to plan the attack and help out in the execution of it.

I flatly refused to do this; I couldn't get involved in the affray. I told her take Ryan, he was a big enough bloke.

"Yes, but he doesn't have any confrontation in him." She spoke to Ryan and got him to come home from work. She briefed him as to what she wanted him to do.

She said, "I want you to go over as a client, get into her place then say you were sorry you left your wallet at home, then leave, saying you will be back soon. In doing so you'll have had a look inside her house and have an idea of a rough layout of the place."

Now, with her being a working girl, she'd probably have a place where the entrance was secluded, which was good for us. She sent Ryan on his reconnaissance mission and he came back with the information and drew a plan for them all to look at. While Ryan was out, Claire got her small army together. This consisted of herself, Chantel, Abbie and little Lee, with Ryan's help.

The plan was simple. The drive was quite long, so they couldn't all walk up to the door together. Ryan would do that on his own as they thought he was a client anyway, just in case somebody should be looking out of the front window. The door was on the side of the property. The remaining four of them would hold back out of sight of the house, then, once Ryan was at the front door and it was opened, he'd stay in the doorway, keeping it open, all the while shouting, "Go, Go, Go!" The four girls would make a rush for the house and once they were all down the side where they couldn't be seen by anybody, they could all pile in and beat up Jill and Woody. "Woody", Claire had found out, was Jill's husband's name.

Once I'd heard the plan I just smiled and said, well you don't need me for anything, I'll be at Maria's flat. I'd already checked to see if she was in that afternoon and she was going to be there, so that was where I was going. The night before I stayed at home while they all went over to the pub. Claire had a big chat with Lettsbe, told him about the plan and what was going to happen. They even got some help from him. Once this was over Claire wanted her sister nicked and shut down so she'd have to move away.

Lettsbe was only too happy to help with the situation. He advised that while Claire was in there, she should take with her a bag of pills, maybe 15 or 20, and place them out of sight somewhere, possibly in the front room. He also knew that Jill smoked and there would be Cannabis in the house but he felt the pills would be a good find for the police, seeing as they were class A.

The police would raid the house first thing in the morning, acting on a reliable tip off. Claire was happy with what was going to happen and they all stayed in the pub for the evening, drinking and getting on the Charlie. The conversation was all about revenge and how she could pay her sister back. It seemed they couldn't wait for their bit of excitement to happen.

FOR THE LOVE OF BRASS

Lettsbe had also told them not to take any weapons, the reason being they'd only be something that could be left behind, plus, he said, "There are enough of you to do what you need to do."

They were to have their raid at 3 o'clock in the afternoon. I, on the other hand, had been to the bank, got the wages for the men and delivered them over to Ron.

It was great having Ron to deal with things, as I was spending more and more time not running my building business and more and more time with the girls. In fact, if it hadn't been for Ron, the building business would have come to a standstill ages ago.

I made my way over to see Maria, arriving there at about 2 o'clock. Claire knew where I'd be for the afternoon and said she'd call afterwards to tell us how it went. I was greeted by Maria with a big hug and a kiss; the kiss, which took place on her doorstep, lasted a little longer than one might expect for greeting a friend. It was more like a kiss your wife might give you after only being married three months, not like the kiss you get after being married 15 years. Those type of kisses for me were non-existent.

We sat with tea in Maria's lounge smoking cigarettes, and discussed what might happen with the raid. Well, with the little information we had on it. We both found it all quite funny and wondered what the outcome might be. We talked about a lot of things, you could do that with Maria. Although she was young, she was very worldly. I always seemed to ask the girls stuff that was related to work, rather than ask Claire. I thought that might be best, the reason being that, if Claire answered, I might not like the answers, so I'd save any questions for the girls, especially Maria.

She told me the job she'd offered me was still open and she hoped one day I'd work with her. I gave her the same answer as before. Mainly we talked about working girls and what they got up to, which was always an education for me. I told her about Chantel wanting a knife and that I'd provided her with one so she could carry out her knife-sex jobs, of which she'd done quite a few now. Maria thought what I'd made for Chantel was a great idea and asked, when I had time, could I make one for her to use, too? She said she had a client she saw once a week who was into knife sex. She'd strip him naked, tie his hands behind his back, bend him over the end of the bed and insert a dildo into him and pleasured him with that, all the time holding a knife against his neck to make sure he stayed down and didn't move. Then she'd tell him not to move and leave him there and come back half an hour or so later and do it to him again; he loved it.

"I'd only be with him about one and a half hours and for this he paid me five hundred pounds. He says his wife doesn't understand, so he has to come and see me." I was smiling as she told me this and asked what else he might get from this. "Well," she said, "it was the whole submissive thing. For him it was like being raped but he'd feel safe knowing that he wouldn't be killed. Sometimes I tell him if he moves, I'll kill him, and he cries with pleasure. He loves it, knowing that I'm in charge." I'd always have a big grin on my face as she told me these stories. "Apparently it's very nice, would you like me to show you?"

I laughed. "No, no. It's okay, thanks. I'll give it a miss today."

Maria talked about sex parties where this sort of thing would go on. Some people loved to watch, some people liked to take part, some people did both. I told her, one day I'll have to come to one of these parties, just for the hell of it. When I visualised some of the carryings on I just found it funny. I think that was why Maria enjoyed telling me things, she said it was the expression on my face, it just made her laugh so much.

FOR THE LOVE OF BRASS

When Maria's phone rang it was Claire; she said the job was a success and that they were all over in Streatham at a café having something to eat and they were going to meet Lettsbe and the Sweeney there. When they were done they'd be coming back over to the pub. Claire wanted me and Maria to meet her there. She couldn't wait to tell us about it and asked for all of us to meet there so we could all go on the piss to celebrate the result.

Once we were all sitting around the tables in the pub and the drinks were flowing, the stories were coming out thick and fast. Each person was trying to tell their part in the attack, but with all the excitement, they were talking and laughing over each other.

Basically, it had gone to plan. Ryan had got to the door and Jill had opened it. Ryan had pushed her back, shouting "Go, Go, Go!" about five times. In no time they were all in and, with the door shut, the two men set about Woody while the three girls set about Jill. The couple got a good hiding and, before Claire left, she placed some packages around the front room and kitchen: something for the Old Bill to find when they raided the place. It turned out the police wouldn't raid the place until the Monday morning but in the meantime there were drinks to drink and drugs to take. Even Lettsbe and the Sweeney arrived and joined in the celebrations with us.

The police, however, did hit Jill's address early on Monday morning. They smashed their way in through the front door to catch them both in bed and, on searching the house, they found quantities of Cannabis, Amphetamine, Cocaine and Ecstasy, so the couple were arrested.

Jill accepted most of the responsibility for the drugs and Woody was released on bail, waiting for a court date. Jill was remanded in custody to await further proceedings and it seemed Claire had got exactly what she wanted, which was one thing in life she was good at. On top of that,

FOR THE LOVE OF BRASS

Lettsbe and the Sweeney got a feather in their cap.

I'd met Claire's friend Nigel a couple of times when we were out shopping; he seemed nice enough, a very inoffensive guy but pleasant in his manner. I'd also become a little friendly with another of her friends, an older guy called Wicksey. He was probably 65 years old and drove a red Porsche. He ducked and dived and dabbled a bit in property, buying and selling. He'd turn up at the Cobden Road parlour for afternoon tea sometimes. This matched his accent as he spoke rather well. He'd helped Claire out quite a lot in the past financially and they'd been good friends for a long time. I often wondered if he was or had been a client but I choose not to ask either of them.

We had great days out in the country together. On weekends away we'd go to places like Winchelsea, Rye and Camber Sands. We'd book into the most lovely old Tudor Inns or B&Bs we could find. We even stayed along the coast at Brighton, Peacehaven, Newhaven and Seaford. We always seemed to be doing something, even if it was just for the one night, or we'd be going somewhere in between doing all the work. I just loved her company and loved being with her.

One Saturday night we were over in Bermondsey and while we were there a shooting had taken place in Portland Road, not that far from our pub: in the Wimpy, to be precise. A man in his 30s was shot in the doorway to the bar. He was hit at point-blank range in the chest and went down on the floor. While he lay there, the gunman stood over him and fired another round into the side of his head. Word on the street was he was new to the area and wanted to supply the manor. We even heard he'd supplied Mr Brown in the past. He started to work the area in a small way, then got a bit too pushy and he'd made enemies pretty fast, so somebody decided he had to go. We also heard that he'd been caught with someone's

FOR THE LOVE OF BRASS

wife and the husband wanted him dead.

Whatever the truth was, the man had been shot and the word went around that I'd done it, or at least it was done on my orders, because it was done in my patch. When I was told about it, I was in our pub standing at the bar having a drink with Claire and some of the locals. Apparently, I laughed when I heard about it, so they put two and two together came up with five, so therefore I must have done it. I had a chat with the Sweeney about it.

"Yes," he said, "I heard it was you! There are one or two grasses about, you know, but we know better. It was a fellow from Walthamstow brought in just to do the shooting. We know who he is but he's on the run at the moment. We'll get him, we always do when it's serious shit like this, so don't worry, you're okay. You've got the credit for it, whether you like it or not, and that suits us. It's in our interests that people think that, it makes people behave themselves better."

Claire's birthday party in November proved to be another completely mental night. We all got together and went up town in three taxis to a rave party which lasted 24 hours. The security on the door didn't search anybody, or made very little attempt to, so people took whatever drugs they wanted in to the party. There was all sorts going on and I'd never seen anything like it. People were completely off their faces but all happy and all dancing in between the laser lights. We all tried to join in as much as possible with the happiness and by the end of it all we'd lost Ryan; he'd wandered off somewhere. Abbie had taken off her knickers and her bra and thrown them at some fellow saying she was too hot. Then we saw the fellow dancing with Abbie's knickers on his head and all she had on was a skimpy top and her mini skirt. I remember her saying she had to give her fanny an airing, it was too hot to handle, laughing as she said it.

FOR THE LOVE OF BRASS

"I can always make some money if somebody wants to look up my skirt."

We all had an absolutely brilliant night. When we got back to Claire's flat I slept for 12 hours straight.

CHAPTER SIXTEEN
UNWANTED VISITOR

It was now around the start of December and the days were greyer and getting colder. Claire asked if I fancied going away somewhere with her, somewhere hot. I told her I thought that would be a good idea and asked where and when, thinking she meant quite soon. She suggested maybe nearer to Christmas which I felt was probably not a good idea because I'd want to spend time with my boys.

Us going away wasn't mentioned again for a while. Ryan was still doing his pick ups and his drop-offs of parcels in between his normal work. I didn't ask about any of that. I didn't want to know, anyhow; I had no interest in any of that. All I knew was everything was going well with the girls and the money was coming in.

There was always something happening or going on; if not with us, then it would be at one of the parlours. A story of some kind to be told, most of which were very amusing, but on one particular day something happened that none of us who were there will ever forget.

A man phoned in to make an appointment to see a girl. He'd not been before. After he'd been given the girl's details, he agreed that he wanted to come along and Abbie arranged with him that he could be here in 30 minutes, which would make it about 3.30 in the afternoon. The time came and the doorbell rang; Chantel went out to answer. The client was a black man aged around 25, he was about 5ft 6in tall with very short hair. Chantel invited him in and showed him into the room. She asked him if he wanted anything like a cup of tea, which she often did. She also asked him what service he wanted and he said he didn't know but what services could she provide? She read out the menu from her memory and he picked the cheapest thing which was called a topless hand relief; I think that's pretty self-explanatory. She took his money then told him to get undressed and lie on the bed, and she'd be back in a couple of minutes. With that, she left the room.

Chantel entered the room where we were all sitting and handed the £40 to Abbie; all this was normal so far. Then she finished her last few puffs on her cigarette, put it out in the ashtray and, with a smile on her face, she left the room. She was only gone for 10 to 15 minutes and when he'd finished he asked if he could have a cup of tea now.

She said, "Yes I'll get you one," and reappeared back in our room, going through to the bathroom to wash her hands. She came out of the bathroom and put the kettle on, leaving the client to get dressed. She told us that he wanted a cup of tea before he left and she came over to get herself a cigarette. With this the door opened and the client came in.

He said, "Is it okay to have my tea in here?"

Claire said, "Yes, that's fine, take a seat," and pointed to a stool that was free. Claire smiled, looking at me at the same time. I was thinking, this is unusual; they normally have a cup of tea while they are in the room to start with if they're going to have one.

He sat down on the stool where he could see all of us. I stood up and said, "I'll make the tea."

I walked towards the kitchen area and he in turn turned his stool sideways so that, with a turn of his head, he could see all of us. Chantel sat down in my seat.

I brought the teas over in two trips while they all exchanged small talk.

FOR THE LOVE OF BRASS

There was nowhere for me to sit, so I stood rolling a cigarette for myself. On the coffee table was a large ashtray, the type you'd find in a pub, along with a carved wooden box. The wooden box had the puff things in it; he asked if we all liked a smoke.

Claire said, "Yeah, when we've finished work we might have a spliff to unwind."

With this, he picked the box up, opened it and looked inside. I noticed one of his eyebrows raise. There were a couple of small bags of grass and a lump of solid puff about the size of a quarter, then there were wraps which usually contain white powder, seven or eight of which could be Charlie or Speed, he wouldn't know but he would know there's a big difference in price.

As he looked, I stood up with two empty cups to make my way to the sink. He put the box down, then reached inside his man bag, which he had slung over one shoulder, and pulled out a big knife, one which might be described as a hunting knife.

He said, "I'm talking this gear along with any money and drugs you have." He pointed the knife towards the girls. Abbie, the poor thing, had a look of terror in her eyes.

Claire said, "We don't have much money."

He turned towards me, keeping the knife pointed towards the girls.

"Where's the rest of the drugs, man? Quick, before I cut one of your bitches."

Claire said, "Give him the rest of our stash so he can fuck off."

"Okay, that's better. Where the fuck is it?"

Claire pointed, "It's in the cupboard."

"Yes, mate, it's in this bottom one."

He moved slightly closer, trying to keep an eye on all of us but keeping the knife pointed at the girls."

"Okay," he said, "get the fucking gear out and give it to me."

"For fuck's sake," Claire said, quite loudly, "give it to him."

I bent forward and opened the cupboard door. I reached in towards the back and felt the pistol grip of the sawn-off shotgun. I lifted it off of its brackets and in one quick movement pulled it out and levelled at his head; the ends of the barrels were about 4ft from his face.

"FUCK ME!" he said. "I wasn't expecting that."

"Now drop the knife, or I'll blow your fucking head off."

This he did immediately. Abbie stepped forward and picked it up. She held it behind her back out of sight. All of a sudden, as if in an instant, this situation became very clear to me. I was holding a loaded sawn-off, pointing at a man's head; behind him, I was aware, stood Chantel and Claire. Abbie was off to one side. My finger was on the first trigger of the gun. I told myself now if for any reason, whatever it might be, I pull is trigger, this man's head, along with the shotgun pellets, are going to be spread all over the back wall. I might even shoot the girls in the process. What would I say to Lettsbe or the Sweeney? I don't think they could sort this out. What could I say in court when I got sent down for murder? The enormity of the situation had hit me and I needed to bring this situation to an end as fast as possible.

I shouted at him, "Sit on the fucking stool," which he did immediately. He put what was left of the gear in his hand on the table. I took the two paces forward to reach him, lowering the gun as I went but still pointing it at his head. I swung the gun forward with both my hands hitting him as hard as I could in the side of his head with the barrels, knocking him off the stool and onto the floor. He let out a big yell and blood started to run down his head. The strike had given him two circular 12-bore size cuts to the head.

FOR THE LOVE OF BRASS

"Take your chain off and empty your pockets; whatever you've got's staying here."

He lifted his gold chain off over his head and placed it on the coffee table and leaned to one side. He put his hand into his pocket and pulled out his money.

"Fifteen quid, is that all you have, fifteen quid?" I looked at the girls and tried to make light of the situation. I said, "I've never done an armed robbery for fifteen quid." Abbie laughed, it was a nervous laugh. The other two just grinned. "Now fuck off, you're dripping blood everywhere. And don't come back," I shouted at him, "and if you want your chain back don't come here, come and see me. I drink in the pub over the road." He went down the hallway to the door and I bet that felt like a long walk, having me behind him with a gun. Once I closed the front door after him I walked back into the kitchen.

"Are you girls all okay?"

Abbie said, "Well, that was exciting," but she was frightened by it, by the whole experience.

Claire and Chantel seemed as cool as cucumbers.

I walked back over to the cupboard and picked up a cloth to wipe the blood off of the barrels. I broke the gun open to make it safe to wipe.

"Wow!" To my amazement, the gun wasn't loaded. Chantel then told us that Lee had found the gun a week or two ago and he'd taken the shells out and hidden them. He was worried if he came home pissed and played with the gun, he might shoot himself, or Chantel for that matter. Chantel had known all along the gun was empty, which is why she'd been so cool about the whole thing.

Plus," she said, "Gary, you were having so much fun, I let you run with it."

FOR THE LOVE OF BRASS

We all laughed. I wiped the gun clean then fitted it back on its brackets. We decided that was enough excitement for one day, so we all went over to the pub.

We told Lettsbe all about the adventures of the day; we also told him to tell the Sweeney and maybe find out any information on the man with the barrel wounds to the side of his head. Lettsbe did tell me that two other parlours in the area had been robbed by a man with a knife, fitting the description of our man.

A couple of weeks later I was in the pub early one evening having a beer with Claire and a few locals when the robber came in, looking around. He saw me, got himself a beer and sat in one of the corners looking out over the bar. Soon after, Lettsbe came in. Claire gave him the nod and matey boy was arrested. Once they got him outside he was searched, then taken to the nick. It turned out he had a little gun on him, a .22 calibre revolver with three bullets in it. He was known to the police, Lettsbe told us, and so was his little revolver, it had been used in a job before. He got seven years.

We were now a couple of weeks into December and Christmas was on its way. We had the working girls do to think of; we called it the firm's Christmas party. We were lucky to get in our venue at such short notice; the firm's do would be held at a Greek restaurant I knew in Thornton Heath. The man who owned the place was called Costas but we all called him the Bubble. I already knew him because I'd done building work for him, fixing up and decorating his kitchen, so he'd been a client of mine in the past, plus he did wonderful food.

Claire and I went shopping for sexy things to put inside the Christmas crackers. Ann Summers was the shop to go to in Croydon; there we bought small vibrators, G-strings in different colours and small sexy

FOR THE LOVE OF BRASS

trinkets to reload the ordinary Christmas crackers we'd bought. We took the crackers to Claire's flat and spent an evening refilling them with the items from the Ann Summers shop. Claire figured these crackers would put a big smile on people's faces when they pulled them. As we worked on the crackers, we also drank our way through two bottles of wine. Ryan was in the kitchen however, cutting and mixing his little wraps and filling them with white powder. He was getting all these ready for the Christmas rush, and a rush it would be. He'd have to have as many as he could ready, not just to supply Lettsbe and the Sweeney but he would be supplying Mr Brown and he would need a lot.

The firm's party soon came around and it was a great night out. The crackers went down really well with everyone, they were all so surprised at the gifts inside. There were enough to go around twice and still we had a few left over, so the restaurant staff got one each; we even gave the Bubble a vibrator and said, "This is for you or your missus." He loved it and we had a fantastic time in there. Excellent food, excellent wine and as much as anyone could eat or drink.

We left the Bubble's restaurant and headed for the Blue Orchid. Once enough time had passed, of which we needed an hour from when we had eaten last, Claire could distribute the desert in the form of an Ecstasy pill. Once that had kicked in, there was no stopping us, we danced and raved the night away.

Dancing and E-ing off our nuts to music like Dr Alban, 'It's my life'; 2 unlimited, 'Get ready for this'; Rozalla, 'Everybody's free' and Felix, 'Don't you want me', along with all the great club music of that time. It was an excellent night we had in there, then it was taxis back to Claire's flat for the party to continue till the sun came up.

Claire still wanted to get away for a break somewhere hot. She asked me again would I go to Greece with her. She wanted the break to go through the Christmas and the New Year holiday period. I told her no, I'd be spending that time with my sons over the holiday.

"Okay, then," she said, "I'll be going with Ryan, then." She'd leave me here to run things while she was away. I must admit I hated the idea of her going away with Ryan, even if he was her husband, but what could I do? I asked her not to go with him but my request fell on deaf ears. I'd now be solely responsible for looking after the girls, picking up money and of course paying the Old Bill each week, for which she'd leave the funds. Also she said, because I was here, I'd still be paid. I made sure the girls knew the score, that I wouldn't be around for Christmas Eve, Christmas Day or Boxing Day. Nor would I be around New Year's Eve or New Year's Day.

Claire left for Greece with Ryan from Gatwick airport two days before Christmas Eve. Ryan was like a big kid because Claire had allowed him to go with her. They weren't coming back until two weeks into the New Year. The night before Christmas Eve, I took Abbie and Maria out for the night to Bermondsey. We had a great night out with my mates from the area; they really loved the girls, said their company was second to none.

After that night, Abbie left to go to her mum and dad's for Christmas and I went home to my house for the next few days. The other girls all had partners or best friends to spend their time with. I had Sharon at my house and I had to put up with her for Christmas, which would mean the silent treatment most of the time and, in between that, pulling faces of disapproval at whatever I might say or do, along with giving me grief of some sort and having a go at me when she thought the boys couldn't hear or weren't listening, but the time over Christmas that I spent with my boys made the whole thing well worth it, regardless of how much

FOR THE LOVE OF BRASS

Sharon tried to spoil it for me.

After Boxing Day I popped over to see the girls, only for two to three hours each day. This would continue until New Year's Eve; however, on one occasion I had a really good afternoon and then the night out with Maria and her mate Lisa. They took me drinking at a big, lovely old pub in Lordship Lane and; once we got the flavour for it, we just kept going. We ended up in a night club in Peckham Rye. I got completely off my trolley that night and I stayed at Maria's lovely big house. I woke up on my own in a great big bed with silk sheets, wondering where the hell am I? I do remember Lisa talking to me before I lost the plot.

Lisa wanted to know why I'd not taken up with Maria, even she thought we would work very well together. She also said Maria thought the world of me. She wanted to know, did I not fancy her?

"No, no. It's not that I don't fancy her. I fancy her to bits, what man wouldn't, she's bloody lovely. It's because I'm with Claire and I love her, that's all it is. It's as simple as that." Lisa made her position quite clear, she wanted to see me and Maria together.

The other evenings I was at home on my own with my boys and no Sharon; she was out with her friends clubbing.

I had a good chat with Abbie one afternoon after she'd come back from visiting her parents. We were sitting in the front room of her flat. She asked me, was the money still coming in while Claire was away?

"Yes, it is," I told her. I'd picked money up this week and would be doing so until Claire came back from Greece.

"I don't know where it comes from exactly," I told Abbie. "I don't know if it's from rents, percentages from the girls or drugs, it could be all three, who knows. Only Claire knows, I guess, but to be honest, I don't really want to know, I don't really care."

FOR THE LOVE OF BRASS

Abbie agreed with me, the less we know is probably for the better in the long run. Then at one stage we were laughing at the thought of the two coppers on our books and that they would get off their nuts with us sometimes. It was as though we were all mates; well, I guess we were. Abbie told me that Lettsbe was in love with Chantel; she quite liked the idea of that and she was fond of him. She also told me how Chantel and little Lee loved each other. Abbie said how nice it was to see and she wished she had a love like that in her life. I explained to her how I couldn't understand how he coped with her working, especially from his flat.

"And working on his bed each day, then they remake the bed each evening and sleep in it together. I really wonder how he deals with that," Abbie said. "There's no way in the world I'd let my partner work!"

Claire came back from Greece; she and Ryan were so brown. Claire was brown all over and I thought of her sunbathing naked with Ryan and wondered what else might have gone on. I didn't like the thought of it all, I told myself, but she was back. I had missed her terribly. Life would now return to normal and it did return to normal, until the end of January.

February began with things seemingly starting to get a bit heavy with the drugs, not just the large amounts passing through Claire's hands but the amount she was taking. She was on it every day. I asked Maria if she knew where all these drugs were coming from. She told me she'd no idea, all she knew was that a man turned up at the work flat with a parcel. She thought he was a cab driver. He dropped it off there, then a little later Ryan would turn up and take it away. I told her I knew she was into the Old Bill for at least grand a week and that she was also supplying them with gear, although I thought most of it was free to them. Well, lately Lettsbe had been off his face every time I saw him. I thought he must be

FOR THE LOVE OF BRASS

getting that all free of charge.

I began to wonder what was going on with Claire. Abbie and Chantel were working as normal from Cobden Road, as were the other girls. I was still picking up money regularly but I was starting to worry now; Claire had started to go missing some days, sometimes all day and sometimes just in the evenings. She'd also started to turn her phone off. She disappeared with her friend Nigel for two days and two nights and kept her phone off all that time so no one could contact her. I asked the girls if any of them had heard from her or spoken to her at all but no, no, they told me, no contact with any of them at all.

When she finally did surface, I saw her for an hour at Cobden Road, then Ryan took her out. I found out later he'd taken her to a sex party where he said she was making money supplying people with gear. Well, that was what he told me although I wasn't believing any of his story at all. I was having serious doubts about the whole thing and I didn't know what was going on. Some nights she would just be gone all night and with no phone on, no one could check to see if she was okay. Nobody knew where she was; even Ryan had a worried look on his face. I'd still be picking up money from Sam, Maria and Holly, while driving the Irish couple around.

I suddenly found I couldn't trust anybody because I didn't know if any of them were covering for her when her phone was off. It was causing me such anxiety and worry. I was trying hard but really couldn't understand what was going on with us. The relationship was falling apart and I was starting to think, this is the worst month of my life ever.

CHAPTER SEVENTEEN
SPILLING THE BEANS

The month of March started and Claire eventually turned up at Cobden Road one afternoon. She'd been on the missing list for two days and she looked like shit. I took her home to her flat and she told me how sorry she was. I stayed with her until the next day. Ryan came home for a while and he showed his concern too. On the next day, once she had had some sleep and a shower, she went into the bedroom to get dressed. I followed her in there; she looked a lot better than she had when I had brought her home. I put my arms around her and gave her a cuddle but I felt a feeling of dread inside me.

I said to her, "I want you to know something."

"Yeah, what's that?"

"I want you to know that I love you very much."

She hugged me back but didn't say a thing. She just gave me a long hug. There was always music playing somewhere in Claire's flat or in the parlours, a radio would normally be on, there would be a radio in most rooms. As she hugged me the radio from the front room was playing a song I really liked, Vanessa Williams, 'Save the best till last'. As I listened, I hugged her even tighter and held her till the song had finished. I think a tear rolled down one of my cheeks.

I left her flat to go home. I felt very sad at the thought of our relationship having come to this. All the signs were telling me we were going nowhere. I went over to Cobden Road the following morning; Chantel and Abbie were just carrying on as normal. There was no Claire and I really started to miss her again. I popped over to see the girls to make sure there were all okay and noticed none of them spoke much. I didn't go to see Maria, I knew she was busy. I'd go over to see her tomorrow.

I'd not seen the Irish couple for two days and I wondered what they were up to. I drove over to Cobden Road. Claire was there, chatting away with the girls as if nothing out of the ordinary had gone on. She suggested we go over to the pub, all four of us. This we did, we all sat there having a beer. Lettsbe came in; he joined us. He loved chatting with Chantel. We all sat there talking, it was as though everything was normal, just how it used to be, but it didn't seem normal to me. I had this sinking feeling in my heart, as though something bad was about to happen. Everybody else was seeming happy and getting on with it. Maybe this was normal, maybe it was just me. I told myself to cheer up, we can have a good evening here, so join in with the others. Yes, I told myself, that's what I'll do.

I was sitting next to Claire. She leaned over towards me so as to talk to me quietly, leaving the other three to talk amongst themselves.

"I want you to know I love you." My heart lifted slightly. "I've something to say to you and I don't want you getting upset or pissed off, okay?"

Claire explained she had an old client who has come back on the scene. He'd asked her to go and see him.

"No!"

"Hold on," Claire said, "he pays me seven hundred pounds a night."

"No!"

"Hold on, I'm not finished yet, let me finish."

"No!"

"I don't have to do anything, just lie with him."

"No!"

"He's old and lonely since his wife died."

"No!"

"He just wants me there as company."

"No! This isn't our deal. You know that, so it's No! You know what will happen if you work."

"What'll happen?"

"You know already. I'll leave you. You know we can't be together if you work."

"Well, it's not working, is it? And it's only each night for one week."

"No!"

"It's just keeping him company for one fucking week. What's wrong with that?"

"No! How many more Nos do you need?"

"Well, I think seven hundred pounds a night is worth it." I could feel myself starting to shake with anger. "I told him I charge a hundred pounds an hour but seeing as how I'll be there all night, he can have the deal of just seven hundred pounds for the night. All I have to do is lie with him."

"No! I'm not fucking having it. You ain't going." I was shaking so much I couldn't pick my drink up.

"Well, I've already booked him in for tomorrow night."

"No! You ain't going."

She looked me straight in the eyes and said, "Yes, I am. I'm thinking of the money. We can go away somewhere nice with that money."

I picked up my tobacco and lighter, stood up and walked out of the pub. I walked down the road towards my van, trying to roll myself a cigarette. I got to the van and tried to light the cigarette but my hands were shaking so badly it was difficult to light. I had to take a big breath and let it out slowly, only then could I light it. I got into van and drove off. I don't know where I went. I just know I got home about three hours later with this heavy feeling of dread again. I was tormented at the thought of this job going ahead and she was going to do it.

The following day I couldn't go over to work, or to see her at Cobden. I was too wound up with the whole thing but by teatime I thought I'd go. Having left it all day, I thought I might be able to handle it a bit better. I needed to go, I don't know why, I just needed to go over there.

It was about 5.30 when I arrived. Abbie and Chantel were carrying on as normal, all seemed good with them. Claire and Ryan were also sitting there. Abbie had got up to make the tea for us all.

I asked Ryan what he was up to and he said casually, "I'm taking Claire to a job shorty."

With this I started to shake again, shake with rage. I sat there quietly, I didn't know what to say to anyone. I had trouble looking at Claire, I just kept shaking at the thought of what she was going to do tonight. To me it was as though she was putting our relationship to the test, the ultimate test, or maybe she was just throwing it all away and I just hadn't caught on yet. Or maybe she wanted to see what would happen.

In a way it seemed she was doing this for fun, almost. Maybe she was thinking, Ryan puts up with my doing whatever I want, we'll see how far I can push Gary. All these thoughts and possibilities raced through my mind but what I did know for sure was that she was going to do this job tonight. The thought of it was making me so anxious and miserable, I couldn't take it any more.

I stood up and walked out to my van, then drove home. I could hardly sleep that night, all I could think of was that Claire was out there working. The thought was tearing me apart and to top it all, she was going out again the next night, and each night for the rest of the week.

I couldn't go over to Cobden Road until the end of the next day. Claire was there when I arrived, sitting with the girls. She told me she had to sleep during the day because she'd been awake all night thinking of me. I don't believe that for one minute, I thought to myself. I told her I didn't want her to go out again that night but she was going regardless and Ryan would be picking her up to take her. My shakes started again. I walked out of the parlour and back to the van. I had trouble trying to unlock the door as I was shaking so much, I just didn't know what to do. I know, I told myself. I drove to a phone box, I got my little book of numbers out and called Maria on her mobile. I asked if I could come over and see her.

"Of course you can, whenever you like, I'll put the kettle on." I parked outside her flat. I was still shaking, shaking enough to make it difficult to roll a cigarette.

Maria gave me a big hug and a kiss when she opened her front door.

"What's up with you? You look really stressed. Come in and have a chill out with me." She handed me a cup of tea and some of it spilt into the saucer, I was still shaking somewhat.

"Do you want me to roll you a spliff?"

"No, no thanks."

"You can have a nice massage if you like." The thought made me smile. Maria smiled too. "Well, at least you're smiling now."

"Yes." I was smiling at last.

"So what's up?" Maria asked.

"Oh, give me a minute, I'll just have my tea first." I noticed my shaking had calmed down considerably.

"Gary," Maria said, "will you come and work with me, you know, with the same deal as I offered you before, which I think is a very good deal?

FOR THE LOVE OF BRASS

You won't want for anything."

I smiled. "No, no, I can't."

"But why?" Maria asked, "Because you're a working girl, I couldn't be with a woman who works."

"Well, Claire works and you're with her; what's the difference?"

"Well, yeah, so it would seem." (I was thinking Maria knew what was going on). She's worked twice now," I said.

"Twice? What are you talking about! She's always worked."

"Yeah, but not while she's been with me."

"That's not true. She's worked all the time she's been with you, which is why I can't understand why you won't work with me. Why won't you work with me? We'd make a great team. Is it because you don't fancy me?"

"HOLD ON, HOLD ON. What did you just say?" I looked at her blankly.

"Oh, fuck! Didn't you know?"

"NO. NO, I didn't. She told me the opposite. I can't believe what I've just heard." I started to shake again, this time uncontrollably.

"Oh, shit. Please don't tell her I told you, please; she'll give me loads of shit over it."

I looked at Maria. "Okay, I won't tell her it came from you, don't worry. I won't say a thing about you. I'll have to think of another way to explain how I found out, then I can confront her with it. Don't worry, Maria, I won't involve you. Thanks for being truthful with me, thanks for that."

And there was me thinking last month was the worst month. This month was getting worse by the day.

"I've got to go now, Maria," I said as I left her flat.

FOR THE LOVE OF BRASS

I didn't know where to go, I just drove and drove, then found myself parking outside my house. I lay in bed that night knowing in my mind it was all over. I've lost a friend or so I thought, I've lost her company, lost a job I enjoyed and I'm on my own now. This is really starting to hurt.

I woke up in the morning and it hit me again, instantly. I had a sick feeling in the pit of my stomach. What will I do, I asked myself? I'll have to go back to being a builder and do that full time; that should take my mind of all this bad situation. Then I thought, I'll go over and see Claire later to have this out with her but in the meantime I need to be able to say I found out from somebody else, so as not to drop Maria in trouble. I know, I'll go and see the girls today to see what I can find out.

I drove over to see Sam. I asked her to her face, did she know that Claire had worked all the time she was with me?

Sam just looked at me and said, "Sorry Gary, she always told us not to talk about it or mention it in front of you, in case it made you angry. She said you were the jealous type and we shouldn't upset you."

This was now feeling like the worst month of my life. Much worse than last month. I thought I'd go to Cobden Road, not expecting Claire to be there because of her being out all night. I guessed she'd be in bed at her flat sleeping. As I walked in, both girls were happy to see me. Abbie offered to put the kettle on. As she made the tea I asked Chantel if I could go into the room with her.

"Yes", she replied. "What would you like from the menu?" giggling as she said it.

I told her, "I'm not interested in what's on the menu."

"Oh yeah?" she says, "got an idea of your own?"

"Yes, I have and it's not what you're thinking. I want to talk with you."

We went into the room with our tea in hand and sat on the bed.

FOR THE LOVE OF BRASS

"Chantel, when you and Claire go to these sex parties, do you sell much in the way of drugs there, you know what sort of amounts?"

"No, we only take enough drugs for ourselves, whatever we might want."

"Oh okay, you don't supply the other people there?"

"Oh no, not at all."

"Oh okay, so how do you both make money while you're there?"

"Through sex of course, how else do you think we make money there?"

"Is it good money?"

"Yes, of course. We make between a thousand and fifteen hundred each per party."

My heart sank, I didn't know what to say. "Can I ask you, did you know that Claire worked all the time she was with me?"

"Yes, of course."

"And you never spoke of it."

"Well, no, that's right, she asked us not to."

"What, you and Abbie?"

"Yes, she told both of us not to. She said it would just upset you, so don't mention it, so we didn't."

Once again I was dumbstruck, lost for words. I sat there staring at I don't know what. I finished my tea and cigarette. I couldn't stay there any more. On leaving I asked Chantel if Claire was coming over later.

"Oh yes," she said, "we're all going to the pub after work and before she goes off to her job tonight."

I left Cobden Road with my thoughts going round and round in circles, trying to make head or tail of it all. I decided to stay out of the way for now. I would walk into that pub tonight and have it out with Claire there and then.

While I was sitting in my van over in Thornton Heath, waiting for the time to pass, I saw Dave, an old mate. I started to tell him of my woes with Claire.

His response was, "Gary, pussy will blow you further than dynamite." Boy, he was right with that. I couldn't agree more, this had blown me up into the air and I'd not come down yet.

Later that day, at around 6.30, I walked into the pub. They were all there sitting around the two tables, laughing and joking. Abbie was singing to a tune that was playing. All I could think of was, I need to have this out with Claire. I need to fix this situation. Claire looked at me as I just stood there staring at her.

"Get yourself a drink and come and sit down." It was at this point I had the sudden realisation, this all means nothing to her. I mean nothing to her and, with that thought in my mind, why would I want to try to sort this out. I turned and walked out of the pub without saying anything. I just walked out. I drove off, not even knowing where I'd be driving to. This is it, this is the day, I told myself. This is it, it's all over. Now I really did feel heartbroken, I felt absolutely terrible inside.

The following morning, after having had hardly any sleep, I sat in my office. I was thinking, I can't believe it's all over with Claire. Okay, I told myself, you need to get busy. Get yourself working properly, keep busy. I had an enquiry come in for a building job, a recommendation in fact, so it was odds on I'd be getting the job. It was to build a large extension to a house over in the Thames Ditton area. I should have been quite happy, the job would be worth a lot of money to me. Instead of feeling happy, I felt absolutely terrible. A feeling of being lost inside, combined with a feeling of disappointment over having been lied to for such a long time.

FOR THE LOVE OF BRASS

I felt anger, frustration and sadness all at once, I felt as if I was broken inside. I told myself, you have had worse times than this in your life so take it like a man. You know you will get over it, so grin and bear it, it will pass.

As I drove the van over to Thames Ditton, I thought, it's nearing the end of March, I have the whole summer to look forward to. A song came on the radio, The Pasadenas 'I'm doing fine now, without you baby'. My thoughts instantly turned to Claire while the song played through. 'Save the best to last' was the next song to play. I think a tear welled up in one of my eyes.

I felt I'd been here before, I'd come full circle. Feeling terrible and driving south along the A3 towards Tolworth.

Déjà vue?

THE END

FOR THE LOVE OF BRASS